FA CONFIDENTIAL

FA CONFIDENTIAL

Sex, Drugs and Penalties: The Inside Story of English Football

David Davies

London · New York · Sydney · Toronto

A CBS COMPANY

First published in Great Britain by Simon & Schuster UK Ltd, 2008
A CBS COMPANY

All images supplied courtesy of the author.

1 3 5 7 9 10 8 6 4 2

Simon & Schuster UK Ltd
1st Floor
222 Gray's Inn Road
London
WC1X 8HB

www.simonsays.co.uk

Simon & Schuster Australia
Sydney

A CIP catalogue for this book is available
from the British Library.

ISBN: 978-1-84737-368-7 (Hardback)
ISBN: 978-1-84737-402-8 (Trade paperback)

Typeset in Garamond by M Rules
Printed in the UK by CPI Mackays, Chatham ME5 8TD

To my girls, Susan, Amanda and Caroline

Contents

Acknowledgements

One Sunday lunchtime during the writing of this book, I sat in front of a television at my beloved Midlands home and watched an old VHS tape my sister Rosemary had uncovered for me. Don't let me bore you with its history. But, for me at least, that tape alone has made telling my story worthwhile.

Sadly, the number of one-parent families brought up over my lifetime has gone on rising. I am the product of one of them after my father died of lung cancer months after I was born.

Of course I had seen still photos of Dad – in the Army, outside our old dairy shop off the Euston Road, in the Council Chamber at Saint Pancras (now Camden) Town Hall, and most vividly on the steps of our church on his wedding day in wartime London in 1942.

But what my sister rediscovered was old cinefilm, transferred on to that VHS, and MOVING pictures of John Edwardes Davies MBE. Yes again on that wedding day. But also rolling around on the grass in the back garden of one of my relations' homes, and playing, as fathers still do, with a baby boy who I now know was yours truly. It was a moment for me, aged almost sixty now, I never anticipated and that I will never forget.

It's almost two years since I retired from the FA. No, I wasn't in a hurry to write mainly because I wasn't convinced I wanted to do the book at all.

Had England qualified for Euro 2008, and not been eliminated in such miserable circumstances by Croatia in November 2007, who knows, I might have kept my peace. But leaving New Wembley that night as the heavens opened, and the Chiltern Line ground to a halt, and like thousands of others I sought shelter where I could – well, I saw the frustration and yes the anger in the faces of so many fans, and I shared it. Why had it come to this?

I still care passionately. Somehow, even long gone from the FA, I feel at least partly responsible. After all, haven't I experienced first-hand how English football, with its FA and Premier League and Football League and all its other leagues, is hopelessly split when it comes to agreeing its real priorities? I am not even sure it has ever actually tried to agree them. How difficult it would be is the one thing everybody is agreed upon. For sure, English football is riven by conflicts of interest. Is it really true, as I was assured by one official at 10 Downing Street, that a former sports minister was so overwhelmed by what he faced that he abandoned plans to force real change inside the national sport? Meanwhile, inside the FA, the parallel universes of the blazers and the senior staff – upstairs and downstairs – live on as the latest former chief executive, Brian Barwick, found to his cost in August 2008.

For the fans, what's worse is that our teams, and not just the national team but also club teams, in my view aren't given the best chance to win. Elsewhere, the development of young players, boys and girls, has been stunted by a football structure that has for too long cried out for real reform. Yes, I was angry that night leaving Wembley, with others, and with myself. But I was also sad for friends in and around the England dressing room.

I decided to go ahead with my story.

A journalist for twenty-two years before my job in football, I surely should have written that story myself and alone. But I am lucky enough to have a new life that makes demands on my time and energy. It was another major reason why I delayed writing. I had no idea how I alone could do it. So this book would not be what it is without the professionalism, dedication and friendship of the *Daily Telegraph*'s Football Correspondent, Henry Winter. I have been truly fortunate to work with him, and I hope I have delivered what I promised. I know how grateful he has been for the transcription services that have processed our many hours of conversation.

So many of our meetings took place at the offices of Wiggin LLP, the law firm that took me on as a consultant after my FA life. Colleagues like John Banister, Caroline Kean, Michael Brader and Richard McMorris have become friends and their support for this book has never wavered. The Wiggin reception team – Louise Slabbert, Lauren Shearing, Tracie Lambert and Mairead Brown – ensured we were never short of tea, coffee or cakes.

My thanks to all of them and to Coutts Bank, another part of my new consultancy life. Ian Turland, Martin Thurnham and Nick Gornall all knew about this book and their encouragement and tolerance over many months has been hugely reassuring and much appreciated. Andree Deane and Fred Turok at the Fitness Industry Association have been similarly supportive.

Of course there would have been no book at all without the backing and passion of Caroline Michel at Pfd, whom I was lucky enough to meet through Greg Dyke. Simon and Schuster, the publishers, meanwhile were always on to a winner with me when their boss in the UK, Ian Chapman, turned out to be as big a Manchester United fanatic as myself. Thanks also to Mike Jones and Rory Scarfe who have put up with my occasional late-night and early-morning cries for help as deadline day approached.

I hope and pray my former colleagues at the FA will find the pages that follow at least worth the read and, even if they don't agree with every word, find plenty to enjoy. Working with them was an unforgettable experience over almost thirteen years and I thank every one of them, even those with whom I had my differences, for the many good times we had. It was a privilege. Beyond the FA too were football friends at home and abroad who urged me to go into print. The football family is spread around the world. Going to some of its outposts in Africa and Asia was probably the most fulfilling part of my FA experience, and the most humbling too. That work has continued for me through Alexander Ross, the football-development company that I part-own with Ben Hatton,

Joanna Burns, Mike Blood and David Sheepshanks. I thank them too for their support.

Ultimately what follows, though, are my words and my experience and my responsibility.

More than anything I hope I haven't stretched the love of my family, and my women – my daughters Amanda and Caroline, and the woman who has stuck by me through thick and thin, my Susan – beyond breaking point. But this book is how it was for me.

Introduction

1966

My life's journey has been shaped by one enchanted day. I was scarcely eighteen, just starting out, but I was there for England's finest hour and the memory never fades. I was there: three words that mean everything. On 30 July 1966, I arrived on my own for the World Cup final but left Wembley the proudest member of the England football family. Every time Geoff Hurst scored, I punched the air. When the final whistle reverberated, I hugged strangers. When Bobby Moore climbed those thirty-nine steps, wiping the mud and sweat from his hands before accepting the World Cup from the Queen, my vision blurred. Blinking away tears, I looked and focused and saw Bobby holding the World Cup aloft. The Jules Rimet trophy belonged to Bobby, to the players, to all England, to me. And when Nobby Stiles did that mad jig, I laughed out loud. Life couldn't get better. These were my heroes, England's heroes. All my working life has been spent trying to re-create the emotions flowing through me that special afternoon. All my dreams in football, all the energy I poured into my work for the Football Association, have focused on England repeating the golden deeds of Hurst, Moore, Stiles and the Charltons. We did it once. Why not again?

As a BBC correspondent and then an FA executive, I embarked on so many voyages of discovery, of pleasure and pain with England. After reporting on the fortunes of Bobby Robson and

Graham Taylor, I worked closely with Terry Venables, Glenn Hoddle, Kevin Keegan, Sven-Goran Eriksson and Steve McClaren as they tried to bring another trophy home. Every passing tournament, every passing manager, brings more grief. The more distant 1966 becomes, the more it troubles me. The growing years of hurt that people sing about carry ever greater resonance with me because I was at Wembley in '66. I remember when England were on top of the world.

My World Cup experience began early in 1966 when I pleaded with my mum to allow me to go that summer. We lived in central London, near Euston Station, an easy hop on the train to Wembley, and I was football mad. The FA offered a deal whereby fans could buy a World Cup season-ticket for the Wembley games.

'I have to be there,' I explained to Mum. 'I have to see England.'

'Remember you have your A-levels in June,' Mum replied. 'If you promise to work hard, I'll help you buy the season-ticket.'

When the tickets arrived in the post, I kept holding them, turning them over and over, knowing I would definitely be seeing my England idols.

'Good,' I told Mum. 'The tickets are near the tunnel. That's where England's most passionate fans go.' Some good banter was guaranteed. The tickets came in little white containers (and are now kept safe in the bank, as precious as any heirloom). On the day of each match, I carefully prised the right ticket from the container and headed across the road to Euston. I loved that train ride: rattling into Wembley Central, glancing across the tracks to see the Twin Towers and then always, always walking down the same side of the road to the ground. Superstition ruled. Same route, same socks, same hope.

I travelled alone, but returned with countless stories for friends. As the tournament began, my mates weren't jealous. Why should they have been? Not many people believed England could actually win the World Cup. Of course, we heard Alf Ramsey declare England would succeed. We knew Martin Peters was ten years ahead of his time. But, unlike now, there was no mass hysteria pursuing England into the World Cup. People were more restrained back then, particularly after the disappointment of the opening stalemate against Uruguay on 11 July. The following morning, I ran out to buy the newspapers. Every report, every comment, every morsel of information was dissected and devoured. The verdict was scathing. John Connelly never played in the World Cup again.

Five days later, the nerves accompanying me to England's meeting with Mexico did not dissipate until a vintage strike from Bobby Charlton. When that thunderbolt crashed into Ignacio Calderon's net, I looked around at everyone near me by the tunnel, and saw real hope. A huge weight lifted off everyone, players and fans alike. Yet even a good victory over France never convinced me England were destined to become world champions. Belief took hold only during the infamous quarter-final with Argentina. 'We can do this,' I shouted to everyone and no one. That collision of different footballing cultures was a rough, tough game. When Antonio Rattin was dismissed, I knew England would get through. Argentina's captain took an unbelievably long time to leave the field. When Rattin finally came towards our end, heading in shame towards the tunnel, I gave him a few choice words. 'Fuck off, Rattin,' I screamed. Not my proudest moment. Rattin was slaughtered by all the England fans around me. Even without Rattin, Argentina ran us very close until Geoff Hurst's late winner. On reaching home, I had a simple message for Mum and my mates about the World Cup. 'We can win this thing,' I said.

And it happened. In an unforgettable semi-final against Portugal, Bobby Charlton scored both goals. My joy knew no limits. The England players who meant most to me were the men from Manchester United Football Club. I loved United. Still do. Much to my delight, Nobby Stiles fought his way into Ramsey's team.

'Nobby! For England!' I kept repeating, unable to contain my pride. Stiles did not let me down, controlling the great Eusebio in the semi.

July 1966 passed in a blur of matches, and endless conversations with fans and friends about the team. The great debating point was Ramsey ignoring Jimmy Greaves when he recovered from injury. Even now, forty-two years later, the rights and wrongs of Greaves's omission stage occasional skirmishes in my mind. Before the World Cup, I watched Greaves create merry hell against United at White Hart Lane several times. One hot afternoon, Spurs pulverised us 5–1. Jimmy cut in from the left, got the ball on to that dangerous right foot and caused havoc. People celebrate the famous George Best goal against Sheffield United, when George ran across the box and curled the ball back and in. They forget Jimmy often conjured up goals like that. Surely he should play against West Germany? Ramsey knew best. Geoff Hurst was the man.

Hurst's repayment of Ramsey's faith is the stuff of England folklore. Too excited to sleep long, I woke early on 30 July. Wembley dominated my thoughts. Running downstairs, I wolfed down breakfast and dashed for the door. The clock showed it was not yet nine a.m., six hours before kick-off.

'Why are you going so early?' Mum asked.

'The train might break down,' I replied.

'It won't.'

'IT COULD!' Mum realised that logic and her son had parted company. Smashing my personal best over the 400 yards to Euston, I leapt on the train. Where was everyone? The train was near empty. Most England fans would arrive at a more sensible hour. I was idiotically early. Who cared? I just walked round and round Wembley, wondering how England would do against West Germany. We had to win. As I bagged my usual spot, behind the barrier to the left of the Wembley tunnel, I reflected on England playing in red. Classy. Strong. On becoming involved with England at the FA, I always preferred England in red.

'That's because he's a Manchester United fan, and he wants everything in red,' came the barbed response from the critics. No. It's just England look better in red, more noble.

The kit sorted, I checked the weather. From boiling sun to pouring rain, Mother Nature launched the full range of her weaponry at us. The final certainly shifted moods. When Helmut Haller scored, my despair at seeing England behind was deepened by the sight of so many jubilant Germans around me. No one thought about segregation. There were no problems, even though the Second World War was still a bitter memory for most of the English present. Many lost friends and family in that conflict. Yet no unpleasantness scarred the atmosphere. This World Cup final beneath the Twin Towers was so grand an occasion that respect defined people's behaviour. Anyway, England soon equalised. I'd visited Upton Park enough times to appreciate what Bobby Moore might do when he took that quick free-kick, floating the ball on to Geoff Hurst's head.

My frequent trips to the Boleyn Ground also fostered an admiration for Peters, who then came to the fore for England. Like most supporters, I had a real soft spot for West Ham. I loved making that journey down the District line, turning right out of the station and stepping into West Ham land. All that noise, all that claret and blue. Matches at Upton Park were always good value. On Boxing Day 1963, I ran out of the station, hurried down Green Street for an 11.15 kick-off, wondering whether West Ham against Blackburn Rovers would produce any drama. It finished West Ham 2 Blackburn 8. Two days later, Ewood Park staged the reverse fixture. West Ham got some revenge, winning 3–1. Ron Greenwood changed the team overnight, dropping Peters, and bringing in a guy called Eddie Bovington. High marks for artistic impression would never be entered against Bovington's name but the switch worked. I felt for Peters. Yet two and a half years later there was Peters, seizing on Horst-Dieter Hottges's poor clearance to make it 2–1 to England.

I began screaming at the referee, Gottfried Dienst, to blow for full-time. England were clearly tiring. Maybe they were weighed down by the nation's hopes. The Germans were stronger. Glancing round at the other supporters, everyone willed England to cling on, everyone whistled to shake Dienst into action. Wolfgang Weber then came sliding in to equalise and my world collapsed. Tears welled up. How could England recover from this body-blow? Too late, Dienst signalled the end of normal time. Jules Rimet seemed destined for a German embrace, not ours. England were in deep trouble. The momentum belonged to West Germany. Famously, fate then rode to England's rescue. Fate and a Russian linesman called Tofik Bakhramov. When Hurst's shot struck the bar and bounced down, no one could see whether it crossed the line.

'OVER!' I shouted. I hadn't a clue. Nor had thousands of other Englishmen and truly we don't know today. This was simply a cry of hope. Roger Hunt celebrated and he was closest. He must know. Surely it was a goal? Holding my breath, I looked towards Dienst, who was heading towards Bakhramov. Their conversation would decide the final. I will never forget how the linesman made this wonderful gesture, spreading out his arms to indicate the ball had entered the goal before spinning out. Yes! 3–2! I thanked God for Tofik Bakhramov. During Sven's time as manager, England visited Bakhramov's homeland of Azerbaijan and the occasion was marked by the unveiling of a statue of the linesman by the FIFA president, Sepp Blatter. The FA contingent present said a silent prayer of thanks to Bakhramov. We are for ever in his debt.

When Hurst then completed his hat-trick, we knew it was all over. Dienst's final whistle confirmed victory. England were world champions.

'Never let this feeling end,' I told myself. 'Never.' Everyone was moved by the occasion – and changed. Two hours of football altered the way English people felt about themselves. We became more positive. Everyone reflects now on the Fifties and early Sixties as 'the good old days', but it was grim for much of the time. The country seemed lost in greyness. The long tentacles of war still wrapped themselves around the nation. The World Cup made a break from a melancholic past. Here was some colour. Here was some glory. The Sixties began Swinging.

Bobby Moore, Bobby Charlton and Geoff Hurst embodied a brave new era. The two Bobbys were the glamour boys of the England XI. Geoff was not a glamorous player but his contribution was immense. Unsung heroes could be found throughout the ranks of those following Bobby Moore up the steps. Full-backs like Ray Wilson and George Cohen. 'I feel an unsung hero,' George once told me. Well, George, you were my hero, and I sang his praises. All of the players were heroes.

My admiration also extended to the losing dressing room. Dignity characterised the Germans in defeat. Still does. When we organised the forty-year reunion before the 2006 World Cup at a Tower of London reception, I talked to Hans Tilkowski and Helmut Haller and they could not have been more gracious about '66. 'England deserved to win,' they both told me. Franz Beckenbauer echoed those generous sentiments. No surprise there. One of the true greats, Beckenbauer is gracious about everything. He belonged to the other side, to the Germans, but I revered Beckenbauer. My life has been blessed with opportunities to meet stars who lit up my childhood. Some are real disappointments. But true legends like Beckenbauer, Sir Matt Busby and Bill Shankly were even greater men than I could possibly have imagined. An unbreakable integrity ran through them. They lived up to the legend. They had time for everybody. That's class. Besides, I can't think Beckenbauer and the Germans begrudge us one World Cup, given how things have worked out since.

The party having finished inside Wembley, it continued on the crowded train back into London. Crushed into the carriage, all I could see were happy faces. Desperate to tell Mum about the day, I dashed from Euston.

'We won!' I yelled as I flew through the front door. 'When are the highlights on?' I needed to see the final again. All fans know the feeling: when something so special has taken place, there is always this nagging fear that it may have been just a dream. As night fell, the BBC provided unanswerable proof that events at Wembley really did happen. During the highlights programme, they cut away to the Royal Garden Hotel in Kensington. The England team had been celebrating. Now they stepped on to the balcony on Kensington High Street. Only a thousand or so fans were outside. Compared to the outpourings of emotion now, the scenes of jubilation in '66 were modest. When England's rugby-union team brought home their World Cup in 2003 they paraded around London. The streets were packed for Jonny Wilkinson, Martin Johnson and the rest of Clive Woodward's team. For the Ashes too. And the gongs followed. One of the scandals of modern sport has been the length of time it took for all the 1966 footballers to be acknowledged. On joining the FA, I received complaints about the treatment of England's 1966 heroes. 'The FA don't do enough for former England players,' was the constant criticism. How right they were. The FA should have done far more for the boys of '66 and others who served England so well, enhancing the FA's wealth and image. I was always sensitive that the FA did not handle former internationals with the respect they deserved. I tried to change that. The sight of Bobby Moore's statue now standing proud outside Wembley fills me with pleasure. Soon there's going to be a bust of Sir Alf in the tunnel. Good. We should cherish these national heroes. And I still dream I will live to see 1966 repeated.

1

Rescued by United

Packed with smiling faces, Wembley lacked one person for me: a father. Striding from the station to the ground, I sneaked glances at lads with their dads by their side, chatting away merrily. How lucky those boys were. They shared the Wembley experience with their fathers. They swapped jokes, stories and thoughts on the match. That World Cup odyssey bonded fathers and sons even closer together. I never had that. I was alone.

When my mother fell pregnant with me in 1947, my father John had just been diagnosed with lung cancer. He died five months after I arrived in the world at the Elizabeth Garrett Anderson Hospital on Euston Road on 28 May 1948. Smoking killed him. To deal with the stress of war, Dad sought refuge in nicotine. He was in charge of Air Raid Precautions for Euston and King's Cross and those transport centres inevitably drew much of the Luftwaffe's wrath. Night after night, London was pounded from the air. When the bombs began falling, it was Dad's job to rush people into air-raid shelters or down on to the Tube platforms. Dad witnessed horrific sights, buildings collapsing, neighbours burning in the carnage. For his bravery during the Blitz, he was awarded an MBE. I was never angry with him for smoking. But I'd have loved to have known my father. He sounded a fine man; fun to be with, everyone said. I missed the things fathers do with their sons: advice, chats, friendship, shared interests, kicking balls, going to the game. We'd have got on pretty well. Dad was a left-of-centre conservative and my political journey, if not on the Tory side of the road, ultimately brought me to share many of his values. Dad did bequeath me one good trait: a loathing of smoking.

I was raised by my mother and my father's sister Teify, 'Auntie Tei' as we knew her, who was divorced and lived with us. In overseeing my development, Mum and Auntie Tei mixed toughness and tenderness. Rising at dawn to run the family shop, Woburn Dairy, on Duke's Road close to St Pancras Church, they worked hard for me and my sister, Rosemary. When I was six, I couldn't pronounce certain words, so Mum even sent me to elocution classes. The speech therapist told me if I got the word right she'd give me a sandwich. The end result was she cured my speech problem but I briefly got a weight problem!

Grafting long hours, Mum and Auntie Tei generated enough money to send me to a private school. In keeping with my early years surrounded by females, they got me into a noted London girls' school, Francis Holland, which took a handful of boys until eight. Not many men can proudly declare they attended the same alma mater as Joan and Jackie Collins, Joyce Grenfell and Jemima Khan. Not many men can boast a school motto of 'That our daughters may be as the polished corners of the Temple'. As I neared eight, Mum searched around for another place to take me. After I'd spent a year at a wonderful local prep school called Arnold House, Mum told me I would be off to boarding school because she and Auntie Tei needed all their time and energy to make Woburn Dairy a going concern. Little did I know the horrors lying in wait when Mum then announced: 'You'll be going to the Royal Masonic School next year.' The entry qualification to this cold place in Bushey, Hertfordshire, was as sad as it was simple: your father must have been a Mason and be either dead or bed-ridden. The Masonic Brethren had sung 'Now the evening shadows closing' as Dad's body was carried from St Pancras Church. As the son of a Mason, I was eligible for Bushey.

The train ride from Euston was dispiriting enough. Crammed into the carriage were boys from all over the country, most sharing the same heartache: we were fatherless. We craved a touch of warmth, a consoling mentor. Pastoral care was not on the curriculum at the Royal Masonic School. On that soul-destroying first day in September 1957, I was ordered to put on a ghastly uniform, grey jacket and shorts. Prison stripes would have been more appropriate. A master attached a label to my jacket, denoting my name, and dispatched me to Junior House. Used to the loving environment created by Mum, Auntie Tei and my sister Rosemary, entering the dormitory felt like stepping into a cell. Twenty-five of us were shoehorned in, complete with school trunks and crates of misery. Already without one parent, I would not see my beloved mother until Christmas, but for one solitary day's release for half-term. My world turned upside down, my cherished routine ripped to pieces and replaced with an unbending timetable. 'Supper is at six,' barked a master. 'Bed at seven-thirty.' What?! Back home, I helped my mother re-stock the shelves until nine, listening to her chatting away. Now, at 7.30, I was in bed, the only sounds being the sobs of distraught children. I wanted to join them, releasing my tears, but I never wanted anyone to hear. Only when every other boy had cried himself to sleep, did I let my own tears flow. I felt desperately alone.

As I lay there, tears flowing, thoughts about my plight raced through my head. How did I get here? How did my parents get to London? Mum came from a proud Protestant family in a 95-percent Roman Catholic village called Moycullen, not far from Galway City. Having lost her parents at a young age, she came to London to live with one of her nine brothers. My father's father came from Tregaron in Wales. In the 1870s, not long after the FA was being formed, my grandfather walked to London, looking for work. Also called David Davies, he found employment in the milk trade in Euston, toiling day and night to save the money to buy Woburn Dairy on Duke's Road. This was a famous old store, once frequented by Charles Dickens, who habitually broke his morning walk for a glass of Woburn Dairy milk and even mentioned the building in *The Old Curiosity Shop*. As the business grew, my grandfather became immersed in politics, being elected Mayor of St Pancras in 1911. He was eventually knighted and a picture of Sir David Davies still hangs in Camden Town Hall. A proud Conservative, my grandfather sat on the local council with such characters as George Bernard Shaw and a young Labour firebrand called Barbara Betts, who became Barbara Castle. Debates were of the turbulent variety but Grandfather admired Barbara, and she him. My father was inspired to enter politics, sitting on the London County Council. John Davies dreamed of becoming an MP; he was even adopted as the Tories' prospective parliamentary candidate for the old Holborn and St Pancras seat for the 1950 general election. Death intervened. My much-loved grandfather passed away in early 1957, so I arrived at Bushey with my heart already badly damaged. On that first evening at Bushey, all these thoughts and raw emotions were running through my mind. Needing the toilet, I left the dorm. The floor was cold beneath my bare feet, so I ran fast down the school corridor. As I returned to the dorm, a teacher came upstairs.

'Go and get your slippers,' he barked.

'Yes, sir,' I responded in the manner we'd been ordered to. Bit odd, I thought. Bit late. I was almost back in bed. Anyway, I hadn't even unpacked yet. My slippers were still in my trunk. I fished them out and walked back to the master. 'Give me one of the slippers,' he growled. I did as he commanded. 'Now bend over.' And this man whom I had never met before, who was supposed to be my guardian, solicitous about my welfare, beat me again and again. Did I imagine he derived real pleasure from the act of brutalising a fatherless, helpless nine-year-old? Did I imagine he smiled even in the gloom? Even now, half a century on, I can feel the blows. The pain was bad, the shock worse. This was my first day at school, my first night away from home. I didn't want to be in this bloody Royal Masonic School. Then an adult comes along and hits me. The callousness of it all still fills me with anger and disbelief.

His appetite for cruelty sated, the master said: 'Go back to bed.' I was too stunned to cry. What would my mother tell me? 'Be strong,' she'd say. She was tough. Now I had to be. That night, I vowed never to be defeated by the sadists or bullies at the Royal Masonic School or when I encountered them later in life, wherever that was to take me. Whenever I hear people say cheerily that 'schooldays were the happiest of my life', I shake my head. They didn't go to the Royal Masonic School. At Bushey, corporal punishment was inflicted on boys almost casually, even for trivial misdemeanours. If I was caught running, when I should have been walking, the result could be pure grief. 'Davies. Come here. Bend over.' Whack, whack, whack. In the middle of one cricket match, a teacher used a bat on a boy. A bat! The boy's crime? Not paying enough attention in the field. This teacher was also a vicar. Boys were too scared to talk, fearing further sanction. One bizarre master in the Junior School seemed to revel in it, not caring who knew. He almost advertised his readiness to thrash boys in class. Hanging from a corner of his blackboard was a half-broken hockey stick, a weapon he brandished with some venom.

No one at Bushey thought I would pass any A-levels, so I was dispatched to see the school careers teacher. 'Davies,' he told me, 'you are absolutely perfect material for banking and insurance.' Rubbish. I couldn't think of anyone less suited, though perhaps some training in these areas might have helped when it came to rebuilding Wembley during my time at the FA. Returning to class, I revealed to my friends what this idiot had proposed. 'Oh, don't worry,' they all replied. 'He told us to go into banking and insurance as well.' All temptation to laugh was offset by the realisation that Bushey too often toyed casually with pupils' lives.

The harsh existence of life at the Royal Masonic School affected me badly. I stood up for myself, but also became withdrawn. My survival plan involved football in general and Manchester United in particular. I retreated into my love for United. My passion for the Reds had started a few months before Bushey, on 4 May 1957. Around seven a.m., a loud noise awoke me in our flat across the road from Woburn Dairy. I tugged the curtains back to observe all these strange men in red and white, rattling the door to the shop. They wore scarves and huge rosettes. I saw Mum crossing the road and talking to them. They did not make great sense. The gist of their scrambled words seemed to be that they were hungry. My curiosity aroused by these exotically dressed folk, I threw on my clothes and ran down.

'We are Manchester United,' one explained to me. 'And we're here to win the Cup.' At least I could understand this man. The others kept falling over and stumbling over their words.

'They're drunk,' Mum whispered to Auntie Tei. I didn't have a clue. I just thought maybe that was how people from Manchester behaved.

'They've just got in on the sleeper from Manchester,' Mum told me. 'Probably tired and hungry.'

These United fans changed my life. Meeting this intrigued young Londoner, they seemed keen on converting me to their religion.

'We're going to do the Double,' said one.

'What's the Double?' I asked. My ignorance prompted much laughter.

'The Double is when you win the League and Cup – and we're going to make history,' explained another. 'We're going to beat Aston Villa today and that's the Double won.'

The possibility of failure did not seem to feature anywhere in United's thinking. Modesty did not trouble them. Maybe United fans haven't changed. On they rattled, praising all the United players. The most lavish tributes were reserved for one hero in particular: Duncan Edwards.

'You want to see this great player, this great Dunc,' they kept saying. My mother reappeared with their sandwiches and the Duncan Edwards fan club headed for the door.

'Get yourself one of these rosettes,' they told me. 'Outside Euston, there's a man selling rosettes. Only one and thruppence.' That princely sum was my pocket money, which Mum gave me the night before. Destiny drove me into a lifelong fixation with

Manchester United. I was determined to blow one week's pocket money on a coloured piece of paper and fabric. Making money had been an annual ritual for me outside Euston, where I had a lucrative penny-for-the-guy pitch in the run-up to Bonfire Night. Spending money outside Euston was a new development. My week's pocket money disappeared in one transaction but I had the rosette. Putting on that rosette was like joining an exclusive club. Walking around London that morning, I felt the proudest person, parading my new allegiance to Manchester United.

As I soon learned about my new passion, the course of true love with United rarely ran true. Watching that Cup final on our terrible TV set was deeply frustrating. Making sense of the wobbly picture was hard enough. Making sense of Peter McParland's dreadful foul on our keeper, Ray Wood, was impossible. Outrage filled my young mind. How could he? I yield to no one in my admiration for Kenneth Wolstenholme, the legendary BBC commentator, but I couldn't fathom his criticism of United supporters for booing McParland. To that child, he deserved it. People always talk about Nat Lofthouse's shoulder-charge the following year, but this was worse. Swiftly I acquired the United belief that opponents are out to kick us off the park.

'That's a foul,' I kept shouting at the TV.

'What is it?' Auntie Tei asked.

'He's just fouled our keeper.' Even through the blurred image on the screen, I saw Jackie Blanchflower going in goal, this fabled giant called Duncan Edwards stepping back into defence and Ray Wood much later hobbling back on at centre-forward. A nobility characterised these players like Tommy Taylor, Roger Byrne, Bill Foulkes and Bobby Charlton. They attacked, had a real go, despite having a stricken keeper up front. Like all true Reds, I was gutted when we didn't win.

'Bad luck,' said friends.

'No, it wasn't bad luck,' I retorted. 'We should never have lost. It was unfair.' But I was hooked on United.

My addiction to United provided an escape from the beatings

and misery of the Royal Masonic School. Three times a week an envelope of newspaper cuttings arrived from Auntie Tei, clippings from the *Daily Telegraph, Daily Express, Sunday Mirror* and *People.* I fell on this package like a starving prisoner on a Red Cross parcel. Contained inside were United match reports. What treasure! When the day's labours were concluded, I enjoyed a few brief moments to myself, sitting on my bed, reading the reports, hunting any titbit about Duncan Edwards.

On one occasion, Mum phoned the school. The date was 6 February 1958, a day etched on the heart of every United fan, the day a team died. On that grim day when United's plane ploughed off the runway at Munich and caught fire, Mum rang Bushey. She was so worried about me.

'Break the news to him gently,' she pleaded with the headmaster. 'He so loves Manchester United. And they say that Duncan Edwards is very poorly.'

Concentration on school work was impossible. Even the odd beating left no mark on me emotionally. My mind focused on Duncan, willing him to live. The suggestion in the cuttings from home was that Duncan would survive. He wore the red of United. He would not be defeated. Losing was not in his nature. The last rites had been read to Matt Busby but he survived. Matt had been pulled back from death's door. Why couldn't Duncan? One God-forsaken morning, a teacher shouted down the corridor. 'Davies, come here.' I hurried up to him. 'Edwards is dead. Chin up.'

Brutally delivered, this devastating news absolutely shattered me. I learned a lesson that day. However emotionally distraught I am over a situation, I try not to reveal my hurt, a useful habit in years to come. Keep it hidden. Keep strong. That night, when the lights went out in the cold dormitory, I allowed the tears to surface. Nothing can be worse than the extinguishing of a candle called hope. Nothing can be worse than the death of such youthful talent. Duncan was gone, his brave battle against those horrific injuries lost. Part of my youth passed away with Duncan Edwards.

That United team captivated people far and wide. David Dein, formerly vice-chairman of Arsenal, once showed me an excerpt from his schoolboy diaries, including his report on United's last game on English soil, the 4–5 match at Highbury on 1 February 1958. A very young Gunners fan on the terraces, David recorded his admiration for the visiting players. Written in red ink a few pages later in David's diary were the names of all the United players who perished at Munich. United had that effect on real football people.

My own overwhelming feeling of sadness melted into a concern over how United would get a team together. My United would fight back. So I longed for news about their next match, the FA Cup tie against Sheffield Wednesday. I pleaded with a teacher to tell me the score. 'Three–nil to United,' he informed me. Match reports soon arrived from Duke's Road, an array of words and pictures. My spirits lifted. United would recover from Munich. Even then, plans were being made for the future. Tossing up in the centre-circle was the Wednesday captain, Albert Quixall, soon to move to Old Trafford. Quixall was to become another hero of mine.

Those 1958 days at Bushey revolved around charting United's FA Cup progress. News of a sixth-round victory over West Brom came through. Then came Jimmy Hill's Fulham in the semis. 'That was my greatest ever game for Fulham,' Jimmy told me thirty years later during our days at the BBC. 'I scored twice.' Jimmy did indeed score two goals but only because he and the ball collided on two separate occasions! United won the replay 5–3 at Highbury, reaching Wembley. The inspiring way the club reacted to Munich was the making of Manchester United as the institution they are today. They owed much to the great Welshman, Jimmy Murphy, who rebuilt the team in Matt's absence. Youngsters were given their chance, a philosophy thrillingly witnessed again under Sir Alex Ferguson. Youth mixed with experience: Ernie Taylor came from Blackpool, Stan Crowther from Aston Villa. Bobby returned from his injuries. These heroes of mine took on the challenge of rebuilding United, of keeping alive a flame lit by fallen heroes like Duncan Edwards.

Having sung 'Abide with Me' at my adored grandfather's funeral in 1957, that haunting melody carries an extra significance whenever I hear its strains on FA Cup final day. In 1958, United lost to Bolton Wanderers but the story engrossed the nation, back then and still now, as the outpouring of emotion on the fiftieth anniversary of Munich in February 2008 proved. When the great Frank Taylor book *The Day a Team Died* was published, I spent what was for me a huge sum of money to buy it. Frank was on the flight. He knew what had happened. I read *The Day a Team Died* over and over again, absorbing as much information about my idols as possible.

I first saw United in the flesh on 20 December 1958. Too young to attend matches on my own, I found a helping hand. Working in an office next door to Woburn Dairy was a lovely man called Ron Jackson. Known to everyone who frequented our shop as 'Ike', for reasons I never knew, he lived near Chelsea.

'David loves Manchester United, and they're playing at Chelsea tomorrow,' Ike told Mum. 'Why don't I take him to the game?'

I nodded enthusiastically before noticing Mum's stern face. 'Will he be safe?' she replied.

'Of course,' promised Ike. 'He'll be with me.'

Mum trusted me on the bus, so I jumped on the No. 30 down the Euston Road, leaping off outside South Ken Tube where Ike waited. We walked to Stamford Bridge through all the posh parts of Kensington, down the Fulham Road and over that small humpback bridge leading to the ground. Plastered across a wall was an advertisement for motor batteries. Even now, fifty years on, I search for the faded paint and my mind rewinds to my first game. Like the ad, everything seemed gigantic. The crowd was enormous, almost 60,000-strong. The noise was immense. After handing over my nine old pennies, the Shed End opened up to me.

'The best position is ten rows back, behind a barrier,' shouted Ike, initiating me in match-day rituals. Standing with Chelsea fans, I peered towards the pitch. Even now I can name the United team: Gregg; Foulkes, Carolan, Goodwin, Cope, McGuinness, Bradley, Quixall, Viollet, Charlton and Scanlon. Mesmerised, I hardly blinked all game. So many little details stayed with me: Warren Bradley's jinking runs, Bobby Charlton's surging breaks, Quixall's hair that turned upwards in a quiff. United won 3–2 and I couldn't wipe the smile off my face. Fortunately, the Chelsea fans who called the Shed their home never worried about a little squirt like me.

Without United, I might have gone mad at the Royal Masonic School. Turning fourteen, and generally quiet, rebellion shaped my daily actions. Challenging authority became as natural as drawing breath. Few at Bushey had much of a spring in their step. The gloomy reality of life was that occasionally sons of one-parent families found their status downgraded to 'orphans'. If Lady Bracknell had made her observation about the carelessness of losing two parents within the confines of Bushey, she would have been chased down the drive by enraged orphans. Boys dreaded a summons to the headmaster's study after evening prayer on Sundays, Geoffrey Dark's or Hugh Mullens's chosen moment for disclosing details of a mother's death. Heart-breaking news was worsened by the manner of its delivery. Called to Mr Mullens's room, boys sometimes wouldn't return to the dormitory that night. An untouched bed carried the same significance as a flag at half-mast. Boys disappeared for funerals and then returned, shell-shocked. No wonder some became psychologically scarred for life. One school-mate of my acquaintance grew up to have a whole *World in Action* devoted to his crimes; he was a drug addict of considerable appetite.

Nurturing model members of society was always going to be difficult at the Royal Masonic School. Bushey was an independent school, but also a charity establishment. No fees were paid by parents. Was I smart or poor? Privileged or unfortunate? God knows. Sporting fixtures encapsulated the confusion. One Saturday we'd be taking on the local state school. 'Posh boys,' they shouted. The next week, we tackled a famous public school. Their barbed comment of choice would be 'Charity boys'. Whenever I played rugby, there was one boy in particular who enjoyed sledging us. 'You've not got a father,' this boy kept saying to me in scrums. 'Your father's dead.'

Bushey was a mixed-up place. Some pupils were destined for Oxbridge. Anthony Andrews headed for fame as an actor. Other pupils slid inexorably towards life's scrapheap, dragged down by serious emotional difficulties. Short of reviving a Dickensian nightmare and rebuilding Dotheboys Hall in Hertfordshire, it was hard to imagine a more traumatic way of raising children. Lads were expelled for the tiniest acts, like nicking the beer from the back of the pavilion at the Old Boys' cricketing reunion. One mate was kicked out just for snogging a local girl. As he packed his bags, the rest of us were given a lecture by Hugh Mullens. This eccentric man warned us of the dangers of female contact with the immortal words: 'A kiss is an invitation to marriage'. Just one kiss and next stop the altar? That creed would have caused a few problems at the FA a few years later. That was Bushey for you. Mad. Masters taught me to swim by throwing me in the pool. Sink or swim.

Persistent offending, even if simply of low-level nuisance value, became a way of life. One Monday morning at Senior School, I was evicted from class in both the first and second lessons and then got 500 lines in the third. 'I must not look at the clock during lessons' I had to write out painstakingly. Having finished those during the break, I celebrated by getting kicked out of double French. The resistance movement was in full swing.

In fairness, quite where I would have gone without the Masonic School I cannot imagine. Fate smiled on me eventually. A father figure appeared. Coming under the guidance of Richard Dilley, one of the masters at Bushey who actually cared, had a profound influence. No one shaped my development more. This wonderful man saw an anguished boy heading for oblivion and pulled me back from the abyss. The first act of Mr Dilley's rescue plan involved phoning Duke's Road.

'I'm worried about David,' he told Mum. 'You'd better come

up.' Mum sped up to discuss my state of mind. Mr Dilley called me into his study. For the first time, an adult listened to my angst.

'What's eating away at you?' he asked.

'I feel hollow without a father,' I told Mr Dilley.

'David, you think you are unlucky,' replied my guardian angel. 'Just think of all those people far worse off than you. Think of Africans starving. Think of people in the war. Far more terrible things happen to others.' How could I argue? Important principles were instilled by Mr Dilley. At last I possessed some rules of engagement for the great conflict called life. 'Treat others as you would like to be treated yourself' was central to Mr Dilley's code – and mine. 'Think before you act' was another tenet. Mr Dilley gave me hope.

With the torch of Mr Dilley's good advice lighting the way ahead, I stabilised at Bushey. Astonishingly, my improved behaviour saw me appointed head of Cadogan House. For the first time in my life I had power and authority over other people. The feudal system of the Royal Masonic School meant I could now inflict corporal punishment on others. There was little chance of me grabbing a cricket bat or half-broken hockey stick and thrashing some petrified first-former to within an inch of his life. The emotional scars I carried made me passionately opposed to corporal punishment. Someone had to make a stand against this cycle of violence.

Inspired by Richard Dilley, I made the rugby XV and skippered the cricket second XI. 'A fairish batsman,' concluded the cricket master in my final report, 'a humane and humorous captain, with some novel tactics up his sleeves'. This usually involved bringing the fielders in and doubling the slips when our bowlers were getting hammered. But on the playing fields, too, the dark cloud of tragedy hung in the air at Bushey. Our hockey team was playing Bishop's Stortford College one day when a ball struck our left-half in the throat. He died. Even by the school's standards for dealing in despair, this was a new low.

Bushey had no football team, but we all competed in wild

kickabouts, house against house. Outside-left was my preferred position with my greatest asset being speed. Unfortunately, the ball had a stubborn tendency not to join me on this rapid journey down the flank. When these house bundles were over, we'd gather around the radio to catch up on more significant results. I counted down the days to freedom, plotting what London matches I would attend in the holidays. Craven Cottage was a regular haunt. I loved listening to Fulham fans yelling at Bedford Jezzard, their manager. A prolific centre-forward for Fulham, Jezzard was honoured with a fans' cry: 'Jezzard – shoot!' During the difficult times of his management years at the Cottage, more fans would shout: 'Jezzard, shoot – preferably yourself!' Humour and drama were always to be found at Fulham, particularly with comedian Tommy Trinder as chairman.

For a fatherless boy, football crowds provided instant companionship. Upton Park offered great noise and goals. A frequent visitor to the East End, my general impression of West Ham under Ted Fenton and then Ron Greenwood was that they would go 4–0 up and lose 4–5 – or trail 0–4 and then stage an amazing escape. Goals were guaranteed. West Ham occasionally featured in my Team of the Week, a section of wall in the attic at Duke's Road. This room was a shrine to football. Scrapbooks were scattered all over the floor. Photographs adorned the wall, cut from *Charlie Buchan's Football Monthly* and the old *Reynold's News*, the first paper to do colour pictures of teams.

Another particular joy was catching the great Gento live. When Real Madrid visited Arsenal for a friendly, I squeezed into the Clock End at Highbury. Like George Best and Cristiano Ronaldo, Gento was the type of winger worth the entrance fee alone. Just him. Just to see him skinning a full-back. I followed Gento's career closely, always checking to see whether he was on television. Even with the poor TV at Duke's Road, the brilliance of Gento and Real Madrid in their European Cup dismantling of Eintracht Frankfurt at Hampden Park in 1960 was inescapable. No wonder 130,000 Jocks, including Fergie, went mad. What a game!

My reverie over football was broken by an annoying need to concentrate on A-levels. Having struck the deal with Mum and Auntie Tei over the World Cup, I knuckled down to acquiring the grades for university, amazingly getting an A in History and a B in English, and getting into Sheffield.

It was at university that I enjoyed my first BBC scoop. Within two years, I was entering the Grand Hotel in Sheffield, microphone in clammy hand, questions churning in my young head. My destination was the suite of Enoch Powell, the politician who'd just stirred so much controversy with his 'Rivers of Blood' speech. Emerging from the lift on Powell's floor, I knew my big break in broadcasting lay just along the corridor. Powell had not talked since causing national outrage with his comments about immigration. This was my chance. Knock on the door.

'Enter.' Walk in. There he was. Enoch Powell. Even though the windows were closed, I could hear my student mates outside, demonstrating against Powell's presence in Sheffield. Lines of police kept them out of the hotel. Inside, all was calm. Powell snaked out a hand. 'Sit down. Have some tea. Cake?'

Powell's willingness to talk stunned me. My weekly student slot on BBC Radio Sheffield was hardly the *Today* programme. It was pre-recorded, rough and ready. Located on the VHF frequency there was some evidence I was the only listener every Saturday at noon. Before going to Hillsborough or Bramall Lane, I proudly tuned in. Broadcasting seemed an attractive career, so when Radio Sheffield advertised for someone to contribute a student show, I jumped at the chance. Too often, the programme was worthy, predictable and a bit dull. It was time to spice it up. Enoch Powell promised fireworks. As my friends shouted at the screen during Powell's infamous speech, I plotted my coup. Powell was due in Sheffield weeks later, and all my mates planned to protest.

'I'll join you,' I said. Then I had another thought. 'The pen is mightier than the placard,' I told them, composing a letter.

'Dear Mr Powell, I understand you are visiting Sheffield and you must appear on my radio programme. This will be going out to a big audience. Yours sincerely, David Davies.'

Even looking at the envelope, on which I had written 'The Right Honourable Enoch Powell MP, House of Commons, London', I never believed my request would go anywhere other than a waste-paper bin. Three days later, my heart leapt. Falling through the letter-hole was a dispatch from the House of Commons, crests and all.

'Dear Mr Davies, I look forward to meeting you in Sheffield. Please come to the Grand Hotel to record the interview at 5pm on Friday, Yours sincerely, Enoch Powell MP.' Blimey! Clutching the letter, I went to see the manager of Radio Sheffield, Michael Barton.

'Michael, I think I should show you this.' The BBC got terribly excited. The interviewing skills of a Sheffield undergraduate were suddenly discussed at the highest level at Broadcasting House. Word came up from London to remind this student to ask certain questions.

'You are going to talk to Mr Powell about his "Rivers of Blood" beliefs?' asked Barton.

'Err, yes!'

The BBC need not have worried. My line of attack was always going to focus on the 'Rivers of Blood'. My friends were unimpressed.

'How can you talk to Enoch Powell?' one asked.

'I have to.' Powell fascinated me. Tea and cake accepted, verbal pleasantries concluded, we began the interview. Powell was spellbinding. With those piercing eyes, corpse-like pallor and huge intellect, he emitted a fear-inducing authority. Sloppy questions were seized on as an affront to his cerebral powers.

'What do you mean by that?' he often countered. Unwilling to call him a racist directly, I began one question: 'Some people say: You are a racist.' Powell swooped on the loose question like a bird of prey. 'Which people said that? Name them.' My stomach tied in ever greater knots.

'Do you stand by your "Rivers of Blood" speech?' I asked.

'Yes,' Powell replied coolly. 'It is my duty to bring these subjects to people's attention. If I have upset people, well, sometimes in life you have to upset people. We are sitting on a huge problem.' The following day, Radio Sheffield ran the exclusive on the noon slot usually reserved for student tittle-tattle. For the first time, we did the programme live. I sat in the studio, fielding calls from people reacting to Powell's views. Radio Four even carried parts on the old Home Service. The reaction was good. Newspapers lifted the quotes. None of them mentioned Powell talked to some tuppenny-ha'penny student. Only the *Sheffield Star* wrote some kind things about me.

'Well done,' said Michael Barton. Usually a closed world to people like me, the BBC suddenly appeared a possible future employer.

Sheffield suited me. People were so warm, locals and students alike. After the harshness of Bushey, this was wonderful. I threw myself into the university football teams and into student politics. Slowly, I emerged from a bruised shell. Reacting to the Royal Masonic School and my conservative background, my drift to the left accelerated. We stayed up late, debating Vietnam. We worried whether the draft would be brought in here almost as much as extending the hours women could be entertained in our rooms at halls of residence. My love of student politics never interfered with my love of Manchester United. In January 1968, I bought a ticket to the European Cup final, not having a clue who would qualify. It was a blind purchase, by postal-order to the FA, as much in hope as expectation of United reaching Wembley. My belief built during the season until United met Real Madrid in the semis. I nipped over the Pennines to watch George Best score the only goal of the first leg one sunlit evening at Old Trafford.

'It's not enough,' I told friends back in Sheffield. 'Here we go again – more bloody heartache. We messed up last year to Partizan Belgrade, who we should certainly have beaten.'

The second leg coincided with our politics-department tour to the European Parliament, at the time situated in Luxembourg. On the Wednesday night, four of us were so keen to find a bar showing the match we scoured Luxembourg, which didn't take long. Finding a café, we sat down on stools and waited for the game. Realising we were United fans, the patron smiled and announced: 'I hate Real Madrid. If you knock Madrid out, I'll give you free food.'

'And what if Madrid knock us out?!' I asked.

'Then you pay!'

Suddenly confident, we tore into the patron's red wine, which was not of the highest standard. Who cared? We were students. United were 1–3 down at half-time, but then made it 3–3 with Billy Foulkes hurtling up the field to score the crucial goal. I was so thrilled. Wembley awaited. Not only did I have a ticket, but a free meal as well. Again, I travelled to Wembley on my own. United should really have lost to Eusebio and Benfica. We would have done but for Johnny Aston, who produced the game of his life on the left wing. Aston was not a fans' favourite. The joke among us United supporters was: 'Aston will run and run, and if they open the gates, he will run right out of the ground!' That night, Aston ran Benfica ragged, eclipsing even Bobby Charlton and George Best.

In between United matches, I began thinking about life after university. One night in my final year, a gentleman from the BBC was booked into the lecture hall to give a career talk. My mates and I piled in; standing room only, lots of anticipation. Everyone fancied a career in the BBC. The Corporation did not select the best ambassador. He was posh, arrogant and clearly aghast at the thought of the great unwashed from Sheffield sullying the hallowed corridors of Broadcasting House.

'Of course, we at the BBC have a traineeship where we take six people a year and, of course, we have thousands of applicants,' came his sermon. 'We have some new scheme coming in, called a news traineeship, which I don't really know too much about, and frankly is not really for you.'

His message was clear: don't waste your time, you Sheffield heathens. 'This man is awful,' I remarked to a friend, as we walked, crestfallen, from the lecture hall. The memory of that BBC guy's dismissive comments bugged me. Proving him wrong would be a thrill. My journey to Broadcasting House was circuitous, including stops at St Peter's College, Oxford, to acquire a Postgraduate Certificate in Education, a spell at the *Belfast Telegraph* and a Thomson's training course in Cardiff, where I met two men destined to become good friends and also greats of the writing game, Ken Follett and Anthony Holden. After a stint at BBC Wales, I was finally summoned to Broadcasting House.

2

George Best and Miss Manchester City

When BBC TV Sport required a presenter to stand in for David Vine at the Benson and Hedges snooker, I prepared for days on end for my debut at the Wembley Conference Centre. The afternoon coverage began well: confident intro, sit back, enjoy the commentary. The four p.m. tea-break arrived, and still things went smoothly. Then the moment came to flick on the video-tape machine to play some recorded action from the other table. Machine One stuck. An explosion of voices burst into my ear.

'David, keep talking. We're switching to the back-up machine.' I waffled on – and on. Machine Two froze. So here was the BBC's major sports programme with no live action, no video-tape, no studio guests, and a rookie presenter.

'Keep talking, David,' came the voice in my ear. 'The players are due back from the tea-break in eight minutes.' Christ. Breathe in. Talk. Thank God, my homework paid off. I sat there, pontificating about the history of the B and H, mentioning the highs of this classic event.

'They're coming back,' piped up the voice in my ear. 'Throw back to commentary.' Blessed relief. I'd survived eight minutes that could have wrecked my career. If I'd frozen like those bloody machines, stuttered, made mistakes or broken out in a sweat, I'd have been looking for new work sharpish. The gallery fell silent in my ear. I'd made it. Exhale. Relax. My ear-piece rattled into life again. 'We've just had a call from Terry Griffiths. In your tea-break history of the B and H, you left out the year he won.' Typical. Sympathy was a rare commodity at the BBC.

I'd started as a news trainee with a spell at BBC Radio Sport, fiefdom of a legendary character called Angus Mackay. The sports room was long and narrow with Angus's office at the end. Occasionally, Angus summoned journalists like me, Des Lynam, John Motson or Christopher Martin-Jenkins to his lair. He pressed a button. BUZZ. A fearsome Scottish voice then boomed over the Tannoy: 'David Davies!' The first time it happened, a few hours into my job as a trainee, my blood ran cold. The forty-yard journey to his office seemed a marathon. Nervously, I knocked and entered. No small-talk, no pleasantries.

Angus launched straight in. 'Davies, they tell me you are very good. But let me tell you, sonny, you are crap.' Heavens above!

'Mr Mackay, I intend to prove you wrong.' Conversation over. Out I went.

Mackay's world, and particularly *Sports Report*, was a tough proving ground. Only the best survived. Fortunately, I enjoyed top advice from a broadcasting master, Des Lynam. Ordered to shadow Des for several days, I followed him everywhere, even into a bedroom once when we shared overnight accommodation at the BBC Club on Langham Place. As a person and a broadcaster, Des inspired awe in equal measure. Working with radio legends like Des and Bryon Butler made me realise how much I had to learn. TV beckoned. Warmly welcomed by the irrepressible Stuart Hall, Manchester became my home for eleven years, presenting and covering countless big stories. Variety was the spice of this professional life. One night, a strike by technical staff threatened the output of BBC Manchester. Then the word came from the NUJ: 'Work normally.' Blimey! How would we fill the half-hour *Look North* news slot? No technical staff, no programme? Surely.

Then some bright spark had a brainwave. 'Basil Brush is in panto at the Palace Theatre. Why don't we get him in?'

Why not?! We had to pad out the show and who better than a fake fox?

Someone called the Palace. 'Would Basil like to earn some extra cash? He would! Marvellous! Can he be in the studio sharpish?'

Good for Basil, he was over in a flash, along with his minder, Derek Fowlds, who became well known starring in *Yes Minister*.

'So, Basil, what are you like at ad-libbing?' I asked Basil. 'We have thirty empty minutes stretching out in front of us.' Despite all his stage experience, it turned out that Basil Brush was rubbish at unscripted repartee. Basil Brush's answers were short, and often accompanied by his catchphrase 'BOOM BOOM'. I wanted to punch him in the throat at one stage. When I ran out of questions, I just repeated them. People thought it hilarious. Martin Buchan, the Manchester United captain and a good friend, called.

'I have just seen the best TV programme ever,' Martin said. 'You and Basil Brush make a great double act.'

'Never again!' I replied.

Out of the studio, I covered the terrible Summerland fire on the Isle of Man, a huge tragedy claiming the lives of more than fifty people in an entertainment centre. 'Get on a plane, get out there, and hold the fort until the big guns get up from London,' our news editor, Freddie Knowles, told me. Arriving outside Douglas at eleven p.m., I came across a scene from hell. Body after charred body was being carried out. The story felt a great break for me, the chance to do national radio and early-morning television before more senior reporters flew in. In truth, my reaction lacked compassion.

'Focus on the stretchers,' I told our TV crew. As I uttered those words, I felt acutely sensitive, ashamed even, that I was intruding on private grief. Also on the scene were relatives of the dead and dying and they objected to a camera crew, recording their loved ones' last moments.

'Fuck off,' some shouted. A bottle flew through the air in my direction. I dodged it.

We risked far worse during the civil unrest in Toxteth and Moss

Side in 1981. Over several nights, we worked between the battle-lines of police and rioters, seeking the most graphic footage and best news angles as bottles rained down on us. 'If you don't fuck off, we'll stick that camera down your throat,' one rioter screamed at me. And that was one of the nicer comments.

One morning, my great police contact, Detective Chief Superintendent Joe Mouncey, a legend in Lancashire police, rang.

'Get over to Morecambe nick,' Mouncey whispered. 'We've caught the Birmingham pub bombers.' Putting the phone down, I raced to Morecambe with a camera crew. I knew the IRA were active again, and had seen the carnage wrought in Birmingham the night before. But why were they on my patch?

'They were arrested trying to board the Heysham ferry to Belfast this morning,' explained Mouncey when I called him back. 'They'll be leaving the station any minute.' Good. These would make fantastic pictures for the BBC's tea-time news. Standing along the pavement was a rather graceful figure. ITN had sent a Manchester-based reporter called Anna Ford, already a respected journalist and clearly destined for greater things than hanging around outside police stations. I liked Anna. Everyone in Manchester fancied her. She was attractive and charismatic but sadly had a boyfriend. Anna and I chatted for a few moments, always aware we'd have to spring into action the moment the Birmingham pub bombers appeared. They soon did. Blankets over their heads, the suspects were shoved into a police van and driven back to the Midlands. The journey from police station to van was over in seconds, but it would make magnificent footage.

'Got it?' I asked the BBC cameraman. His pause horrified me.

'Sorry,' he said finally. 'The camera jammed.' I went ballistic. As Anna Ford swanned off down the road with her crew back to Manchester, I stood there speechless. Desperate times called for desperate measures. Ingenuity is a journalist's best friend, along with his contacts. I rang Mouncey, explaining my predicament.

'The BBC have no pictures of this great piece of police work,' I told him, little realising the alleged Birmingham pub bombers would eventually be cleared. 'Leave it with me,' replied Mouncey. 'Stay outside the station.' Sure enough, half an hour later, another six people emerged from Morecambe police station, their features again hidden under blankets. Again they were bundled into a police van that had just pulled up. That footage formed the lead item on the BBC news at six and nine, and I basked in the rare glow of BBC management praise. Anyone comparing my pictures with Anna Ford's ITN version could have noticed one startling difference: the suspects' shoes were different. My 'suspects' all wore the same boots, which was no surprise. I fear they were all bobbies based at Morecambe nick who did me a massive favour.

Covering crime, politics and football, I really was building up the perfect CV for working at the FA, particularly when BBC Manchester gave me the unexpected chance to present religious programmes. In Wythenshawe, Manchester, one Sunday morning, my inquisition of the Bishop of Durham live on air was interrupted by the noise of slates being removed from the church roof.

Of my many roles in Manchester, the most enjoyable was becoming the BBC's unofficial George Best correspondent. George would go missing, and I'd hurtle round town looking for him. It became a ritual. First stop, the Grapes pub.

'Anybody seen George?'

'No!' On to Blinkers, Slack Alice or various trendy menswear stores.

'Anybody seen George?'

'Not since yesterday.' Off to Mrs Fullaway's, his old digs. Knock on door.

'Is George in?'

'No.' Off to Paddy Crerand's, George's occasional base. No joy. And so it went on. Sometimes we headed to the Cliff, United's training ground, waiting outside those huge red metal gates in the forlorn hope George might turn up. George's incorrigible pursuit of women and later drink vexed a range of United managers. Matt Busby was always gracious. Meeting Busby was everything I dreamed it would be and more. Imagine every compliment ever bestowed on Matt and then double it. That was Busby. All charm and integrity. He was a wise owl who absorbed the views of others. 'Matt listened to us,' Paddy Crerand told me. 'He brought players out of themselves. We were in awe of him.' So were we reporters, waiting at the Cliff gates or outside Old Trafford. Busby would emerge, a benign look on his face but say nothing about George's whereabouts. Typically, Bestie was holed up in a hotel with his latest squeeze. Staff at the hotel, looking to make a few quid, tipped reporters off, so we'd all speed there. Within minutes, camera crews would besiege the hotel. Standing next to the heaving scrum, I'd solemnly deliver a piece on the latest episode in the George Best soap opera.

George became more than a news story to me. Being young and single, I happily headed off into Manchester's club-land, spending some great evenings with him. George was bright, funny and good company but he always seemed slightly lost, always searching for something. After he retired the first time, he was persuaded back to United by Tommy Docherty. The Doc was so pleased with himself.

'It's never going to last,' I told Freddie Knowles and Tom German in the BBC office. Watching George at his return press conference at Old Trafford, I thought this was a guy who'd won the European Cup, who must look around the team and see lesser players than when United were at their height under Busby. Denis Law and Bobby Charlton were gone or going. 'There's no one of their ability left,' George told me later. After George's death, I always wondered how Sir Alex Ferguson would have handled Best. People depict George as hurtling inexorably towards oblivion but I genuinely believe someone strong like Ferguson might have rescued him. Fergie could have kept Best motivated.

'How do you live with the fame?' I boringly asked Best once. We were in a night-club and the noise momentarily dropped. George shrugged those slender shoulders, and smiled as some stunning girl eyed him up. As a fan, I loved George Best and was troubled by his off-field life. But it would have been wrong to lecture Best about the desperately sad wasting of a God-given talent. Best meant the world to me. When he scored those six goals at Northampton, I was there. My sister Rosemary married a farmer in Northamptonshire, so I cunningly tied in a trip to see them with a visit to the County Ground. What people forget is that Best's six goals that day did not come on a bowling-green surface like those that Wayne Rooney and others play on today. Northampton's pitch was a muddy field that looked like cows had just trampled across it. George danced around the divots.

North-west teams ruled England, often Europe, during my time in Manchester. Liverpool were immense and a joy to work with, particularly Bill Shankly. Every interview I conducted with Shanks provided a rich seam of material glistening with nuggets. 'If Belfast ever had a team like Liverpool the Irish problem would be solved quickly,' Shanks once told me before an FA Cup semi-final replay. 'The Irish people would unite behind such a team.' Personally, I thought the Troubles were slightly more complicated but it showed Shanks's view of Liverpool. A force for good, a force so strong it could bring peace to Belfast.

Like Busby, Shanks was another legend who didn't disappoint. I understood why people described Shankly as a 'messiah'. Blessed with a great aura, he knew how to work a crowd. Fans loved him. Watching Shanks milk the applause of the Liverpool fans after winning the 1974 Cup final, I had no inkling he was about to stand down. News of his retirement was one of those JFK moments. Some months after he retired, I went to interview him at his modest terraced home not far from Anfield. His wife, Elsie, opened the door, ushering me into a house packed with Liverpool mementoes. It was hard to believe he had deliberately left Anfield. Bill sat there in his Liverpool tracksuit.

'So what are you up to?' I asked him.

'I still get to games,' he replied. Typical. Shankly's life still revolved around Liverpool. People often spoke about how early Shankly arrived at games in retirement, as if he could not shake off the match-day ritual. I rang Tommy Docherty.

'I'm concerned about Bill,' I said.

'Look, I'm concerned as well,' said Docherty. 'What is he up to?' The Doc was probably not the ideal person to pontificate on others' lives, but he was genuinely worried. Shankly seemed bereft without football, which made his retirement even stranger.

Unlike Shankly, Bob Paisley was not a journalist's dream. I did the first ever TV interview with Bob as Liverpool manager and it was not my finest hour. It was not even close to an hour. One minute five seconds of it was usable. It was the most difficult interview of my career until 1977 when Kenny Dalglish brought his thick Glaswegian accent down from Celtic. Bob's accent was not the problem. He just didn't say anything. A short sentence here, a couple of words there. 'Listen, Bob, no one is going to shoot you here,' I told him. No difference. I couldn't complain. Bob was a lovely man. He just never sought the limelight like Shanks. Paisley downplayed any hysterical acclamation of his own abilities, which were immense. Watching training at Melwood, I saw there was no secret to Liverpool's success. Their football was just a celebration of simplicity. 'Pass and move,' Bob would say. 'Pass and move.' All day long.

The players responded because they appreciated how important Paisley had been to Shankly. Promotion from the Boot Room seemed right. 'It's amazing in there,' Stuart Hall kept telling me about the renowned Boot Room, that small space hardly much bigger than a cupboard in the main stand at Anfield. 'It is one of the most important rooms in football. If you get invited into the inner sanctum, seize the opportunity with both hands.' After one match, an invitation was extended. Acutely aware of the honour, I entered the Boot Room slightly nervously. 'Beer or whisky?' offered Roy Evans. What a privilege, what warmth of welcome, especially for a Manchester United fan.

The wily old birds within the Boot Room made it unique. Liverpool's brains trust gathered there. I knew them from European trips, real football men like Ronnie Moran, Joe Fagan, Roy Evans and Tom Saunders, an old schoolmaster. They were all so approachable, sitting in their den, gossiping about football. I travelled all over Europe with the boys from the Boot Room, eulogising about this 'pass and move' philosophy in action from Tbilisi to Paris. On Liverpool trips, you couldn't move for characters. The secretary, Peter Robinson, was a master at dealing with the complications thrown up by travelling in Europe in the Seventies, particularly when the Iron Curtain had to be parted. The Russian Bear was rarely helpful, though. Liverpool always flew Aer Lingus, but the Soviets refused to permit a foreign plane to land in Tbilisi when Liverpool were drawn with Dinamo. 'An Irish plane cannot come here,' came the word from the Soviets. 'You must fly on the glorious Soviet carrier, Aeroflot.' Clever. Liverpool had to hire an Aeroflot jet. Hard cash only. So for the first time in aviation history, Aeroflot flew a plane into Merseyside to take Liverpool to Tbilisi. Even worse, the plane stopped off at Moscow on the way, which was a massive detour. The Soviets just wanted to knacker Liverpool. It worked. Liverpool got stuffed.

The collision between Liverpool and Manchester United in the 1977 FA Cup final was massive news for BBC North West. Television Centre still looked down slightly on their regional stations, but they had to provide us with passes and studio time for a final involving our two biggest clubs. After the final whistle, I battled my way up to the gantry. All the icons of British broadcasting sat there. Jimmy Hill was in full flow, delivering his verdict. David Coleman was presenting. Famous voices addressed the nation. I was twenty-eight, still a novice, but I needed to deliver my report. They all looked at me. Who was this interloper? Graciously, they paused, allowing a newcomer to do his work. For four minutes, with the eyes of Hill and Coleman focused on me, I ad-libbed into a camera. When I finished, they gave me a standing ovation! Brilliant. My confidence soared to the stars. Someone must have mentioned it in the corridors of BBC power. Within two months I was covering matches for *Grandstand.*

If *Grandstand* offered the weekend treat, the North West provided my daily bread and butter. Manchester City occupied me for a while, particularly during Malcolm Allison's second coming in 1979. Even though United were hardly dominating football in the Seventies, City still felt in their shadow. I was on the team coach once when City played at Borussia Monchengladbach. We headed up the drive of this German hotel when a City director, Ian Niven, shouted: 'Stop!' The bus lurched to a halt, everyone aboard being thrown forward.

'Stay here,' commanded Niven, before leaping out and running to the hotel. Our curious gaze followed him. We soon realised why. Niven pointed angrily at the words spelled out above the front door. 'The Holiday Inn Welcomes Manchester United'. City directors were incensed.

Niven gave the management of the hotel an almighty bollocking. 'Manchester City are not coming into your hotel until that's sorted. We are not Manchester United.'

The bus stayed still, no one moving until 'United' disappeared, and 'City' appeared. Only then did Malcolm lead the players into reception.

At Maine Road, I fell in love with a stunning blonde model called Susan Cuff, recently crowned Miss Manchester City. One of Susan's friends entered her for the competition, where she talked passionately about her love for City. That surprised Susan's friends and certainly her father, a huge United fan. I was a die-hard Red but love can cross the grand divide. Even more impressive than her Miss Manchester City garlands was the fact that within months, in 1975, Susan had become Miss Great Britain. That rather put the City award in the shade. When she was not collecting tiaras and garlands, Susan worked in television, as a hostess on Derek Batey's ITV show *Mr and Mrs.* At Maine Road, our eyes made contact. I smiled and got back to work, covering Manchester City. She smiled and got back to being Miss Great Britain.

Cupid was played by Cyril Smith MP, twenty-seven stone of pure Rochdale personality, whose by-election victory for the Liberals I'd covered.

'Listen, David, I need you to come to the town hall on Friday night to judge Miss Rochdale Carnival Queen,' Cyril said a month later. 'You'll enjoy it. Lots of beautiful women.'

'I'll try to be there.'

'You'd bloody better.'

Entering the magnificent Rochdale Town Hall with snow settling up the sides of the building, I immediately noticed everyone had a partner. Cyril mentioned nothing about bringing a partner. As I stared at all the couples, Susan glided through the door with her boyfriend, a very wealthy owner of supermarkets in Manchester. As a partner of one of the Carnival Queen judges, he was ushered into the mayor's parlour for warm sherry, which he was welcome to because I hated it. Watching him leave, I made a bee-line for Susan.

'I saw you at City last month,' I said.

'I saw you on *Look North*,' she replied. Good start, I thought. As Cyril led us to the judges' table, I made sure I sat next to her. We chatted all evening, having such a laugh that Cyril announced: 'David, Susan, shut up. You are supposed to be taking this seriously.' Cyril's intervention made little difference. After the voting, we all sat down to dinner. Susan's boyfriend reappeared, plonking himself down next to her. My single status was brutally highlighted by the empty space next to me, and my discomfort was only partially relieved when a bloke from Piccadilly Radio wandered over and sat there. I ignored him. I was too busy trying to chat to Susan as her boyfriend glowered. Things seemed to be going well.

'I've a driver here, do you want a lift home?' I asked Susan. Her boyfriend butted in.

'No thank you, I have my Rolls-Royce outside and Susan is coming with me.' Perhaps I'd been pushing my luck. Miss Great Britain was probably out of my league, as I was reminded by Nick Clarke, a BBC Manchester colleague whose wonderfully expressive voice became a treat on Radio 4 until cancer took him from us. 'David, previously your standard had been Miss Merseyside and North Wales Electricity Board!' laughed Nick. When the lights went out with Miss Manweb, not much had happened.

But in the local launderette a few days later, I bumped into a friend from university, Max Franklin. 'Hey, you know you met Susan Cuff last week,' said Max.

'Yes! Do you know her?'

'Sure, she plays at my tennis club,' replied Max. 'I saw her yesterday and you have to ask her out.'

'You must be joking. She's got a boyfriend and he's got a Rolls-Royce.'

'Don't worry about him or the Rolls-Royce. They've split up. Now's the perfect time to call Susan.'

'I'll think about it over the weekend.'

That Saturday, I did my usual match for *Grandstand* and then tore up to the Lake District to do a film with a promising young athlete called Sebastian Coe. The weekend had gone so well that, as I drove back to Manchester on the Sunday evening, I thought: 'Bollocks, I'll do it. I'll ring Susan. She's fun.' On Monday, Max gave me Susan's number and I arranged to take her out on the Wednesday. By the end of the evening, we were sitting in my Toyota in a lay-by near Rochdale and I asked her to marry me. 'Yes,' she replied. 'And what took you so long?! I told Dad after meeting you at that Miss Rochdale Carnival Queen event that I'd met the man I was going to marry.'

Miss Great Britain marrying a *Look North* reporter, ITV embracing BBC, was always going to be a good story so we had a news conference at the BBC in Manchester. Afterwards, Freddie Knowles hauled me into his office.

'I'm only going to tell you this once: it's not love, it's lust,' Freddie said.

'Bugger off, Freddie.' Thirty-one years later, Susan and I have maybe proved him wrong.

We were married one sunny Saturday in July 1977 in St Ann's Church in the centre of Manchester. I remember so many people came to see Miss Great Britain get hitched they stopped the traffic. Tommy Docherty was a guest, forty-eight hours before Manchester United sacked him. Thankfully the two events weren't connected.

I gained a mother-in-law that day, Dorothy. And a father-in-law, Peter. He became the father I never had.

I threw myself back into work at the BBC, a home to all creatures great, small and bizarre. John Cole, the legendary BBC political editor and West Ham supporter, invited me to join the Corporation's team at Westminster. One evening I was due to do a live voice-over into the first item on the *Six O'Clock News*. So I took my place in the studio, next to the main presenters Sue Lawley and Nicholas Witchell. Sue began reading the headlines, about the poll tax, and all appeared calm. Suddenly, just as Nicholas was about to read his headline, there was a commotion and two female gay-rights protesters ran into the studio, shouting 'Stop Clause 28'. Lesbian No. 1 handcuffed herself to a camera cable. Lesbian No. 2 tried to get on screen, but the producer quickly flicked to an image of the House of Commons as Sue coolly carried on reading the news. What do I do? All my training as a reporter had never prepared me for lesbian insurgents. Lesbian No. 1 was being dealt with by management, who'd rushed on with a hacksaw to cut off the handcuffs. So did I tackle Lesbian No. 2 and become unable to talk when Sue came to me in thirty seconds? Nicholas had already leapt on Lesbian No. 2. It was quite a sight, the distinguished, carrot-haired Witchell sitting on this woman and shoving his hand over her mouth to keep her quiet. Sue kept going, reading Nicholas's headlines. Because viewers could hear the protesters, Sue had to make an apology. With a very British stiff upper lip, Sue said: 'I'm afraid we have rather been invaded by some people who we hope to remove shortly.' I sat stoically in my seat, waiting for Sue and hoping that Witchell would see off Lesbian No. 2. As he did, I completed my two-minute piece without fluffing a line. Somehow, I managed to keep a straight face, because I was desperate to burst out laughing.

My work continued to switch between news and sport. In 1989, Brian Barwick, then head of football at the BBC, came to see me at Pebble Mill in Birmingham, where I'd moved to present BBC Midlands news. He got straight to the point. 'David, I want you to be England correspondent,' Barwick said in that bluff way of his. 'There are some big games coming up, including Sweden. Wherever England go, I want you to follow. I want a proper relationship with Bobby Robson. All the things you are good at. If all goes well, you'll go to Italia '90.' So I hotfooted it to Stockholm for England's World Cup qualifier. On the eve of the big match, Bobby was so determined to hold a private training session that he kicked the press out of the Rasunda Stadium. Bobby failed to appreciate one peculiarity of the Rasunda: the stadium had a lunch club overlooking the pitch. All the journalists piled in there to inspect Bobby's not-so-secret practice, enjoying a decent meal into the bargain.

With qualification for Italia '90 soon achieved, I attended an interminably long World Cup group-stage draw in Rome in December 1989 which was enlivened by the chance to interview Luciano Pavarotti. The great tenor was utterly charming, and a skilled diplomat when faced with inquisitors from all over the globe.

'Mr Pavarotti, what is your dream final?' I asked him.

'My dream final is my beautiful Italy against your England,' replied Pavarotti.

'Perfect. Thank you, Mr Pavarotti.' How gracious. This would make terrific TV back home. 'Pavarotti Backs England' – I could see the headlines emerging from my film. As we packed up our kit, a crew from Holland approached.

'Mr Pavarotti, we are from Dutch TV, who would you like to see in the final?' the reporter enquired.

'I would like to see my beautiful Italy against your Holland in the final,' Pavarotti responded. Thrilled, the Dutch reporter thanked Pavarotti and moved on. Next up was a confident German crew.

'Mr Pavarotti, we are from German TV, who do you think West Germany will face in the final?' came the inevitable question. Followed by the inevitable answer from Pavarotti: 'My beautiful Italy will play West Germany in the final.'

The BBC's decision to adopt Pavarotti's rendition of 'Nessun Dorma' as the theme music to our World Cup coverage was inspired. A few have claimed credit. Brian Barwick thinks it was Brian Barwick. Des Lynam thinks it was Des Lynam. The person who really deserves credit is Philip Bernie, an assistant producer at the time. Phil first used 'Nessun Dorma' at the end of the World Athletics Championships in Rome in 1987 and again for the World Cup draw in Rome. With Brian's and Des's full support, Bernie pushed for 'Nessun Dorma' for the BBC coverage of Italia '90 and it proved the sound of the summer. It took football to opera-lovers, and opera to football-lovers.

Getting close up to England at Italia '90, stars' quirks came into focus. I detected Gary Lineker was not overly keen on training. 'Gary has a bad toe,' Bobby Robson would announce. So Lineker missed work-outs, spending the morning in the pool. Crafty! Lineker knew what worked best for him: he was like a panther, resting for long periods and then stirring into life to kill off some poor goalkeeper. In those days, I found John Barnes a bit distant. Liverpool's classy winger never gave me the impression of enjoying the World Cup or enjoying being away from home. Terry Butcher was terrific company, although I had to build some bridges first. Butch told me he was incensed by some criticism from Bob Wilson on BBC Breakfast TV. Bob had condemned Butch for a headbutt during the pre-tournament draw with Morocco. 'I'm not speaking to the BBC because of Bob Wilson,' Terry told me. Butch eventually relented. Thank God. He was always good value on camera.

So was Olga Stringfellow, the faith-healer who made a controversial visit to the England camp. 'I can cure Bryan Robson,' Olga promised. Bryan was plagued by injuries. Olga arrived in Sardinia at 11.30 p.m. and I was dispatched to interview her. What became immediately apparent was that Olga had enjoyed her in-flight hospitality and she proved a particularly lively interviewee, concluding with another pledge: 'I will rid Bryan Robson of his injuries.' Shortly afterwards, Bobby came up to me and ITV's

Jim Rosenthal in the hotel to give us some important news. 'Bryan's out,' said Bobby. 'He can't continue.'

Bobby was always straight with me and Jim, keeping us abreast of team developments. The great debate still clinging to England's Italia '90 adventure was exactly who suggested the successful change to a sweeper system against Egypt. Even now, it is accepted by many pundits and fans that it was a classic case of 'player power', that a delegation banged on Robson's door, pleading with him to introduce another centre-half, Mark Wright. 'It is my idea,' Robson stressed to me and Jim at the time. 'And the players agree with me.' Bobby was completely convinced he was the architect of this tactical masterstroke, and I believed him. It saddened me to see Bobby leave England after the World Cup, taking over at PSV Eindhoven. On 31 August, I received a lovely letter from Bobby on PSV note-paper. 'I was a little sorry to leave the Football Association but perhaps, overall, it was time to go,' Bobby wrote.

> Italia '90 was a pretty good finish to depart on and as you know we were pretty close to going all the way and actually winning 'the thing'. What pleased me most, however, was that the England performances restored our pride, reputation and credibility back in world football. Winning the Fair Play award was a magnificent achievement by the players in such a prestigious and competitive tournament and a feat they thoroughly deserved. By the end some of the younger players were magnificent and should be a force for the country's football in years to come. PS: After England, this should be a piece of cake!

I continued to cover England, now managed by Graham Taylor, but was also given the chance to present *Match of the Day*, the broadcasting equivalent of being handed the England captain's armband. So on 11 December 1993, I fulfilled every football-mad broadcaster's dream and presented *Match of the Day*. Gary Lineker was on pundit duty along with equally eloquent Alan

Hansen. Preparing for that show, I thought of the programme's history. Continuity ruled. The first match was Liverpool–Arsenal, black and white, Kenneth Wolstenholme in his clipped-tone pomp. Now it was Liverpool–Arsenal, colour, Barry Davies in his inimitable style. The keeper of the *Match of the Day* flame has been Niall Sloane, the current head of football. He has restricted alterations, preferring a tweak to the presentation here and there, but avoiding radical change. Some within the BBC crave a revolution in the *Match of the Day* domain. I suspect it will come. For now, Niall, Gary and Alan remain on the barricades in defending this unique show. The schedulers are the real problem. *Match of the Day* is at the wrong time,' Des Lynam told me years ago. 'It needs a regular, earlier slot.'

With Hansen and Mark Lawrenson on the sofa, and when Barwick was editing, *Match of the Day* was accused of a Liverpool bias. This bizarre debate, still rumbling today, has always puzzled me. Anyone genuinely believing that a Merseyside mafia exists at the heart of BBC TV Sport, putting Liverpool first, slaughtering Manchester United, is wrong. Niall Sloane is a United supporter. Peter Schmeichel worked on their programme and his allegiance is very much to Old Trafford. The stand-off between United and the BBC is purely down to an unflattering film about the football agency work of Fergie's son, Jason, made by BBC News and Current Affairs. Ever since, Fergie has refused to speak to the BBC. His anger is entirely understandable. A proud father, Fergie took the criticism of his son very personally. I know how incensed he was. Many parents would have reacted similarly. The BBC impugned Jason's integrity. I just wish they would find a settlement. Alex doesn't yield lightly.

Less fractious than the BBC–Fergie tension was the Motson–Davies rivalry that provoked endless comment in newspapers. Each wanted to cover the World Cup final, the FA Cup final, England games, but only one could do so on TV. At Italia '90, I was close to Barry when he was informed by the BBC hierarchy that he would not commentate on the final. Barry was devastated. I understood. For Barry, it must have felt like climbing up Everest, and then being ordered home in sight of the summit. Barry has great attributes, and many admirers, but he is so different to Motty. John sees football as a sport while Barry views it as theatre. When Motty is building up to a commentary, he becomes like a player: all detailed preparation and tunnel vision. Euro 2008 was supposed to be Motty's final tournament for the BBC, but I am sure he will pop up in a commentary booth somewhere. But a whole new generation of commentators are bursting through and they deserve a chance. John Murray and Simon Brotherton are excellent. I just hope they receive more nurturing and encouragement from the BBC than my generation did.

It was to Motty that I turned for advice when the FA contacted me about working for them. We were in Rotterdam in 1993, as the life drained from Graham Taylor's regime.

'The FA want me to fight their corner,' I told him.

'Do you want to leave the BBC?' John asked.

'I've been to World Cups,' I replied. 'I've presented *Match of the Day*. I've covered general elections. I've interviewed every PM going back to Harold Macmillan. I've done just about everything and more I ever dreamed of. I'm never going to be you or Des Lynam, and will I ever get this chance again?' I was forty-four. It was time for the poacher to turn gamekeeper.

3

The Old Curiosity Shop on Lancaster Gate

Entering 16 Lancaster Gate in 1994 was like stepping back into 1894. As I walked into the FA reception at 8.55 a.m. on 28 February, I felt I'd been in more modern museums. A fading portrait of the Queen, painted when she was very young, stared down. Copies of the *Telegraph*, *Mail* and *Times* lay in a neat row on an ancient table. Behind glass on rather dusty shelves stood silver trophies from bizarre places around the world, some of which no longer existed. A replica of the Jules Rimet trophy had pride of place, highlighting England's under-achievement since 1966. The FA offices reminded me of old merchant shipping companies I'd filmed in Manchester, scared of the changing world outside their heavy front doors. Rather forbidding women sat behind a wood-panelled desk, apparently guarding the place. 'Sorry, what is your name again?' they asked. They didn't seem to be expecting me. Eventually, I was allowed in and shown to a small cubby-hole of an office, containing a chair and a table. Terry Venables had just joined as England manager and was fond of saying: 'I walked in to the FA and found the cupboard was bare.'

'Terry,' I told him, 'you're lucky to have a cupboard. Luxury!'

My initiation into the extraordinary tensions characterising life at the FA began in earnest that evening. Football-mad MPs hosted a dinner at the House of Commons and I was keen to hear a speech by Joe Ashton, chairman of the all-party group on football. From my days as a BBC political correspondent, I knew many of the MPs like Ashton, so an enjoyable evening was guaranteed. Ashton stood up to address an audience of politicians, journalists and assorted football folk, including members of the FA hierarchy. We'd all had a few wines, so the mood was distinctly convivial. 'I'd like to say how delighted we are that David Davies has joined the FA,' Ashton began. 'We are confident he'll make a real difference.' Trevor Phillips, the FA's commercial director, was upset and walked out. Christ! What had I got myself into? Ironically, Trevor was to become one of those people I liked and most respected.

Day two bore out my fears. The governing body of English football ran from nine to five, Monday to Friday, with an hour off at lunch-time. Now, I was fully aware that football itself operated twenty-four hours a day, seven days a week, and was usually very busy at weekends. I could see the potential problem. 'The FA closes down at weekends!' I whispered down the phone to my wife Susan. 'It's unbelievable. Don't they know there are a lot of games on Saturdays? We might need to react to something, but no one will be around! Crazy!' By five past five that day, 16 Lancaster Gate had emptied. I was in my office, and the caretaker, John Crabtree, appeared.

'Would you like a pot of tea, Mr Davies?'

'Yes, I would. I'm going to be here working for a while. Tell me, does everyone really go home at five p.m?'

'Oh, yes, Mr Davies, except Pat Smith.' Pat was a wily, immensely hard-working administrator on whom the chief executive Graham Kelly relied utterly. Starting as a secretary and ending up as deputy chief executive, Pat was almost certainly the most influential person within the FA without having any public profile. I was to grow to respect her, and to enjoy her company immensely.

That day I sat back, enjoying the tea, and reflected on how on earth I'd entered this Old Curiosity Shop. Two chairmen were really to blame, Peter Swales of Manchester City and Doug Ellis of Aston Villa. Both knew me well, and understood my desire to influence the sport I loved. When the FA advertised for a new press officer, Peter and Doug thought of me.

'You'd be good at it,' said Peter.

'You'd be able to work inside the game and have an impact,' added Doug.

Why not? I liked a challenge. Putting on my best suit, I went to see the FA chairman, Sir Bert Millichip, at his home near Birmingham. 'Sir Bert, I don't believe you need a press officer,' I told him. 'You need more than that. After the government and the monarchy, no one gets more column inches than the FA. But you don't have a big press office. You need a director of communications and supporting press officers. I would be interested in the position if you were interested in making the job more substantial.' I wasn't going to leave a good career in TV just to sort out tickets for the press and release statements on when the next Ian Wright disciplinary hearing was. But did the people at the FA want someone of my profile? Some of them didn't, as I soon realised during my three interviews.

The appointment panel was made up of the four leading men in the FA. Bert I knew. I had previously met the vice-chairman, Chris Wilcox, and Arsenal's Sir David Hill-Wood, the chairman of the finance committee. But it was Graham Kelly, the chief executive, whom I realised quickly was going to be an awkward customer. 'Do you want to build a proper communications team?' I asked Kelly during each of my interviews. Graham was clearly ambivalent. Certainly, his opposition to my appointment was clear from the outset. He thought I was too expensive so he tried to undermine me. The FA offered me slightly more than my BBC salary, and even when I accepted, Graham tried to recruit someone else for less. Two weeks after shaking hands with Sir Bert, I discovered Kelly offered the job to Ray Stubbs, a colleague at the BBC and a close friend of mine. I thought Kelly's behaviour was outrageous.

'You know you're not wanted there,' Graham Taylor warned me before I started at Lancaster Gate.

'Graham, I've worked that out for myself!' I laughed. Taylor heard from people he knew at the FA that Kelly and others were manning the barricades against me. 'If the intention is to frighten me off, then I'm even more determined to see this through,' I told Taylor.

'Good luck!' Taylor said.

'You'll survive three months,' Martin Edwards, the Manchester United chairman, predicted down the phone. Martin knew the FA machinations well. 'You'll not put up with it. It'll drive you mad.'

'Martin, I'm pretty resilient. And I believe I can make a difference.'

'Good luck, then!'

Alex Ferguson made contact. 'I knew you were a Manchester United fan!' said Ferguson. 'It will be interesting to see how a United supporter gets on at Lancaster Gate!'

I received some nice letters of congratulation, including one from my bank manager, who finished thoughtfully by recommending 'Mr Blobby for England manager'. The legendary journalist, Brian Glanville, also called. Whenever our paths crossed in press-boxes, we'd always got on. A veteran observer of English football life, Glanville's contempt for the FA ran deep. 'I am absolutely astounded,' Glanville said. 'What on earth are you going there for?'

'Someone has to do it!' I replied. 'I can't sit on the outside, forever moaning about the FA. I'm going in to change it. Surely you approve of that?'

'Good luck!' Glanville laughed and rang off. Everyone was wishing me luck, and then laughing. What had I let myself in for? At least my card was well and truly marked. At least I knew I was walking into an ambush. Some members of the FA senior management, like Trevor Phillips, believed I was coming on a huge wage, so I sensed resentment from them. Sitting with Venables at Lancaster Gate, I confided my game-plan.

'I have two aims,' I told Terry. 'The first is to give you the best chance to be successful with England. The second is that I want to be a catalyst for bringing this organisation not into the twentieth century, but into the twenty-first century.' Terry laughed as well. We both knew revolutionising the governing body of English football was a formidable objective.

'But it can be done, and there are other people inside and outside Lancaster Gate who can help do it,' I added, perhaps too obviously trying to convince myself. The look on Terry's face suggested that my 'mission' to reform the FA was very much of the 'impossible' variety. Sir Bert also warned me that the FA was impervious to change. 'David, we've tried to restructure several times, look back to the Seventies and Eighties, and all attempts foundered,' said Millichip. 'It won't happen.'

Lancaster Gate was part-museum, part-asylum, part-heartbeat of the game. The building was a warren designed by confused rabbits. Getting lost was easy. Strange people popped up here and there. One man lived in a tiny cubicle, the wall wrapped around him. 'He can't move,' Terry remarked. 'Not much use in an emergency!' Terry and I christened him Head of Fire Alarms. Another quirk of 16 Lancaster Gate was the very strange double door at the front. This entrance had a life of its own. If it didn't like the look of you it trapped you. One evening, leaving late, I got stuck between the outer and inner doors.

'John Crabtree!' I shouted, hoping to attract the caretaker's attention. Silence. Crabtree was upstairs. I was going to spend the night there. Try again.

'JOHN CRABTREE!' Eventually he came down and freed me.

Apart from when the doors ensnared me, the eerie silence in many parts of the building was the most noticeable characteristic of the FA offices. Terry and I were also astounded by another Lancaster Gate trait, probably because of our backgrounds, him in dressing rooms and me in newsrooms.

'Have you noticed something, David?'

'What, Terry?'

'The staff.'

'The staff?'

'Yes, David, so many of them have their desks facing the wall. It's depressing. They need cheering up.'

'OK, Terry. Where shall we start?'

Terry and I strove to lighten the mood. One April Fool's Day, the pair of us sent around an internal memo announcing: 'Due to accommodation difficulties at Lancaster Gate, Mr Venables's department and Mr Davies's department will be relocated to the Helepi Restaurant from next Monday. For an appointment with Mr Venables and Mr Davies, please contact the restaurant and the waiter will make a reservation.' This wind-up might entertain one or two, or so Terry and I thought, but not everybody. They were too entrenched in the past to appreciate a more relaxed approach to life and work. Change was going to be difficult. The FA seemed a hopeless case. Management team meetings were rare, so problems were allowed to fester. Even more oddly, my post never arrived until mid-afternoon. When it finally landed on my desk, all the letters had been opened.

'Why does my post arrive late and opened?' I asked Sue Ball, my PA, whose deep love for football was split between Cardiff City and the grass roots.

'The post gets opened downstairs,' Sue replied.

'But it's my post!'

'Mr Kelly reads it.'

'What?!'

At the next management meeting, which took an interminable time in coming, I raised the Great Tampered Post Scandal. Addressing Kelly, I declared: 'Can I ask, Graham, what does the FA have in common with Her Majesty's prisons?'

'Er, I don't know.'

'You have your post opened.'

Glen Kirton, who was overseeing the build-up to Euro '96, collapsed in hysterics. Graham certainly didn't. Letter-opening was an ancient tradition dating back to the days of Denis Follows, the FA secretary in the 1970s. Either Graham or Pat Smith went through everyone's post. Entering Graham's office was always an experience. On his desk would be letters, packages and committee minutes stacked up high like the Empire State Building. Graham would peer around them. If the letter was stamped 'personal and confidential', they were not supposed to open it, but occasionally private letters would appear on my desk opened. I'm sure it was an accident. So I called for a vote on the post. 'It's all an incredible waste of everyone's time,' I told the management team. 'I can't believe you find my post interesting.' Perhaps they did. 'I propose that this practice be abandoned.' Only me and Glen and Trevor Phillips voted in favour. The Postal Three lost out to the Phantom Letter Openers. The mad old system continued. Lancaster Gate's postal system descended into complete and utter madness when the FA eventually entered the email age. Around lunch-time, I'd receive emails about post I hadn't even seen yet. Bonkers.

Very quickly I recognised the great joy of life inside the FA was meeting its characters: Roy Baker in Finance, who wanted to buy me an abacus to 'help with your expenses'; Saty Gahir, who transformed this Luddite into something near computer literacy; Mary MacLennan, whose life was too often made miserable by the latest edict from the Protocol Committee; and many more.

Charles Hughes was more problematic. I did not get on with the FA's Director of Coaching and Education, an austere figure who patrolled the fourth floor of 16 Lancaster Gate. He was a former schoolteacher, so we had some common ground after my stint at Oxford and as Education Correspondent at the BBC, yet we remained worlds apart. At the sporadic and irretrievably ghastly management meetings, regular rows erupted between Hughes and Trevor Phillips. Glen Kirton was never a fan of Charles either so he'd wade in. Frustration appeared Hughes's constant companion. Frustration that Kelly, not he, was chief executive. Frustration that I was allowed into the building – not FA material, I heard. Frustration that he was often criticised in the press. Hughes wrote this weighty tome about tactics, *Winning Formula*, which expounded the delights of direct football as he saw it, the long-ball game to his critics. He was occasionally interviewed, and usually came across as slightly eccentric.

'If you want positive media coverage, you have to do more to transform the perception of you,' I told Hughes. 'Can I suggest something? You should glue a ball to the corner of your office ceiling, so when someone comes in to interview you and asks: "What is that?" you can reply: "It's the long ball". That might lighten the mood.'

'For Heaven's sake,' replied Hughes, dismissively.

Attending one committee meeting on women's football, I argued for greater investment. 'We need a commitment to a women's professional league and a major publicity campaign,' I said. 'The more women who become involved, the more secure the future for the whole of football. Let's get women into football, and coming to games.'

'We have tried all that,' said Hughes in his dismissive way.

My blood boiled. How wrong Hughes was. During my time at the FA, women's football became part of the landscape of sport. Hope Powell's team reached the last eight of the World Cup, their games carried live on the BBC. England hosted the women's Euros. When friends in other sports complain there is too much girls' football in schools, I think of Hughes's intransigence with a smile.

I am sorry my heart did not bleed excessively on the day Hughes left Lancaster Gate. Once the FA appointed Howard Wilkinson as technical director, Hughes's powerbase was threatened. Inevitably, Kelly dithered over how to handle Hughes's departure. Even by Kelly's standards, the hesitancy was remarkable. I went into Graham's office to draft a press release about Wilkinson's pending arrival.

'And what should I say about Charles Hughes's position?' I asked, not unreasonably.

'Nothing yet,' replied Kelly. 'His position is still under discussion.' Very odd. Classic FA. Anything to avoid confrontation.

Hughes eventually moved out. I regretted he didn't have a leaving party or perhaps I wasn't invited. He managed to alienate the big clubs. He rarely went to matches, so there was little dialogue between Hughes and Liverpool, Manchester United, Everton, Tottenham Hotspur and the other leading clubs. *Winning Formula* was never accepted as a winning doctrine by clubs. It was certainly a winning formula for Hughes as the book sold worldwide.

Of all the strange characters I encountered in the Old Curiosity Shop that was 16 Lancaster Gate, Graham Kelly was comfortably the most curious. I'd met this decent, complicated man before, having conducted the first ever TV interview with him when he became the Football League's secretary after Alan Hardaker. Back then at Lytham St Anne's, the League's old base, I found Kelly uncharismatic but enthusiastic. On meeting him the next time at Lancaster Gate, Kelly had changed. He was still uncharismatic but I detected his enthusiasm levels had waned. Everyone within the FA was shocked when he succeeded Ted Croker, an inspiring, warm man, everything Kelly wasn't. Kelly did love the game deeply and so did I but there the similarities ended. Kelly soon began describing me as 'Leader of the Opposition'. He knew immediately I wanted to transform the FA but he seemed ambivalent about the task. When he joined Lancaster Gate, Kelly had probably himself dreamed of modernising the FA. No longer. He seemed to have given up on change. I felt like a young architect coming in to renovate a famous building and discovering an elderly retainer barring the way. What changed Graham Kelly? Why had he become so rooted in the past? Over the years working with this strange man, I came to the conclusion that Kelly had been profoundly affected by the Hillsborough disaster of 1989. On that fateful day that claimed the lives of ninety-six Liverpool supporters, being chief executive of the FA must have been incredibly difficult. Hillsborough happened on his watch. Kelly cared about football, and would have been devastated at the carnage on the Leppings Lane End. As his sport plunged into crisis, the chief executive of the FA seemed incapable of responding strongly even though he bravely faced the cameras. On the anniversary of

Hillsborough, Kelly always mentioned it in the office. Hillsborough was the shadow that followed Kelly. It would have only been natural for Graham to ask himself whether he was at fault in any way. Should he have acted differently? After Hillsborough, Kelly definitely considered whether he should stay in the job.

He, along with Pat Smith and Charles Hughes, never really received the recognition they deserved for forcing through the formation of the Premier League. But I fear Kelly recognised the FA itself would never change, that the parallel universes of elected FA Councillors and staff would never work together towards change. It was well-meaning, well-connected volunteers versus full-time employees. Tension ruled. Graham lost himself in committee meetings, sometimes two or three a day. Many councillors looked down on him. They were upstairs, he was downstairs. Ken Bates was quite open about this feudal set-up.

'You're downstairs,' he informed me as the Director of Public Affairs. 'You're downstairs,' he reminded Kelly, the chief executive. Occasionally, those upstairs made the FA management team of people like me, Kelly and Trevor Phillips believe we were not just 'downstairs' but somewhere beneath the cellar. Kelly never aspired to be upstairs. He was happiest putting on an England tracksuit and nipping off into Hyde Park for a kickabout with FA post-room staff. At games, he felt more at ease on the terraces than in the directors' box. Passionate about Blackpool, Kelly was also a familiar sight at non-League grounds as well as professional ones. A good person, Graham's heart was in the right place but he increasingly cut an isolated figure at Lancaster Gate. The painful truth was that football had moved on whether Graham Kelly liked it or not.

My biggest criticism of Kelly was that he was so elusive. Always. I wanted to work with the chief executive, not against him. But where the hell was he? 'Where's Kelly?' became my daily catch-phrase. I understood his private life was complicated. He set up home near Peterborough with the former wife of one of the FA

Councillors, and would disappear back there. He arrived at Lancaster Gate early, and left early. Of course, it wasn't a nine-to-five job but that was hardly a help to me unless I changed my lifestyle and body-clock as well. When a football crisis broke out, it often didn't have the decency to take place during Kelly's hours of work. So I spent ages tracking Kelly down. 'Where's Kelly?' Often when we were abroad with England, Graham sauntered off for a stroll. At France '98, he ambled off in Marseilles and ended up in the middle of a riot.

Kelly was an enigma. Terry Venables once bumped into him strolling down Lancaster Gate, puffing on a huge cigar.

'Happy days, then, Graham?!'

'Life couldn't be better, Terry, couldn't be better.' No explanation. Nothing. He just walked on.

Glanville always called him 'Kelly the Jelly'. Graham laughed off his bumbling image but inside I think he was hurt. He was an administrator, at his best organising the minutiae of competitions not debating, deciding and leading. Glanville's 'Kelly the Jelly' observation stuck.

Football would have benefited if I'd worked harder on my relationship with Kelly. I did try at times. After breakfast at a Tory party conference in Brighton one year, I said to Graham: 'I'll come back to London with you.' He was driving, and looked horrified at the prospect of an unwanted passenger. Graham liked being alone. As we meandered through Sussex and Surrey, heading towards Lancaster Gate, Kelly tried to avoid my attempts at conversation. I chuntered away, determined to make him open up. The journey was marked by occasional exchanges but it was hard work. On arrival at Lancaster Gate, the staff were amazed.

'You have not come back from Brighton in Mr Kelly's car, have you?!' one asked.

'Yes.'

'He likes to travel on his own, you know.' Only in the surreal world of the FA could my behaviour in seeking a lift be seen as weird, not Kelly's for trying to stay silent.

'He couldn't have invited you.'

'He didn't.'

On his good days, Graham would crack a joke with me. He was blessed with a decent sense of humour, occasionally at his own expense. He didn't take himself too seriously. He'd given up on change but I was new. Forget him, I thought, leave him behind. Let's drag the FA forward. There were difficult days, times when I railed against the tortoise pace of action at Lancaster Gate. I felt ground down by the resistance to change, but always fought back. It required all my cunning to circumvent some committees simply to get decisions made. Some Council members felt they were the only ones responsible enough to take important decisions. But could they? Out in the shires! Sometimes they came in once a month. The FA needed to reach conclusions on issues every day, sometimes every hour. It was easy for Councillors to berate staff for taking decisions 'beyond their authority'. It was also easy for staff to denigrate Councillors they rarely saw and who sometimes had no understanding of the issues. Nowhere was it written down how this relationship between Councillors and staff was actually meant to work. The result was that far too often it didn't.

On the rare occasions the FA moved quickly, complaints would fly in from the Councillors. 'The commercial department are exceeding their authority' was a common complaint. 'Please remind Trevor Phillips not to exceed his authority. He should wait until Councillors are present.' It was laughable. I felt for Trevor. He wanted to crack on with deals, and had to wait for permission. I couldn't consult either. Dealing with 24-hours-a-day, seven-days-a-week news, I had to make up policy on the move at times, making sure that whatever I said would find a sympathetic echo with the majority of the Councillors. This was no way to run a sport, let alone a business.

In those early days, Lancaster Gate was just corridors containing committees. Will Carling's infamous remark about the Rugby Football Union being run by 'fifty-seven old farts' doubled me up with laughter. Only fifty-seven! Count yourself lucky, Will! Sir

Bert soon after his eightieth birthday called me into his office and asked: 'David, I keep reading Joe Lovejoy in the *Sunday Times* writing that "the FA have more old buffers than St Pancras Station." What does the man mean?'

'Well, Chairman, I think he means that the FA is not the youngest organisation in the world.' Sir Bert understood slightly better when Joe started referring to the FA's 'Blazered Buffoons'. Good, intelligent minds could be found amidst the old buffers and Blazered Buffoons, who rightly resented their public image. People like Ted Powell from Herefordshire, Fred Hunter from Merseyside, Barry Bright from Kent and many others had real insight into the game and cared about football at all levels. Others of the so-called 'amateurs' were lawyers and building-society executives of high quality. They did not need lectures from one or two representatives from the professional game who came from somewhat less distinguished backgrounds.

After cajoling Sir Bert into announcing his departure as chairman after Euro '96, and ensuring he left with thanks all round, I'd hoped one of two people might succeed him. Frank Pattison, a Durham lawyer, was rightly well respected by most Council members. Sadly, for his own private reasons, and following growing exasperation with the machinations of some of his fellow FA board members, Frank withdrew from the organisation altogether. Outside the FA was Sir Roland Smith, the chairman of Manchester United plc, a man with a huge business reputation. Sir Bert and Sir Roland discussed it. But in those days, neither United nor Sir Roland had a chance of election to the Council itself, a crucial prerequisite of the chairmanship. The FA had to wait a decade for a chairman – an independent one at that – in Lord Triesman who promised the gravitas and leadership the organisation craved. Back in the mid-Nineties, a firmer hand was needed with the number of men behaving badly in English football.

4

Men Behaving Badly

When Eric Cantona leapt over the hoardings at Selhurst Park on 25 January 1995, and kung-fu-kicked a less than charming Crystal Palace fan, I turned to Terry Venables's right-hand man, Ted Buxton, and remarked: 'It's going to be a busy old night.' And week, and month, and year, and more. From the moment I joined the FA, I seemed to be fighting a fire a day. In the period either side of Euro '96, headlines raged around Cantona, Bruce Grobbelaar, George Graham, Paul Merson, Tony Adams, Euro '96 tickets and Brighton & Hove Albion. At times, the national game seemed in meltdown. At times, I awoke despairing over what would be the latest episode of football's Men Behaving Badly.

The Cantona affair was the most extraordinary. Any controversy involving Manchester United always doubled the media firestorm. Even as a super-Red, I sensed immediately what Eric had done would be indefensible. Within seconds of Cantona landing on Matthew Simmons, the mobile in my pocket came alive, reporters and radio stations demanding reaction from the FA. I stayed up into the night doing interviews. 'A stain on the game' was my message. In the morning, the first request to talk came from IRN at 05.25 and the calls never ceased. Arriving at Lancaster Gate, there appeared a cast of thousands outside, wanting news. The interest in Cantona's transgression was massive. The story led the bulletins, covered front pages. Swift contact with United was vital to co-ordinate our response. Tracing Martin Edwards to the Royal Lancaster Hotel, I found United's chairman talking tough. 'We are thinking of an indefinite suspension for Eric,' Martin said. 'Banning Eric altogether.'

The initial perception that Eric had assaulted an innocent bystander changed when stories emerged of what Simmons was alleged to have said to Cantona. He abused Eric's family. OK, but professional footballers earning huge amounts should not react to some verbal abuse with kung-fu kicks. Martin realised the seriousness of Eric's conduct but, when he returned to Manchester, he softened his stance. 'Eric will be banned until the end of the season,' Martin announced. Not 'indefinite'. Not 'altogether'. United had had an emergency meeting somewhere in Cheshire and Martin must have spoken at length to Alex Ferguson. United continued to back-pedal on Martin's original hard-line on Cantona. 'Eric can play for the reserves while he's suspended, can't he?' United's chairman then asked me.

'No!' I retorted. 'Wait for the disciplinary commission to rule.'

I feared some confusion at Old Trafford. Martin was clearly feeling the heat from Ferguson, who understandably wanted his best player in action. Ferguson got it into his head that when Martin told me they were suspending Cantona for the season, I replied: 'If that happens, that will be it.' Namely, no more punishment for Eric. That was clearly beyond any authority I had. Martin and the club's solicitor, Maurice Watkins, never believed I would have made such a comment. Alex later reiterated his belief to a Sunday newspaper, which angered me. Why would I say something I couldn't deliver? I had no influence with disciplinary commissions and never claimed to. My complaint produced a simple response from Martin. 'That's Alex,' he said.

A week later, as the commission prepared to convene at Sopwell House Hotel in Hertfordshire, I met Bobby Charlton, the United director, England legend and a wise man sensitive to the public mood. 'There is a very strong anti-Cantona feeling around,' Bobby said. 'It's going to be a very difficult time for Eric.'

Too right. On the eve of the commission meeting at Sopwell, I needed a drink and some convivial company. I knew one man wouldn't let me down, Mike Parry, the senior FA press officer now of talkSPORT fame. Mike was rumbustious, not everybody's cup of tea, but he was fantastic to work with. No. 3 on the *Sun* in Kelvin MacKenzie's era, Mike was ebullient, unpredictable, a terrific journalist with a tabloid hack's nose for a story and a great sense of humour. Parry was just the pick-me-up I needed before the world's media besieged us the following morning. 'Come on, Mike, let's go for dinner,' I said. Parry needed little persuading. The Cantona commission dominated our table-talk. 'It's so difficult to predict,' I said. 'Eric will be punished but for how long and how much, God only knows.' We should have asked the next table. Sitting there, enjoying a good dinner, was the Archbishop of Canterbury, Robert Runcie. 'Good evening,' I said before losing the nerve to ask whether the FA could borrow some divine guidance on Cantona.

Friday 24 February dawned. By nine a.m., thirty photographers encircled Sopwell. Thanks to the support of Geoff Thompson, the then Disciplinary Committee chairman, I enjoyed access all areas of football and was allowed to sit in on all disciplinary hearings. Three men would decide Cantona's fate: Thompson, the commission chairman, assisted by Gordon McKeag and Ian Stott. Cantona's presence mesmerised me. Every United fan loved Cantona, and I was no different. Collar up. Arrogant strut. A rebel with a cause, United's cause. Cantona always had much of Denis Law about him.

United were first represented by Maurice Watkins, a lawyer I rated very highly whose influence within football at home and abroad grew year by year. Watkins explained that United pleaded 'guilty with mitigation'. Cantona had stayed silent so far.

'We haven't heard from Mr Cantona,' said Thompson. Oh

God, I thought. Prepare for fireworks. I recalled a previous French FA hearing when Cantona smacked an official in the face. Anything was possible here. Apprehension filled me. 'Would Mr Cantona like to add anything?' said Thompson. He would. In perfectly good English, Eric delivered the most astonishing speech I've ever heard.

'I would like to apologise to the chairman of the commission,' Eric began. 'I would like to apologise to Manchester United, Maurice Watkins and Alex Ferguson. I would like to apologise to my team-mates. I want to apologise to the FA. And I would like to apologise to the prostitute who shared my bed last night.'

What?! Maurice and I looked at each other. Maurice's face was a picture. He registered what Eric said. Eric, meanwhile, kept going, apologising to everyone else who knew him. Had I honestly heard that? At least two members of the commission certainly hadn't grasped it! Cantona was taking the mickey. He had to be. His apology to a non-existent prostitute was, I think, a prelude to his remark later about 'when the seagulls follow the trawler'. The commission continued, eventually punishing Eric with an eight-month ban and £10,000 fine. Ferguson went nuclear. United thought the suspension too harsh, the media deemed it too soft, so maybe it was just about right. The *Daily Mirror* panned the FA with their main football writer, Harry Harris, placing us in the gutter with Cantona. When Harry next called, I said: 'It's amazing people like me in the gutter actually own mobile phones that work!'

Ordered to do community work as part of his civil punishment, Eric threw himself into it with gusto. On his return to the United ranks, Cantona slotted back in effortlessly. The team I supported since 1957 always fielded mavericks who did something different, who were worth the gate money. Eric found his natural theatre at Old Trafford. After twenty-six years without the title, Cantona was the catalyst.

'You've bought who?!' my mates said in 1992, taking the piss.

But even by Fergie's high standards, Eric's arrival from Leeds United was inspirational. As a person, Cantona was quite complicated. He pretended not to speak English and refused interviews, but after the FA Cup final win over Chelsea in 1994, Cantona conducted an interview in perfect English. Outside Old Trafford one day, I watched Eric signing autographs happily for twenty minutes. United people told me Eric did that regularly. After his 'trawler' outburst, it didn't surprise me to see Cantona eventually take up acting. Eric saw life as a stage with himself in the middle, moody and magnificent, the spotlights highlighting his noble features.

Cantona provided the most spectacular episode in the Men Behaving Badly series, a sequence that started with the Grobbelaar investigation. I heard rumblings on 9 November 1994 that the *Sun* were running a large story, potentially damaging to football. Mike Parry and I stayed late at Lancaster Gate, ready to spring into action when the *Sun*'s first edition dropped. 'Bloody hell!' I said when I saw its astounding story. The extent of the research was substantial, referring to specific games that they alleged Grobbelaar and others had thrown. They mentioned the famous Wimbledon match with Hans Segers in goal, when Wimbledon were 2–0 up against Everton yet somehow managed to lose 2–3. On the back of the *Sun* story, the outcry was unbelievable. 'Suspend them,' came the cry. 'Ban them *sine die*.'

'If this is true, we have to act,' I told Graham Kelly. 'If there is even a whiff of corruption, Grobbelaar and the others shouldn't play until the matter is cleared up. Surely we can enforce that.' Senior management at Lancaster Gate differed. Lawyers got to them. 'He's innocent until proven guilty,' came the word from on high. I tried to argue my corner. 'Innocent or not, the allegations are so serious, those involved can't just play on as if nothing has happened,' I said. 'By doing nothing, the FA will be slated. The credibility of the game is at stake.' Nothing. The FA assumed their default ostrich position, head in the sand, hiding behind the well-worn if strictly valid excuse of 'we are powerless unless the club acts against them'. The FA needed Grobbelaar's club, Southampton, to make the first move. Those were the rules, according to the lawyers.

'If you really want to know what is going on at Southampton, talk to me and not other people,' Lawrie McMenemy always advised me. No one knew feelings on the south coast better. So I rang Lawrie.

'There is no desire to see Grobbelaar stopped from playing,' Lawrie told me. I rang Keith Wiseman, the Southampton chairman.

'There is no guarantee we would suspend Grobbelaar even if he were charged by the FA,' Wiseman told me. Hardly helpful. That was an eye-opener to me.

'We are powerless, Mike,' I told Parry. 'This whole sorry mess just shows up what is wrong with the FA. How can you be a real governing body in this position?'

Despite the FA's inertia, events did accelerate. On 14 March 1995, Grobbelaar was arrested with Segers, John Fashanu, a woman and a Malaysian businessman. Cameras, predictably, accompanied the police on their raid, a tactic that always made me uneasy. I had been the beneficiary of police tip-offs at the BBC, but I still think it is too much for show. 'When this case comes to trial, I wonder whether the defence barristers will make a meal of the raids and cameras,' I said to Parry.

When Grobbelaar, Segers and Fashanu all played on, I went to see Kelly again. 'Graham, my job is to protect the image of the game,' I said. 'I have to balance our old friend "innocent until proven guilty" with the wider interests of English football. Letting Grobbelaar play on damages the game. I like Bruce. He's a real character and football needs characters. But there is a need for leadership on this issue. The FA must be strong.'

Kelly did not appear to have a view. All he saw were the shadows of lawyers. Some might argue today that the FA's refusal to act was vindicated as Grobbelaar and the rest were never found guilty. The real damage was done to the FA's reputation as guardians of the game, and our ability to lead.

Like Lancaster Gate, the FA rule-book in the 1990s belonged to the Victorian era. Poor old Nic Coward, the organisation's highly talented lawyer, was forever vigilant. Coward knew the rule-book would be shredded to pieces by any half-decent QC in court. We became neurotic about betting. The Sir John Smith report on betting, that I'd urged Kelly to initiate, was a compelling piece of work. Sir John concluded that people in football shouldn't bet at all. The problem for the FA was how to enforce it. 'I won't even buy a scratch-card if it worries you, Nic,' I told Coward, only half-jokingly. Nic saw me as one of his great disciples and I followed his betting ban scrupulously. Few others in football did. Footballers do bet on football, some incredibly heavily.

'Football in England isn't bent,' I insisted to Nic. 'Throwing games in eleven-a-side is immensely difficult in practice. I don't believe a goalkeeper could get away with that for any significant length of time. His team-mates would dig him out.'

Gambling on the game became a huge issue. Thirty years ago, nobody could have predicted people in the Far East betting on the time of the first corner, free-kick or throw-in. Charlton Athletic's floodlights were infamously tampered with. Fortunately, Peter Varney, the chief executive of Charlton, moved very quickly. He realised the damage the situation could do to the club, and football generally. If all clubs are as vigilant as Charlton, the game will remain clean. Vigilance is vital.

Bungs were the other big fear in the era of Men Behaving Badly. The George Graham case that came about shortly after the Grobbelaar allegations distressed me and embarrassed football. I liked George and knew him pretty well. When he became Tommy Docherty's first signing at Manchester United, I interviewed him. Ever since, we had often chatted, particularly in the build-up to the 1993 FA Cup final, when he managed Arsenal. George was also a good friend of Terry Venables, so we occasionally met up. Sadly, the moment George was accused on 11 December 1994 of accepting a bung from the Norwegian agent Rune Hauge, any social contact dried up. Sacked by Arsenal, George was then charged by the FA and a disciplinary meeting was convened at the Watford Hilton. On arriving at the hotel the night before, I discovered to my horror the key rooms allocated to the commission had been taken over by two families. They were eventually persuaded to move out, though not before some harsh words were exchanged with the hotel management. Problems continued. One of the foreign witnesses failed to turn up. His colleagues confided he'd just been sentenced to a jail term. Later that evening, I organised a meeting of the FA team. 'What shall we do if George Graham walks out?' asked our brief, Brian Leveson QC. 'What will the FA do? Technically, George Graham is out of football, so beyond the FA's jurisdiction.'

'Christ,' I replied. 'Don't even think about it. Graham Kelly has landed me in it again. Well, we just have to hope George doesn't walk out.'

We were in good hands with Leveson. He was a formidable barrister, at the peak of his game and soon to prosecute Rose West. Spiky but humorous and human, Leveson was capable of creating moments of pure theatre. During the commission, the QC produced a suitcase containing imitation money amounting to the six-figure sum handed over by Hauge to George in a London hotel.

'What did you think it was for?' Leveson asked George.

'A Christmas present,' George replied.

'Presumably, you gave him a pair of socks,' shot back a QC on top form.

During the first break, I talked to the FA's solicitor, Raj Parker.

'I think Leveson may have gone over the top, counting out wads of money in front of the commission,' Raj observed. I didn't agree. Back in the hearing, the defence team called the Leeds United manager, Howard Wilkinson, to give a character reference for George. Howard was very well-meaning but Leveson gave him a real grilling. Despite all the pressure, and the seriousness of the allegations, George's demeanour impressed me. He stayed very calm. During one break, I bumped into George in the loo. He was upbeat. 'Your QC is a Liverpool fan,' smiled George, 'and I always do well against Liverpool.'

When he faced Leveson, George stuck to his 'unsolicited gifts' defence. Maybe George felt that having given the money back and been dismissed by Arsenal he had paid a big enough price already. His hopes of no more punishment disappeared the moment Leveson got his teeth into Hauge. Giving evidence in support of George, the agent was an unmitigated disaster. He refused to answer many questions, which was not helpful.

'Have you given money to other managers?' Leveson asked.

'I am not answering that question,' Hauge replied, time and again.

Arsenal's position was heard as well. Ken Friar, their secretary, proved an excellent witness for Arsenal. Their chairman, Peter Hill-Wood, was less impressive. Public performances were never Peter's forte but his integrity stood out. The commission then delivered its verdict, banning George from football for a year. Two years minimum had been my expectation. As I announced the ban to the media outside, one of George's friends shouted at me. He had been drinking champagne all afternoon. I doubt George cracked open any bubbly that night; he could have received a longer ban but it was still pretty humiliating. The whole experience was dispiriting. George and I are civil when we bump into each other now but our friendship never really recovered. In the wake of the George Graham affair, I expected more bungs cases. I believe bribes definitely go on but they are so difficult to detect, let alone prove.

Another instalment of Men Behaving Badly emerged from Arsenal around the same time. Football endured Paul Merson's very public confession of cocaine, gambling and boozing. Talking to people associated with Arsenal's talented England winger, I felt the alcohol and especially the drugs element of the unholy trinity were overplayed when revelations materialised in November 1994. Paul's problem was betting. The whole scandal was essentially a human and personal battle, similar to the failure of George Best and Paul Gascoigne to deal with addiction. Like George and Gazza, Merson was a fundamentally decent guy struggling to handle fame. Merson was loud and fun, slightly over the top. When he revealed the depth and nature of his assorted compulsions, I helped to organise a meeting between Graham Kelly, Paul, George Graham, Arsenal's secretary Ken Friar and the chief executive of the players' union, Gordon Taylor.

'Merson is in a precarious state,' Arsenal warned me. Message understood. The FA had to keep that meeting as discreet as possible. If a swarm of reporters and snappers ambushed Merson, no one knew how this emotionally fragile young man would react.

'Please avoid a circus,' Arsenal pleaded.

'OK, the meeting will be in central London and I'll inform everyone of the venue an hour before we start,' I promised. A subterfuge operation was launched with two dummy locations booked near Lord's and Edgware Road. The real destination was the Football Trust's old HQ adjacent to Euston Station. On 1 December, the day of the meeting, Gordon Taylor's mobile kept flicking into and out of life as he disappeared into tunnels on the train into Euston.

'Gordon, it's at the Trust,' I gasped, at what felt like the tenth attempt. The operation seemed to be working but as I walked into the Trust offices, I bumped into a BBC radio reporter completely by chance, interviewing someone. Nightmare. Our cover was seconds from being blown. Merson was about to enter the building. 'Don't be late for your meeting,' I told the reporter, who checked her watch and walked into another office. Thank God. She was moments away from the big story of the day. As she disappeared, Paul came in with George and Ken. George clearly felt under real pressure. He couldn't understand how anyone could slide into such depths of addiction as Merson. Beginning the meeting as hawks, Kelly and I finished as doves. Merson was caught bang to rights. He admitted everything. We realised he had got on to a downward spiral and it was mainly betting dragging him down. A little boy lost, Paul was contrite, fearing for his future. All those big gestures on the pitch at Wembley, simulating knocking back pints of lager, were just bravado. I felt for him.

'I'm surprised you're this sympathetic,' Mike Parry said to me later.

'Look, Mike, point one: the most important thing is to sort Merson out. Why go wallop? That won't help. Look at him. He's distraught and destroyed. Point two: how is he going to get out of this spiral? He has mentioned some pretty heavy people demanding money back. Jesus, he's got in with a strange crowd.' Mike became a huge ally of Paul's. The FA decreed there would be no immediate punishment, a controversial decision. Arsenal effectively suspended Merson by sending him to a drug counselling clinic, which looked after him incredibly well. On his return, we organised a news conference so Merson could talk through his experiences, maybe urging people to keep away from drugs and gambling. 'You look great, Paul,' I told him. He did. Unfortunately, the sheen of strength was superficial. To my complete surprise, as the cameras rolled and reporters asked questions, Merson broke down, bursting into tears. I should have thought in advance that might happen. I should have reacted more quickly and showed I cared for Paul, which I did. Merson just wanted to get the hell out of there.

A drinking culture clearly pervaded parts of the Gunners dressing room. Tony Adams was a fascinating character. When I covered Arsenal for the BBC at the 1993 FA Cup final, I went to Tony's parents' home and met his father, sadly now passed away, and mother. Tony's father had done well in life, making a bit of money, but his pride and joy was his footballing son. 'I'm so proud of Tony,' he told me. In their back garden, Tony's parents had this fantastic, designer pond system packed with all types of exotic fish. Admiring all this elegance and sophistication, I then looked across at raw-boned Tony. It felt incongruous.

After losing to Germany at Euro '96, Tony was desperately upset. He was up all night. Bumping into Tony in the morning, he looked rough. I was still shocked to read a headline in the *Sun* on

Friday 13 September 1996 that 'Krauts Drove Me To Booze'. He'd apparently gone on an almighty bender after that defeat. This surprised me. Tony never drank excessively at Burnham Beeches when England trained there. We'd have an occasional beer in the evening. He was just Tony: loud but no trouble, just good company. Tony was not drinking himself silly in the team hotel. If anything, I admired his restraint. With his marriage in difficulty, Tony must have been under real strain. The moment the tournament was over, he clearly let rip and hit the bottle big-time.

Eventually, he addressed his demons, checked into a clinic, and dried out. The transformation was extraordinary. Tony Adams Mark I had been full on, all action, up for a party. Tony Adams Mark II, the survivor of alcoholism, was transformed. Tony is highly intelligent, but I was still startled by the strong way he tackled his alcoholism. Tony was always very self-critical, always analysing his performances, and now he turned this trait on his personality flaws. Tony Adams Mark I had not been the greatest reader of books. Tony Adams Mark II was almost Poet Laureate, devouring literature. He allied his natural intelligence with a desire to educate himself, a process that may have started during his incarceration for drink driving. Prison shocked Tony.

'Grim' was how he described it to me.

'I can understand,' I replied. 'I've done films in there, and it horrified me.'

Another episode damaging the image of English football occurred during the run-up to Euro '96. The job of Trevor Phillips, the FA commercial director, was to make sure if he possibly could that every Euro '96 venue was sold out, easy with England, more difficult with the likes of Bulgaria and Romania. Talk of tickets on the black market began in April, still two months before the tournament kicked off. Such talk was potentially highly embarrassing for the FA, which had trumpeted that it would be able to trace back any ticket sold over the odds. I feared being asked to resume the 'Inspector Knacker' role I'd already performed with FA Cup final tickets. This involved me and others meeting up with various dubious characters, buying up their tickets on a budget the FA gave me, and then enabling those who sat in the warm at Lancaster Gate to name and shame their original recipients. Luckily, for Euro '96, professional sleuths were employed. On 18 April 1996 I was asked by Graham Kelly and Pat Smith to hold a discreet meeting with a Metropolitan Police contact. The Met were already on the case. 'We're going to raid some premises where we believe there may be activity around black-market tickets for Euro '96,' my police contact told me. Several days later, the raids followed. When questioned, the ticket agencies involved invariably claimed they had permission from the FA to sell them. Some, it seemed, actually did. Worse still, the Met took TV cameras on their raids. Euro '96 was seen to be mired in controversy. For those caught up in all this, including those working at the well-known National Sporting Club based at the Café Royal in Regent Street, it was a horrendous experience.

'Graham, we have what could be a major scandal on our hands,' I told Kelly. 'We've said for two years we can trace and source every ticket on the black market even when the trail leads back to ourselves.' What emerged was that tickets had been released ultimately to hospitality companies with Trevor's authority but without the knowledge of anybody else at the FA. There was no evidence whatsoever that Trevor sought to make money from this. He just wanted to shift tickets for less attractive matches so he offloaded them to various outlets which then intended to sell them on. When Graham spoke to Trevor, he protested he had done nothing wrong. Graham thought differently. Events moved quickly. 'It's done,' Graham said barely twenty-four hours later. 'Trevor's resigned. He was very emotional.' He would have been. I always liked Trevor and enjoyed his company. Despite that bumpy beginning to our relationship when he seemed to take offence at Joe Ashton's praise of me at Westminster on my first day at the FA, we became good mates and laughed a lot at some of the bizarre things that happened inside Lancaster Gate. I was glad he found a new and very successful life in South Africa.

Immediately after Trevor's departure, a Euro '96 crisis group met up in my front room. 'The situation is worse than we thought,' Graham explained. 'There may be a host of bulk ticket deals that breach our own rules. They are hugely damaging to the FA.' Also present was the person in overall control of ticketing, Pat Smith. I'd rarely seen her so depressed. Several times, I thought Pat was about to shed a tear or two. She talked of resigning herself.

'Who benefits from that?' came the immediate response from Nic Coward, Glen Kirton and myself. My view was that we needed to act quickly to limit any public perception that Euro '96 was in any sort of crisis. Remarkably for the FA, the story took five days to emerge publicly. But on 7 May it did. The contacts books of journos Harry Harris and Charlie Sale struck more gold.

'Any hope of separating Trevor's name from the ticket issues is probably hopeless,' I said. 'But in the interests of the tournament, let alone Trevor, we should try.' And we did. The credibility of Euro '96 was damaged before it began but, thankfully and somewhat surprisingly, less than some of us feared.

Of all the fires I had to fight during that period, the most complicated was the long-running saga of Brighton & Hove Albion. The intentions of businessman Bill Archer towards the club were unclear. Archer was in dispute with Dick Knight, someone who became a great mate of mine. Brighton's plight filled me with despair. They moved out of the Goldstone Ground, and their very existence seemed threatened under Archer.

'We have to get involved,' I told Nic Coward and Graham Kelly repeatedly.

'For us to intervene would set a precedent,' replied Nic, ever the lawyer.

'But we cannot afford not to move on this,' I argued. We reached a compromise that the FA would not become involved directly but would encourage mediation and pay for it. On contacting the CBI, I talked to Bill Marsh, who operated their short-sharp-shock mediation service. 'Bill, we have this complicated situation at Brighton with Archer and Knight,' I said. 'I need you to broker a deal so Archer can leave and Knight can run the club.' Marsh tried his best. The mediation became not so short, and not so sharp.

Dick invited me to one of the many public meetings in Brighton. 'It'll be quite rough, you know,' Dick said on collecting me from Brighton Station. 'The FA are not popular down here.' When I entered the night-club, the setting for the meeting, I was welcomed by 1,000 Brighton fans chanting 'The FA have done fuck all'. After waiting for the boos to die down, I took the microphone. I knew what I was about to say might antagonise Kelly and Coward, but I had to get involved.

'I will fight for Brighton,' I promised. 'The FA move in mysterious ways, but I can assure you that I will move heaven and earth to make sure Brighton survive. To allow a club of Brighton's tradition to die would be a disgrace. I will fight for you all the way. One of my friends at school was a passionate Brighton fan. He lived and breathed the club. So I understand what Brighton means to you. I promise you this: you do have a friend at the FA.'

Silence ensued, ended by a standing ovation. Brighton fans knew that at least someone at Lancaster Gate was emotionally involved in their predicament. When I returned to HQ, word had got around about my speech. A certain frostiness was in the air. But sod it.

'What are the FA for?' I asked Kelly. 'We should be involved in situations like this. We are the guardians of the game. The Goldstone Ground is history but the club needs support to survive. I know the FA are not a police force, and we can't just go into a club simply because we don't like the look of someone. But Brighton are a challenge we need to meet. I don't know whether Bill Archer is good, bad or indifferent. I do know that Dick Knight has some finance, and could take over the club. Dick is a real supporters' person, just the person you want running your club. I'm going to stick in there.' I left Graham's office, feeling very much on my own over Brighton. To this day, I've never understood why Graham, who cared about grass-roots football so much, always seemed loath to get involved in saving Brighton.

Of course, the FA couldn't just rustle up a few tanks, roll down the A23, along the promenade and rebuild the Goldstone Ground. So it was left to me to coax and cajole all parties. Eventually we got a new board together with independent directors, including Sir John Smith and Lord Richard Faulkner. I gave evidence for Brighton at the public inquiry for a new stadium at Falmer. I passionately believed in Brighton's cause. In truth, I wish I'd found the time to champion more clubs whose futures were being threatened. But so much of my time was taken up with England.

5

Terry

When Terry Venables was first seriously considered as England manager, Lancaster Gate legend has it that Sir Bert Millichip responded: 'Over my dead body.' Sir Bert needed some convincing. Two good friends of mine, Noel White, soon to be chairman of the FA International Committee, and his predecessor the late Peter Swales also disagreed vehemently with Venables's appointment. 'Too much baggage' was their united concern over a coach who, at one stage, figured in a list of legal disputes that would have drowned most mortals. When Terence Frederick Venables arrived at 16 Lancaster Gate, not everyone rolled out the red carpet.

While I served my notice period from the BBC, Sir Bert quizzed me about Terry's suitability. 'Jimmy Armfield has been round the country, canvassed the views of lots of people and he believes Venables is the best man for the job,' said Sir Bert. 'My one concern is Venables seems to have sailed a bit close to the wind at times. Look at the problems he's having with Alan Sugar at Tottenham. Their relationship has obviously soured. I'm being urged to take Venables but I need to know what you think? As FA Director of Communications, you'll have to deal with any fall-out.'

'Chairman, the question is do you have a better coach than Venables in mind?' I asked Sir Bert. 'Until and unless Venables is found to have done something wrong, I cannot see why you shouldn't appoint him if you think he is the right coach. Do you think he is the best coach?'

'Yes,' replied Sir Bert and rang off. He offered Venables the post at an extraordinary meeting at the Football League's old HQ off the Edgware Road in London. As they were about to sign the deal, Venables and Millichip became aware of a commotion outside. Sirens blared, tyres screeched as a couple of police cars pulled up. Standing on the window ledge straight across from an astonished Millichip and Venables was a woman about to jump. Fortunately, she was talked inside, but I often felt that was a warning to anyone about to sign his life away as England manager. Think before you leap.

Terry did sign. 'Terrific,' I told Susan. 'I really fancy working with Terry. Point one: He's a top coach. Point two: he's fun.' I spoke from hugely enjoyable experience, starting with Spurs' famous FA Cup final triumph over Nottingham Forest in 1991. After the semis, the BBC called a meeting of the main people at *Match of the Day* and *Football Focus.* Reporters were assigned to each finalist, so Tony Gubba and I tossed a coin to decide who covered Forest or Spurs. 'David, we don't need a toss of the coin,' said Gubba. 'I'll do Tottenham and you can do Forest.' Tony probably thought that because I lived in the Midlands at the time I'd want Forest.

'No, I want a toss of the coin,' I insisted. So Jimmy Hill flipped a 10p piece in the air.

'Heads,' I called.

'Heads it is,' said Jimmy.

'I'll go with Tottenham,' I said. 'I'll follow Venables.' One coin, one correct call, launched a wonderful relationship with Terry. If I'd said 'tails', my life might have been so different. Scarcely had the coin dropped my way than I was off to see Venables. First stop was the Holiday Inn, Liverpool, where Spurs were staying before a game at Anfield, shortly before the Cup final. Venables had agreed to meet for a chat. He seemed friendly enough over the phone but nerves still pursued me through the foyer. Venables was such a massive name in the game. He could not have been more welcoming. He seemed to enjoy meeting new people. We chewed the fat for an hour, laughed a lot. 'See you at the Royal Lancaster,' Venables said as we parted. Thank God. I was in. The Royal Lancaster was Spurs' Cup-final base. Arriving with my BBC crew on the eve of Wembley, I noticed some very distinguished figures entering the hotel.

'Heavens above, it's the 1966 World Cup boys,' I said excitedly to my cameraman. 'There's Gordon Banks! Bobby and Jack Charlton! Geoff Hurst!' All the legends were there for a 25th-anniversary reunion, minus Bobby Moore, sadly absent as he bravely fought cancer. Seeking out Venables, I asked: 'Terry, can we film the players meeting the '66 boys.'

'Of course,' Terry replied. 'I'll bring the team down.'

As the BBC cameras rolled, Spurs players like Gary Lineker, Gary Mabbutt and Paul Gascoigne mixed with the men for ever etched in Wembley folklore. Gazza ran around like a particularly energetic puppy. 'He's everywhere,' I said to Terry. He smiled and shrugged his shoulders. 'That's Gazza,' Terry laughed.

'It's not the most relaxing venue for a Cup-final team,' I said to Susan later that night. 'It's so different from the secluded places Manchester United always choose.' Nothing seemed to trouble Tottenham, even though Terry was involved in the time-consuming process of buying Spurs with Alan Sugar that very weekend. In the breakfast room the following day, an eagle eye was required as Gazza threw bread rolls around. 'Erik!' shouted Gazza. A doughy missile flew Thorstvedt's way. The keeper dropped it. That had better not be an omen, I thought. After breakfast, I took Lineker and Mabbutt over into Hyde Park for some filming. With the clock ticking ever louder towards kick-off at Wembley, they could not have been more relaxed and helpful.

Back at the Royal Lancaster, Terry invited me on to the team coach.

'Sit at the back,' he said. 'You should be safe there.' Safe? I soon discovered what he meant. Gazza was manic, charging up and down the bus, singing, shouting, joking and jousting with the other players. He was in full prank mode, pulling faces and ruffling hair. He was wound up like a coil, ready to unleash. Even now, the image of Gascoigne's mad tackle on Gary Charles early on in the final remains painfully fresh in my mind. It wrecked Gazza's knee and damaged his career. 'What has he done?!' I shouted. Journalistic instinct took over, dragging me to the tunnel, searching for the stricken Gascoigne. This was massive news. As the camera crew and I arrived in the tunnel, we saw Gascoigne being lifted into an ambulance, which then sped off, sirens wailing. 'Where's Gazza gone?' I asked around. 'Northwick Park Hospital,' someone suggested. Duff information. Gascoigne was hurtling towards the Princess Grace Hospital.

According to all the talk in the papers that morning this was Gazza's last game for Spurs before he moved to Lazio. Now look at him. The fates of football could be vicious. When Spurs then beat Forest, Venables announced: 'We're taking the Cup to Gazza.' Everyone piled on the bus, me included, rushing to the Prince Grace. On the journey to central London, my admiration for Gary Mabbutt grew by the mile. Tottenham's captain should have been savouring his moment of glory, looking in joy at the Cup which stood proudly on the dashboard. Gary should have been waving back at all the people who saw the victors' coach. Mabbutt was more concerned about Gazza's injury and how he would cope with it. On arrival, I sought out the nearest doctor. 'Can we get a shot of Gazza with the Cup?'

'No,' came the answer, carrying a clinical finality. 'No cameras.'

After Princess Grace, it was back to the Royal Lancaster. As we pulled into the hotel's small drive, players and staff jumped off and were mobbed by the hundreds of very merry Spurs supporters on the pavement. Being at the back of the bus, I was last off. 'Hey, you've left the Cup,' I shouted after them. Terry and his players couldn't hear. The party beckoned them. Even the bus driver had gone, leaving just me and the oldest piece of football silverware in the world. The FA Cup and me. I couldn't leave it. 'You're coming with me,' I said to the Cup. So I stepped off the bus, holding the Cup. The crowd went potty. My own love affair with the Cup began in 1957, and the besotted reaction of the Tottenham fans reminded me again of the trophy's power. Anyone who doubts the nation's deep passion for the FA Cup should be there when people are in close proximity to it. The Old Pot casts a spell. I felt like a bodyguard for a Hollywood star, everyone reaching out to touch, to get a picture, just to get close to this silver celebrity. 'You forgot this!' I laughed as Terry walked into the BBC's interview room on the first floor. In future years, when the FA used this suite for disciplinary hearings, I would sit there during the more interminable moments and smile to myself at the memory of handing the Cup to Terry Venables, one of the most fascinating men in football.

'Terry has a grasshopper mind,' people always said, arguing that Terry jumped here and there, never settling. I knew what they meant.

'He has an interest in lots of subjects,' I always replied, 'and can talk in depth about many.' Terry loved football with a passion, would talk about the game with anyone. Over a few glasses of wine late at night at the dinner table, Terry would show me how he wanted Alan Shearer and Teddy Sheringham to work in tandem for England by moving the salt and pepper pots about. He was a real football man, incredibly knowledgeable about the sport and blessed with this great ability to articulate his ideas simply. No wonder players adored him. They knew he could play as well. Growing up, I watched Terry at Chelsea, Spurs, QPR and Palace. He had obvious talent. As I got to know him, sometimes I thought Terry knew everyone in London, not just because he was naturally sociable but also because he was recognised everywhere. He sang with the Joe Loss Orchestra at the Hammersmith Palais and Terry is a classy crooner, the East End Sinatra. He was and is one of life's great enthusiasts. Even in the difficult times, I felt much better for knowing Terry.

Even though I was still winding down my contract at the BBC, the task of hosting Terry's inaugural press conference fell to me. When I saw the hundreds of journalists gathered in the Banqueting Hall at Wembley, my stomach tightened. I needn't have been nervous. Venables was a star, answering every question with a smile, satisfying every demand for interview. He loved it. Later, I sought out his dad, Fred, for a chat. Fred was beside himself with happiness. 'I'm so proud,' Fred kept saying. Every time England played at Wembley, the Venables family were out in force. They were real London people, great characters and deeply patriotic.

Heading towards Euro '96, I was desperate for Terry to succeed. Life was not easy. A hullabaloo about Terry's financial affairs pursued him into Lancaster Gate like an ill wind. The list of all the court issues he was involved in reached double figures at one stage. Some of Terry's problems, I fear, were brought on him by the acts of associates.

'Are you absolutely sure you are happy with the people you are surrounding yourself with?' I asked Terry several times.

'Yes. When I was out on my ear, they stood by me.' Who was I to criticise that? Venables was incredibly loyal.

Was he really worth two BBC *Panoramas* and a *Dispatches* programme on Channel 4? 'There is a vendetta against me,' Venables insisted. I was never sure there was a conscious vendetta against Terry. Several people inside football simply didn't feel he was a fit person to be England coach, regardless of what was or wasn't proven against him. Terry divided people. No one was ambivalent towards Venables.

On joining the FA, I walked into the bungs inquiry conducted by Rick Parry, Robert Reid and Steve Coppell. One of the transfers they looked into was Teddy Sheringham's move from Forest to Spurs, then managed by Venables. As chief executive of the Premier League, Parry was based in Lancaster Gate, so we often talked. 'I'm worried about the Sheringham story and the links to Terry,' I told Rick. 'The inquiry is going on for ever and it does not help England.'

On 21 December 1995, Rick warned Kelly: 'The inquiry on Sheringham could still be a problem in terms of Terry.' Rick is pessimistic on his good days, but his bleak assessment troubled me deeply. I discussed the predicament with Kelly.

'It's exhausting, this constant fear that at any moment we could get landed with a crisis around Terry's position,' I said. 'I am really concerned about this. If they make serious allegations against Terry, his position could become untenable. When on earth will they report? They should end what has been whipped up into a witch-hunt. I want them to put up or shut up.' All the time, it was drip-drip claims, understandably upsetting Terry. 'It's farcical,' he said.

Heading home for Christmas, my mood was deeply miserable.

'This is the calm before the storm,' I told Susan. 'I'm very depressed over where we are going with the bungs inquiry.'

'Are people on the take in football?' she asked.

'I've no proof. But I do know of one chairman who, I am assured, took a bung from a TV company to make sure his game was covered. If things are so serious, the police should deal with it. The FA, the Premier League – these are not police forces.'

I would have preferred that Terry had not arrived at the FA with so much baggage, but I couldn't rewrite history. His media supporters outnumbered his media opponents, though not in the noise they made. Day after day, for long periods, his business and private life seemed to be fair game on the back pages. 'I don't read the papers,' Terry said. He did. Every England manager except Sven-Goran Eriksson claimed he never looked at the newspapers. Barring Sven, they all did. It's human nature to learn what people are saying about you. They also need to know what the players are reading. A resilient character, Terry still bruised. 'Anything that upsets Dad or my daughters upsets me,' he said.

Some of the newspaper coverage was poisonous. On the morning of an England game against Norway in Oslo on 11 October 1995, Terry woke to a mock-up picture of his head in a noose on the back page of the *Mirror*. Oslo was always going to be rough.

'David, tomorrow will not be pretty,' predicted Terry on the eve of battle. He was right. It was a grim 0–0 and the papers went to town on England again. I hated this world of cruel headlines, writs, claims and counter-claims. England being caught in the war between Alan Sugar and Venables was a constant frustration. Embarrassing to the FA, it was a time-consuming diversion for some of us trying to give the players the best chance of success. One day in 1995, after another barrage of headlines detailing the messy breakdown of Venables's business relationship with Sugar, I'd had enough. I went into Millichip's office.

'I want to try to sort this out,' I said.

'Go ahead,' Sir Bert replied. That night, I mentioned my determination to bring Terry and Sugar together to my former BBC colleague, Brian Barwick.

'Stay out of it,' advised Brian.

I couldn't. Something had to be done. I called on the conciliation services of the CBI run by Howard Davies, a good friend and big Manchester City fan for his sins. 'Howard, you are aware of this Venables–Sugar thing,' I said. 'I'm desperate for someone to mediate between them. It is debilitating for the FA, for England, for Terry and for Sugar. It's ghastly. Our chances of winning Euro '96 will be damaged if this mess continues.' Howard investigated possible ways to ease the tension between Venables and Sugar, but even the CBI's skills were not enough.

Venables and Sugar remained at war. I sought out another potential peace-maker from the august offices of the Queen's solicitors. Farrar and Company provided one of their very best lawyers, Charles Woodhouse, to broker a truce. Everyone started optimistically but when they got into the detail of the dispute, it all foundered again. So I returned to Millichip. 'Sir Bert, you must personally intervene with Terry because he is our employee and tell him to take part with Sugar in this mediation process,' I pleaded.

It was a gamble. Millichip's previous interventions had actually not been particularly successful. At the FA, we had what I termed Brian Woolnough's monthly 'Sir Bert' story in the *Sun.*

An experienced and excellent journalist now at the *Daily Star*, Brian is an astute watcher of England. He developed this routine of ringing Millichip on the eve of internationals, giving the *Sun* a strong back-page lead. Good tactics. Always well-meaning, always polite, Sir Bert always gave Brian a line. The ritual, I imagined, went like this: 'How are you, Sir Bert? It's Brian Woolnough here. And how is Lady Barbara?'

'Very good, Brian, we are all looking forward to the game.'

'How do you think Terry is getting on?'

'Early days, Brian, but I don't want to get into a discussion about that. We are all optimistic.'

'You must be a bit irritated about this row between Terry and Alan Sugar?'

'I don't want to say anything about that.'

'But surely day after day?'

'Of course, I wish they would sort it out.'

Bingo. Brian had his story. Brian's interviewing skills landed me with some humdingers of headlines to deal with, and some early starts in England team hotels abroad or our usual base, Burnham Beeches in Bucks. Occasionally, my hotel-room door would shake to a firm knock. Terry would be standing there. No shoes, no socks, unshaven. In a few hours, the coach of the England team would be suited and booted, organising a team in front of 80,000 people, with the eyes of a huge television audience on him. He would be calm and in control. Yet here he was in shorts and a T-shirt, holding up the back page of the *Sun*, which screamed: 'Belt up Tel, says Bert'.

'You couldn't make it up,' I would say. That was our Woolnough moment. Eventually, it became a running gag between Terry and me: 'What's Brian got out of Bert this time?!'

Millichip did encourage action over Venables and Sugar. To get them moving, I published the letter about the FA's plea to both of them to sort things out. Venables's quarrel with Sugar hung over England and was settled only after Terry left the FA. Sugar was only part of Terry's problems. Terry was involved in a succession of court cases, and was eventually banned from being a director for seven years. The spotlight burned so strongly on Venables's off-the-field activities partly because England were hardly setting the world alight on the pitch. As Euro '96 hosts, England had no competitive games, so it was friendly after dire friendly. That is the major downside of having a tournament in your own country. As Euro '96 neared, the decision was taken that England should warm up in the Far East. I raised more than an eyebrow. I raised some serious questions.

'Why are we preparing for a tournament at home against European opposition by playing games in China and Hong Kong?' I asked Kelly. He shrugged. 'It's Trevor's idea.' Commercially, the trip made sense. Trevor Phillips made money for the FA from the two games. Terry thought disappearing to the other side of the world might take the pressure off the players. Being away from the national debate about tactics, and Alan Shearer's lack of goals, would be an advantage.

'We need to get away,' Terry said.

'Well, we can't get much further away than China and Hong Kong!' I laughed.

'I wonder what the pitches will be like?' Terry mused. Good question. Our scouts soon informed us the pitch in Beijing was 'shocking'.

'We need to persuade the Chinese to improve the pitch,' said Terry. 'We need to send someone over to have a quiet word. It sounds like a job for Ted.' Ted Buxton was a Venables friend, scout, all-round diamond character and possessed with what he often reminded us was a distinguished war record fighting in the Far East jungle.

'I hope Ted never fought the Chinese!' I remarked to Venables. 'We're sending someone to Beijing who might have killed some Chinese.'

'Ted will be fine,' Venables insisted. And he was. 'Mr Ted', as the good people of Beijing hailed him, utterly charmed the Chinese. Everyone from their FA, to the ground staff at the

Workers' Stadium, to hotel staff, all loved Buxton. By the time England landed, the advance FA party called 'Mr Ted' was the Hero of Beijing. In local eyes, he had saved the game, and saved face for them. Under the eagle gaze of 'Mr Ted', the pitch was quickly tarted up, he approved its viability, and celebratory firecrackers were let off. Terry and the England players found it hilarious arriving at the hotel to be greeted by hundreds of Chinese chanting: 'Mr Ted! Mr Ted!' As a friend of the People's Republic of China, there was none greater than Mr Ted.

A trip of constant surprises, some good, some bad, had started in style. Doc Crane's anti-jet-lag pills worked well. I felt perky, which I needed to be during a rather lengthy speech by Noel White at the ritual banquet laid on by the Chinese. Terry's take on Noel's speech was succinct. 'Nightmare,' whispered Terry. At least I had the consolation of sitting next to the celebrated Italian referee, Pierluigi Collina, who was charming but confused. One thing fazed him. 'I cannot believe the size of China,' said Collina. 'Everything is so big.'

Even the local Wall. Gary and Phil Neville and several other players went to visit the Great Wall, unlike West Brom's John Trewick in the Seventies, who famously stayed in his Peking hotel arguing that 'once you've seen one wall, you've seen them all'. Gary and Phil were keen as mustard, even helping some of the less athletic photographers up to the Wall when the cable-car broke down. It turned into the trip from hell. The local guide took the players in the wrong direction, sending them on an exhausting, very extended tour.

'Unimpressed' was Terry's verdict after his players hobbled home.

'How on earth did the guide lose the Great Wall?' I asked. 'You can see it from the Moon.'

England's trip to the Wall was described as a 'shambles' by Alan Green, the Radio Five Live commentator. When I heard, I called Greeny and we had a real ruck. David Dein, a member of the International Committee, told me that Greeny had been complaining about the trip, so I was ready for an argument. Some media people dish out criticism every day yet become all sensitive when it is returned in their direction. Over tea in Hong Kong, Greeny and I quickly made our peace.

The one bright spot on the Great Wall débâcle day was morning sightseeing around the Forbidden City with assorted FA dignitaries like Dein, Noel White and Keith Wiseman. 'It's just like Lancaster Gate,' I muttered under my breath.

The Magical Oriental Mystery Tour continued. With Gary and Phil in the starting line-up for the first time, England beat China 3–0 and it was off to Hong Kong. We touched down into pure chaos, local fans going crazy over the England players. For a brief period, I really worried about their safety. Fortunately, we reached the hotel in one piece. I didn't fancy ringing up Manchester United or Liverpool to inform them one of their precious players was coming home on crutches after being injured in the crush or clipped by a rickshaw. Mindful of the players' condition, Venables announced: 'The journey was exhausting. So we won't train this afternoon.'

'What?!' I replied. 'We are due at this private club to train. There will be a storm if we don't turn up. Hong Kong people will consider it a snub.'

'No,' Terry insisted. 'We're not going whatever the repercussions.' Venables was adamant and I respected the coach's wishes, but I was right. An almighty storm engulfed England the next day. The Hong Kong papers ripped into 'arrogant' England, asking whether we thought we were too special for their pitch? It was just the type of classic PR clanger I was trying to prevent the FA from making. Time for a charm offensive. The following day, after eventually training, I told the players to go around handing out badges and signing autographs. Mission accomplished. Smiles replaced scowls on local faces. The match against the Hong Kong Select XI was not England's finest hour; we scraped only a 1–0 win and the bus wrapped itself around a taxi on the way back to the hotel. At least the players found it funny. Terry remained in a serious mood, agonising over who to leave out of his squad for Euro '96. I knew Peter

Beardsley was out. He came to my room and we talked for twenty minutes. Thank God, he was not likely to pan Venables for ending his Euro '96 dream. Beardsley held a press conference to announce his England retirement. When the journalists applauded a player who had been a valuable servant to his country, I looked across at Venables, whose eyes moistened. Axing good people was tough. Robert Lee, Jason Wilcox, Ugo Ehiogu and Dennis Wise were also omitted. Dennis's reaction was unbelievable. I thought he would go crazy. Instead, he told Venables: 'Good on you, Guv'nor. I didn't expect to be here in the first place!'

Some players were showing the strain of missing family and friends. Gazza came up to me and showed me the flowers his son Regan had sent him. 'To Daddy, I miss you, Happy Birthday' read the card. Gazza burst into tears. So did I. It was my birthday the following day and I was missing my daughters, Amanda and Caroline. Everyone was pretty shattered, so Terry announced the players could have a night out before the long haul home the following day.

'Are you sure, Terry?' I said. My instincts feared trouble.

'They've earned it,' he replied. I went to bed, full of misgivings, wondering what was going on in other parts of Hong Kong. The next day was a long one before the evening flight home. Some of the players looked very jaded. Still, I thought, they can catch up on their beauty sleep on the thirteen-hour flight home. Boarding the Cathay Pacific jet, I prepared myself for a nice relaxing time. The players were upstairs, I was downstairs. Perfect. Time to get some shut-eye. In the middle of the night, I nipped to the loo. For some reason, I climbed the stairs and bumped into an upset Gazza. 'What's up?' Gazza wouldn't answer. Clearly something had happened. Once again he looked tearful. At breakfast, Noel White woke Terry, who was none too pleased to have his sleep interrupted. 'There's been a complaint upstairs,' said Noel. 'Your players have been up to something.' Terry went off to have a look but things seemed to have calmed down. At Heathrow, everybody went their own way for a four-day break until the squad gathered for the tournament itself. Those four days, during which it was impossible to contact everybody, and so equally impossible to be certain who was to blame, were a nightmare. I hadn't been inside my front door half an hour when a telephone call confirmed the FA were embroiled in absolutely the type of crisis I'd wanted so desperately to avoid.

A hurricane whirled around the England team. TV headlines proclaimed that the players did £5,000 worth of damage to a screen on the plane. Someone at Cathay Pacific had clearly been on the phone, pointing the finger at Gazza and Robbie Fowler, amongst others. Bedlam ensued. My birthday was wrecked. I hit the phones. Noel White assumed the FA default position: batten down the hatches. Graham Kelly assumed Kelly's default position: elusive. I was on my own with this mess. Terry rang. 'What's all the fuss?' he enquired, clearly believing Cathay Pacific had overplayed the incident. Jamie Redknapp called: 'I'm innocent but I'm besieged at Mum and Dad's with reporters and photographers everywhere. What do I do?'

'Stay calm, stay inside. I'll sort it.' But how? All of us had gone in different directions for our so-called days off.

'At least the storm can't get any worse,' I said to Susan. Yes, it could. The following morning brought another blizzard of awful headlines, this time accompanied by photographs of the players' night out in Hong Kong. They seemed to be celebrating Gazza's birthday with some enthusiasm, including having drinks poured into them while sitting in some contraption called the Dentist's Chair.

'Anything in the papers?' Susan asked.

'Gazza's tummy is rather prominent,' I replied. 'There are a lot of ripped shirts. Robbie Fowler and Steve McManaman seem to be enjoying themselves.' Pictures of people partying rarely look pretty in the cold light of day. 'Gazza will be slaughtered by the press again.'

David Platt called, clearly shocked. 'I've never seen anything like it,' he said. 'I can't see a way out.'

'Nor can I, Platty, but we'll find one.'

The next day, 31 May, the tempest raged on. A poll in the *Daily Mirror* claimed '86 per cent want Gazza expelled from Euro '96.' God, if they only knew how fragile Gazza was. I dreaded him reading that. A distraught Gazza soon rang. 'Everyone is accusing me of breaking the screen. Why are they picking on me?'

'We'll sort it, Gazza. Everything will be fine. You'll have a great tournament. You can show everyone then.' Craving reassurance, Gazza seemed to lack trust in anyone, even those supposedly close to him.

'Stick in there until Sunday night and then when you get to Burnham tell everything you know to Terry.' Mention of Venables seemed to calm Gazza. Terry was like a father-figure to him. Gazza's agent talked of suing newspapers for accusing his client of damaging the plane. I felt that would just fan the flames.

Terry called. 'I've not heard from Kelly,' said Terry, who was getting battered in the media for not upbraiding his players. I stood up for Terry. People didn't know the facts. Terry was abroad, the players were in twenty-three different places and, by the way, we were nine days from the biggest tournament for England since 1966. Here we were, on the eve of a tournament the country was desperate for us to win, and the media was slaughtering the team and the coach. The only tactic was to battle through until the team re-assembled. To clear my mind, I headed to Bisham Abbey to check out the media centre the FA had built for Euro '96. It was magnificent, a gleaming white tent fit for a wedding, or a divorce judging by the current state of relations between players and press. This was my pride and joy, based on my own experience covering football around the world, and what journalists needed.

'It's perfect,' I said to Michelle Farrer, the England team administrator who'd accompanied me. Michelle is an FA institution, regarded with affection and respect by generations of players and successive coaches. England couldn't function without Michelle, who makes sure everything runs smoothly off the pitch.

'Oh, my God,' I shouted. 'But there's a problem.'

'What?' Michelle asked.

'We'd better get those pictures down for a start.' I pointed at life-size photographs of Gazza and Fowler, the men in the eye of the current storm. It wasn't in the players' interests to be so prominent at this moment. Arriving in the marquee foyer, the first thing journalists would see would be inescapable pictures of Gazza and Fowler. On day one of Euro '96, those pictures would be back-page news. We had to change them for someone less controversial.

'Where's a picture of Gareth Southgate?!' I pleaded.

D-Day dawned. 2 June. Time for answers. Quieter than usual, the players gathered at Burnham, chastened, even, I sensed, a little frightened. The inquest began. I knew whatever we did would be scrutinised in depth: 'How will the FA deal with the vandals of Cathay Pacific?' That's what the public and press wanted to know. It was an evening of endless huddles involving Venables, Macca, Gazza, Robbie Fowler and others. Exasperation built within me. For days, the players and Terry had been in the public stocks, having everything thrown at them without reply. Now, we needed answers.

'It's the worst of all worlds, no one is admitting responsibility,' Terry told me.

'We're five days from the tournament and we have to draw a line under this,' I replied. 'Is anyone going to help? Some of the FA people want to chuck Gazza out of the squad as a sacrificial lamb, taking the heat off the team. But how can we possibly justify doing that? He hasn't even admitted responsibility for the bust television. We could be hanging an innocent man.'

'Right, if no one is going to own up, everybody has to pay,' said Terry. 'We're going to make a large contribution to charity.' The senior players agreed to Terry's compromise. That was a start. As I listened to Terry, an idea formed in my head. If no one owned up to being responsible, then surely everybody is responsible? No individual was prepared to take responsibility. So it had to be collective responsibility. Good teams stick together and accept blame together.

At breakfast the next morning, I made my proposal to Terry.

'Why don't we explain that we feel there's a collective responsibility here,' I said. 'All the squad apologise. All take the blame.'

'OK,' replied Terry, after a pause. 'Let's try it.'

Waiting until 5.30 p.m., I knew an announcement then would give us a free run at the *Six O'Clock News*. I walked down Burnham's drive, the rain dripping from the trees, and stood at the gate. Addressing the media hordes, I read the statement, heard the gasps at 'collective responsibility' and headed back to the hotel. Job done. But how would it play? At last beginning to unwind, I sat in the bar enjoying a drink with Terry, Don Howe and Bryan Robson. My peace was shattered by my phone.

'David, hi, it's Rob King here.' It was dear old Kingy, the popular football correspondent of the Press Association now, sadly, no longer with us. 'David, I have to tell you I rang Sir Bert at his home. I want to tell you how the conversation went.'

'Oh yeah, Kingy, go on.'

'I asked Sir Bert: "Have you seen tonight's developments?" Sir Bert replied: "I knew all about it. David rang me and told me about it. I am not quite sure what 'collective responsibility' means but David says it's a good idea."'

'Kingy, well done. What do you want me to say?'

'David, clearly the chairman doesn't understand what collective responsibility means.'

'We all understand what it means and, Kingy, so do you. Everyone is taking responsibility and that's it. Finish.' Returning to the bar, the look of thunder on my face was familiar to Terry.

'Sir Bert?!' Terry laughed.

'Yes. He has landed me in the shit.'

'Again?'

'Again.'

As it turned out, the *Sun*, a frequent vehicle for the thoughts of Chairman Millichip, was particularly supportive of 'collective responsibility'. Their editor, Stuart Higgins, decided the Cathay Pacific story had run its course. In true *Sun* fashion, it was time to get behind the lads. The *Guardian* hailed 'collective responsibility as a PR masterstroke'. If only we had been that clever. A real gamble, it was the only solution we could think of.

Cathay Pacific intensified a siege mentality in the England camp. 'We can turn this to our advantage,' said Terry, ever the cunning managerial fox. Terry knew criticism of the squad could be used to bond them closer. All the players felt tarred with the same media brush, and they refused to talk to the press. Eventually, I persuaded Shearer and Southgate to come down to the media centre. 'Move the agenda on,' I urged them. 'Focus on the tournament.' Thank God for Alan and Gareth, real rocks in a storm. Upstanding pros, they would have had nothing to do with Cathay Pacific but accepted collective responsibility for the good of the team. They were prepared to face the music, even though someone else had written the lyrics. Gazza still raged over his treatment. 'I never want to speak to the media again, even if I score a hat-trick in the final,' he told me.

'Let's see.'

My room at Burnham Beeches was like the Samaritans sometimes. Just before Euro '96 kicked off, Paul Ince walked in, clearly distressed. 'Thomas has just been in the rehearsal for the opening ceremony and he's come home in tears,' Incey began. 'He said they were nasty to him.'

'What? Who?' Then I remembered. Paul's son had been nominated to take part in the festivities. Apparently, Thomas became slightly overwhelmed, started crying, and Euro '96 staff had not handled the situation well. Cue distressed father and son. 'I'll sort it out,' I promised Paul. Some people around the England camp didn't get on with Incey because he was a bit loud, with all that 'Guv'nor' stuff. But I liked Paul, who was also a bloody good player. He ought to have scored more goals for United. He certainly had the talent. During my time with *Football Focus*, I made a film at his house and realised there were many layers to Incey. Far from the cocky Londoner often depicted, he had a serious side and thought about the future. 'I want to be a manager one day,' he told me. Even knowing about his ambition, I was still surprised when he was managing in the Premier League with Blackburn Rovers scarcely two years after starting his second career. But Incey was always a leader.

Terry had no shortage of them. When he became England manager, a debate rumbled on over whether Tony Adams or David Platt should be captain. From an early stage, Terry went with Tony. He just saw Tony as a well-known leader at Arsenal. His turbulent life off the pitch was still largely his private property at that stage. 'He's an inspiration for Arsenal,' said Terry. 'He can bring that leadership to England.' In the dressing room and in the tunnel, Tony was right in there, stirring everyone up. Tony saw Euro '96 as his moment of destiny, that he would succeed Bobby Moore as the man to lift a trophy at Wembley.

Shearer was also a leader. The critics hounded Alan for a lack of goals all the way to Euro '96, but I knew this tough Geordie would deliver. Alan had a depth of determination that I have witnessed in few other players. So when he scored against Switzerland in England's opening game of Euro '96, I wasn't surprised. Shearer was made for big stages; the tougher the task, the more Alan fronted up. A 1–1 draw with the Swiss was hardly the most heroic start to Euro '96 but at least we could concentrate on the football now.

With a point in the bag and Scotland up next, it was time to throw off the hair shirt and go on the offensive. Who on the coaching staff could let rip at the press and had the respect to get away with it? It sounded like a job for Bryan Robson. 'Robbo, will you do the press today?' I asked. 'You know them all well and can defend the players. It will also give Terry a break.' Bryan did not let us down, charging into Bisham and lambasting the press. 'Write about the football' was a polite summary of Robbo's words.

After all the stress of the past fortnight, I needed to let off steam. When the ITV guys like Jim Rosenthal suggested a night out in nearby Marlow, I organised a raiding party from Burnham. Much wine was taken. Fortunately, I kept some of my senses about me. Shortly before midnight, Ted Buxton announced: 'I have found a little place with a karaoke machine.'

'Taxi,' I shouted. As much as I liked Mr Ted, I would never

have survived a night of Golden Oldies. Good move. The eve of the Scotland match proved intense. Craig Brown, the Scotland coach, called early. He'd heard I was campaigning for a minute's silence for those who'd died in the Dunblane massacre. 'I'm supporting your call for a show of respect,' said Brown. 'We must do something.'

'Craig, I agree, but the problem is your FA. I'm told the Scottish FA don't want such a gesture three months after the event.' We both couldn't understand why. I felt sorry for Craig, who passionately wanted a mark of respect for Dunblane. I always got on well with Craig. 'You're a miracle-worker,' he said to me. 'I don't have someone like you fighting for me.' Typical Craig, over-generous, but at the time a much-needed boost to morale.The man I fought hard for, Terry Venables, was under immense strain. Criticism still dogged England over Cathay Pacific and the uninspiring draw with Switzerland. Terry's demeanour was hardly improved when I almost killed him on the roundabout outside Bisham. This car, speeding through from the M4 to the M40, came flying out of nowhere. Fortunately, I veered out of its way. If I hadn't, the England coach would have departed Euro '96 somewhat earlier in a coffin. 'That was a bit close,' remarked Terry when he finally recovered the power of speech.

A car scandal of another sort did hit England. When Skinner and Baddiel recorded their famous video for 'Three Lions on a Shirt', they took some footage of life at Burnham. A still frame was taken from the video showing my car, nothing special in that except the tax disc was out of date. The England manager was being driven around by the FA's Director of Communications in a vehicle that had no legal right to be on the road. When the players realised, they gave me fearful stick, calling me 'law-breaker', 'criminal', everything.

Match-day, 15 June, arrived and the calls began early. 'Tell Terry I wish him well,' said Bobby Robson. What a great gesture from a great man. He knew Terry would be feeling the pressure. The papers had been full of 'Battle of Britain' headlines, and Terry faced a hellish time if England lost to the Auld Enemy. At Wembley, I sought Terry out in the tunnel.

'Good luck,' I said.

'I don't need good luck,' he replied. 'I need some Trebor Mints. Can you find some?' Was there no end to my duties? Mints duly located, I turned to concentrate on the game. A good result and performance against Scotland were vital to shift the attention completely back to football. Crucially, David Seaman saved a penalty. Sadly, Jamie Redknapp, one of football's good guys, had not been fit enough to start. Poor Jamie. He was so unlucky. Injury seemed to stalk him with England. At his best, Jamie was a match-winner. England just never saw enough of Harry's boy. England still had Gazza to conjure up some magic and he certainly did it in style against the Scots. When Jamie finally came on, he set up Gazza, who juggled the ball over Colin Hendry and then volleyed it past Andy Goram into the net. I was out of my seat, punching the air. If a Brazilian had scored that, it would have been lauded as a classic and everyone in England would have lamented, 'Why can't our players do that?' Some could. Gazza could. His celebration was as notable as his goal. Gazza lay on the ground, arms outstretched while Teddy Sheringham squirted a water-bottle into his mouth. Now that's refuelling! Gazza's answer to all those who had lectured England's players over their drinking in Hong Kong. People speculated that it had been rehearsed, but it was a spur-of-the-moment reaction. Teddy and Gazza just saw the bottle and came up with their double-act.

A few more drinks were downed that evening. Terry gave the players the night off, but no one abused the privilege. I stayed up to watch *Match of the Day* with Terry, Ted and Robbo amongst others in the bar. Just before the game started, one of the Burnham Beeches staff members popped her head around the corner and said: 'David, there's a call for you at reception.' I wandered over and picked up the phone.

A voice barked down the other end: 'It's Colonel Sanders here. I live on Grove Road, overlooking Burnham Beeches. My two daughters are worried about the noise. Trust it's not going to last much longer. My wife and I are going to bed early.' I was stunned. England had just beaten Scotland. The whole nation was celebrating. Diplomacy took over and I thought I'd better apologise. Always good to keep the neighbours happy. 'Very sorry, Colonel,' I replied. 'You are aware the England football team are staying here and it has been a very good day. But of course we don't want to cause any offence.'

Still startled, I went back to the television lounge.

'You won't believe this,' I announced, 'but someone called Colonel Sanders who lives next door has called to complain about the bloody noise!'

No one really seemed interested. Ted, Terry, Bryan and Macca were watching the match. When it finished, I trooped upstairs to bed. Scarcely had I settled under the covers than the bedside phone burst into life. It was the England coach.

'David, we need you down here pronto,' said Venables. 'We have a big problem.' Through the window, I caught the flashing light of a police car. Trouble. I tumbled downstairs to be greeted in the hall by Terry, England's head of security Ray Whitworth and two constables from Thames Valley Police, one male, one female.

'Mr Davies, are you the senior person here?' the policeman asked. What on earth was going on?

I finally got my brain working. 'Well, Terry is the England coach but I suppose I'm the senior FA person.'

'Could we have a private word, sir?' We all headed into a room off the main lounge.

'Mr Davies, we have had a very serious complaint from Colonel Sanders, whose two daughters have been shocked to see a blond-haired young man running naked across the lawn.' Gazza, I sighed. He'd dyed his hair almost white. Bloody Gazza!

'Who could this possibly be?' asked the policeman.

Before I could answer, his female colleague spoke up. 'Mr Davies, we need an identity parade.'

My heart fell further. We'd survived Cathay Pacific, we'd beaten the Jocks. Life should have been good.

'Where will this be?' I asked.

'Now. Outside on the lawn,' replied the WPC.

'Now?! It's midnight. It's dark.'

'That's good, sir, because it will not attract attention.' My fuse began to shorten, not with the PCs, but with Venables and Whitworth. They sat there, in silence, letting me deal with this problem.

'Who exactly is going to be in the identity parade? And who will be looking at them?'

'Everyone in the hotel, sir, and we will ask Colonel Sanders to come over with his daughters.'

'But there are sixty people staying here. I can't just go round, waking them all up, telling them we're having an identity parade in the middle of the night.'

'All right, sir, we'll do it in the morning. I'm sure Colonel Sanders won't mind waiting until daylight. It might make identification easier. We'll return in the morning and if you can have everyone lined up outside on the lawn.'

Sarcasm took over. 'Before breakfast or after?' I asked. 'Look, I'm terribly sorry but most of these people in this hotel are amongst the best-known people in this country.' I pointed to Terry. 'As a matter of interest, he is attempting to win the second-biggest football tournament in the world. And I'll have you know that I'll be contacting the Chief Constable of Thames Valley Police.'

That was it. I'd played my ace card. That would surely end this farce. Instead, everyone burst out laughing, including the police, and also players like McManaman listening at the door.

'You utter bastards!' I shouted. In the great history of England wind-ups, this ranked as one of the best. At breakfast, everybody knew.

'Met any nice policewomen lately?' came one shout.

'How's Colonel Sanders?' came another.

'Oh, you lot think you are so bloody clever!' I retorted.

If the England players felt more relaxed, Terry remained on edge. 'We've got so little time to prepare for Holland,' he said. 'The game's on Tuesday.' Terry knew the whole country was watching him and the team. Even in sleepy Bucks, the interest in England was overwhelming. When the players went for a stroll around Burnham village, they were mobbed. Craving privacy, I ordered screens to be erected around the hotel. Photographers and reporters were parked at the end of the drive, bumper to bumper along the country lane. Fans arrived in ever greater numbers, so I organised a rota of players to nip out and sign autographs.

No wonder Terry was tense: the moment England went out, he was off. The situation was ludicrous. Ever since December, we'd been living with this reality. Back then, Terry kept asking the FA: 'What's happening after the Euros? Will my contract be extended?'

Sir Bert had grown to admire Terry as a coach and a person. Unfortunately for Terry, the chairman of the International Committee Noel White remained deeply sceptical. After the Holland–Ireland play-off at Anfield on 13 December, Noel was stopped in the car-park by Rob King from the PA. Noel suggested that Terry really needed to prove himself at Euro '96 before any contract could be considered. Terry was apoplectic. He wanted to confront Noel and Sir Bert about it. When they all met, Terry's mood soured even further because they never gave him the guarantees he wanted. Everyone decided to cool off and consult again after Christmas. After the break, with the press all asking 'When's Terry meeting Sir Bert to discuss his future?' Terry bumped into the chairman in the lift at Lancaster Gate.

'Has the International Committee's attitude changed?' Terry asked. 'Are you prepared to give me a contract after the Euros?' In the course of their short journey in the lift, and then brief walk along a corridor, Sir Bert sadly informed Terry that White and the International Committee were not budging. No decision would be made until after the Euros.

'Right, that's it,' Terry told me. He knew he had few allies in the building. Graham Kelly wasn't going to fight for him. I would, but on my own I couldn't change White's mind. Over the previous few months, I'd enlisted the help of players like Gazza to push Terry's case in public. One day at Burnham, I sat Gazza down in an armchair, which was the only way to hold his attention, and told him: 'Look, anything supportive of the coach would be helpful.' Gazza loved Terry and often made complimentary remarks about him. It wasn't enough. The FA effectively asked Terry to audition for his own job at the Euros.

'The FA have gone wobbly on me,' he sighed.

'I agree,' I replied. 'It's crazy, but what are you going to do?'

'I want to stay in England, if only for Dad's sake. I want to find a club to have a real go at the League. If I can't find the right club in England, I might go back to Spain.'

'You might just get the last laugh. I don't want you to leave anyway.' All the off-field issues had taken their toll. Sugar, the DTI, and other court cases were a burden. Terry would have been less than human if they hadn't distracted him. His strength during Euro '96 was remarkable.

Without question, the high point was England's final group match against Holland on 18 June. That morning the staff had to contemplate that if we lost, the tournament was over for England. The reality was gloriously different. Gazza, Teddy, Alan and the rest produced a thumping 4–1 win over the stunned Dutch. England's dressing room was fantastic, all the players singing 'football's coming home' and throwing each other into the bath. I listened to the fans revelling in England's new anthem and envied Skinner and Baddiel. They'd written a song that had caught the imagination of the nation, of everyone from fans to footballers. 'Football's coming home' added immeasurably to the atmosphere at Wembley. I thought back to 1966, and, believe me, Wembley did not shake with as much emotion and noise as it did at Euro '96.

At the final whistle, I stared in amazement at the scoreboard.

Netherlands 1 England 4. Entering the Banqueting Hall, I found Susan in tears, overcome by the sheer brilliance of the performance and the day. I held back my own tears. I wanted to kiss a lot of people. Results like that make sane men lose all restraint. Amidst all the jubilation, one person stayed very composed. Terry was very low-key. Maybe he was stunned by the achievement. Maybe his mind was racing ahead to the knock-out stage. Maybe he was also thinking that he would soon be walking away from all this.

The rest of the country went potty. A fax from the Prime Minister, John Major, arrived within twenty minutes of the final whistle. 'Congratulations' it read. Victory adorned the front pages of the morning papers. 'The greatest England performance in 30 years' was Fleet Street's consensus. Was it really just two weeks ago that the team were villains, boozers and a national disgrace? The papers now hailed them as heroes. We still had to be on our guard. Only on Planet Gazza could the nation's most-loved footballer manage to have a ruck with a *Mirror* photographer while out fishing. No one dared ask Gazza whether he had caught any snappers that day. The newspapers were all over England. Editors like the *Sun*'s Stuart Higgins kept calling, requesting stunts of varying degrees of silliness, anything to associate their paper with England's success. One photo-shoot request involved some players and a lion. 'Too dangerous,' I told Stuart. 'Too damned silly.'

'Three Lions' obsessed press and public alike, although I'd made one disturbing discovery when inspecting England's famous crest.

'These lions are bloody asleep,' I remarked to Terry.

'What?!'

'Look, the lions are asleep. Their eyes are shut.' I could just imagine the headlines if anybody else noticed. 'Dozy England' would have been one of the politer ones. Getting on the phone to the FA designers, I said: 'We must wake up the three lions. Can you re-do the graphic?' The creative wizards weaved their magic and the three lions now boast wider eyes than before. Pleased with my handiwork, I was shocked to receive a letter from an England fan who claimed: 'Dear Mr Davies, people keep singing about the Three Lions, but they are not lions, they are leopards.' This was one debate I chose not to get involved in.

England's lions were about to acquire some cunning. On the Friday before the quarter-final, with most players now prepared to talk to the media, Terry was happy to confuse the Spanish.

'The *Sun* and *Daily Star* have asked for Sol Campbell to talk to the dailies,' I told Terry. 'Shall I put him up?'

'Yes,' agreed Terry instantly and I knew why. Sol had almost as much chance of starting against Spain as I had. Chatting to reporters afterwards, I was delighted when one remarked: 'Terry must have some clever new tactics involving Sol.' Returning to Burnham, I heard from Noel, who was not relishing the flak as one of the men who'd forced out Terry Venables, the country's new darling. 'Don't you think I was right?' Noel said. I had known Noel for almost twenty years, since my BBC Manchester days. I thought he was wrong, and said so.

'Noel, unless something is proven against Terry, that rules him out as a coach, some way should have been found to keep him. It's the country's loss.' Noel walked away. Sadly for Noel, the criticism intensified the next day, 22 June, when we beat Spain on penalties. Of the thousands of games I've attended in my life, none exhausted me more than this. For the shoot-out, I perched next to Phil Neville. David Seaman was such a good shot-stopper, most people probably felt we had a chance. The atmosphere was unbelievable. As each Englishman walked forward, the support screamed by every England fan grew more vociferous. I sensed Lady Luck had turned. Spain had a goal disallowed that on another day might have stood.

When Stuart Pearce scored his penalty, Wembley went utterly mental. Everyone knew what a cathartic moment it was for Stuart, who'd missed against West Germany at Italia '90. All that emotion built up over six years was released with one guttural scream from Stuart that could have emanated from his beloved Sex Pistols. The sound almost knocked me over and I was fifty yards away. But that was it for Stuart. Turin was out of his system. Afterwards at Burnham, he was calm, certainly calmer than everyone else. Victory was like a pump of adrenalin attached to every player's vein. All of the team believed that if Stuart's demons had been so exorcised, there was every reason to dream about a Euro '96 winner's medal. Stuart fascinated me. His great mate was the studious, unfailingly polite Gareth Southgate. That opened up my eyes to the real Stuart Pearce. To mix with Gareth, Stuart could not have been simply the one-dimensional, tough-tackling full-back nicknamed 'Psycho'. They loved the same music and went off to see the Pistols during Euro '96. Stuart had been really hard to get to know; he rarely opened up, a trait of many of Cloughie's players, but when he did, I realised what a strong character he was. Stuart needed to be strong to take that penalty. I had shut my eyes. Fortunately, he didn't.

Life became even more manic. The days building up to the Germany semi passed in a sleepless blur. Burnham Beeches lacked air-conditioning, June was ludicrously hot so any chance of a decent kip melted in the night. Strange creatures were also appearing during the night. At the bottom of the hotel garden, BBC and ITV had erected a studio and Terry was talking live to the BBC late on the Sunday the day after the victory over Spain. Suddenly, these figures in white sheets came running past, waving their arms, pretending to be ghosts. Watching, I knew from their running style who the phantoms of the Burnham opera were. It had to be Gazza and Robbie. Inside the hotel, everybody was watching and loved the moment. Those studios were a magnet. Gary and Phil Neville loved nosing around the BBC vans.

The Monday morning after victory over Spain, the papers really let rip with England mania. Sadly, the *Mirror* went too far, even by their own admission later. Referring to our imminent meeting with the Germans, the headline 'Achtung Surrender' demanded what it got: disdain from us and condemnation from just about everyone else. For those of us with friends within the German camp, it provoked embarrassment as well. Thankfully, people like Horst Schmidt and Wolfgang Niersbach, German FA executives and real football men, did their best to laugh it off, whatever they really felt. Crucially, the fans behaved. The tournament was about football, nothing else.

When England are on a roll, the power is incredible. At Euro '96, it seemed everybody wanted to be a part of it. On the day of the semi, I received a call from Whitehall.

'The Home Secretary Michael Howard is a big football fan and wants to go into the England dressing-room after the game,' came the request.

'No,' I replied. 'That's rather like Terry Venables asking to meet the Chancellor after his Budget speech. It's not going to happen.'

Every detail of the match assumed immense importance, particularly with a couple of significant tosses. Terry, myself and the TV producers gathered in Burnham's garden to decide which host broadcaster would interview Terry first after the final whistle. The flash interview would then be shared by both ITV and BBC. The ITV producer tossed the coin and his BBC opposite number called.

'Heads.' Heads it was. The BBC would conduct the flash interview first. Just as we concluded this time-honoured ritual, ITV's reporter Gary Newbon came bouncing down the garden.

'This can't have happened,' Gary said. 'Who tossed the coin?'

His producer spoke up. 'I did.'

'But you can't,' retorted Gary. 'I'm the ITV tosser.' Venables and I fell about laughing. On returning to the hotel, I had a quick word with our kit-man. Later on, Terry presented Gary Newbon with a shirt emblazoned with the words 'I'm the ITV Tosser'.

Another toss carried even greater weight. On the Monday, I went up to London to the Royal Garden Hotel for the tossing of the coin between Sir Bert Millichip and the president of the German FA, Egidius Braun, to decide who wore which colour. Sir Bert called wrong. We wore grey. Nightmare. Grey had somehow become England's second-choice colour. Not surprisingly, nobody owned up to having championed it, though the blame had to lie somewhere between the manager, the FA commercial boys and girls and Umbro.

All my life, I have preferred England in red. People say that the 4–1 over Holland was in white, the 5–1 over Germany in Munich was white, but red suits England best. We won the World Cup in red.

Next day, I went on Radio One to debate the issue with Chris Evans, the DJ I'd known from my BBC Manchester days.

'You can't let England play in grey,' pronounced Chris, voicing the horror of the nation. What could I say? It was nobody's fault and everybody's. Collective responsibility again perhaps!

If the kit was criticised, Venables's stock had never been higher. Jimmy Armfield, the FA's special adviser on England matters, arrived at Burnham with an idea. Jimmy loved floating ideas. I always listened. 'Why not keep Terry on as technical director,' Jimmy suggested.

'Jimmy, it's a non-starter and it's too late. Graham Kelly would not consider it. Hoddle [Venables's successor] would hate it. Terry wouldn't take it.' I paused. 'As for Noel White . . .'

A date with destiny and the Germans now awaited Terry and England. The fans believed. Burnham was besieged. Steering out of the hotel to go fishing, David Seaman drove over the foot of one young fan. 'Quick, get him into the hotel,' I said. We brought the poor little boy in and showered him with gifts. He soon cheered up. Leaving Burnham on the coach for Wembley, the scenes were memorable. Fans hung out of trees, leaned precariously over the parapets of bridges, anything for a glimpse of the nation's heroes as they made their way to their greatest test. I sat with Phil Neville, whose company I always enjoyed. The familiar journey down the M40, then left to Wembley, passed in a flash. In the tunnel, I took my ritual trip towards Terry. 'Good luck,' I said. He seemed less tense than before the Spain quarter-final. The weight of expectation sat less heavily on his shoulders. Terry was ready. So was Wembley. Everyone sang. Everyone waved flags. Even amongst the FA dignitaries in the Banqueting Hall, a buzz could be detected. I found Susan and we looked at all the famous people flocking into the room. Mick Jagger! Moments after taking up our seats, Shearer scored.

'We can make this,' I said to Susan. Stefan Kuntz equalised and the drama really kicked in. Extra time. So close. Darren Anderton hit the bar. Gazza missed by inches. Penalties. I dashed down to pitch-side and sought out my lucky charm, Phil Neville. Looking back feels like reopening an old wound. England's first five penalties all went in. Then Gareth stepped forward.

'What is Gareth doing taking the sixth penalty?' I asked Phil. Brave old Gareth. He volunteered. Terry had been adamant about who he wanted to take these kicks. 'I want those who are up for it,' Terry told the players. And Gareth was. Paul Ince and others were less keen. I understood. After Gareth's miss signalled the end, England's dressing room was deathly quiet. Nothing could be said, no consoling words could heal the hurt. This was the worst part of my job, rallying a distraught coach and his players to talk to the media when their dream had just died. So had mine. My heart went out to Terry, Gareth, Gazza and all those shattered individuals sitting in front of me. Many I now regarded as friends, not colleagues. We'd shared an amazing adventure that ended so suddenly, so cruelly. My own few tears didn't matter. Gazza was gone, lost in gloom, replaying that moment of his near-miss over and over again. When they reflect on the day, England's players should remember it with pride.

A devastated Gareth was in the corner, allies like Stuart rallying round. One of my own trusted assistants, Joanne Budd, always great in a crisis, was a huge Crystal Palace fan and knew Gareth well.

'I let my country down,' Gareth said.

'You haven't, Gareth,' Joanne, Stuart and Terry all told him. 'You performed fantastically well all tournament. It could happen to anybody. A keeper goes the right way and "bingo". Don't blame yourself.' Gareth was beyond comforting. If only that was to have been the last time I was to experience bloody penalties. The sad retreat from Wembley began. The bus interior was dark, signalling the lights had gone out on our tournament. As the coach moved as slowly as a hearse away from Wembley, Stuart picked up the microphone. 'That was my last England game,' he announced.

'Thank you for everything you have done. Thank you for giving me a fantastic experience.' Everyone burst into applause. The reality sank in more, this really was the end for some.

I then took the microphone. As senior FA person present I had to say something but I doubt my words registered. 'It has been a privilege being with you these past few weeks. You so nearly did it. Take pride in what you have done. It was an unforgettable experience.' For a moment, I thought of mentioning there was always the 1998 World Cup. I wanted to give a broken-hearted squad hope and focus. Then I looked at Terry, a lump formed in my throat and I couldn't talk of the future. Terry was going. On reaching Burnham, the security had disappeared. Fans were up the drive, in the garden, everywhere. Eventually, they left but few of us felt like going to bed. Some of the guys, like Tony Adams, stayed up all night. Tony did drown his sorrows after the Germany game, but he might like to know he didn't drink any more than anyone else. The mood was maudlin. I felt so depressed, particularly when I heard there had been some disturbances in Trafalgar Square. It was what I'd feared after that 'Achtung Surrender' headline. Thankfully, it was contained. I joined Terry for a drink in his inner sanctum with his closest lieutenants, Ted, Bryan and Don. They knew it was the end of an era. As he left the bar, I looked at Terry, and my admiration grew again. Terry was not shell-shocked by defeat. His innate resilience remained.

Waking up in the morning, Burnham looked a mess. No damage could be detected but cups and glasses were strewn everywhere. Walking down the corridor, bumping into players emerging from rooms, bags packed, saying their goodbyes, deepened my depression. I sought out Terry, because he still had one onerous obligation to discharge.

'I don't want to do the press conference,' said Venables.

'You have to.'

'What have I new to say?'

As we parked at Bisham, Terry repeated: 'David, I just don't want to do it.'

'Come on. The last time.'

And of course, Terry was magnificent, warm and humorous. At the end, as he stood up to leave, the correspondents all applauded him. His biggest critics, like Harry Harris of the *Mirror*, chose to stay away, rightly. I still had some debriefing for the media, so Terry drove himself back to Burnham. I walked him towards the car. A lot of tears were shed in the car-park at Bisham. 'Thanks for the journey,' I said. 'We'll always be friends.'

'Always,' said Terry.

6

Glenn

'You'll like Glenn,' Jimmy Armfield told me after scouting the various candidates to succeed Terry Venables. 'But he is stubborn.'

'I don't mind him being stubborn,' I replied. 'I just think he's too young for the job. He's thirty-eight. Being England coach should be the climax of a career. It's a job for an experienced man. It's going to be difficult for Glenn. He has only ten, twelve games a year. He has to deal with gaps between games that could be as long as three months. He has young children. If the team get tonked in one of the qualifiers for the World Cup, his kids will get a hard time in the playground.'

Jimmy was back on his original point. 'Remember that, David,' Jimmy repeated. 'He's stubborn. Mark my words.'

I did. A good reader of men, Jimmy always made sense. Stubborn. The word stuck with me all the time I worked with Hoddle. And Jimmy was right. Hoddle was not my first choice, and not simply because he was relatively inexperienced in management terms, certainly compared to Terry.

'Who would you like as England manager?' Armfield and Graham Kelly both asked me.

'Alex Ferguson,' came my instant reply. 'He's the best. It's a job for an older person. I've talked to Sir Roland Smith at United and he certainly didn't say: "Lay off our manager." That's encouraging.

Roland seems to think that because Alex has been at United for ten years, and done very well, that that could be the shelf life of a club manager. It strikes me Alex is not out of the question. But I do struggle to see Fergie leading England out at Hampden.' Jimmy went off to see Ferguson. 'He doesn't want the job,' Jimmy reported back. Pity. If Ferguson had wanted to become manager of England after Euro '96, the job was his. Absolutely. Ferguson was tickled by England's interest. He would have done a brilliant job; he had international experience, having managed Scotland at the 1986 World Cup. There certainly would have been no player withdrawals from United. Disappointed by Ferguson, Jimmy continued to tour the country for the FA. Close to Kelly, Jimmy's role still slightly worried me. Was this tapping up? Were we breaking our own rules? Everything happened in the open and no one complained. Jimmy is so popular in football, every manager invited the former England captain into their office. It was an amazing tribute to Jimmy's reputation that no one felt the FA were tapping up managers. Of course the moment he sounded anyone out, news spread quickly. A few contenders emerged for the job. 'They should go for Robbo,' Venables told me. Bryan Robson assisted Terry at Euro '96 and was popular with the players. 'The continuity will be good for the team.'

One morning, Terry and I headed to Glasgow to watch Gazza in an Old Firm match. At Heathrow, we bought all the papers, and were greeted with the front-page splash in the *Sunday Express* that Frank Clark would be the next manager of England. Astonishing. Reporters confronted me in the terminal.

'Is it true? Has Frank Clark got the job?'

'Off the record: bollocks and garbage,' I replied. 'On the record: bollocks and garbage.' One paper quoted me, provoking a complaint in the next FA Council meeting. 'Should our spokesman be using language of this nature?' asked one Councillor. Such language passed my lips more than once and always to kill a story stone dead.

Gerry Francis, the Spurs manager, was also in the frame. Jimmy definitely saw him. Someone claiming to be close to Kenny Dalglish called me, saying he might be interested. Kenny had just stood down as Blackburn Rovers manager. But Jimmy and the FA wanted Hoddle. Clean-cut with a decent reputation from Chelsea, Hoddle had been such a magnificent midfielder that dressing-room respect was surely guaranteed. Because of his youth, Hoddle still looked like the wonderful player he had been. The FA experienced a brief fracas with Chelsea's chairman, Ken Bates. Understandably, Ken didn't want to lose a good manager but we were confident of Glenn's arrival. He desperately wanted to become England manager. Ultimately, Glenn may reflect the job came too early but there was no way he was going to turn down the chance to lead England.

Glenn was formally announced as Terry's successor on 2 May 1996. His coronation was in the Royal Lancaster at four p.m., so we met around the corner at White's Hotel beforehand. Getting Terry and Glenn to put on a show of unity was vital. Wary about Glenn, Terry was far from keen on this joint news conference. Terry didn't want to leave, so was naturally resentful over the succession.

'Glenn will be a distraction at Euro '96,' Terry said to me before he arrived at White's. 'I don't want him around the camp.'

'I understand, Terry. But let's have this announcement now, weeks before Euro '96. Let's get all the potential issues out of the way. Look, I want you to come to this news conference. What are we here for? To win Euro '96. What we don't want is two months of Venables v. Hoddle. The best way to make sure that doesn't happen is to have this public show of support for each other.' Inevitably, Terry put on a bravura performance for the cameras.

Glenn wanted to observe his future players. He appeared once at training at Bisham Abbey during Euro '96, sensibly staying well in the background, sitting on a tree. Itching to work with the players, Glenn was frustrated. If life was weird at Bisham, the whole managerial transition back at Lancaster Gate was completely surreal. 'When does Venables move out of his office and

Hoddle move in?' I was constantly asked. Glenn actually brought some stuff into the England manager's office at Lancaster Gate during Euro '96. Terry didn't think the transition was very well handled. We were treading on eggshells.

'I'm driving to Ascot to see Glenn Hoddle,' I told Susan the day before the Germany semi-final. 'Terry's time is ending. It's desperately sad. I'll see what Glenn thinks. He might not want me as part of England's future. It may be time to leave, anyway. I'm so tied to Terry, I'm not sure I want to work for another England manager.' Meeting Glenn in his favourite hotel, the Royal Berkshire, I came straight to the point. 'You might be better off appointing someone new, Glenn, someone not associated with Terry. I understand if you want a fresh start.'

Glenn also got straight to the point. 'I want you involved,' he said. 'And I want to be even-handed with the media.' I knew how difficult that was in practice but I warmed to Glenn immediately. Hitherto, my experience of Hoddle had been admiring his sublime football talent. As a Manchester United supporter, I learned to appreciate good footballers and Hoddle was a class act.

'You've been great for Terry, and you can be great for me,' said Hoddle. His enthusiasm affected me. I could work for this guy.

'What plans do you have for England?' I asked.

'Paul Ince might be captain,' Glenn replied. 'I really rate him.'

Glenn was busy. When England bowed out of Euro '96, Terry was followed out of the door by Ted Buxton, Dave Butler, Don Howe and Mike Kelly, the goalkeeping coach. Glenn brought in a lot of people. Steve Slattery, Glenn Roeder, Ray Clemence, Gary Lewin, Terry Byrne and Peter Taylor. His no. 2 was John Gorman, the organiser on the training ground, and Glenn's trusted sounding board. John is a lovely man, as straightforward as Glenn was complicated. Any idea that all the off-field issues would disappear the moment Terry departed was laughable. Glenn's brother Carl, now tragically dead, attracted some cruel publicity about his private life, days after Glenn took over.

Initially, Glenn charmed everyone. He was fresh, enthusiastic, keen to build on the success of Euro '96. Everyone took to him. Well, not everyone. Along with Graham Kelly, Glenn and I attended a reception at Downing Street shortly after Glenn's appointment. No. 10 had this wonderful Irish lady who took your coat. Glenn was slightly behind Graham and me as we handed our coats over. 'I don't know why you're all wasting your time with all these managers,' said this Irish lady. 'The man who should be manager of England is Jack Charlton.' We laughed. Hoddle didn't hear. He wouldn't have worried anyway. He had a stubborn streak. Jimmy told me.

Most people were upbeat about Hoddle and I caught the mood. When he named his first squad to face Moldova on 1 September, Matt Le Tissier and David Beckham were in. Everyone approved. What wonderful ball-players! Glenn was trying to build an England team in his own image. Alex Ferguson upset him very quickly though, pulling Phil Neville out two hours before the squad for Moldova was announced. 'Welcome to England, Glenn!' I said to Hoddle, who was angry with Ferguson. 'You'll get used to these withdrawals. It was worse in the past. Bobby and Graham never knew who was going to turn up.' Glenn was receiving a crash course in England politics.

Reaching Moldova for this France '98 qualifier, I saw the first evidence of Glenn's renowned interest in matters religious. Neil Harman, the very likeable football correspondent of the *Daily Mail*, had found this orphanage in Chisinau. 'I would really appreciate Glenn and the players raising money to improve its conditions,' Neil told me. That's precisely what happened. Glenn was particularly moved by a television film he saw about conditions inside the orphanage. Hoddle appreciated football could be a power for good. He always helped out with visits to orphanages or meetings with Red Cross people. His Christian streak showed in his desire to help others. Hoddle's spirituality intrigued the media, and I became a bit sensitive. One day, Umbro held an England kit launch at Wembley Conference Centre and I turned up in advance of Glenn. As I alighted from the taxi, I noticed a double-decker bus parked outside the entrance with 'God Save You' emblazoned across it.

'The press will have a field day if they see that,' I shouted to Steve Double, the new press officer.

'It's quite funny,' he laughed. It was, but . . .

'Find the bloody driver and get that ruddy bus shifted.'

As we were learning about Glenn, he was discovering the extraordinary demands of the so-called 'Impossible Job'. In Moldova, Glenn's players watched the under-21 game the day before theirs. When the heavens opened, the seniors all climbed into the press box. Gazza managed to be photographed pulling down Ince's shorts. The next day, the tabloids were crammed with pictures of Incey's bottom. He was livid. So was Hoddle, who gave Gazza a bollocking. 'I'm not going to make a big fuss about it,' Hoddle told me. If it had been Terry, I would have made a joke about Incey needing to turn the other cheek but I didn't know Glenn well enough. Everyone was very circumspect. Messing about was not tolerated by Hoddle.

'Training is so bloody serious,' one of the players confided to me. 'It's not much fun.' The change of tone between Venables and Hoddle could hardly have been greater. Terry liked a good laugh but all the jolly japes were left at the training-ground gate. Terry really controlled training. So did Glenn but less sympathetically in the players' eyes. 'It's like he's trying to distance himself from us,' one player told me. 'He played against some of us.'

Glenn and Tony Adams were not bosom buddies. At one news conference, they both sat at the same table with Glenn leaning forward and Tony leaning back. My mind kept going back to Jimmy Armfield's advice. Glenn was stubborn. Hoddle's regime was stricter than Terry's. The players generally stayed together without a break when there were double-headers – two matches in ten days. Trips home became rarer, although sometimes wives, girlfriends and families were invited to stay overnight at Burnham Beeches.

'The contrast with Terry is pretty marked,' I told my wife

Susan. 'But perhaps that's good. I do worry how he'll react to results going against him, if they do. I'm not sure he's aware how intense the players are finding him.'

Sometimes his choice of language got him into problems. Andy Cole 'needed a few chances' before he'd score a goal. Michael Owen 'wasn't a natural goalscorer'. The comments were maybe true, but neither was well received.

'But I'm impressed by Glenn's serenity,' I told Susan after returning from a 2–0 win in Georgia. 'I'm not sure he fully realises the pressure. He's just having his honeymoon period. It could turn and he will feel it. I think Glenn's quite sensitive. But then aren't all England managers?!' It was true. No England manager I've met was thick-skinned like Shankly or Fergie.

In qualifying for France '98, our key game was Italy at home on 12 February 1997. Hoddle went to great lengths to keep his team plans quiet.

'It'll leak,' I warned him.

'It had better not,' Glenn replied. 'If the press want to make my job more difficult, they'll tell the Italians our team.' As Glenn was realising, a familiar ritual occurred on the eve of games, a frustrating one for England managers. Within an hour of the manager naming the team at the hotel, players told agents, who informed journalists. News spread fast. The worst ones for leaking the team were squad members not in the starting XI. Their annoyance spilled over. They whinged to their agents, and it all kicked off. On the morning of the Italy game, I headed off to a Downing Street reception. In the cab, the radio carried an interview with Matt Le Tissier's brother, chuffed to bits over Matt's selection to face Italy. 'So much for the secret plan,' I muttered to myself. 'Le Tissier's brother has told the world.'

Back at Bisham, Hoddle was incandescent at the blowing of his plans. 'I can't believe he's just given the Italians our team,' said Glenn, who'd been hoping to surprise the Italians by using Matt. Glenn was not angry with Matt, just his brother. Matt was so laid-back, I'm sure he just laughed. Matt was fun, articulate, well rounded, like that other Channel Islander, Graeme Le Saux. Bright guys, Matt and Graeme kept football in perspective. Glenn's mood was not improved by the 0–1 defeat to Italy. In a subdued dressing room afterwards, Glenn had a word about the team leaking, but he would have preferred to let the dust settle and talk to the players the next morning. No chance. Clubs demanded their stars back straight after the final whistle. A fleet of smart cars pulled up outside Wembley and transported them home.

'I can't believe how well you treat your players,' a foreign player once said to me.

'Well, if you've played for your country the least your country can do is get you a car home.' England's players were well looked after. The staff, the team behind the team, tried to address every detail. FA Councillors constantly complained about cost and there being 'too many staff with England'. Under Glenn, numbers grew significantly. More medics, physios, masseurs and media staff. 'They're needed,' I argued with the Councillors. 'The game has changed. If we are going to qualify for France '98, and do well there, we have to give the players the best support.' Sir Clive Woodward did the same with England's rugby team, encountered similar scepticism, ignored it, and won the World Cup in 2003.

The morning after the Italy defeat, Glenn was angered to read newspapers comparing him to Graham Taylor, claiming he tinkered with his teams. 'I don't want the press on the team plane anymore,' Glenn said as we built up for the return match with Italy on 11 October 1997. 'And David, I want you to fax all the sports editors and ask them not to print our team line-up.' I did well to hide my scepticism. Glenn was in full flow. 'And I want a base in Rome which is isolated. I want distance between the players and everybody else.'

As we flew out of Luton, Hoddle was engrossed in his horoscope in the papers. 'Very accurate,' he told me before outlining his pre-match tactics. 'David, I want to create as much confusing speculation about the team as possible.' Operation Southgate and Beckham was launched, with much disinformation given about their supposed injuries. Glenn was determined to leave nothing to chance. England stayed in a training centre outside Rome with excellent facilities. The media hotel near by was less impressive. I forgot to check whether the locals held a very jolly fruit and veg market there at the crack of dawn every Thursday. Which they did. It's not something I considered asking the hotel owner. 'By the way, will our media be woken by the sound of carrots being offloaded from the back of a lorry?'

'And another thing,' Hoddle requested. 'No tabloids for the team. You can have them, but not the players. Just *The Times* and *Telegraph*.' That meant one thing. Knocks on my door at all hours with players hungry for the tabloids. David Beckham and Gary Neville insisted on raiding my room to read the red-tops. As the game loomed, Glenn was remarkably relaxed, snoozing on the coach to the Olympic Stadium. How he slept I don't know. The noise was unbelievable, sirens blaring and Italians screaming at us. Our outriders were so fierce they kept whacking all the cars with their truncheons to get out of the way. Italian fans were gesticulating at us. In terms of abuse, the Italian supporters outside the Olympic Stadium were up there with the Scots welcoming England to Hampden, or the Welsh greeting the England bus at Cardiff's Millennium Stadium. One Italian seemed nervous. 'Look,' I said to Hoddle after we'd run the gauntlet and reached the tunnel. 'There's Cesare Maldini.' Italy's coach, resplendent in a bright red polo shirt, stood on his own, drawing deeply on a fag. 'He looks apprehensive,' I added. Maldini's mood was nothing compared to mine as England clung on. Needing just a point, Hoddle's cautious tactics were working well. When Paul Ince's head was split open, we had the nightmare of our physio Gary Lewin trying to get into a locked dressing room. Gary sprinted back the 100 yards to the bench, shouting: 'Where's the key?' We located the groundsman, who handed it over. (Ever since then, England have had a pre-match routine to establish the dressing room can be swiftly accessed.) Fortunately, Gary was fit and he returned to Incey quickly, got into the dressing room, stitched him up and got him back playing again.

Just as well. Incey delivered the England performance of his life. With Incey back on, I gave up sitting on the bench, and roamed the running track, willing the referee to call time on a 0–0 draw that would take us to France '98. 'Just blow the bloody whistle,' I kept shouting, earning my first warning from a Uefa official. I ignored him. My emotions were flowing too strongly. Rome was in the days before electronic boards revealed the amount of minutes added on. 'How much bloody time?' I raged at the official. It seemed like seven minutes. Then Ian Wright hit the post.

Wrighty scoring would have been special. He was a player I'd grown to know well, primarily through his regular disciplinary commission appearances. One day, he was involved in a ruck at Leicester City and I attended his disciplinary case at the Moat House at Elstree. Ian arrived with a lawyer, David Dein and Gary Lewin, who also worked for Arsenal. Gary in a suit was a new sight to me. 'It's my FA disciplinary commission suit,' Gary would laugh. He needed it with Wrighty on Arsenal's books. Barry Bright, Mr Disciplinary Commission from Kent FA, was in the chair as we all gathered around this very long table. The hearing meandered along. As the referee gave evidence, Ian began scribbling something. Walking around the table, he slapped down this folded piece of paper in front of me. Everyone looked at me, thinking what the hell's that about, what's in the message? Wrighty sat there with a straight face. For many minutes, I ignored that piece of paper. Eventually, curiosity overwhelmed me. Inside was Wrighty's succinct verdict on the referee's evidence.

'THIS IS COMPLETE BOLLOCKS'.

I giggled. 'Any chance, David, we could share in the joke?' enquired Barry Bright. I glanced at Ian, who was muttering: 'Oh, for fuck's sake.'

'No joke, just a private note, Mr Chairman,' I replied. Ian always cheered me up. He loved representing England, really appreciating the honour. I'd just wished he had scored in Rome, ending the tension. When he struck that post, Italy sped down the other end. My language deteriorated further. I swore at everyone, at the referee, at the entire Italian nation and particularly at Christian Vieri as his head made contact with the ball. Vieri must score. World Cup dream over. Nightmare. Somehow, Vieri's header went wide of David Seaman's goal. David didn't move. 'Yeah, yeah,' David told me afterwards. 'I knew it was going wide.'

'You must be psychic,' I told David. Everybody else in the Olympic Stadium believed that header was destined for the net. Rome was a triumph for Hoddle. He had an inner confidence that was not insubstantial, and he was right on so many things. Rome was tactically inspired, one of the great England post-war displays. How many times had such games been lost?

Sadly, Glenn's tactical victory was followed by a great personal defeat. Shortly afterwards, I was back in Worcestershire, relaxing at the pub with jubilant friends, when Glenn called. 'I'm splitting with Anne,' Glenn said. 'We've fallen out of love over the last ten months. I can't live a lie or I'll probably have an affair in the next six months, so I'm moving out. Can you make an announcement, asking for some privacy?'

'Of course,' I replied. Privacy? Fat chance. The press will go to town on this. 'ENGLAND HERO'S HEARTACHE'. I could imagine the headlines.

'Why the hell do I have to do this?' I asked Susan in frustration. 'It's so personal. Hardly anybody will believe there isn't another woman but Glenn is adamant there isn't.' I believed him. With a heavy heart, I got to work. I called Kelly and new chairman Keith Wiseman to warn them of incoming missiles. I phoned Anne, one of the most painful calls I have ever had to make. She was angry and shocked. Her husband had gone to Italy and returned wanting a divorce. Clearly, when Glenn was sitting in his room in Rome, he resolved to take action over his marriage. Part of me admired the way he focused on being decisive over England's date with destiny in the Olympic Stadium and also his private life. At 8.30 p.m., I finally issued a statement to the Press Association, calling for the media to leave the Hoddles alone. Within seconds, my mobile glowed with calls and messages. Within half an hour,

Hoddle's house was besieged by journalists. So much for the privacy tack. England are always massive news. Six months later, Glenn was pictured on holiday with his new girlfriend, Vanessa. The intrusion angered him.

Other issues soon began to concern Glenn in the build-up to France '98. England almost lost Alan Shearer for the tournament, following the furore over an incident with Leicester City's Neil Lennon. Shearer was accused of stamping on Lennon and calls proliferated for England's captain to be charged. I talked to Alan's agent, Tony Stephens, a good man whom I trusted implicitly.

'Alan feels so strongly about the way he's being treated that he's thinking about pulling out of the World Cup,' said Tony. 'Alan feels he is being victimised because he is England captain.' Feelings ran high. Alan told Glenn he was considering withdrawing. 'What are the FA up to?' Glenn asked me, exasperated. 'Do they not want us to win the World Cup? How can they do this to England's captain?' Here was an absolute classic case of conflict of FA interest. On the one hand, the FA were the governing body, responsible for discipline. On the other, they ran the England team. Once, I had to announce the results of a disciplinary decision against Sol Campbell, which left him hugely aggrieved, and twenty-four hours later I had to ask Sol to talk to the press in the build-up to an England match. It was madness. The Shearer case triggered particular chaos. After the usual problem of locating Graham Kelly, there was a very unsatisfactory meeting between myself, Graham and Glenn.

'The incident has to be looked at,' said Graham. 'There is going to be a charge but, David, can you sort out the consequences?'

'Thanks.'

With the World Cup looming, the FA charged Alan.

'Other countries would sweep it under the carpet,' people kept saying to me. 'Why don't you?' We couldn't. The FA had to act. They had to treat Alan like any other player. I was caught in the middle. Alan was a friend. He was a bloody good player, tough but fair. Off the pitch, Alan had a great sense of humour. I always found it bizarre, his reputation as Mr Bland. Alan resented that image, understandably. Nowadays, I watch him on *Match of the Day* and know he is winding up Alan Hansen and Mark Lawrenson. We would play pranks on Shearer. Before one tournament, Alan was secretly consuming the odd ham sandwich between meals. We were at Burnham Beeches, so I had a quiet word with room service. Every half-hour throughout the day, a ham sandwich was delivered to Alan's room. I never knew where they all went. Alan was a wonderful servant to England, which is why the Lennon controversy hurt so much. The word 'charge' desperately offended Alan. He felt his integrity was being questioned. Glenn released a statement in support of Shearer. Mercifully, I managed to persuade him to omit his criticism of the FA. 'The FA are undermining my player going into the World Cup,' Glenn told me. But he didn't say that so emotively in his statement. Kelly was still upset. 'It sends out a contradictory message to the FA's position on Shearer,' said Graham.

For one horrible period, I feared England might lose Shearer and Hoddle – in protest – just weeks before the World Cup. Still, the chaos continued. When Glenn announced his squad for the World Cup, one reporter asked: 'When is the Shearer case being heard?' I stepped in. I couldn't have the England coach lying. The secret hearing was already under way at Hillsborough. 'It will be held very soon,' I said disingenuously. Within hours, the disciplinary commission announced: 'Case not proved.' Shearer was in the clear. Anticipating a backlash from the papers, I decided to prepare myself for the first editions with a fish and Sancerre dinner with Nic Coward, the FA lawyer, around the corner from Lancaster Gate. So much for a relaxing evening. I ended up in St Mary's Hospital A&E department with a bone stuck in my throat. Perhaps I deserved it. I sat there alongside a variety of druggies for three hours before I was finally seen to. At three a.m., I was discharged and walked home, collecting the first editions, which were kinder than I expected.

People still speculated on whether pressure was placed on the commission to go soft on the England captain. False. FA commissions are scrupulously honest. When David Dein was on the FA board, people always claimed the FA might be lenient on Arsene Wenger or harder on Alex Ferguson. That never happened. In my experience, they were always fair, truly independent but not always right. Critics of the system, usually among clubs, said: 'Amateurs should not be hearing these cases.' OK, let's get the professionals in but do United want representatives of Arsenal, Liverpool or Chelsea hearing their case? No. The critics then say: 'OK, let's get in fair-minded, respected ex-pros like Gary Mabbutt and Trevor Brooking.' Now, I'm friends with Gary. I'm friends with Trevor, whom I've always known as 'the elegant Brooking' as he was so often described by commentators during his graceful playing days. But disciplinary hearings occur all the time. The list of people of their background, calibre and character is not lengthy.

With the Shearer furore thankfully over, Hoddle turned his meticulous eye for detail to preparations for France '98. Glenn was concerned about club cliques forming with England. Manchester United and Liverpool players found it difficult to knock three bells out of each other on a Sunday afternoon at Anfield and then be all lovey-dovey on Sunday night at Burnham Beeches. 'I want them mixing more,' Glenn said. So he re-arranged the table plans. Round tables were out. Long tables were in.

Glenn also tackled the newspapers. We organised a golf day at Stoke Poges, where Glenn pleaded with the sports editors to go easy on the players. 'Look,' Glenn said, 'if you're going to run any stories about players' private lives, if you've been storing them up, run them before we get anywhere near France.' Glenn's compassion for his players was very evident. When David Seaman's private life was then splashed across the *Sunday People* during the early days of the World Cup, he was upset for David as well as angry for the damage it might inflict on England. 'I'm livid,' Glenn said. 'We asked them not to.' Seaman was always fairly phlegmatic. He is just what you want a keeper to be: calm in a crisis. Still, the episode sent him into his shell for a while.

On my way home from Stoke Poges, the *Mirror* editor Piers Morgan called. 'We want you to speak to Glenn,' said Piers. 'Glenn's daughter Zoë has written a letter to us, basically saying "Lay off my dad". We don't want to publish it but we want Glenn to know it's happened.' I phoned Glenn, who was gobsmacked. We all felt sympathy for Zoë. Her letter showed their close relationship. The *Mirror* were honourable and supported Glenn. 'We'll back Glenn through thick and thin,' Piers promised. And they did.

Less smooth were relations between Glenn and Pat Smith, the deputy chief executive, over travel and administrative arrangements in France. I tried to bring the pair together. Graham Kelly seemed uninterested in the deteriorating state of Glenn's relationship with Pat, which irritated me. The administrative and executive team behind the team was important. We were all in it together to bring the World Cup home.

Seeking the perfect preparation, Glenn was very keen on nutrition and brought in an expert called Dr Jan Rougier, who assessed everything eaten and recommended vitamins for the players. 'There will be no cereal, only toast and poached eggs at breakfast,' Glenn decreed.

'No cereal?' moaned a few players. Glenn was convinced it made a difference. Lunch-time on match days altered noticeably. Fish and chicken dominated. Bread was nowhere to be seen. Glenn was a disciple of that professor of proper preparation, Arsene Wenger, having played under him at Monaco. 'Arsene taught me so much about the right preparation,' Glenn said. 'I owe so much to Arsene.'

Creatine, a powder that improves stamina, was supplied to England players as we built towards France '98. 'I believe in creatine,' said Glenn. 'So does Arsene.' From the little I knew, creatine was pretty controversial stuff. During the build-up to France, I was relieved England's use of creatine never became public knowledge. Doc Crane passed it. The players accepted it, even though it apparently made some of them fart. Creatine appeared to work.

England did get stronger as the tournament wore on. They were buzzing going into that game against Argentina in St-Etienne. The following year, the FA's own diary even carried an advertisement for it. 'Creatine. The Power. New. Direct from the USA. Scientifically supported. Research proven. Give yourself the competitive edge.' So much for secrecy.

Glenn did things his way. He partially traded on his reputation as a wonderful player. 'I can do it and you know I can do it' Glenn seemed to be saying at training. Being young, Glenn was less sensitive to others. He had his ups and downs with Tony Adams and Teddy Sheringham, Venables stalwarts. Glenn was a man of contradictions. He would be introverted, almost morose, and then suddenly burst into being the life and soul of the party.

'Hoddle has no sense of humour,' some people said to me.

'That's ludicrous,' I replied. 'Glenn just doesn't show it in public.' I certainly warmed to Hoddle.

Faith was a major issue with Glenn. I raised the issue on one of our many car journeys between Bisham and Burnham.

'Glenn, people keep telling me you are very religious. Are you?' I asked.

'My faith is very important to me,' replied Glenn, who'd become religious as a player when England visited Jerusalem. 'I don't go to church much but I believe in the importance of the spirit. I believe in karma. I believe in reincarnation.' Ageing and losing friends have made me hope there is an afterlife. What I really didn't understand about Glenn's faith was how Eileen Drewery fitted in. Most religious people would dismiss a faith-healer like Eileen. Terry wouldn't have given her five minutes. My only previous experience of a faith-healer was of Olga Stringfellow at Italia '90.

'Your back problems will recur,' Olga told me months after I'd had a major and, I thought, successful operation. She was right. But then back problems often do recur.

'Eileen has a capacity to heal,' Glenn explained.

'I had better see her, then,' I replied. Full of scepticism, I still felt I should find out what all the fuss was about. I doubted Eileen's laying-on of hands transmitted any strength, but if it made Ian Wright and Darren Anderton feel better, then good. Still, I realised the image problem Eileen presented. During his days advising Tony Blair, Alistair Campbell famously observed 'we don't do God'. I understood what Alistair meant. The Blairs are religious people but faith has become controversial. England is no longer a nation that respects people's faith or at least its traditional faiths, which is a huge shame. When FA chairman Geoff Thompson spoke of his faith, he was ridiculed.

'Glenn, steer clear of talking about Eileen and faith,' I always said to Glenn before news conferences. Then a question would come in about Eileen, I'd try to stop the line of attack, but Glenn would often say: 'No, David, I want to just answer that.' When Glenn talked at length about Eileen before the World Cup, I knew all the reporters would snigger. 'England are flying to France on a mumbo jumbo jet' read one paper. The *Sun*'s back page was 'Come all ye faithful'. The *Independent*'s was 'Welcome to the Voodoo woman'. Some players were similarly cynical. When she laid hands on Ray Parlour's head, he replied: 'Short, back and sides, please.' Incey was a non-believer in Eileen. So was Robbie Fowler, who turned on the TV when Eileen laid her hands on his head. The FA International Committee were incredibly sceptical but for another, more predictable reason. 'Who's paying?' was their usual reaction.

I talked to Glenn about the reaction. 'Eileen gives us a better chance at the World Cup,' replied her number-one supporter. She was a character. Affable and not averse to a drink, Eileen didn't take herself too seriously. She arrived at Burnham Beeches in the evening, placed her hands on the believers' heads, and went home. The FA never paid her. Glenn did. Hoddle was adamant that not taking Eileen to France '98 was his biggest mistake. Eileen's absence would not have been in my top-ten England mistakes at that World Cup.

Another controversial figure soon appeared at training. We had already met Mr Peperami at our World Cup training base in La Manga. He was an eight-foot sausage who used public events to promote his brand of salami. A week later, Glenn and the players were training at Bisham when our new friend re-appeared. Having hidden in the bushes for a time, Mr Peperami ran across two rugby pitches, fell over the advertising hoardings and joined in a kickabout between the players. No one saw him coming. We should have done really. He was quite distinct. Wearing a red, white and blue bobble hat, he had bulging eyes, one bigger than the other. Mr Peperami's fashion sense was limited, basically a pair of Union Jack Y-fronts. Hoddle and the players thought his arrival was hysterical.

Our security man, Ray Whitworth, was less impressed. He stormed over and grabbed the human sausage.

'What do you think you're doing here?' asked Ray, grappling with Mr Peperami. 'You can bugger off.' The players were now beside themselves with laughter. 'I'm not going to stand here any longer talking to a sausage,' Ray shouted. He managed to drag Mr Peperami away. By then, some players were on the ground, rolling around laughing. For a few days afterwards, players like Shearer greeted Ray with: 'Met any good sausages recently?' Wherever we travelled in the world after that, I often asked people to go up to Ray and ask: 'Are you the famous security man who talked to a sausage?' Ray took it well.

Some light relief was welcome in the build-up to the World Cup, particularly after the Sheringham episode. Teddy had nipped off to Portugal for a quick break and been photographed in a bar at six a.m. Glenn was spitting with anger. Some people around the camp, and in the FA, even wanted Teddy thrown out of the squad. Teddy was called to Glenn's room at Burnham Beeches. He had some explaining to do.

'Why on earth have you put me in this situation?' Glenn asked Teddy. 'What were you doing?'

'The reason I was there at that time is that they socialise at different hours in Portugal,' Teddy replied. This argument was never going to sway Hoddle, who administered an almighty bollocking to Teddy. Glenn was tough. Stubborn. He made Teddy read out a statement, apologising. Teddy felt humiliated.

'Glenn is making a mountain out of a molehill, David, I shouldn't have had to do that,' Teddy told me afterwards. 'I've only done it because I want to play in the World Cup.' I sympathised with Teddy, a good person, terrific company and hugely popular within football. He would have genuinely believed that he was off duty, that people sleep through the afternoon in Portugal and then head out into the night. Yet six a.m. was a bit excessive. Maybe today he would agree.

Glenn wanted everything running smoothly before the World Cup. No stories. No fuss. He even organised a game against Caen behind closed doors when we arrived in France. 'I want to have a proper match,' Glenn said. 'In secret.' When England arrived at the Caen stadium, two reporters, Graham Hunter and Rob Shepherd, were waiting to greet us. The whole game was hardly a PR winner, but England won 1–0, with a Paul Scholes goal. Already a United favourite, Scholesy fascinated me; he was pretty shy, and hated seeing himself on TV, yet he came alive on the pitch. More significantly, Scholesy scored in England's opening win over Tunisia in Marseilles before the team headed to Toulouse to face Romania.

'I have a bad feeling about this game,' said Glenn on the coach on the way to the stadium.

'So do I.' Our fears were borne out. I was behind the bench, screaming such abuse as Romania's winner went in that our chief security man, Brian Hayes, told me afterwards: 'You are a Category C hooligan.' Outwardly, Hoddle handled the adversity well. He was upbeat, but returned to his room to reflect deeply on the defeat.

'Get some sleep,' I told him.

'I am getting enough sleep,' Glenn replied. I was never sure he got enough. That worried me. But Glenn always looked good. He kept himself really fit and was always very smart. Glenn was still young. At World Cup draws and UEFA congresses, I realised how young Glenn was when I saw him with other national team coaches. When he lined up with the other thirty-one coaches before France '98, Glenn looked like a player.

'Don't you wish you were still a player?' I asked Glenn late one night at France '98.

'Yes,' he replied. 'I wish I was.' He could still do it. The quality of Glenn's technique was inescapable in training.

Before England's third game, against Colombia in Lens, we booked into Château Tilques, a wonderful place near the coast that the Gestapo liked so much during the war, they commandeered it as an HQ. The plan was for the wives to join us. Everybody seemed quite jolly but I was going around, muttering: 'We've won one game, we've lost one game. If we make a mess of this, we're out. Colombia aren't duffers. We'd better win. We can't take anything for granted in this bloody business.'

On the way to training at the Stade Félix Bollaert on the eve of the game, Glenn told me: 'Michael Owen's ready. He will start against Colombia.' After training, Glenn and I were driven back to Château Tilques. It proved a not so magical mystery tour.

'Does he know where we are going?' Glenn asked as we kept passing signs to Calais. The Channel Tunnel grew closer and closer.

'Excusez moi,' I ventured. 'Château Tilques?' The driver said nothing. Marcel Marceau was behind the wheel and we seemed to be heading out of France.

'This could make a great picture for the press!' I laughed. 'Hoddle flees France.' Calais loomed. 'If we get into the wrong lane here, we're in the Channel Tunnel.' Fortunately, at the last moment, Marcel turned away and found a back route to Château Tilques.

Match-day dawned and the previews in the papers were hardly friendly. Glenn was skewered in some, so I made sure the hotel staff hid the papers. But the mood lifted when Darren Anderton and David Beckham scored to ensure a terrific night. The mood improved even more during the party with the wives and girlfriends back at Château Tilques. The players had earned some

R&R. Some relaxed by playing cards. Newspaper accusations of their gambling huge amounts irritated the players during the World Cup, they were to continue well beyond Glenn's tenure as England coach. For me, playing cards is the most tedious activity of all time. Players did gamble on cards but stories of mammoth sums of money flying around within the England hotel were rubbish. More interest was aroused by the sweepstake, with players putting in a fiver or tenner and predicting the score. Sometimes, there would be a big horse-race back home that we watched on a giant screen. Alan and Teddy would go round taking bets. There was nothing new in that. Peter Shilton and Bryan Robson did the same in a previous England generation.

People occupied themselves in different ways. One morning, I went to a British military cemetery near Lens where 3,000 soldiers were buried. I was very conscious of being with a team of young Englishmen playing so close to where so many young Englishmen fell during the wars. Even before England landed at France '98, I'd flown with Bobby Charlton to visit a war cemetery that stretched as far as the eye could see. The sheer number of people buried there was unbelievable. I looked at the ages on the graves, and they were all late teens, early twenties, the same age as Owen and Beckham. It was a sobering moment.

Both Michael and Becks were to hit the headlines for rather different reasons in St-Etienne, the setting for England's second-round game against Argentina. 'I have a good feeling about this game,' Glenn said as we neared the ground. 'Everybody looks strong and fit.' They did.

The day before, Doc Crane had told me: 'The fitness levels of the players are incredibly high.' England's preparations were surely now paying off.

'We are well prepared,' Glenn told me in the tunnel before kick-off. 'We can beat Argentina.' What an occasion! What a match! Michael's dribble and goal were sensational. At 2–2 I still felt confident, sitting as I was next to a worse-for-wear member of the International Committee. Even down to ten men with Becks's infamous dismissal, England performed fantastically. I couldn't bear the tension any longer in the stands. I had to get down to the dug-out. Standing between Teddy and Steve McManaman, I leapt up when Sol Campbell headed in. When the referee, Kim Milton Nielsen, ruled the goal out for a foul by Alan that no else saw, I went ballistic. My language was a disgrace. 'It's only a game,' Teddy remarked. Only a bloody game?! It felt like life and death, and I wasn't even playing. When Nielsen blew for the end of extra time, Macca turned to me and said: 'Seaman saves penalties for fun and Incey won't miss.' Incey took some stick for not taking a penalty at Euro '96. I prayed he wouldn't miss.

'If there is a God and he supports Hoddle, we'll win now,' I told myself. I wasn't that convinced. A sense of foreboding filled me. As David Batty and Incey missed, God didn't seem to be supporting Hoddle. Walking into the beaten England dressing room afterwards was one of the worst experiences of my life. Tears flowed down some faces. Others just sat there, numb. It was a horror scene. Glenn had to attend a press conference. Some FIFA people dragged us into this room, where there was a stage for the coaches. It was a joke. Loads of Argentinians were dancing on this platform.

'This is ludicrous,' I screamed at the FIFA official. 'Get them off so Mr Hoddle can talk.' It was disrespectful. Glenn was shattered, right on the edge, and now we faced a delay while the stage was cleared.

'I have never seen you so angry,' Brian Woolnough told me afterwards.

Glenn's dream was over. Everything he had worked so hard for had gone up in smoke. It was painful. The Argentinians were not only partying on the stage. When we got outside to the car-park, their players were already on their bus, going crazy with delight. At the sight of England players, they began gesticulating and chanting. Our players were infuriated by the Argentinian taunting. It was unsporting, aggressive and set tempers boiling. England players would never, never behave like that in victory. All the wives and girlfriends were present, standing horrified as the Argentinian footballers gestured. I was so proud none of the England players reacted.

Back at our La Baule base, everyone drowned their sorrows. Some players, like Alan, went without their sleep but not without their golf. Alan was out on the course at six a.m. while others nursed hangovers. No one could be blamed for drinking that night. What else was there to do? You want to numb the pain of defeat. England were out of the tournament, unluckily and controversially. Dawn arrived and I still drank. I felt for Glenn and his players, good people kicked in the stomach by fate. Minutes after heading off to bed at seven a.m., my mobile rang.

'Who on earth is it, this early?' I said as my hand searched around on the bedside table for the phone. Have they no respect?

'Mr Davies, it's British Airways here. Would you like to travel home on Concorde? Everybody's so proud of the team. Giving the team a flight home on Concorde is the least we can do. But it will be an hour later than you were planning.'

Hoddle was fast asleep by then. There was no chance of me waking a devastated coach to finalise our travel arrangements out of a tournament he dreamed of winning. 'Fine, I've never been on Concorde, let's do it,' I said and put the phone down. So we flew home in style. The joy of experiencing Concorde was somewhat marred a couple of months later when BA tried to stick the FA with a bill for the extra fuel.

After France, I really worried about Glenn. He was so low, unable to do anything, watch any more games. The reality of his split from Anne now came into sharp focus. During qualifying and the tournament itself, Glenn was caught up in the whole obsession of winning the World Cup. Emerging from that tunnel, Glenn looked around and saw what had changed. His whole life.

Nothing seemed certain any more. Even 16 Lancaster Gate was in upheaval. On the night of St-Etienne, a fire blazed through parts of the FA offices. It wasn't arson, simply building work that went wrong and left a couple of floors seriously damaged. Most departments had to move out to Wembley. Just to add to the air of uncertainty, the *Observer* published a story claiming I was to leave the FA to join Alastair Campbell at No. 10. It wasn't the first or last such story. 'It's news to me,' I always replied when asked. And it was.

Rumours had been circulating about my future. I felt at a crossroads. On the eve of St-Etienne, I talked to Graham Kelly in the garden of England's hotel. 'Look, Graham, I really don't want to stay beyond the end of this year,' I said. 'I want you to know that. I don't know what I'm going to do but I don't want it to come out of the blue.'

Kelly just looked bemused. 'Why are you doing that? Why do you want to leave?'

'The FA are not changing quickly enough for me,' I said, 'and I don't have enough influence at the top. I'm never invited to executive committee meetings.' I knew full well why. Let's keep David in his place. That was their thinking. But to do my job properly – to represent and defend the FA in public – I needed to hear issues first hand. Anyway, after arriving back in England, I had a more pressing project than revolutionising the FA. Glenn had asked me to write a book with him on France '98, and we needed to get cracking to hit the publisher's deadline. This was to be the infamous *Glenn Hoddle: My 1998 World Cup Story.* Eager to resume working, I phoned Glenn. I found a man still in mourning for France '98.

'It's been terrible since coming home,' Glenn said.

'I know. But we need to finish off the book.' We'd been working on the diary during France '98, grabbing a few hours here and there. I never felt the book would be controversial. England managers had written World Cup books before. In 1986 and 1990, Bobby Robson produced a World Cup diary ghosted by the respected journalist Bob Harris. Other reporters commented that this gave Bob special access to the England manager, but Bobby's books still came out with little fuss. Unlike Glenn's. The idea came from Glenn's agent, Dennis Roach. Hoddle went along with it. They found a publisher, André Deutsch, and discussed the book with me over lunch in a restaurant at the back of Lancaster Gate. 'Well, David, why don't you write this book with Glenn because that will be the least controversial thing to do,' Dennis said. Famous last words. Remembering the tensions that Harris's connections with Bobby had caused, I agreed. It would be easier for the FA's Director of Public Affairs to write the book for Glenn rather than employ one of the football correspondents. Fair enough. Glenn went to Kelly for permission. 'That's fine,' said Kelly.

So the furious reaction when the book emerged was illogical. We'd told the FA. The press knew Glenn and I were producing a World Cup diary. Nobody had written a word of criticism. If this had been *The Secret Diary of Glenn Hoddle Aged 40¾ Aided and Abetted by the Awful David Davies* then we would have been fair game. If Glenn and I had surreptitiously compiled this diary and then sprung it on an unsuspecting world, then, OK, a spiky response from the press would have been more understandable. If it had been a secret, my position would have been indefensible. But everyone knew. Some at the FA got hot under the collar. Even a friend like David Sheepshanks, the Ipswich Town chairman and executive-committee member, was unimpressed.

'Are they doing it in FA time?' asked Ken Bates. No, no, no. I told Ken the truth.

'Ken, the truth is we do this book sitting in airports, late at night, weekends, on the phone, whenever we can, right? So unless I'm not allowed to do anything else in my life, then it is surely OK. By the way, I've been given permission for this, Ken, and if you've got a problem please speak to the chief executive, not me. And Ken, as you endlessly tell me, I'm an employee, right?'

'Not for long if I have anything to do with it!' Ken replied. I couldn't tell if Ken's tongue was in his cheek. He used to call for my sacking so regularly, I just never knew.

Serialisation, about which I wrongly never asked to be consulted, sparked the conflagration. The book went in the *Sun* and they inevitably intended giving it the full treatment. I began to worry about the book's likely impact when I received a call from the *Sun*'s chief sports writer, Steve Howard. I was waiting outside a hospital ward in Birmingham, where my daughter Amanda was undergoing an operation, when Steve phoned.

'David, I just want you to know that at last I've read an interesting football book,' said Steve.

'Thank you, Steve.' I headed back to Amanda, enjoying the compliment but then realising I was in for a lively few weeks. Serialisation in one paper inevitably antagonises the rest. The timing of the serialisation, 10 August, was awkward. Pride in England's World Cup performance had faded. The memory of that stirring victory over Colombia and the ten-man defiance against Argentina was ebbing. Disappointment at bowing out was kicking in. Critics were now writing: 'Well, actually, we didn't do that well in France and it must be the manager's fault.' They looked for a way to bash Hoddle. Unintentionally, we provided them with a huge stick. Some managers piled in. At Blackburn, Roy Hodgson had a go at Glenn over his handling of Chris Sutton.

When *Glenn Hoddle: My 1998 World Cup Story* came out, many columnists vilified us, even accusing Glenn of taking his eye off the World Cup ball because he was distracted by the book. What rubbish. Even during a full-on tournament, the England manager was allowed a few hours' spare time. Claims that Glenn deceived the press during France '98 to keep stories back for the book were also wide of the mark. The most extraordinary criticism came from the *Guardian*, not one of the usual attack dogs of the football press. They suggested I should have censored more of the book! Being lectured by my old profession, journalism, on the need for censorship I found painful. Surely the media believed in freedom of expression?! I couldn't believe that they felt we had been too open. They called the book 'an appalling breach of confidence'. But where? The book was not 'crammed with dressing-room secrets'. If I'd written a bland account of a traumatic, rollercoaster tournament, I would have been pilloried. England fans deserved more detail than 'we had breakfast, had a laugh, were crap at penalties and came home'. The book went to No. 1 because Glenn was honest in it.

On reflection, though, writing the book was wrong. No ifs, no buts. Wrong. Wrong. Wrong. My first mistake was naïvety in not realising that the media climate had changed since Bobby's books in 1986 and 1990. The media were more intense, more critical. A World Cup diary was always going to attract censure unless England brought the trophy home. I should have known. A perception also grew that Glenn held information back during France '98; that wasn't true, but the book allowed that theory to take hold. Another error. We were also accused of breaking secrets, of publishing privileged information that should have remained in the dressing room. That charge was unfair. Glenn would never have betrayed his players. But the mere publication of a World Cup diary gave the impression of revealing secrets. The reaction deeply upset me.

'I'm angry with myself,' I told Susan. 'I let personal ambition to do a book, and my own journalistic instincts of what makes a good story, run over my sense of what was right and wrong. If the England players pummel me, I really will think about leaving.' Some England players were certainly unimpressed. Graeme Le Saux was very critical. So was Gary Neville. Both were players I counted as friends. 'The book shouldn't have been written,' Gary told me. Yet the players knew Glenn and I were writing it. Not one of them came up during France '98 to complain about what we were doing. Graeme and Gary were displeased but hardly mutinous. None of the players said: 'Look, this is totally unacceptable, you and Glenn have betrayed us.' If they had, our position would have been absolutely untenable. But I regret the fuss and damage the book caused. I was naïve not to think we might be pulling a pin out of a hand-grenade. At the very least, Glenn and I should certainly have tried to have more control over serialisation. Glenn, lucky man, was away on holiday during the worst of the uproar. On his return, England reported on 18 August in preparation for a game with Sweden. Walking into the media room at Bisham Abbey that day felt like entering the lion's den. The huge number of reporters present stunned me. The questioning was brutal. Every time Glenn tried to move the subject away from the book, one of the reporters immediately dragged it back. Only then, during that merciless grilling, did I fully appreciate how much damage the book was doing to Glenn and me. In all my twelve years at the FA, writing that World Cup diary was my biggest mistake.

After training, I talked to senior players like Alan and Gary.

'You know when you normally meet up with England, it's usually a player at the centre of a storm,' I said. 'This time, it is Glenn and I.'

Some players, like Alan, thought it hilarious.

'You've spent so long defending people and now you need a bit of defending yourself,' Alan laughed.

Within Lancaster Gate, some people called for my resignation. Paid to see the downside of everything, I hadn't with the book. I was probably saved from the sack by the fact that I had gained permission from Kelly. These were truly nervy times, however. A few weeks after serialisation, the FA's executive committee met and I had been tipped off that the book would be discussed. David Sheepshanks voiced his disapproval forcibly. Funnily enough, the book actually ensured I remained at Lancaster Gate. Frustrated by the organisation's refusal to modernise, I had told Kelly that I was thinking of leaving. I couldn't now. Everyone would have thought it was because of the book.

Bizarrely, within weeks, my fortunes at the FA were transformed. The sudden departures of both chairman Keith Wiseman and Graham, following what the majority of the executive committee regarded as 'actions exceeding their authority', left a void. My heart was hardly broken to see Kelly go, but he certainly wasn't corrupt. Nor was Wiseman. Offering finance to the Welsh FA for their support of England's bid to host the 2006 World Cup without sufficient backing was an unwise political manoeuvre. It still surprised me that people at one end of the deal lost their jobs while their counterparts at the other end didn't. Clearly, the atmosphere was more fevered at the FA than at the Welsh FA. A few FA people had been looking to ease Kelly out of Lancaster Gate, and this gave them their chance. Nic Coward, Michael Cunnah and I took over, effectively as joint acting chief executives. Those first days were like a South American revolution. We moved into offices containing files about ourselves that we never knew existed. There were internal memos, detailing why Graham was so opposed to my appointment, long discussions about my salary and the manner in which I was recruited.

Meanwhile, pressure still mounted on Glenn. Going into Christmas, the press were chipping away at him. The results hadn't been good enough. To improve his image, Glenn and Dennis Roach decided to do some interviews with individual journalists. In the build-up to a game with France on 10 February, Glenn talked over the phone to Matt Dickinson, at that time the respected chief football correspondent of *The Times*. The interview appeared on 30 January and caused carnage. I had no inkling of the pending storm. My role in the FA had moved on. I didn't listen in on the interview. In the light of the ensuing mayhem, somebody should have done; but I trusted Glenn. He was a grown man – not every interview was monitored. After a busy Friday in London, I had returned to Worcestershire. Bryan Richardson, then chairman of Coventry City, and the Sky presenter Richard Keys came over for dinner with their wives. Moments after they arrived, Glenn called. Someone had tipped him off about the line *The Times* was running in the morning from Matt's interview. It was all about the disabled paying for their sins in a former life. 'I've been misinterpreted,' said Glenn. Somehow a football interview turned into a discussion about reincarnation. 'I thought it was off the record,' Glenn added. Suddenly it was my responsibility again. As usual with FA crises. How on earth could I put this fire out? The moment *The Times*' first edition dropped at eleven p.m., all hell broke loose. At two a.m., my phone was still ringing with reporters from other papers seeking reaction. 'We have a serious problem,' I told Susan.

I encouraged Glenn to make lunch-time television appearances but the incoming tide of revulsion over his comments quickened. Glenn and I met at Highfield Road that afternoon. Coventry hosted Liverpool and Glenn was there to watch some players. Noel White, the chairman of the International Committee, was a director of Liverpool, so he was there too and talked to Glenn at half-time. I knew Glenn was in real difficulty, having spoken to a range of editors and sports editors and understood their critical stance towards him. Even Glenn's friends at the FA might struggle to save him now, I felt. My mobile went into meltdown on the Sunday – seventy-one calls, a personal best.

'Today's papers are not as critical as I feared,' I told Glenn after flicking through the Sundays. 'But, Glenn, what you have to do is have an all-in news conference, tackling this issue head-on.' Glenn was not keen. He was listening to others more than me. Calling around the FA, I managed to organise a meeting on Monday to discuss the crisis. Noel White didn't seem to understand the urgency of it. Yet any hope of controlling events was soon dashed. Alastair Campbell called on Monday morning.

'The PM is going on *Richard & Judy* and is bound to be asked about Hoddle,' Alastair said.

'Well, let the PM know everyone involved is getting together this evening to sort out the problem,' I replied. But my heart was pounding over-time. I knew Glenn was doomed when I tuned into *Richard & Judy* and heard Blair asked: 'If Glenn Hoddle has said what he is reported to have said, should he go?'

'Yes,' replied the PM. The London *Evening Standard* immediately splashed on the PM's devastating verdict: 'Hoddle must go says Blair'. In an ideal world, the PM should probably not be getting involved in debates over the future of the England manager, but Blair had to operate in the real world. He was asked the question. If he'd ducked it, the headline in the *Standard* might have been: 'Blair doesn't care about disabled'. After the PM's intervention, I struggled to conceive how I could rescue Glenn now. He might have survived if he'd fronted up and said sorry with no ifs or buts. I felt frustrated and confused. Glenn has done work for the disabled over the years. He said something similar about reincarnation before on Radio Five Live without causing a furore. Results were good back then, and Glenn rode a wave of popularity, so no one was looking to bring him down. Glenn was entitled to his beliefs but he also had to be sensitive to other people. Glenn did not mean to offend so many people but he did. He was rapidly losing friends at Lancaster Gate. There were strong views that he should never have talked about reincarnation.

'But I never said those things,' Glenn insisted to me. I have never questioned Matt Dickinson's trustworthiness. It was an impossible situation. That Monday evening at six p.m., a group of us convened in my bedroom at White's Hotel. Media opinion was highly critical of Glenn and the PM was against Glenn, so the mood was not good. The meeting involved Dave Richards, David Dein, Noel White, Geoff Thompson and myself. David Sheepshanks was in contact from Barcelona. Noel and David Dein sat on the fence. The rest were against Hoddle. Within minutes of the meeting starting, it was abundantly clear to me that the overwhelming majority felt Glenn's position untenable. Glenn had supporters in the building but too few. The FA felt deeply embarrassed by the reincarnation remarks. At ten p.m., Glenn and Dennis Roach came into the room. We had a half-hour meeting in a last-ditch attempt to keep Glenn. I found myself having to lead a desperately difficult conversation. The majority wanted Glenn to accept various conditions if he was to stay as England coach. These I spelled out to him.

'No. 1: Make an apology. No. 2: Hold a news conference. No. 3: Agree that non-football statements are off-limits. No. 4: Remove Eileen Drewery.' I stopped talking and looked at Glenn. I knew Glenn would never accept such conditions. He was stubborn but genuine. The meeting broke up without a resolution. Everybody agreed to sleep on it. I crashed out knowing the following day would probably be Glenn's last as England coach. I hardly slept. My mood didn't improve when I got into Lancaster Gate next day to find no Dave Richards. Inexplicably, he had returned to Sheffield without telling me.

Piers Morgan called from the *Daily Mirror*.

'If you back Glenn, we will,' Piers said.

'Piers, I genuinely do not know how this is going to work itself out,' I replied.

'What are his chances of surviving?'

'Pretty low.' My instinct was that Glenn's predicament was unsalvageable but I clung to hope. Hoddle was privately preparing for the worst. The sack duly arrived. People rightly ask: 'Did David Davies betray Glenn Hoddle?' I don't believe I did. Glenn Hoddle let himself down with whatever he said about the disabled in a football interview. Never for a moment did Glenn mean to be callous. Events conspired to make his position impossible. Ultimately, his fate as England manager was wretchedly cruel.

7

The Genius and Madness of Gazza

At an unforgettable tribute dinner for Sir Bobby Robson in July 2008, just about everybody's most loved England manager repeated his long-held view that Paul Gascoigne was 'daft'. And he added, 'Do you know, Gazza never could understand why his sister had two brothers, and he had only one.'

England's brightest diamond in the 1990s was sadly its most flawed. Watching Paul Gascoigne relaxing at England's World Cup base in Sardinia as the decade opened, I noticed him becoming friendly with a waiter who served him cappuccinos at all hours of the day, each laced with brandy. Graham Taylor's subsequent comments about Gazza's 'refuelling' lit the beacon of concern within the game. During the build-up to Euro '96, Terry Venables and I agonised about him. He was the classic English footballer: bored easily. Down-time did Gazza's head in. For this genius of a player, it was not the matches that were the problem, it was filling in time between kick-offs.

During one international break at Burnham, Gazza seemed particularly down. So Terry and I tackled him. 'What's up?' we asked one evening after dinner. 'Money and home,' shrugged Gazza. It was a tearful exchange. Terry and I shook our heads in disbelief. Surely, Gazza's money was being looked after. Did he have enough? Was it being invested properly for his future? Gazza didn't seem to have any idea. His life heaved with complications. He seemed controlled by an addictive personality: boom or bust, excess or abstinence. Extremes of behaviour defined England's best footballer. Lazio didn't help; never was an English player less suited to living abroad. The tales from Lazio are legendary. One centres on the day Gazza stole the Lazio coaches' whistles, and distributed them round the necks of various sheep in a field next door to the training ground. Holidaying in Portugal one year, Susan and I bumped into Gazza. He was a mess. I was so anxious, I rang those who really cared for him, people like Terry and his then agent Jane Morgan. 'He's completely on his own out here, and his behaviour is weird,' I told them. 'He's going for runs in the midday sun. He then goes from restaurant to restaurant. He's not drinking, just eating.' One night, he was adamant he wouldn't leave a restaurant until he had purchased a fish – from the goldfish tank. Gazza was a lost soul and needed help. Terry tried. Jane tried. So did Glenn Roeder. So did Incey. Most of us let Gazza down. I blame myself. I blame everybody. The alarm bells certainly rang early enough.

'Gazza simply was not prepared for what happened to him at Italia '90,' I remarked to Terry one day. No one could argue with that. The sudden explosion of interest in this likeable, emotional Geordie was extraordinary. One moment he was an up-and-coming England international. The next? Everybody on the planet knew him. Gazza's brilliance on the road to the World Cup semi-finals illustrated his special talent to every football fan. His tears in Turin, his heartache at that booking and then defeat, moved every human being. Paul Gascoigne the Footballer became Gazza the Icon. Days after the World Cup, Gazza was a guest on Terry Wogan's TV show. He was young, modest, witty, a star – that was then. His life was taken away from him and turned into a soap opera. Could anyone have controlled this wild comet? Maybe if he'd gone to Manchester United, coming under Fergie's benevolent control, Gazza might not have slipped off the rails. Who knows? Maybe if he'd spent longer under Terry, he might have found an even keel. Gazza was like a favourite wayward son to Terry. The situation was so frustrating to his friends. Gazza was foolish, infuriating, but blessed with a heart of gold. One day I was struggling to sort out a family holiday.

'I can't decide where to go,' I mentioned to Gazza.

'Leave it to me,' Gazza said. 'I know a great hotel in Italy.' He got on the phone, fixed everything up and it was a top holiday. Typical Gazza. Warmth flowed through him. I lost count of the times I defended Paul to the hilt within the FA and to newspapers planning on running another knocking piece. Paul was worth protecting. Euro '96 was the last time England saw Gazza almost at his best. At times that wonderful summer, he even relaxed off the pitch.

'Good,' Terry would say. 'Gazza's off fishing with David.' Terry knew that if Gazza was sitting on a river-bank next to Seaman, he'd be happy. It seemed odd, someone so hyperactive willingly disappearing fishing. But Gazza loved it. David and Gazza became best buddies at Euro '96, the laid-back Yorkshireman and the madcap Geordie wiling away the hours between games on a secluded reservoir near Burnham. Those moments provided the calm in the storm of Gazza's existence. Those storm-clouds gathered after Euro '96. On 17 October, I picked up the *Daily Mirror* and read with horror details of Gazza's attack on his wife, Sheryl. The paper included graphic pictures of a bruised Sheryl. I immediately switched into crisis-management mode. What would Terry's successor, Glenn Hoddle, do? What would the FA tell him to do? Glenn was about to name his squad for a World Cup qualifier in Georgia. Could we take Gazza and risk a running side-show of protesting women's groups?

'Where's Kelly?' I asked. 'Where's Wiseman?' Keith Wiseman had succeeded Sir Bert as chairman and I needed to talk to the new man urgently. England's best-known player being accused of wife-beating represented a crisis for the FA. The organisation had to provide some leadership on such a sensitive issue. Glenn needed guidance.

'I feel terrible for Sheryl,' Glenn said. 'But how do we deal with it?' I outlined the problems in taking Gazza to Georgia.

'Point one, Glenn: if you pick Gazza, a bloody great media circus will follow us to Georgia and back. So is that fair to you and the other players? Point two: should you take a moral stance and leave Gazza out?'

'I'll think about it,' replied Glenn, clearly determined not to be bounced into a decision. As Glenn wrestled with the choice, the FA hierarchy were noticeable by their absence and silence. The newspapers immediately saddled up their high horses. Gazza was crucified and Hoddle didn't escape either. 'How can a Christian select a wife-beater for England?' enquired the *Daily Mail.* The fires around Gazza and Hoddle burned fast. Situations like this cried out for a decisive chief executive to put out these fires. Come on, Graham. What a mess. My depression deepened with news that Matthew Harding, Chelsea's benefactor, had perished in a helicopter crash on 22 October. I knew Matthew a bit, a decent guy and Chelsea-daft. Life throws people together at times, and a small bond is made. I bumped into Matthew on the platform at Blackpool North railway station on the way to a Labour party conference. We chatted for ages and Matthew's intelligence and enthusiasm for life made a deep impression. Now he was dead. Glenn felt the loss even more deeply, having known Matthew at Chelsea. 'I want to go to Matthew's funeral,' Glenn said. 'Let's put back the squad announcement twenty-four hours.' Fair enough.

Everyone kept having their say on the Gazza situation. Sir Bert, by now the former chairman, delivered his verdict through Brian Woolnough in the *Sun.* 'I'd have blocked Gazza's selection,' Sir Bert said. Glenn still hadn't made up his mind. Finally, I managed to round up Hoddle, Kelly and Wiseman for a summit on 28 October at the Compleat Angler, a wonderful hotel by the river in Marlow near Bisham. 'I don't want to be told what to do,' said Glenn. He clearly expected us to order him to leave out Gazza. None of us did. The coach must decide. And Glenn certainly did. 'Rock bottom. Gazza's in' read the headline in the London

Evening Standard. My instinct had been that Gazza should have been left out. But Wiseman and Kelly were content to leave the decision to Glenn. When I picked up the papers the following day, vitriol poured forth. Most of the flak was aimed at Lancaster Gate for not giving a stronger lead. When Gazza arrived at Burnham, I immediately sat him down.

'I'm sorry,' said Gazza, genuinely remorseful.

'Paul, we have to address this,' I said. 'You have to talk to the media tomorrow. Front up, sort it out.'

'I'll only talk to TV,' he replied. 'I don't trust the press.' Eventually, we compromised on a mass conference with Glenn sitting alongside Gazza, by then a bag of nerves. Woolnough wondered aloud if Gazza would walk out rather than answer his questions. Gazza stayed in his seat and dealt comfortably with all questions. The hurricane seemed to blow itself out.

Inevitably, many observers tried to analyse the cause of Gascoigne's problems. For me, he didn't feel secure off the pitch. Gazza had low self-esteem. One evening, when England were in Nantes for the 1997 Tournoi de France game with Italy, I had a long talk with Gazza after the game. He was miserable.

'I want to quit England,' he told me. I was shocked. England meant everything to Gazza. He adored the banter, the friends. He loved the training and the games. He was one short of his half-century of England appearances.

'Why?' I asked.

'After I get my fiftieth cap, I'm off. I'm always being slagged off. Whatever I do, whatever I say, people slaughter me.'

I didn't know how to calm him down. I scoured the hotel for Glenn Roeder, Gazza's confidant and one of Hoddle's assistants. Roeder sat and talked to Gazza, lifting his spirits. When Gazza returned to his room, I chatted to Roeder.

'Paul's existence seems an absolute nightmare off the pitch,' I said.

'Gazza has no life,' Roeder replied. 'But he's not seriously thinking of giving up England. He's just fed up.'

'It sounds like a plea for help,' I remarked. The following morning, another bloody tornado blew in. Gazza was fuming at the papers again.

'What is this about Hoddle saying I should quit Rangers and play in England?' Gazza asked me.

'I'll look into it.' It transpired that English papers had lifted comments Glenn made to the French media, and maybe something had been lost in translation. Maybe not. Try explaining that to an enraged footballer.

The dark dogs of depression chasing Gazza picked up pace as the World Cup came into view. On 15 May 1998, Hoddle and I were flicking through the papers over breakfast. 'Oh, no, look at this,' I said. One of the tabloids contained a picture of Gazza falling out of a restaurant late at night. The following day, Gazza was apparently still at lunch in late afternoon. I rang his number. No answer. Probably sleeping off his hangover somewhere. Glenn was furious. For the first time, I believed Glenn might leave Gazza out of his France '98 squad. I knew what a story that would be. Massive. It would lead every bulletin. I also understood what it would do to Gazza – break his heart. The story took a further twist when the *Daily Mirror* published a picture of Paul guzzling a kebab at two a.m. in Soho with the DJ Chris Evans. My phone almost melted under calls from the *Sun*'s Stuart Higgins. 'We are running stories on "Hoddle reads riot act to Gazza",' Stuart said. Higgins was right. Hoddle's anger intensified. Wolfing down kebabs in the small hours with a bunch of celebrities is no way to prepare for a World Cup. Gazza's behaviour was unfathomable. After all the injuries his body had sustained, Gazza knew he'd lost that special ability to take games by the scruff of the neck. His future in football worried him. 'So why damage your fitness with kebabs?' friends warned him. Glenn's face almost contorted with rage at dealing with another Gazza mess. He was clearly losing patience. That frustrated Gazza's friends in the squad, players like Incey and Wrighty. They felt Glenn should be more understanding. Yet no one in the dressing room seriously thought such a gifted footballer would be dropped for France. Gazza understood that his relationship with Hoddle was under great strain. He didn't feel Hoddle supported him in tackling his problems. They had Tottenham in common, a reputation for being great entertainers, but little else. Gazza and Glenn could not have been more contrasting characters. The people who conjured up the most magic from Gazza's talent were those great man-managers, Bobby Robson and Terry Venables, older men. Their relationship with Gazza was almost father–son. Glenn was closer to Gazza's generation and struggled.

D-Day approached. England flew out to La Manga with Glenn needing to drop seven of the thirty-strong squad. This attractive Spanish retreat proved the scenic setting for one of the biggest personal confrontations in England's footballing history. Initially, all seemed well between Hoddle and Gazza. On Tuesday 26 May, the sun again warmed La Manga, and the players flocked to the hotel pool. Having sweated hard in training, they deserved a break. Hoddle, though, had strict rules on how long Gazza and the lads could spend out in the sun.

'Too much sun drains them,' Glenn explained to me. When he was out of ear-shot, Doc Crane revealed: 'Glenn was the worst for sneaking out for extra sunbathing when he was a player!' On 27 May, we briefly left La Manga to fly to Casablanca for a World Cup warm-up against Morocco. The coach was only 200 yards from the hotel when somebody shouted: 'Where's Gazza?' He hadn't reported in time. The bus turned back to collect him. It was his birthday, which might have explained why he was late.

'Maybe he's been celebrating,' someone said.

'Maybe he has been on the phone to Sheryl,' added somebody else.

'Glenn, can you go back and get Gazza?' Hoddle asked Roeder.

Roeder brought Gazza to the bus. I looked at Gazza, then glanced at a seething Hoddle. A collision course was set. Gazza was in his own world by then, his mind 1,000 miles away, distracted by events at home. When he read an article in the *Sun* on Sheryl's 'new man', Gazza plunged into a deeper depression. Even a hilarious moment the following day failed to cheer him up. It was my birthday, and at dinner a beautiful blonde wheeled in a cake. Only after inspecting the woman very closely did I realise it was Peter Taylor, whose make-up was almost perfect.

Gazza's life continued to unravel in La Manga and Casablanca. The day before we headed back to Morocco for a game with Belgium, Gazza spent most of the afternoon on the phone. 'He's meant to be resting,' Glenn fumed. Things worsened in Morocco, first for me, then Gazza. As I walked near the pitch, some Moroccans threw a bag of piss at us. Urine soaked my shirt and trousers. Before kick-off, Gazza stood in the centre-circle, again talking on his mobile. This was madness. Glenn was about to whittle down his squad and everyone was on their best behaviour – except Gazza. Glenn made up his mind not to take Gazza to France on the flight back from Morocco on the Friday evening. Back at La Manga, Glenn told the players: 'Enjoy the weekend, play some golf and I'll tell you on Sunday evening.' In the hotel bar on the Saturday night, Gazza was on the karaoke big-time. Glenn had given the players permission to have a couple of beers, a limit exceeded by Gazza. On Sunday morning, Glenn confirmed his bombshell to me on the way into breakfast. 'Gazza's out,' he said. I nodded. I wasn't shocked. The rest of the world would be. Knowing we had to make contingency plans, I called my assistant Steve Double into the hotel library.

'Steve, somebody is going to have to fly back tonight with the dropped players,' I said. 'I need you to go with them, because it could be lively.'

'Why?'

'Guess who's out?'

'Phil Neville? Dion Dublin?'

'And?'

'I don't know.'

'Gazza.'

'What?!' Steve was stunned. A notice-board in the La Manga dining room detailed which player had to go to Glenn's room at which time, starting in mid-afternoon. Until then, the players were allowed a round of golf. As they disappeared to the fairways, I spoke to Glenn Roeder about Gazza. He was torn. Roeder was part of Hoddle's coaching staff yet he was extremely close to Gazza, who relied on him. Now Gazza was about to discover his grim fate. When he went in to see Hoddle, mayhem ensued. Informed he was cut from England's World Cup adventure, Gazza went mad. On hearing the commotion, I ran out of my room and witnessed the carnage wrought by a wild Gazza. Flowers and vases were strewn all over the corridor. In one corner, Gazza was being comforted by Incey and David Seaman. Glenn's room was a mess. 'I thought he was going to hit me,' Glenn told me. Gazza had kicked a chair over and punched a lamp, showering the carpet with glass. Glenn was standing in the middle of the room, talking to John Gorman about getting the glass tidied up before the next player walked in. At that moment, I knew for sure we had to find a better way of telling players their World Cup or European Championship dreams were over. La Manga built up the pressure to such a pitch that Gazza just exploded. I talked to Hoddle in advance about how he would tell the players. I told him how Venables handled it. But every manager does things their way. In later years, managers have shown more sensitivity to a player's feelings. Ultimately, there is no easy way to notify a player that he is surplus to requirements. I felt bloody sorry for the others omitted in La Manga, for Philip Neville, Nicky Butt, Ian Walker, Dion Dublin and Andy Hinchcliffe. Of course they dealt with exclusion better than Gazza but their heartache was as deep. Talking to those players who remained in Hoddle's squad, I sensed the unease at the way the omissions were handled.

Gazza's absence sparked some initial outrage back home. Chris Waddle criticised Glenn, his old friend and team-mate. That didn't surprise me. Gazza, a friend of Chris's too, evoked strong feelings. To this day, I regard Gazza as a friend but I fear for him.

In 2008, his public humiliations, drunk or sober, on the streets of London or in his native North East make me weep. In my last days at the FA, I sent Gazza to Botswana to use his fame to campaign against HIV/Aids. As usual, he was brilliant in public with children. Privately, his demons exhausted all of those travelling with him. Gazza's ill. I still discuss him with Terry Venables, who was called in by the Met Police in 2008 to talk some sense into his old midfielder. It's an uphill battle. As Terry says endlessly: 'Only Gazza can save Gazza.'

8

Kevin

'I've a gift for you,' announced Mohamed Al Fayed, handing me a Harrods bag as we stood in his opulent office on the fifth floor of the world's most celebrated store. As executive director and effectively chief executive I was on an England mission, seeking the Fulham benefactor's permission to talk to his manager Kevin Keegan. Suddenly, Al Fayed offered me this present.

'Can I open it?' I asked.

'Absolutely,' he replied.

'It's a gold bar,' said Al Fayed as I unwrapped it.

'And it's made of chocolate,' I said, relieved. I dreaded the headlines: 'FA man accepts gold bar from Harrods boss'. Al Fayed had been the centre of attention for allegedly offering gifts to Tory MPs. 'I'll keep this in the bag!' I laughed with Al Fayed. Arriving back at Lancaster Gate, I encountered a Sky crew lurking on the step, looking for updates on the search for Glenn Hoddle's successor. The papers had linked Al Fayed's most famous employee with the vacancy; fortunately, darkness was falling and they didn't notice my Harrods bag.

'Anything happening, David?' the reporter asked.

'We're making a bit of progress,' I replied. And we were. Inside Lancaster Gate, only one person voiced any doubts about Keegan. 'I certainly want Kevin considered for the job,' said Howard

Wilkinson, our technical director, who was covering as team caretaker. 'I'd just be happier if Kevin had all the coaching badges.' Howard was sceptical about Kevin's credentials. 'I'm not sure how tactically sound he is,' Howard added. As technical director, he was building a coaching system that required coaches to be fully qualified. Kevin wasn't. I believed Howard fancied the England job himself, making his temporary control permanent. He was an engaging character who liked a story, a cigar and a glass of wine or two. He was vastly removed from his image of a dour Yorkshireman, a perception he felt harmed him.

Within Lancaster Gate, there was talk of Howard working in tandem with Brian Kidd. Under Noel White's chairmanship, the International Subcommittee considered Howard's candidacy. He did have a chance but fairly quickly they decided they much preferred Howard continuing as our highly regarded technical director, working on the Charter for Quality designed to revolutionise youth development. Having made known his concern about Kevin, Howard understood we had to get on with the appointment, although he still thought we rushed it. With Howard's case rejected, Noel, Dave Richards, David Sheepshanks and David Dein began discussing other candidates. The process was complicated by the FA chairman Geoff Thompson being in New Zealand and Australia. He had only become chairman in December and the trip had long been booked. I was pleasantly surprised his absence wasn't more widely criticised in the media.

'Who do you think it should be?' Dein asked me.

'Fergie,' I replied, repeating the view I had aired before Hoddle was installed. But was the timing any better now? No! I still made a short, exploratory call to Old Trafford. The reaction was emphatic. United were going for the Treble and they would not appreciate any distractions, thank you very much. I reported this to the FA. Arsene Wenger's name was mentioned. Dein always got it in the neck over the FA and Wenger. David was Arsenal's vice-chairman, as well as an FA man responsible for finding a new England manager. David would never have blocked an approach from the FA to his manager. He couldn't have done anyway. If the majority wanted Wenger, David would have been outvoted. Discreet soundings were taken over whether this highly regarded Frenchman was interested. The word back from Arsenal was that Monsieur Wenger was perfectly happy there. That was sad. Arsene would have made a fantastic England manager. I always found him very inspiring, with a good sense of humour, far removed from the dug-out figure who rails at referees, then claims he never saw a bad challenge by one of his players.

'How is it that you never seem to see some of these incidents?!' I asked Arsene at an NSPCC event once. 'Have you got an eyesight problem?' Wenger laughed. In return, he expressed the opinion that the FA picked on Arsenal.

'I think Arsenal are being victimised,' Wenger said.

'I don't believe it, Arsene,' I replied. For all his occasional conspiracy theories, Wenger fascinated me. Slightly introverted, deeply thoughtful, Wenger wanders around grounds an hour before kick-off, chatting to people, having a cup of tea, always polite. Come kick-off, Wenger has as many red mists as Ferguson. Suddenly, the storm will pass and he reverts to this charming, intelligent man. Talking to Wenger, I understood how shocked he had been by the physicality and lack of professionalism in English football when he joined Arsenal in 1996. What was also clear was how much he loves English football. 'I want to stay at Arsenal,' he always says to me. If Wenger ever becomes an international manager, it will be of his native France.

Back in 1999, no huge desire existed within the FA to appoint a foreigner anyway. Bryan Robson was considered before we concentrated on Kevin. Outside Howard's office, most enthusiasm in Lancaster Gate seemed reserved for Keegan. He was English. He'd done very well at Fulham, pretty well at Newcastle. Kevin's 'I'd love it' outburst against Ferguson in 1996 was mentioned. Was he too emotional? Well, surely we wanted someone with passion. The memory of Newcastle melting as United turned up the heat that season was also discussed. Just about everybody on the selection subcommittee seemed to be satisfied Keegan was tactically proficient. Surely he had taken Newcastle virtually to the pinnacle of the Premier League so why shouldn't he have tactical nous? 'It will all end in tears,' Geoff Thompson was quoted though as saying in the *Daily Telegraph*. Calling from Sydney Harbour, Geoff denied saying that. The mood in Lancaster Gate was incredibly pro-Kevin. At lunch-time on 12 February 1999, Howard and Noel contacted me to authorise an approach to Keegan. Much to everybody at the FA's amazement, things moved fast. That chocolate gold bar would soon be mine! Ringing a contact at Harrods at two p.m., I secured an audience with Al Fayed for four p.m. On my way to Harrods, Brian Woolnough called from the *Sun*.

'Anything occurring with England?' Brian asked.

I tried to sound relaxed. 'We're progressing, you know.'

'Is anything going to happen this weekend?' For a moment, I wondered whether Brian had developed psychic powers.

'Not this weekend. Maybe next week.' I couldn't tell Brian everything but I also never lie. So I carried on into Al Fayed's regal office. I'd come for a manager, not a gold chocolate bar.

'We'd like to talk to Kevin about him becoming the coach of England,' I said, half-expecting Al Fayed to tell me to 'buzz off'. Happily, he didn't.

'I cannot stand in the way of you talking to Kevin about the job,' said Al Fayed. 'Kevin is a patriot. I am a patriot. If England want to talk to Kevin, you have my permission. I will talk to Kevin first. Then you can talk to him after Fulham play United on Sunday.' United won the FA Cup tie with a goal from Andy Cole. That delighted me but can't have pleased Kevin, who sold him to Fergie. Worrying slightly what Kevin's mood would be, I headed out to enjoy a Valentine's Day dinner with my wife Susan at Scalini, a restaurant around the back of Harrods. After a few bites of food and sips of wine, I couldn't wait any longer. Leaving my meal, I stepped out on to the pavement and called Kevin. I knew him from his Liverpool days, and always found him friendly.

'Well done on losing to Manchester United!' I began. 'Great result!' Kevin roared with laughter. He remembered my affiliation. He also knew why I was calling, and it wasn't to wish him Happy Mother's Day.

'Can we come and meet you?' I asked.

'Of course,' Kevin replied.

'When's good for you?'

'Come up tomorrow.'

'OK. Let's do it.' Jubilant, I immediately rang Noel and Howard.

'Kevin's happy to see us,' I blurted out. 'Let's meet at Darlington tomorrow and go and see him.'

'That's quick,' Howard remarked, still reluctant, I sensed. Both he and Noel were astounded by the speed with which our pursuit of Kevin was developing.

'We have to move fast,' I told them. Now that I was executive director of the organisation, I was determined the FA's days of dithering were over. 'If we can pull off the coup of getting Kevin as England manager it will be great for the team and great for the FA's image,' I said. 'Kevin will enthuse people. He always does.' So the pincer movement on Kevin began. I made the first train out of King's Cross to Darlington. Noel travelled from Manchester, Howard from Sheffield. We were soon driving into the Wynyard Estate, heading towards Kevin's home. His wife, Jean, whom I got to like a great deal, welcomed us. Kevin appeared, overflowing with bonhomie as he led us into the spacious lounge. What struck me about the Keegans' house was how lived-in it was. It felt a real home. After a few pleasantries, Kevin, Noel, Howard and I got down to business. Kevin had an immediate shock for his guests.

'I'll help my country out but I don't want the job full-time,' Kevin announced. 'I'll do three or four games until the end of the season. But that's it.' We were taken aback. Kevin left the room, leaving the three of us to consider his proposal.

'Look,' I said to Howard and Noel after a pause. 'We all know what Kevin is like. He'll love this job. Once he gets a taste, he'll want to do more than three or four games. He'll get the bug.' I was desperate for Kevin to become England manager. He had a good track record; even those who never supported Newcastle respected what he did at St James's Park. The country would rally behind him. Kevin was the People's Choice. So we agreed with Kevin's request. Negotiations began immediately on the deal. Nic Coward and Mike Cunnah represented the FA, with Neil Rodford leading the way for Fulham. Complications soon blew up. At one point, I thought we might lose Kevin. The sticking point was money. When Bobby Robson managed England, he was not the best-paid person at the FA. Ditto Graham Taylor and Terry Venables. The chief executive was always the highest-paid employee. Good for Graham Kelly. Glenn Hoddle changed all that. Keegan was looking to take it on again. We had a bit of a wobble but eventually agreed terms. Members of the selection subcommittee were well aware of how generously Premier League clubs had begun rewarding their managers.

Everybody seemed thrilled when Scholesy celebrated Kevin's first game with a hat-trick in a 3–1 win over Poland on 27 March 1999. Al Fayed came to Wembley and presented me with a huge Fulham scarf in the Banqueting Hall.

A deal done for four games, Kevin changed his mind after three. We were in a hotel room in Budapest on 28 April, when Kevin said: 'David, I want to be coach full-time.' I was taken aback. I'd hoped he'd become smitten, never realising it would be so soon.

'OK, that's fantastic news, Kevin,' I said. 'You know how highly we all regard you.'

'But, David, I want to bring in Arthur Cox full-time.'

'I'll talk to the International Committee.' They refused.

'Cox is sixty and Keegan already has Derek Fazackerley,' came their answer. 'Why does he need someone else? It will cost us money.' That view was wrong and I felt for Kevin. Somehow, probably, I should have found a way to make it happen. Arthur was his trusted ally, his sounding board. Arthur did join England, but not full-time. At least we had Kevin on board permanently.

England were still fortunate to qualify for Euro 2000. Sweden did us a huge favour by beating Poland in Stockholm when even a draw would have sent the Poles through at our expense. I sat with Kevin in a deserted Sunderland boardroom, watching that game on TV. Outside, half-a-dozen camera crews waited in anticipation of England's demise. When the Swedes scored, Kevin stayed remarkably calm. Much to my embarrassment, my own whoops of delight were picked up by the microphones outside the door. We survived a play-off with a Scottish side well up for revenge for Euro '96.

With the Scots back home, England headed to Euro 2000. The atmosphere around the camp was good. The suggestion that cliques emerged under Kevin only later became accepted wisdom. The new chief executive, Adam Crozier, mentioned it after Kevin resigned. I never saw any real divides in the England dressing room. Did the Manchester United, Liverpool and Arsenal players socialise in individual groups? Yes. Was there hostility between those players? No. They were not bosom pals but they certainly weren't at each other's throats. England's squad seemed happy. Kevin spent more time socialising with the players than Terry or Glenn ever did. When Kevin walked into a room where the players were, it was like an electric charge going through the place. He had that presence. Kevin bantered with them, played cards with them, a harmless exercise blown out of all proportion in the media. All the talk of gambling dens at Spa, England's Euro 2000 base, was ludicrously overdone. Did a number of players play cards a lot? Yes. Alan Shearer and Michael Owen liked cards. Were they sitting around, wagering wads of notes on cards? Not to my knowledge. Players need to fill down-time between matches, and card-schools are not the greatest evil. But I did ask Kevin about the gambling. 'There is absolutely nothing anybody should be concerned about,' Kevin said. 'You know, people play cards.' Kevin enjoyed cards and I never felt it was damaging. These were players already earning fortunes.

Kevin was one of the lads. People wanted to play for him. Kevin liked the squad because there were some real characters in it. Robbie Fowler and Steve McManaman were very clanny, always together.

'Where's Robbie?' someone would ask.

'With Macca,' everyone would answer. And life was always fun when McManaman was about.

'I used to watch you on television,' said McManaman, aware of my career at BBC North West. 'If I didn't do my homework, I was made to watch you!' We regularly exchanged insults. I was sorry McManaman wasn't recognised as a truly special player for England. When Steve was on song, he was bloody excellent. But watching him around the hotel at Spa, I never felt Steve enjoyed international football temperamentally. He got bored during tournaments. Such a naturally bright guy required more to stimulate his mind than hotel life.

At Spa, Kevin held a meeting every morning. Everyone piled in: Howard, Les Reed, the security people and Michelle Farrer. We used to bring cakes and biscuits and sit around plotting. The meetings worked very well. Unfortunately, the results at Euro 2000 were less impressive. But we did take a 2–0 lead against a team as good as Portugal before shipping three goals. We beat Germany, admittedly not the best German team in history. England then made a hell of a mess of the game with Romania. And we were out. Keegan was criticised by Martin Keown, who wrote in the *Daily Telegraph* that the England manager was 'tactically inept'. Martin was entitled to his opinion – and maybe later events vindicated him – but it was not a view shared by everybody in the dressing room. A number of the players, particularly senior ones like Shearer, were upset by Martin's comments. England's players liked and respected Kevin.

After Euro 2000, an inquest was held internally. Remembering the euphoria after England defeated Germany, no one felt Kevin should lose his job. The FA are traditionally loyal to managers. They stuck with Ron Greenwood and Bobby Robson during tough times. They kept faith with Kevin. On arriving as chief executive in January 2000, Adam Crozier inherited Kevin. Adam could have bombed Kevin out after the Euros, but stuck by him. We all did. 'Kevin just needs more help,' Geoff Thompson was reported to have remarked. If Geoff made what was a reasonable observation, I was concerned by how Kevin would react. Help? The chairman was implying Kevin wasn't up to the task on his own and required a helping hand. 'It's very difficult for us as lay people to tell a football manager he needs help,' I said to David Dein. 'That's quite a big thing to say. Kevin believes in the staff around him and still wants Arthur Cox full-time. But bringing in some other coach as well he would see as undermining him.'

Geoff's reported view was quietly forgotten, probably wrongly. The FA could never have imposed an experienced coach on Kevin. He was happy to go on, guiding England as the focus turned to Japan and South Korea. Everyone knew how high the stakes were as England prepared for the opening World Cup qualifier on Saturday 7 October 2000. The opposition were Germany, old enemies. The match marked Wembley's farewell before the bulldozers rolled in (eventually). We wanted to bring the curtain down on a positive note. A good start to our 2002 qualifying campaign was vital.

My confidence drained away as the week wore on. Shortly before the build-up began, Kevin's mother passed away. I wanted Kevin to have the maximum time to do what sons must do when they lose parents. I worried about how this emotional man would react. Would he be in the right frame of mind to take training, to pick the ideal team? Yet Kevin turned up at Burnham Beeches in a remarkably positive mood. The tension really kicked in on Thursday, forty-eight hours before kick-off. Kevin informed the press that Steven Gerrard would play against Germany. Steven himself spoke. After the news conference, Keegan took a private training session with the players at Wembley. No cameras, no media. England managers are obsessive about secrecy before the game. During the open sessions, the opposition might have a spy watching. So Kevin was determined England's final practice should be behind closed doors. Few knew Stevie picked up a small injury. I certainly never knew, so I never informed the media. At eleven p.m., Kevin told me Stevie was out, which was awkward as the morning papers were going to be packed with Kevin talking about how keen he was on Gerrard.

Friday saw a hostile media hunting Kevin. The news conference at Burnham was a nightmare. David Lacey, the *Guardian*'s esteemed correspondent and not a gentleman given to confrontation, acted as media spokesman and let Kevin and me know his anger big-time.

'Kev, you deliberately misled us,' David said. 'You told us Gerrard was playing but he's not. You should have told us the moment you knew Gerrard was injured.' Kevin was gobsmacked. A savaging by the *Guardian* was a rare experience.

'This is the slippery slope, Kev, if you're misleading people,' concluded Lacey.

'I've obviously upset Mr Lacey,' responded Keegan. 'We didn't mean to mislead you.'

'We've noted it down, Kev,' Lacey concluded. 'We've noted it down for future reference.' I couldn't wait for the ordeal to end. When we escaped the bear-pit, Kevin let rip. He was seething.

'It was not a bloody conspiracy to deceive the media,' Kevin said. 'I don't know why you bother about any of this lot.' The day's shocks had not finished. Kevin had decided to play Gareth Southgate in midfield. Southgate? A centre-half? In midfield? I think it was a surprise to the nation, and not least to Gareth himself.

Friday's horrors kept coming. That evening, I tuned in to *Hold The Back Page*, the Sky show featuring journalists discussing the week's big issues. Kevin's decision to start Gareth in midfield was ridiculed by everyone around the table. Their verdict was that Kevin couldn't survive if England lost a vital qualifier to Germany in the last game at the old Wembley. Thanks. Kevin hardly needed reminding how important the match was. My phone trilled almost violently. A furious England manager was on the other end. 'Are you watching this?' asked Kevin. 'It's disgraceful. They have just told my team to the Germans. Whose side are they on?' Kevin was incredibly worked up. I tried to calm him. The last thing England needed was a manager at war with the world before a key qualifier against Germany, with Finland to come four days later.

'Kevin, after next week you won't have to talk to them for ages,' I said. 'Get this game and Helsinki out the way, and then it'll all go quiet. Don't worry about the press. Who cares? Just sleep on it. Just go and win the game. Then life's easier.'

My forebodings worsened. Before a match England dared not lose, Kevin was clearly distracted. Worrying about him and the game, I hardly slept. In the middle of the night, I looked out of the window and watched the rain fall. Even the new dawn brought little lightness. The skies were coloured a filthy black. London beckoned for a meeting, but I delayed my departure from Burnham. I had to see Kevin, to show my support and wish him luck. My heart dropped even further when an unshaven England manager walked into breakfast. He looked unwell. The sparkle I loved about Kevin had gone. He had the weight of the world on his shoulders. We're going to struggle against Germany, I told myself. The manager didn't look ready for the challenge. Kevin mentioned the Sky programme again.

'I can't believe what they were saying,' said Kevin, still wound up.

'Look, Kevin, just forget it, right? Let's just worry about today. We'll deal with all this after the game.' I did my best to cheer him up. A man who wore his heart on his sleeve, Kevin needed to be positive. England's dressing room would instantly detect the manager was feeling the heat. Criticism did get to Kevin. Far from thick-skinned, Kevin found the level of scrutiny that went with England very difficult. He was hurt by what happened at Newcastle, and the disparaging comments lobbed at him for walking away. Kevin remembered those who supported him and those who didn't. The criticism on the morning of the Germany game depressed Kevin further. At breakfast at Burnham, England's management and players devoured the papers. Ray Clemence read everything. Kevin's plan for Southgate had hardly been well received. I hated the media that day.

Another bloody omen then filled me with even more dread. I never saw Kevin before kick-off to give him my usual 'good luck' message. The match bore out my worst fears. Dietmar Hamann scored for a German team that was far from great, England lost, and the old Wembley closed down in humiliation. Even the heavens wept for England. As the game ended, I remembered the FA had organised a huge firework display. Oh, no. As a disconsolate Kevin trudged from the field, the rockets fizzled up into the monsoon. Oh, my God, I could see the headlines already: 'Damp squibs' and worse.

No one at the FA could have predicted what happened next. I went down into the South dressing room to see Kevin. Even with the bitter taste of defeat in his mouth, Kevin had to face the cameras. He had to voice his belief that England would qualify for the World Cup. On entering the dressing room, I couldn't believe the scene. Steam poured out of the showers, making it difficult to see who was where, but I glimpsed Kevin in one corner. Tony Adams, David Beckham and other players sat around in various states of undress. They screamed at me.

'David, you tell him not to do it,' shouted Tony, who was completely fired up.

'David, he'll listen to you,' pleaded Becks, who was in tears.

'What?'

'Talk to him,' Tony said.

'Who?'

'Kevin!!' Tony and David both yelled. They didn't need to tell me what Kevin had done. He'd thrown in the towel. I knew it. I looked at Kevin.

'Don't leave. You have to stay.'

'No, no, no,' Kevin replied. 'I'm off. I'm not for this.'

'This isn't happening,' I thought. I wasn't prepared mentally for such a situation. Think fast. Calm things down. Lock away the emotions. Shift into work mode.

'Come on, let's go,' said Kevin, 'I'm ready to face the press.'

'No, you're bloody not,' I retorted. 'We're having a talk before you go anywhere near the press.' Where on earth could we find that was private? The tunnel? Crawling with television reporters. The dressing room? Heaving with emotional players. The bath area? I couldn't hold a vital conversation with an England manager as players dived into the water. Only one option presented itself. The toilet cubicles. A dramatic moment in England's long football history occurred in the ancient loos of a stadium facing demolition. The impending destruction could almost be smelled in the air. Dragging Kevin into a cubicle, I shut the door behind us. We stood there, facing each other. Kevin and me.

'You can't change my mind,' Kevin said. 'I'm out of here. I'm not up to it. I'm going out to the press to tell them I'm not up to it. I can't motivate the players. I can't get the extra bit out of these players that I need.' At that point, I knew that all the pleas of David and Tony, all my appeals, would fall on deaf ears. Kevin's mind was made up. What struck me most about Kevin was his composure. He was finished with England. Game over. Reign over. Even though I knew I was wasting my time, I tried my hardest.

'You can't leave now,' I said. 'What the hell are we going to do in Finland?' Kevin shrugged. 'You'll sort it out. It's best I go now. When I walked off the pitch, I looked up at the fans and felt they didn't support me anymore. I'd lost the fans.' I knew how much that would hurt Kevin. For the People's Choice to have lost the people was too much to bear. Kevin cared passionately about England. Was he being weak in walking out? No. I felt his decision took immense courage. First, owning up to not being good enough was pretty brave. Second, other managers might have hung on, knowing one day they would get the sack and a nice pay-off. That was never Kevin's way. He was a man of principle, a creature of instinct and his instinct told him: GO.

I appealed to his patriotism, to his loyalty to his players. 'Kevin, why don't you sleep on it?'

'No. I want to go now.' Kevin moved to open the cubicle door, which wasn't exactly far.

'Wait,' I said, pulling him back. 'I'm sorry. We're not going anywhere. I'm bloody responsible for the situation now. I'm not having the people who employ you hearing that you are off from the bloody television. We have to let them know first.' That was only right. I dreaded the image of all the FA hierarchy gathered in the Banqueting Hall, drinking their tea, eating their sandwiches and then listening to a breathless reporter on the TV revealing the England manager had resigned. Noel White and the International Committee deserved to know first. Adam Crozier had to be informed. A fire burned around England and we had to tackle it quickly, without the media fanning the flames first.

'You're staying here and I'm going to find them and get them here,' I told Kevin. Mobile reception was minimal, so I went out into the tunnel, looking for an internal phone. Milling outside the dressing room were people like Michelle Farrer, the team administrator, and the TV reporter Clare Tomlinson, who'd left the FA for Sky.

'What's going on?' Michelle asked.

'Where's Kevin?' enquired Clare. 'When's he coming out to talk?' Clare's producer was probably screaming for some post-match reaction from the England manager.

'He just needs a bit more time,' I replied. That was completely false but I had to win us some time. Finding a phone, I got through to Adam and Noel. 'You'd better get down here fast,' I said. 'It's Kevin.' Down they came. 'Keep walking, say nothing,' I'd told them. Clare and all the reporters in the tunnel now knew something was definitely up. The sight of the FA's decision-makers piling into the England dressing room clearly signalled something serious had happened. Quickly, I briefed Adam and Noel. There was obviously no room in the cubicle for all of us, so Adam, Noel, Kevin and I decamped to the dressing-room area. By then, all the players were in the bath. The players had stopped pleading with Kevin. They knew it was over.

'Do you really want to do this?' Adam asked Kevin.

'Adam, I just can't take the team further,' Kevin repeated. Adam and Noel knew it was over. Kevin went off to explain his reasons to the media and thanked the FA for our support. I respected Kevin for saying that. It was true. We had all backed Kevin. He had been left alone with the team. No interference. No pressure. Of course, if Kevin had then lost in Helsinki, I doubt he would have survived but I admired his decision to walk now, even though it gave all of us an almighty headache. Not many nations lose their coach in the middle of a World Cup qualifying double-header. Kevin left Wembley, severing his association with England, stopping briefly at Burnham to say goodbye to his staff. I stayed behind at Wembley, sifting through the wreckage with members of the International Committee. Adam was impressively decisive.

'Let's meet properly in Finland, but for now we'll put Howard in charge for Helsinki,' said Crozier. Howard was on his way to the under-21s' base at Sopwell House. On hearing about Kevin's resignation, he almost drove off the road. News spread fast. Even as Adam, myself and the International Committee members were leaving the Banqueting Hall, calls were coming in, putting names forward as Kevin's successor. He'd hardly been gone an hour but already agents and friends were promoting certain individuals. The whole process of appointing an England manager was about to occur again. People accused the FA of having no contingency plan. How could we? England are not like a bank. You cannot have the England manager knowing the FA have a replacement ready to step in. Paranoia would run rife. Contingency plans are difficult; anyway, who expects their most famous employee to resign in the loos?

Under Howard, England drew in Helsinki. Even if Ray Parlour's shot had gone in instead of hitting the bar, Howard would still never have got the England job. Adam already had other plans. As I waited for Howard to begin his post-match news conference, I looked at our World Cup qualifying table and saw England had played two, no goals, one point. Even Albania were above us. Another shock lay just round the corner. Wilkinson sat down and uttered the immortal phrase: 'Maybe we should let the 2002 World Cup go and concentrate on 2006.' At that very second, I wanted to stand up and scream. Oh, that's bloody brilliant! Let's forget about qualifying for the 2002 tournament in Japan and South Korea! Let's just say we are not good enough, we're going to run away and hide and reappear with a better team for 2006! As ever, Howard meant well. In the media, it would look terrible. I couldn't believe what I'd heard. The press would slaughter Wilko for flying the white flag over 2002. Glancing at the writers, I caught the eye of Martin Samuel, now of *The Times* but then of the *Daily Express*. This was always dangerous because Martin made me laugh. He was giggling over Howard's not very cunning plan. The irony was that Howard's scepticism over Kevin's technical prowess on his appointment had proved justified.

England landed home at four a.m., and when I reached my flat at the back of Lancaster Gate, I immediately turned Sky News on to check whether the nightmare was really happening. Yes, it was. There was the table. England were bottom. We needed a manager of substance to inspire the players, to go where Kevin Keegan couldn't and wouldn't take England. And we needed him desperately.

9

Sven

When we all sat down in Helsinki four days after Kevin's dramatic resignation, Adam Crozier didn't waste any time. Howard Wilkinson was elsewhere in town, preparing the team for the World Cup qualifier against Finland, and Adam was looking further ahead. He produced a huge blank piece of paper, pinned it on the wall and listed candidates to be the next England manager. Noel White, Dave Richards, David Dein and myself chipped in with suggestions. Very quickly there were twenty names from home and abroad. Before the conversation advanced far, I wanted one subject addressed straightaway. 'What about Terry Venables?' I asked. Since Wembley, to nobody's surprise, Terry's name had attracted considerable support in the media. Terry's friends in the press could always be relied upon to champion his cause. A long silence ensued. Eventually, one by one, they said it: 'You can't go back.'

'I've taken several calls since Wembley from people who disagree,' I responded. 'They want Terry back.' Over the following days, I had a series of private conversations with the others about Terry. But from that early moment, I knew we weren't going back.

'We should go foreign,' ventured Dein. Was he about to offer Arsene Wenger from his own club Arsenal? No. 'What about Sven-Goran Eriksson at Lazio?' Dein continued. 'I talked to

Athole about Sven.' That was no shock. I knew David and Athole Still had been in contact less than an hour after Kevin's resignation at Wembley. Even at the FA, events can move fast. David had long known Athole, Sven's adviser and friend. David backed Sven and I quickly gained the impression that Adam was keen on Sven. The moment Adam broke with FA tradition and actually began listing criteria for the post, I thought everything pointed to Eriksson. 'The right person must have a consistent track record of success,' Adam insisted. 'He must have dealt with big-name players. He must be able to deal with the media pressure.' Sven ticked all those boxes. Other names did make Adam's famous piece of paper. For all the 'don't go back' caveats, Venables was on it. So was Arsene, Alex Ferguson, Marcello Lippi, Bobby Robson, Fabio Capello and Roy Hodgson. Adam also scribbled down younger English names like Peter Taylor, Bryan Robson and even an untried, untested Alan Shearer.

'But first we need somebody for the Italy game,' Adam mentioned, focusing on England's imminent friendly in Turin. Between Adam and myself we came up with the idea of Bobby Robson as caretaker, assisted by two young coaches in Taylor, the Leicester City manager, and Steve McClaren, Ferguson's no. 2.

'We have to talk to their clubs,' said Adam. I phoned John Elsom, Leicester's chairman.

'Can you release Peter for a week?' I asked. John, ever helpful, agreed. So far so good. 'Fergie might be more difficult,' I said to Adam. But not only did Alex agree to see us, he immediately took to Crozier. Maybe it was a Scottish thing. Maybe it was because Adam, as always, was good company. 'Can we borrow Steve?' Adam asked. Looking at Alex, I feared a blast of the notorious hairdryer. He could have sent us packing but he didn't. In agreeing to our request, Fergie probably saw it as a good opportunity for Steve. Talking to Ferguson, we also knew England was out of the question for himself. Sir Roland Smith, who several years earlier had not discouraged me from putting forward Alex's name, this time told me off for distracting him hours before a big game.

The final hurdle was Newcastle. We found Bobby incredibly keen, which was hardly a shock. A special man, Bobby's patriotism runs deep and he jumped at the chance. He had unfinished business in Turin, scene of England's semi-final heartbreak in 1990. Although the understanding was for a temporary role, Bobby felt it could lead to a full-time position. The hero returns! Newcastle's chairman, Freddy Shepherd, feared that once Bobby got a taste of England again, they would never see him back. On 21 October, we had a huge to-do with Newcastle. 'We can't let Bobby go,' said Freddy bluntly, ending the matter. Bobby was as furious as we were disappointed. We still had Peter and Steve to take charge for the trip to Italy.

With Turin sorted, Adam and David Dein resumed the search for England's full-time boss. I canvassed Tony Adams, Alan Shearer, Gareth Southgate and others about the dressing-room view, a move criticised by some of the International Committee. 'We don't support talking to the players on matters like this,' Dave Richards told me. I felt it right to consult. The feedback was: no. 1 scenario, Terry coming back; no. 2, Ferguson or Wenger; no. 3, the right foreign manager. Terry still aroused too much opposition at the FA. Wenger and Ferguson had ruled themselves out. But the players' willingness to work under a foreigner was good news as a certain Swede was coming through at a rate of knots. The job was Sven's for the taking.

The FA also polled fans, discreetly gauging likely reaction to the appointment of a non-Englishman. Little hostility could be detected – provided the new man spoke English. Wenger had changed the perception of overseas managers; England fans were now more open-minded. Armed with that intelligence, we felt Sven would be given a chance. Newspaper criticism spilled notably from the widely read column of Jeff Powell in the *Daily Mail*. An experienced Fleet Street operator always fair to me, Jeff's view was perfectly valid. The coach of the England team should be English. English for Jeff equalled Venables. But talking to people within football, I heard the widespread view that the best-qualified person to succeed Keegan was foreign. Other than Terry, where were the English managers? Kevin, by his own admission, had been found wanting.

'Can you get me Sven's record as a manager?' Adam asked. I prepared statistical documents about Sven, Roy Hodgson and Peter Taylor. Enquiries were made into Sven's background, the usual personal checks. To my knowledge, the FA never asked Sven: 'Do you have any skeletons in your cupboard?' Why the hell should a governing body investigate the love life of a distinguished coach? Sven's reputation was untarnished by any hint of wrong-doing or corruption. Yes, our soon-to-be new manager had a new girlfriend called Nancy Dell'Olio, who sounded quite colourful, but why would we be bothered about that?

'Let's get him,' was Adam's approach. Along with David, Adam flew to Italy in a private plane to meet Sven. The deal to bring Sven to England was sealed in the Rome flat belonging to Dein's daughter, Sasha, who spoke Italian and was studying there. Sven and Athole drove a hard bargain, which the FA agreed to. Believing he was getting the best, Adam was prepared to pay for it.

My choice of restaurant on Monday evening 30 October proved propitious. I was half-way through an Italian meal around the corner from Lancaster Gate when Adam called. 'We've got Sven,' said Adam, unmissable excitement in his voice. 'David and I are on our way back. Sven's staying on with Lazio a bit longer.' When Adam landed, he called again. 'Nightmare flight,' he said. 'We got hit by an electric storm coming into Luton. I thought we were going to die.' The FA got their coach but almost lost their chief executive and most high-profile board member. 'Anyway, we need somebody to fly back out and bring Sven over for a press conference. You go.'

'I will,' I agreed, 'as long as I don't have to go on your bloody plane.' I did. Fortunately, the weather was fine on the Wednesday morning as I climbed into this tiny jet with Sasha Dein. Her knowledge of Italian would be useful. Bank-holiday sleepiness clung to the Italian capital, except near the Olympic Stadium. Serie A was in business.And Lazio were expecting me. 'If you win,

Sven will accompany David back,' Adam had agreed with Lazio's president, Sergio Cragnotti. 'Sven will give a press conference early on Thursday and then fly straight back to training with Lazio. If you lose, Sven will not fly to us.' What happened if Lazio drew was left vague.

My secret mission was going well. At the private airport outside Rome, no one noticed a representative from England and the attractive daughter of an FA bigwig quietly arriving. At the Olympic Stadium, the mission began to lose its secret element. Outside the VIP car-park, a jobsworth stood as unyielding as one of the many statues that guard the route to the ground. Inevitably, loads of photographers and camera crews lurked by the gates, looking to snap stars arriving to see Lazio. They kept peering into the car, and soon twigged it was 'the man from England coming to take Sven away'. I imagined the headlines: 'FA man blocked outside Lazio'. My cover was blown. Signor Gate-man refused to budge. 'Sod it, let's walk in,' I said to Sasha. With a Sky camera crew zeroing in on me, my attempt at nonchalance was not easy, particularly when I casually strolled round to collect my raincoat from the car boot and cracked my head on the door. Operation Bring Sven Home was not running smoothly. Lazio gave us seats in the directors' box, a kind gesture that allowed photographers to find me more easily. The Italian media were on the case as well. Fact and fiction raced around the Olympic Stadium. Was Sven leaving for good today? Who was this classy woman sitting next to the man from England? I was very aware of people staring at Sasha and me.

At that moment, Sven wandered out of the tunnel to take his place in the dug-out. He waved warmly in our direction. 'I pray he wins,' I remarked to Sasha. 'If Sven loses, we leave empty-handed. And God knows what happens if it's a draw.' At which point Lazio went one down. 'This is all going swimmingly well!' I added. Lazio still trailed at half-time. Cragnotti was behind me, doing a series of interviews with Italian crews.

'Sasha, can you go and find out what the hell they are talking about?' So off Sasha went.

'No alarm,' she said. 'It's all very pleasant.'

'Thank God. Now all we need is a couple of Lazio goals.' Lazio equalised, and then Fabrizio Ravanelli came on and scored the winner.

'God's on form,' I thought. Time to find England's new coach. Lazio were as good as gold. Any frustration they may have felt at losing Sven was well hidden. An official led me to Sven. Absolute mayhem reigned outside the dressing rooms but Sven was completely relaxed. I introduced myself.

'Sven, I am David Davies from the FA. It's good to meet you.'

'Hello,' said Sven. 'I'm looking forward to the flight.'

'I've arranged a car to take us to the airport.'

'No,' Sven replied. 'I have my car here. I will drive us. I know where the airport is. You come with me.'

'Fine!' Waving goodbye to Sasha, I jumped into the four-wheel-drive belonging to the first foreigner in history to be responsible for England's football future. We hadn't gone 100 yards down the road when Simon Greenberg rang. Now Chelsea's Director of Communications, Simon worked for the *Mail on Sunday* back then. 'David, can you confirm you are being driven through Rome by the highest-paid taxi driver in Western Europe?!' Simon asked. Sky had shown me getting in Sven's car. I told Sven. He laughed loudly. 'Very funny!'

As we sat down in the plane, Sven took my copy of that day's Italian newspaper and wrote: 'To my new friend, David. Sven-Goran Eriksson.' Keen to reciprocate the gesture, I dug out the bottle of champagne I'd smuggled on board. We toasted the future. On that flight, I discovered that Sven was completely different to his image. He was not a cold fish. He was not a distant Swede. Sven was thrilled to be England manager. 'I have such respect for England,' he said. 'Enormous respect. I know the players of England are very good. I am excited. I look forward to working with them.' Listening to Sven talk, I quickly gained the impression that he might be somewhat daunted by the task. Despite all the hype about huge salaries the truth about Sven-Goran Eriksson was that he was slightly insecure. He was thrilled but maybe a little surprised that his career had taken him where it had. This guy from a small town in Sweden, little Torsby, didn't always have huge self-confidence.

After landing at Luton, we drove to Sopwell House in preparation for the following day's official unveiling. Sven was well received. Only one person demonstrated against him, the famous 'John Bull', a fan given to marching up and down outside Soho Square with his placard. I was the devil incarnate to 'John Bull'. He was always taken aback when I used to wander across for a chat. He was a Brummie well known outside the troubled Longbridge car plant near my West Midlands home.

Whatever the critics claimed, Sven went on to do well as England manager: 40 wins and only 10 defeats in 67 matches. England qualified for all three tournaments under Sven. When we lost in Moscow under McClaren, a few people remarked to me: 'Well, you must have experienced that, a qualifying defeat in some distant place.'

'Actually, no, I hadn't,' I replied. 'Sven rarely lost qualifiers.' We did lose in Belfast, when Windsor Park was rocking. Mainly we were fine. Sven's first away game came in the weird land of Albania on 28 March 2001. For years cut off from the world under Enver Hoxha, Albania had been that European novelty, a country whose regime was closer to Beijing and Chairman Mao than to Moscow. The only Western films deemed unlikely to corrupt Albanian youth were Norman Wisdom's. When I learned this, I smiled. We could have some fun here. During my BBC years in Manchester, I did a film on tax exiles in the Isle of Man and met Norman. Finding a number for his PR people, I asked: 'Would Norman like to come to training and meet the England players when we get to Tirana.'

'He'd love to,' they replied. We were used to our players being mobbed at training sessions but when Norman Wisdom arrived, the Albanians went crazy. They loved him. Norman was unbelievably popular. I made sure he was introduced to Peter Taylor, whom Sven had brought on to his coaching staff. One of Peter's many talents was a brilliant impression of Norman Wisdom. 'Go on, do your Norman Wisdom,' the players beseeched Peter in Tirana. Initially, Peter went all coy on us, which was unlike him. Eventually, he did his best 'Ooo, Mr Grimsdale', much to the delight of Norman and the players.

Apart from that moment of light relief, Tirana was chaos. England stayed in a hotel on the pot-holed main drag that was constantly noisy. The weather swung between baking hot sunshine and teeming down with rain. Dear old Sir Brian Hayes, our security expert, got terribly worked up about the crowd permanently gathered outside, and sometimes inside, the hotel. Strangers wandered around seemingly everywhere. Welcome to international football, Sven. At the ground, the pitch was a mess. Spotting Albanians lobbing missiles everywhere, I sought sanctuary on the bench. A lighter hit my shoulder. I flinched. 'Calm down,' said Steve McManaman, whose tranquillity amazed me. Albanian fans were throwing everything. Ashley Cole was struck by lipstick. But England won, a splendidly recurring theme on the road with our new Swedish coach.

Memories of another away qualifier under Sven will for ever be in English hearts: Germany in Munich. 'The one thing we don't want to do is lose an early goal to the Germans,' I said to Michael Cunnah as we walked into the Olympic Stadium on 1 September 2001. We duly did. Michael and I were seated behind Nancy Dell'Olio and a friend of hers, who took out a lamp when the German goal went in. She began rubbing it. 'Don't worry, it's going to be fine,' she said. 'England are going to win this game.' She kept rubbing it as Michael and I looked on in astonishment. As Michael Owen made it 1–1, Nancy's friend just rubbed harder and harder. Then Steven Gerrard scored that fantastic goal to leave England 2–1 up at half-time. My mind flooded with bizarre thoughts. As a veteran of England's Eileen Drewery era, I didn't know how to react. I hadn't known Sven and Nancy very long and here was a friend of hers, seeming to demonstrate magic powers.

Pray God, no cameras. Perhaps Nancy's friend ought to be on the bench? When the score reached 4–1 with nineteen minutes left, my natural manic depressive's reaction reflected how long I had been at the FA. 'God, what will people say when it's 4–4?' I remarked to Michael Cunnah. Only when England's fifth went in did I begin to believe we could hold on. I kept looking at this woman rubbing away at her lamp. Over a glass of champagne with Sven afterwards, I said: 'You know you won the game because Nancy's friend had a magic lamp.' Sven groaned . . . and then laughed.

After results like Munich, England's players took even more to this quiet Swede guiding them from the devastation of Keegan's last day. 'Sven's great strength is he has taken the emotion out of running the England team,' Gary Neville explained to me. 'Previously, everybody was a fan. Sven steps back and analyses.' His style of management was very informal. Sven moved amongst players, having a word here or there. The press would scream: 'SVEN SUMMONS STARS TO CRISIS SUMMIT MEETING'. But the 'meeting' was often just a chat, sitting on the grass after training. Eventually, Sven's unemotional demeanour on the touchline became a stick to beat him with. 'He doesn't care!' came the criticism. Nonsense. Sven cared as deeply as a manager like Barry Fry who charges down the touchline like some demented human being. I think the world of Barry and that's the way he shows his emotions. Sven's nature was easygoing, but I saw him angry, saw him act ruthlessly. A tough streak runs through all top managers. Sven dropped people. He discarded David James, for example. Players knew when he was disappointed in them. Just because he sat passively in the dug-out didn't mean he was detached from events. When David Beckham stepped up to take that last-minute free-kick at Old Trafford against Greece on 6 October 2001, everyone saw plenty of emotion from Eriksson. At 1–2 down, I feared England's World Cup hopes were history. Only a few seconds remained to claim the draw to secure qualification to Japan and South Korea. I loved those long-gone days at Old Trafford where it always seemed that injury time was dependent on how Fergie's watch was working that particular day. Electronic boards are rather boring now. Fortunately, the good people at United had given me a seat with plenty of room to run up and down if England scored. When Beckham's free-kick sailed in, I cavorted with the best of them, hugging Paul Barber, the FA commercial director now at Spurs. Sven's appointment was proving a success.

A national icon, England's new coach fascinated the media. We warned him. 'The media will be obsessed with everything about you, professional, personal, everything,' Adam told Sven. David Dein and I reiterated the message.

'Sven, we will have press conferences when football will not be the first, middle or indeed the last subject that comes up,' I told him. He laughed.

'I can't believe that,' Sven replied. He soon found out. Sven's private life proved a rich seam for newspapers to mine. In April 2002, the story broke about Sven's affair with Ulrika Jonsson. We had all been at Lancashire County Cricket Club for a Prince's Trust do the morning after a Champions League game at United. Sitting next to Ulrika, I found her lively company. I've always enjoyed women's company more than men's and quickly noticed Sven was the same. Sven was in the fortunate position that a remarkable number of women found him attractive. They tell me when Sven talks to a woman he makes her feel she is the only woman in the world. He shows an interest and is funny, qualities women seem to warm to. Sven was never the Ice Man as portrayed, and certainly not with women. When Sven zoomed in on Ulrika, my instinct was that their relationship was never going to lead to anything apart from an increase in newspaper sales. England were big news. So was Sven, a leading man in a soap opera that captivated the world. When Ulrika's au pair came out with some supposed revelations, Sven ignored them, his habitual way of defending himself. As the arc-light of the media burned on him, Sven never flinched. He disliked having his private life dissected by everyone, but he put on a very brave face in public.

'In Italy and Portugal, they criticised me only for football,' Sven said. 'Here, we have a press conference and they ask me about my private life! David, I think you should deal with the press conference and then I will come in when the journalists want to talk about football.'

'Sven, what you must understand is that there is an extraordinary appetite for celebrity tittle-tattle,' I explained. 'The papers consider your private life fair game.'

'Well, I cannot believe people are really that interested in my private life,' he said. 'Why?'

'Because it's great fun,' I said. 'It's your fault; if you were duller, people wouldn't be interested.' Sven laughed. Only towards the end of his time with England did Sven begin to think his private life might be considered exotic to other people.

'I am a single man,' he told me during the Ulrika affair. 'Why cannot I see other women?' Sven regarded himself as a single man. 'What's the issue?'

The issue was Nancy Dell'Olio, who lived in Sven's house and considered them a couple. Whenever a story emerged of Sven and another woman, Nancy's reaction was wonderfully defiant. She dressed up and looked ever more glamourous. Nancy was 100 per cent Italian style wrapped up in a stunning red suit. The cameras feasted on her.

Nancy was fun. I loved gossiping with her about the FA, football, travel and her work with Truce International. Nancy wanted to save the world. This was no ego trip. Nancy cared. As personalities, Sven and Nancy are chalk and Gorgonzola. Nancy is fiery and fragile. Sven is controlled and strong. Whenever they emerged from a restaurant, and were pounced on by the paparazzi, Sven frowned. Nancy smiled. She enjoyed the publicity. She was as happy to see a camera as Sven was unhappy. Always an attractive woman, Nancy loved seeing her picture in the papers. I like people who add immeasurably to life's rich tapestry. I was also intrigued about what was the glue that kept them together.

Colourful in clothes and thoughts, Nancy was great copy for

interviewers. One evening, Sven and I were in a black cab hurtling down Piccadilly when we both spotted a billboard bearing a startling headline. 'Nancy and Sven: we're having babies'.

'David!' Sven eventually said when he regained his composure. 'This is news to me!' Nancy had given another interview.

Predictably, Sven and Nancy's love life provoked some pretty bitchy coverage. Some of those who regarded themselves as traditionalists at the FA admitted to being embarrassed by the publicity. I don't think the public moralised that much. They just thought: 'Good luck to you, Sven, but just keep on winning.' And England generally did, at least until they got to quarter-finals. In fact, Sven enjoyed a lengthy honeymoon period by the usual standards of England coaches. Our public opinion polling showed how popular he was, and people didn't even know the private charity work he did. Generous financially, Sven quietly gave significant donations to good causes. 'Of course he should,' the cynics will cry. 'He earns loads of money.' The answer to that is Sven was also generous with his time. When Sven travelled around the country watching England players, I laughed when people criticised him for leaving early. This is what happened: I would lead him down the stairs, through reception, head for the car-park, turn round and there would be no England coach. He was signing autographs, sometimes scores of them.

'Sven, you've definitely been accepted by the English,' I told him one day.

'Why?'

'Alistair McGowan and Rory Bremner have mastered you!' Sven took the next opportunity to watch the programmes. He loved Ronni Ancona's impression of Nancy. On one trip, some England players got hold of a DVD of a McGowan show and passed it around the team hotel like precious contraband. Players disappeared, watching McGowan mimic Sven so brilliantly, before returning, their faces wreathed in smiles. One night, the DVD was on in the masseurs' room, and the players in there were chuckling away. Completely absorbed in the programme, they didn't hear the door open behind them. Only when this light Scandinavian laugh was emitted did they turn round. Sven stood in the doorway, smiling away.

Japan beckoned. 'I don't think we will win the World Cup,' Sven told me as we flew out, 'but we will do well. This is a magnificent job but it is also very, very difficult. I try to build a team and then I lose a player. I lose Gerrard. I lose Neville.'

For a change, England's tournament build-up was relatively low-key. No dentist chairs. No damaged hotel rooms. I raised a glass to Roy Keane for taking the spotlight off England. After Roy fell out so spectacularly with Mick McCarthy, the feeding frenzy centred on the Irish camp. 'Did you organise this diversionary tactic?!' our security man Ray Whitworth asked me. Sven was amused that everyone suddenly ignored England because of Keano.

'It's a hell of a blow for the Irish losing Keane,' one of the players remarked. When Keane talked about how poorly the Irish players were treated in comparison to England's, that went down particularly well with the FA staff working overtime behind the England team. Giving the players the best chance to repeat 1966 was my constant aim.

Searching for the perfect base in Japan, we travelled far and wide inspecting hotels. Every place we visited said the same thing: 'We've already had one federation here.'

'Who? The Germans?'

'No. The Dutch.' Holland failed to qualify but it showed their attention to detail. Finally, I chanced upon a secluded hotel called the Westin on Awaji Island near Kobe. The one problem was the constant noise and pollution from some very visible earthworks next door. 'ENGLAND PLAYERS POISONED' was not the headline anybody wanted at World Cup 2002. The local mayor became my best friend when he suspended work there during the tournament. Brian Scott, England's travel manager, soon arrived to check on the Westin. Awaji so excited me, I had an idea waiting for him. 'If England fly in to Kobe, don't you think it would be great if Beckham landed here by boat?' I suggested. 'It would look fantastic. England's captain on the bridge, leading the team on a great adventure. *Treasure Island* and all that jazz.' Brian loved a boat trip but he wasn't convinced. The straits between Kobe and Awaji looked rather choppy, I had to admit. It was also the epicentre for the Kobe earthquake in 1995. The Beckham Boat Plan was quietly shelved. Goldenballs arrived by coach.

Awaji was a huge success, though. The players loved it, as did the Japanese kids riding up and down in the lifts all day, hunting for autographs. 'Go and explore Awaji,' I urged the players. When we took the three keepers, David James, David Seaman and Nigel Martyn, to a local school, the children were left speechless at how tall these visitors were. They kept looking and staring in disbelief. David James joined me and Gareth Southgate at a temple. We experienced a tea ceremony, gaining an insight into a different culture. Players like Gareth and David don't want to hang around the hotel all the time. They want to expand their minds. 'The biggest problem with most English players is what they do between matches,' Sven told me. 'They get bored so easily. Why do they need a games room with so many funny machines in it? Why don't they talk and read and enjoy TV? You don't have this problem so much in other countries.' Sven wasn't the first and certainly won't be the last England coach to struggle with players' 'downtime'.

Matches soon arrived to occupy them. After an opening draw with Sweden in Saitama, England flew to Sapporo for a grudge match with Argentina. Ill-feeling from St-Etienne still lingered, and our players were particularly pumped up. 'We're going to do Argentina,' the players kept saying. Even though the squad lost warriors like Paul Ince and Alan Shearer, the hunger remained huge. Sven didn't need to motivate the players. Argentina were overcome and Beckham enjoyed his moment of redemption, converting the winning penalty. A draw with Nigeria in Osaka took England into the knock-out stage. We could draw breath.

Travelling around Japan gave me an opportunity to get to know

Sven's valued assistant, Tord Grip. When Sven stayed calm, Tord very often didn't. That was why they were such a good blend. I loved Tord to bits; he was warm, witty, with a great curiosity about the world. On one flight, we sat down next to each other, took out our books and both burst into laughter. My book was on the Taliban. Tord had the Swedish translation. On another flight I treasure the memory of Tord playing his accordion, which he took with him everywhere. Athole Still, Sven's agent, was also a fascinating character, a former swimmer and opera singer of some repute. After winding Athole up, I'd ask him to sing. What a voice he had. A terrific singer with a great repertoire, Athole can still hit all the notes.

Music was often in the air in Japan. In one of England's hotels, a group of us, including International Committee members, were sitting in the bar when Noel White, chairman of the International Committee, found the hotel piano too tempting. Noel wandered across to illustrate his talents on the ivories, and he's pretty good. The only problem was that Sven and England's coaching staff were holding a meeting near by, and couldn't hear themselves think because of Noel's ragtime blues. Rarely had I seen Sven so perturbed. How do you tell the man whom you suspect agreed your wage demands that he should pipe down?

After beating Denmark in Niigata, England ran into the elegant juggernaut of Brazil. When Ronaldinho's cross-shot sailed over David Seaman's head, my heart went out to the big Yorkshireman, a lovely bloke and bloody good keeper who never deserved this. From my schoolboy years, goalkeepers have always fascinated me. Most must be bonkers but nicely bonkers. Of course, there's glory in saving a penalty but keepers are known for their mistakes, which tend to be fatal. 'If I'd played to be a hundred, people would still remember that Charlie George beat me in the '71 Cup final,' Ray Clemence, England's goalkeeping coach, told me. Mad but true. Clem was one of Liverpool and England's greatest ever keepers. He understood how keepers are always a split-second from ignominy, which was why he rushed to David, a broken man in floods of tears.

Where it all started, outside the family shop and dairy off the Euston Road in London, Grandpa and my father on patrol in 1948. Months later, Dad was dead.

Davy Crockett invades the Euston Road, 1952.

Correspondent, Presenter and stand-in for Stuart Hall, *Look North* 1975. The hair's real.

Miss Great Britain 1975. Susan Cuff at the Motor Show had yet to meet her greatest challenge.

Miss Great Britain 1975 with the man of her dreams.

Charity Match, 1976, organized by Tom Pendrey MP at Stalybridge Celtic FC. 'Stuart Hall's Layabouts' included then-Manchester City Manager Tony Book, then-Manchester United manager Tommy Docherty, myself, plus Nick Clarke and Tony Wilson, both great broadcasters now dead.

General Election campaign 1987 with Dr. (now Lord) David Owen for the BBC's *Nine O' Clock News.*

ansfer to BBC Midlands Today, 1988. Fee Undisclosed.

Debut with the England team for the BBC at Italia '90, Peter Beardsley, Peter Shilton and Gazza.

Graham Taylor and friend at Fiumicino Airport in Rome during Italia '90. Both were eventually to endure life at Lancaster Gate.

Where's Gazza? With Terry Venables on our first trip together to the Olympic Stadium in Rome in February 1994.

With England in Hong Kong hours before the infamous dentist's chair incident pre-Euro '96.

Legend has it that the last Prime Minister before Tony Blair to visit Lancaster Gate was William Gladstone, who used to pop in very late at night. Graham Kelly looks concerned.

On the staff minibus at La Manga prior to World Cup 1998.

Glenn Hoddle behind the shades explains why Gazza will miss World Cup 1998.

A not unusual start to the day outside The FA, 1999.

ghten up, Howard. With Technical Director and occasional England Coach, H. Wilkinson, at embley 1999.

Reunited with Kevin Keegan, whom I'd known as a player, during his first stint as manager of Newcastle. Venue: House of Commons.

Suits meet players pre-match at Wembley; England vs. Scotland in November 1999. Hair loss was a serious danger during an FA career.

Euro 2000 in Charleroi with my first and only wife, Susan. The stand behind appeared to shake when England scored against Germany.

’n the bench in Tirana, Albania 2001. Steve McManaman next to me had an uncomfortable evening.

Bringing together Fergie and Sven for the NSPCC, April 2002.

Gifts from a Japanese Temple at World Cup 2002. Note the 'happy jacket'.

Adam Crozier gets his man – with Sven, 2002.

;uest of the Afghanistan FA in Kabul months after the departure of the Taliban. Their stadium still ›rovided evidence of the atrocities committed.

›rsenal vs. Southampton at Cardiff, May 2003. The first FA Cup Final indoors with the roof on – as ›e sun shone outside.

Sven and Mark Palios meet the most famous woman in the world at Buckingham Palace 2003.

'Ask Sven', a charity breakfast for the Prince's Trust at Old Trafford Cricket Ground in 2003. Ulrika Jonsson (2nd left) had spent the previous night in Manchester as well.

'ootball Writers Dinner at the Savoy, January 2004. Palios, Bevington, Richard Keys of Sky, Ray
'tubbs of the BBC and myself plus partners, including Faria Alam. 'A jolly evening' according to the
'Aail on Sunday.

'gland Team congratulates Sir Trevor Brooking, Portugal 2004.

Football and footballers as a power for good. David James, Rio Ferdinand and Gary Neville in Lilongwe, Malawi, in May 2005.

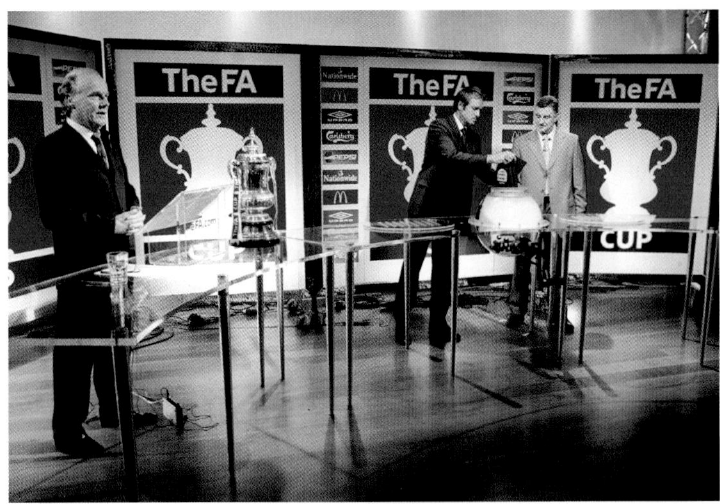

The FA Cup Draw, the nation's only programme live on terrestrial and satellite TV, BBC and independent radio. John Scales and John Aldridge doing the honours.

WAGs alert – Elen Rives and Carly Zucker (partners of Frank Lampard and Joe Cole) with Nancy Dell'Olio and my Susan at World Cup 2006.

Mission accomplished. A day trip from Baden Baden to Manchester and back confirms Wayne Rooney will be part of World Cup 2006 despite his metatarsal. England doctor, Leif Sward, and security man, Terry Wise, were with us.

Davies, Barwick and Brooking – still dreaming of World Cup success in Germany, June 2006.

Sven on the way to his last training session with England before World Cup elimination, on penalties again, in Germany.

A new era? But not for long. Steve McClaren with his England captain, John Terry, weeks after I left Soho Square for the last time, October 2006.

Plenty of ups and downs, but keep smiling.

What went wrong against Brazil? To my dying day, I'll believe the absence of Gary Neville was a huge burden to England. Against Brazil, Gary would have raged, fought and got the team going. Was Beckham 100 per cent fit after his metatarsal travails? No. 'We have nobody better,' Sven said. 'We haven't got a better person for free-kicks, corners and crosses.' Would a more tactically inspired coach have found a way back against opponents, even Brazil, down to ten men? 'Yes, for certain,' screamed Sven's critics, growing in number that day. Privately, we'd all worried about the players' fitness levels. Compared to other nations in Japan and South Korea, England players lacked conditioning and stamina. The only player with a really good fitness level was Owen Hargreaves, who played in Germany at the time. The long, unrelenting English club season certainly took its toll that hot and steamy Friday afternoon.

As ever in the wake of tournaments, the period after Japan was full of raw pain and uncertainty. To much sadness, Doc Crane left. 'I thought we had a leaving do for you after France '98!' I told him. 'We'd better have our leaving present back!' Immediately, I missed the Doc, a lovely man. Everybody adored him. Doc Crane would stand on the bus, take the microphone and tell a terrible joke. The players just fell about laughing. It was the Doc. He cracked people up. I sensed he hadn't enjoyed the Japan World Cup as much as others. Indeed I later learned that differences of opinion within our medical team had been a feature of that expedition. Sven ensured it didn't happen again.

After Japan, Sven came under greater scrutiny. On 12 October 2002, Ulrika picked a sensitive moment to bring out her book *Honest.* England were in Bratislava where all hell broke loose on the eve of the Euro 2004 qualifier against Slovakia. A fan was shot on England's hotel doorstep. Fighting erupted outside. David James filled his 'down-time' by filming the trouble out of his window. Now Ulrika's potential bombshell was about to land. I talked to the new Director of Communications Paul Newman about Ulrika's book. 'Do we know what's in it?' I asked Paul. 'I can't believe Sven would talk about the players to Ulrika.' He hadn't. Ulrika rose in my estimation. She could have put salacious material into her book simply to sell it, but she didn't.

Life was always interesting with Sven. On 12 February 2003, England faced Australia in a friendly at Upton Park. 'I'm going to play one team in the first half, and another in the second,' Sven said. Under FIFA rules, Sven was completely at liberty to do that. Nil–two down at half-time, Sven told the players none were staying on, and several weren't happy. Typically Beckham and the rest wanted to rectify the mess. Sven wouldn't be swayed. He sent out another team and got slaughtered by the press, particularly when four people wore the captain's armband at the old home of Bobby Moore. The outcry perplexed Sven. 'When else am I supposed to experiment?' he asked. 'When am I allowed to see other players?' I pointed out the national sensitivity towards the England armband going around like pass-the-parcel. 'I have to keep my word to the club managers,' Sven said. Clearly he had understandings with people like Alex Ferguson, promising them certain of their stars would play only a half. He always kept his word.

'I am beginning to believe England are not the number-one priority of English football,' said Sven. 'We need all the clubs to support England.'

'I agree. I'll get the managers together.' John Barnwell at the League Managers Association and Dave Richards at the Premier League delivered. Fergie and Arsene came, so did Gerard Houllier from Liverpool. Kevin Keegan, then with Manchester City, called me. 'David, I'm not coming but you know what I think about England,' said Kevin. 'I haven't got any players in and around the England team at the moment, but you know I'll always support England.'

The managers all sounded sympathetic to England's plight – with reservations. 'I will always support England in competitive games,' said Ferguson. 'It's matches in April that are the problem because of the Champions League and the Premiership.' Surprisingly, none had issues with August friendlies. April friendlies were already on the way out at FIFA's behest. Arsene also had a request. 'When you have double-headers why won't you have matches on the Friday and the Tuesday?' asked Arsene. 'That allows players to get back earlier for the following weekend matches.'

'Arsene, take where you live, in London,' I replied. 'The Metropolitan Police do not like England games on Friday, Saturday or Sunday evenings.' Policing considerations weren't the first thing most managers thought about. Common ground was found and we all agreed to meet again. Sadly, it never happened.

The surprises kept coming with Sven. In July 2003, he was snapped going into the London home of Roman Abramovich, Chelsea's owner. 'Sven, I'm not upset you talked to Chelsea,' I said. 'I'm just upset you didn't bloody tell me.' Some long-standing friends at Chelsea were also rather slow in remembering the facts of their meeting with Sven. Those pictures caused chaos. Some within Soho Square were angered, with people chuntering on about how much Sven earned, wasn't he happy, shouldn't he show some bloody loyalty? When it had happened with Manchester United, I really had to calm them down. 'We should take it as a compliment that our coach, the man we appointed, is wanted by big clubs,' I told them. 'Sven's star is high. Naturally, clubs want him. And, by the way, it's not just English clubs. Barcelona and Inter Milan have enquired about Sven.' That was true. Sven was target no. 1 for many big clubs.

Sven was unfazed by the outcry. 'People ask me, so why can't I talk to them?' he mused. And why not? At the heart of the complaints was that England were so special it was treason to talk to anyone else. 'Well, in the real world, everybody talks about their future,' Sven said. 'It doesn't mean I'm running off to Manchester United or Chelsea.' Sven was also wary of people at the top of the FA. 'David, if I lose a few games these people will think nothing of getting rid of me,' Sven said. 'So it is interesting for me to hear what else is going on. If people approach me, does it mean I will leave England? Have I ever told you I want to leave?'

'Never.'

Sven's critics claimed he was the best-paid coach in the world. He certainly wasn't. People kept reading that Sven earned £5m a year. He didn't. He would have needed to win the World Cup every year to make £5m. We joked about it at Soho Square. 'What figure is Sven on this week?!' I laughed. Sven never took all the money talk seriously, but I found all the 'greedy Sven' jibes debilitating. The managers of leading Premier League clubs, like Manchester United and Chelsea, earned more than Sven.

Some English critics forgot what a star Eriksson was globally. Being with Sven abroad was like accompanying royalty. Everyone wanted to grab a word, an autograph or a photo. No wonder big clubs pursued him. Yes, Chelsea offered him the job. Yes, he was close to Abramovich. Yes, United were very interested in him. Yes, Sven would have loved to have been United manager. And, yes, I fought hard to keep him. 'Sven, you're doing a great job here,' I told him. 'If you bring home the World Cup, do you realise what a god you will be in England?' Sven understood. If I'd berated Sven, I could have been accused of hypocrisy. UEFA approached me about leaving the FA to work for them. Ultimately, the prospect of living in Switzerland seemed a bit far-fetched. I'm a bit of a home bird really.

Sven's loyalty issue rumbled on. When Mark Palios became chief executive after Adam Crozier, he called me into his office. 'I want a contingency plan on what we should do, who we should go for, if Sven leaves,' said Mark. So I examined the track record of ten or so candidates, including Fabio Capello, Marcello Lippi, Martin O'Neill and Sam Allardyce. No one was approached, it was just a plan for action. But I did tell Mark: 'I keep coming back to the person best qualified for the England job is the person who is in it: Sven.'

On the pitch, Sven had to steer England through a tricky qualifying campaign for Euro 2004, with Turkey a real danger. Bad blood flowed between English and Turkish fans. Leeds, Manchester United and Arsenal all ran into trouble with

Galatasaray. Tragically, two Leeds fans were stabbed to death out there. By the time we reached the fixtures meeting in Istanbul to sort out our Euro 2004 qualifiers, relations between England and Turkey were pretty raw. Sven stayed at home. He was happy to leave such meetings to his trusted assistant Tord and me. Our fears were soon realised. Their FA briefed the local press that England would play in Istanbul last, a coup for Turkey. 'No chance,' I told the Turks. A slanging match broke out between us. The other countries looked on in such amazement that eventually I apologised to them. Tord became so angry with the Turks that he threw a banana across the room. In the next break, I rang Sven. 'It's got so bad that Tord is launching fruit at the Turks.' I then went on an offensive with the Turks. More strategy, less fruit. 'Our flight is at four o'clock, thanks very much, so we must leave,' I told them. 'We'll have to get UEFA to draw lots.' The Turks almost exploded with rage as Tord and I walked out. Sod's law, when the lots were drawn, England ended up in Istanbul last! Tord's banana flew in vain.

Affronted, the Turks were particularly insulted when we turned up without our fans. 'Don't you think we can handle a big game?' they said. We decided not to take up our ticket allocation because we feared England supporters would be ambushed. With Turkey pursuing EU membership, the situation was very sensitive. Government became quietly involved and a decision was made to travel without supporters. Fans' groups understandably worried about a precedent being set. But it was the right call. The players enjoyed another good away day under Sven, getting the point to ensure England fans went on an even better trip: Portugal.

Before Euro 2004, Sven and I worried what shape the players would be in. In February and March, we embarked on a mission through the corridors of power to rescue England's drained players. 'We need a winter break,' Sven kept saying to anyone who would listen. This would be too late to help England at Euro 2004, but it could be in place for the 2006 World Cup. Sven and I addressed the Premier League chairmen, who voted 19 to 1 in favour of the principle of a break in late January. Only Richard Murray of Charlton Athletic opposed it. Sven then presented our case to the Professional Game Board of the FA. He was very persuasive. 'What I'm proposing is in the national interest,' he told the most powerful group of people in professional football. 'It is for the benefit of your players, your clubs and, yes, for the national team as well.'

Sven then played his ace: some stunning research by the highly respected Professor Jan Ekstrand at Linkoping University near Stockholm. With UEFA's backing, Ekstrand compiled a report comparing injury levels in those countries with a winter break, like France, Italy, Holland and Spain, to those without, namely the Premier League. 'The project found that during the last three months of the season the injury risk was four times higher in teams without a winter break,' Sven informed the Professional Game Board. 'That is the physical price we pay. We don't know about the mental and psychological price.' Sven was really into his stride, utterly convincing, and I felt his audience shedding any scepticism. As club people, they had watched some of their stars, like David Beckham, limping off with metatarsal breaks in the second half of the season. 'How can Italy, Spain, France, Holland and Greece and all the top European countries be wrong in having a winter break and England right in not having one?' said Sven.

His proposal for a thirteen-day break in January, missing only one weekend, with seven days' complete break followed by six training, was approved by the Professional Game Board. Next up was Ken Bates's Challenge Cup Committee, who weren't opposed to the winter break but certainly weren't prepared to do anything to help England in terms of scrapping Cup replays. Otherwise, the majority backing for a winter break lifted Sven's spirits.

'David, we have the support of the chairmen of the Premier League, the support of the Professional Game Board and the support of the FA Council,' said Sven. 'We surely will get a winter break?'

I preached caution. 'Nothing is simple in English football,' I replied. 'We could still run into problems.'

We did. Sven and I ran into a very charming, very astute roadblock in the form of Richard Scudamore, the redoubtable chief executive of the Premier League. Outwardly neutral, Richard effectively obstructed a plan that would have breathed life into jaded England internationals. Scudamore had committed to so many live televised games that it was a struggle to fit them in. I understood his dilemma. Sky Sports' managing director, Vic Wakeling, fought TV's corner. Having shelled out more than a billion quid, Vic didn't want the season messed with. In his heart of hearts, this shrewd and highly successful Geordie probably felt a winter break would help England but not Sky. After inspecting the fixture-list, Vic wrote to me on 15 April 2004, concluding: 'We are a long way from making this work.'

Sven was dismayed. I had to explain the Premier League and TV method behind the madness. 'If you spend January in the Far East, right, you can't see any French football, any German football, any Italian but the good old English are ploughing ever onward,' I told Sven. 'It's about showing games live in the Far East and in England. That's why they don't want a winter break.' For a winter break ever to come in, all those powerful club managers who do want to press the pause button in the fast-forward season must insist a January break is included in the next TV contract when discussions resume in 2009. Back in 2004, England players had to hobble towards Portugal.

Euro 2004 mixed pleasure and pain, England's usual summer cocktail. After losing to France in Lisbon, England put on a far better performance in defeating Switzerland. In Coimbra, German TV picked up Alexander Frei spitting at Stevie Gerrard. Shortly before Stevie and the rest were due to face Croatia, Michelle Farrer received a crazy email from UEFA. They explained they were considering disciplinary proceedings against Frei and instructed Stevie to give evidence the night before the Croatia game. Simple as that. Ask Stevie to leave the camp, spend hours in a UEFA disciplinary commission room, when he should have been resting up! Madness. Or were they serious? Michelle immediately informed

Sven, who went ballistic. 'Our players are not going anywhere before a game,' said Sven. 'It is crazy. David, sort it out.' I talked to UEFA, who remarkably hadn't realised Stevie had an imminent work appointment with the England national team against Croatia. Stevie was loath to give evidence anyway; Liverpool's captain was not the type to squeal on other players. 'Can we give you a written statement?' I asked UEFA. Eventually, they agreed. Reluctantly, Stevie gave his version of events, the statement was dispatched to UEFA and Frei was banned. Stevie duly played against Croatia as a quarter-final place was won.

Confirming Ekstrand's verdict on how brittle England players became from March onwards, Wayne Rooney then broke his metatarsal against Portugal. With Rooney, we might have won. When John Terry's goal was, I thought, ridiculously ruled out, I'm afraid my language would have shocked a docker. The inevitable penalty embarrassment followed. As the inquests began, Ivan Carminati, England's fitness expert, declared he thought Beckham wasn't fit. Ivan's comment didn't stun me. I don't think David himself felt he was right, either, but who would have done better? The depression around the England camp took time to disappear. Sven's spirits were lifted by a supportive message from Tony Blair, who told Sven that he should be proud. Those two got on well. Whenever Sven and Blair met at functions, they had this running gag about their job prospects.

'You'll be gone first!' the Prime Minister would tell the England manager.

'Well, I think you'll be gone first!' the England manager told the PM.

The PM got it right, but not by much.

When the dust settled on Euro 2004, Sven cast around for ways of strengthening his England squad. By chance, FIFA opened a window of opportunity, allowing countries to register players born elsewhere but who had lived a certain amount of time on their shores. 'I like Carlo Cudicini,' Sven told me. Chelsea's keeper was an obvious target for England. He'd never represented Italy, met the residency requirement to play for England and was obviously a class goalkeeper. Prompted by Sven, very serious consideration was given within Soho Square to recruiting Cudicini. But Clem was particularly concerned about Sven's pursuit of him. As England's goalkeeping coach, Clem told Sven it would destroy our own keepers. 'Can you also find out about Steed Malbranque, Edu and Louis Saha?' Sven asked me. I wasn't sure what the public reaction would be to an Italian, a Brazilian and two Frenchmen coming into the squad, but I did Sven's bidding. However, all my discreet enquiries to clubs and agents led to nothing. Miraculously, the moment our interest became known, Saha was called into the next France squad and Edu was summoned by Brazil.

Denied a winter break, Sven pleaded for a decent preparation period before the 2006 World Cup kicked off. He was determined England's players should have better fitness levels than in previous tournaments. We hatched a new plan. It involved an informal and swiftly arranged meeting with Sepp Blatter. FIFA's president was staying at Claridge's, so Sven and I popped in for tea and a talk. 'Mr President, we are not here on behalf of the FA,' I stressed. 'Sven and I are here as people concerned about the health of national-team players. Sven believes passionately in the need for a four-week break before major tournaments.' Sven spoke eloquently about how vulnerable players were to injury.

'I absolutely agree with you,' said Blatter. 'We must have a four-week break before the World Cup.' Lo and behold, a FIFA decree came down from on high to that effect. Brilliant. My heart then fell through the floor when our chairman, Geoff Thompson, wrote to Blatter, saying: 'You know we support a four-week break but we would like a dispensation for teams in the FA Cup final to have only a three-week break because of the opening of the new Wembley.' An English initiative with special dispensation for flipping England! Sven went apoplectic about Thompson. So did I.

'Do you realise how much this undermines our case for a decent break before the World Cup?' I asked Geoff. 'This is an almighty spanner in the works.'

'I hadn't realised,' replied Geoff. Meekly, he claimed he had been under pressure from elsewhere within Soho Square. I was astonished. Here we were trying to revive England, being let down by our own people. It was crazy.

Barriers were erected everywhere. Again my friend, Richard Scudamore, was opposed to us. I sensed his closest colleagues, Mike Foster and Philip French, now Senior Advisor at the DCMS, were less anti, and ultimately recognised the strength of our case. 'The England manager's job shouldn't be full-time,' Richard Scudamore and, on occasions, Dave Richards would suggest.

'Scud, that's just lunacy,' I'd always reply. 'The logic that the England job shouldn't be full-time when most other national team jobs are escapes me.' Dave Richards sometimes agreed with Scud, sometimes with me. Those who felt Sven shouldn't be full-time argued that the England manager only had six or seven competitive games a year. 'And why do we need friendlies?' they added.

'If we don't have friendlies, England will never play teams from outside Europe other than in World Cups, if we're lucky enough to qualify,' I replied. 'We'd be mad not to have friendlies against Brazil or Argentina.'

Sometimes, frustrated at running into walls when I was trying to help England, I took work problems home. Susan was unimpressed, understandably so. I was endlessly on the phone, endlessly on edge. I lived the job. I lived to help England, to give other people the memories I took from Wembley in 1966. 'I can't go on like this,' I told Susan a couple of times. 'Do I really want to kill myself, banging away at trying to give England a chance of a better future when others don't feel the same?' Every time I contemplated chucking it in, the squad would meet up, all the banter would start again and my love affair with England would resume. Whenever I turned up at the England camp, and saw Sven, the players and the staff, I realised how privileged I was.

Christmas 2005 was the best and worst of times. Early in December, I was in the House of Lords, enjoying a festive drink with Tony Banks, the former Sports Minister and one of the wittiest men I've ever met. Tony was delighted to have been made a lord. 'They asked me what title I wanted,' said Tony, 'and I replied: Lord Banks of the Thames!' As well as a wicked sense of humour, Tony shared my view of how football could be a power for good around the world, so I asked him where I should take Sven on a goodwill visit, a place where Sven could bring some hope and publicity. 'Take Sven to Botswana,' Tony responded immediately. 'They have a terrible HIV/Aids problem. Sven could help raise funds and awareness.' Tony knew people in Botswana and promised to arrange the trip.

When I called him, Sven sounded keen and we agreed to talk with Tony again when everyone returned from their Christmas breaks. Sven went to Sweden. I headed off to Australia with the family. But two days before flying home, I received a phone-call from Jane Bateman, whose development work for the FA in so many countries is a source of real pride and prestige for the organisation. The tone of Jane's voice immediately betrayed something awful had occurred. 'Tony has collapsed and died in America,' said Jane. Tony's death was a huge shock. He was a brilliant but often infuriating Sports Minister and his death left a hole in politics.

More bad news ensued when I was tipped off that Sven was about to be exposed by the 'fake sheikh' in the *News of the World.* Sven had been taped on a boat in Dubai making apparently indiscreet comments about his interest in a job at Aston Villa and about bungs to managers. Totally predictable carnage followed. When the story broke, Brian Barwick, our latest chief executive, immediately asked some of us to hurry to Soho Square for a crisis meeting. Athole Still came as well. Although Brian respected Sven as a coach, his mood was obviously now anti-Sven. Brian had never really built much of a relationship with him, and had always hankered after a coach of his choice, not Adam Crozier's. Sven's contract was until 2008, but it was obvious Brian wanted him out after the 2006 finals. Brian asked me my view.

'One of three things could happen at the World Cup,' I began. 'One: we are going to do really well, which I hope, and we might even win it. Two: we could do really poorly and then Sven's position is untenable. Or three: England could do somewhere in between, where again Sven's position would be untenable.' Privately, I felt that even if Sven did well, at least reaching the semis, he would walk anyway. After five years, he had already become almost the longest serving national team manager in the world. Whatever happened on the pitch, Germany was going to be the end of the road for Sven and England. What was disappointing to me that day was that several months earlier, I'd produced a document for Brian, urging a resolution of Sven's future then. I'd assumed he would be going after 2006.

But now Brian moved very quickly. 'Sven's contract will be terminated at the end of the World Cup,' Brian informed Athole and Sven's lawyer, Richard Des Voeux. A pay-off was discussed. Having unwittingly helped cause the furore by organising Sven's trip to Dubai, Athole and Richard were negotiating from a position of considerable weakness. Brian was pretty fired up over Sven's behaviour. However, there was never any chance Sven would be fired there and then. 'We must focus on the World Cup,' Brian said. He was right. It would have been pointless changing managers months before a tournament we felt we could win. We all knew Beckham and the rest of the players still backed Sven.

The whole fake sheikh farrago was bloody annoying, though. 'How on earth did you get caught up in this?' I asked Sven later in the day.

'I just went on this trip to Dubai, it was arranged by Athole,' Sven replied.

'But, Sven, you have no proof of the corruption you were talking about?' I asked. He hadn't. No one could substantiate whispers of dodgy deals. What Sven unwisely told the fake sheikh was the type of gossip always circulating within football. There is a naïvety to Sven, a trusting streak and he got burned by the fake sheikh. Sven would often muse aloud about football, and he was taped doing just that. But how big was his crime? Did I think Sven would abandon England to join Villa before the World Cup? No,

I certainly didn't. Sven had enjoyed a few drinks. For all his annoyance at falling into such a pit, Sven never lost any sleep over it.

The real burden for him was the turmoil in his private life. His relationship with Nancy was not working out. She didn't want to split up with him. He felt a responsibility towards her, having gone through what they had, when she left another man for him. Sven's unhappiness nagged away at him in Baden-Baden, England's World Cup base. Heading into Germany, I knew Sven was privately deeply unhappy with the direction his relationship with Nancy was going in. Sven was distracted during the tournament. Sven's a friend, and I hated seeing him as down as he was in Baden-Baden. I tried to jolly him up. 'Think of how the fans behaved towards you at Old Trafford,' I reminded Sven. At the end of his final game in England, the 6–0 defeat of Jamaica at Old Trafford before we flew out, the fans chanted his name. So he walked towards the centre-circle, in that slightly embarrassed way of his, to respond to the fans' applause. He gave a little wave, a nod of the head and retreated. Sven never saw himself as a special one.

If Sven was privately downcast, England's mood was positively flying on the way to Germany. Sven even decided to take it upon himself to rid me of my fear of flying. 'Go and sit in the cockpit,' Sven commanded. So I did. The pilot let me take the intercom.

'The first piece of bad news for everybody is that I'm in charge of this plane,' I announced. 'The second is to say "happy birthday" from the cockpit to Trevor Brooking.' This was a long-standing joke I had with the elegant Brooking; wherever we went, I tried to organise birthday greetings for him. Trevor was now seventy-five years old, according to my announcement. All the players laughed, as did Sven, but I remained worried about his inner mood, and some of the critical barbs increasingly flying his way. After five years with England, Sven was accused of having taken up residency in the comfort zone. Perhaps that happens to most public figures after a time. I don't accept it happened to Sven. 'This World Cup is a great opportunity,' Sven told me. For all his melancholy over his private life, Sven felt confident about the World Cup.

Not many people disputed his squad. OK, there was a debate around Theo Walcott, Arsenal's teenager untried even at club level. OK, perhaps he should have taken a striker from Spurs reserves, Jermain Defoe, or a forward from Charlton Athletic, Darren Bent. Otherwise, his squad was well received. He had a core of players he trusted. Sven was loyal to players, maybe too loyal. 'Loyalty is important,' Sven always told me. 'I believe I selected what I thought was the best team for the day.' Funnily enough, some of those who criticised Sven for chucking around caps like confetti against Australia at Upton Park now accused him of being too loyal. That's football. Theo apart, few argued about Sven's final squad. Before Sven announced his party, he and Nancy came over to dinner with Susan and me at our new flat in north London. They arrived in a black cab with the paparazzi trailing them as usual. Nancy and Susan quickly caught up on gossip, so Sven and I stepped on to the balcony. When Sven relaxed, he was fun, very open, liked a drink, and a talk, particularly now. 'David, how do you think people will react if I take Theo Walcott to the World Cup?' Sven asked.

'They'll react!' I replied. We both laughed.

When I then met Theo, I realised how young he was. He made me feel incredibly old. Theo's parents, great people, were younger than me. It felt so different from when Sven took a teenage Wayne Rooney to Euro 2004. Theo was completely different to the bullish Rooney.

'How are you finding everything with England?' I asked him a few days into our stay at Baden-Baden.

'Fine,' he said. But he looked slightly lost.

Steven Gerrard, I knew, was unimpressed with Theo's choice but Sven had made his judgement. Would having Defoe or Bent at the World Cup have changed our fortunes? No. Anyway, how was Sven to know when he selected his squad that Michael Owen would be carried off and Wayne Rooney sent off? If Theo had come on during the World Cup, the criticism would have been less. He almost did. 'I was about to use Theo,' Sven told me after the draw with Sweden that carried us into the last sixteen, 'but then Gerrard scored and I wanted to be more defensive.' Stevie had given England the lead with five minutes left but sadly we couldn't hold out.

After Michael suffered that terrible knee injury against Sweden, I had the awkward task of phoning his Newcastle chairman, Freddy Shepherd, to discuss the predicament of a player he paid handsomely. The reaction was likely to be pretty splenetic, so I got my sympathy and diplomacy in first. 'I want to say how sorry I am about what has happened to Michael,' I told Freddy. Newcastle's chairman made it quite clear that his club would require substantial compensation. 'You haven't heard the last of it,' he said. Unlike most countries, England insured players but not sufficiently, according to many of the biggest clubs, Newcastle among them. Ultimately a compromise was reached, and FIFA were part of that. Insuring and compensating clubs for the use of top players in internationals was an ever more controversial issue during my FA years. Around the world, many national associations just cannot afford the costs involved. FIFA and UEFA always had to be the answer.

Having beaten Ecuador in Stuttgart, another quarter-final with Portugal awaited. As the players gathered to board the coach for Gelsenkirchen, I sensed real optimism. Sure, there was respect for Portugal but Sven's players definitely believed they could reach the semis. Being superstitious, I was always wary of omens with England, though. As we came off a slip road on to the Autobahn towards Gelsenkirchen, an out-of-control car shot across in front of us, burying itself in a bank. Our bus screeched to a halt. Hours before the kick-off of a World Cup quarter-final, England players were parked on the hard shoulder looking at the wreckage of a car. Luckily the occupants were OK. We finally set off again. This was it. Each man knew he had to deliver. Each fan knows what happened next. Rooney dismissed. St-Etienne revisited. Heroic display by ten men. Penalty fiasco. Again. England's departure from the 2006 World Cup was the biggest disappointment in my life. Questions raced around my mind. Should Sven have brought Walcott on against Portugal? Possibly. But the team were doing OK with ten. Aaron Lennon had a great chance. After Rooney was sent off, Sven was amazingly phlegmatic. Other managers would have ripped into the ref. Not Sven. 'It wasn't to be,' Sven told me. 'It was fate.'

He was crushed inside, though. The burden of responsibility on behalf of the English public got to Sven big-time. That Saturday night in Baden-Baden was like a wake. No one got paralytically drunk, but players and staff all had a few drinks. Coaches and senior staff sat together until three a.m. with long periods of silence. Sven was absolutely distraught. At 2.30 a.m., everyone somehow managed to lift themselves for a presentation to Michelle Farrer on her birthday.

In the morning, the pain hadn't eased. If anything, it was worse. I packed, avoided watching television and rushed downstairs to check my bags in before the WAGs arrived at ten a.m. Seeing Steve McClaren, I suggested a final coffee and chat. 'You know, I expect David to pack in the captaincy, probably live on television,' I said to Steve. I had no advance knowledge. Together, we watched spellbound as Beckham did just that, and Sven went through the purgatory of a farewell news conference. I knew what it was like as well for Adrian Bevington, the FA's Director of Communications, sitting by Sven's side. I'd recruited Adrian as a young press officer from Middlesbrough only a few years before. Now here he was in front of the world. Been there, done that – it hurts like hell.

'I'm also waiting for the first person who says the players "don't care enough about losing",' I added to Steve. Another prediction that soon came true. A few days later, Clive Woodward criticised the footballers' apparent lack of passion. I was shocked by that. I wanted to say to him: 'Clive, you need to meet some of these guys.' England players were heartbroken by the horror of Gelsenkirchen. After the final whistle, I saw John Terry and Rio

Ferdinand close-up – both in tears. Beckham trudged back into the hotel after announcing he was handing back the England captaincy – in tears. For the rest of the day, I rarely saw Beckham not in tears. Everyone hurt.

Flying home, the wound deepened. England's plane made two stops, Stansted and then Manchester for the northern boys. Susan and I were picked up at Stansted and driven to north London, passing all the flags outside people's homes in Tottenham, Manor House and Finsbury Park. Debris was piled everywhere. Decorations hung limply outside pubs. Inevitably, the driver wanted to talk about Eriksson's tactics. I didn't. Every cab resembled a mobile interview room where I was grilled endlessly about Sven, Becks, Rooney, penalties, WAGs, the works. The inquisition was so persistent I gave up cabs and rode buses everywhere. That was worse. People kept asking me about England. My pain was particularly deep. My last chance of helping England had gone. I'd already decided I was leaving the FA in September. On reaching the flat, I received a text saying England's flight onward from Stansted had been delayed. Then another relayed info that it was being diverted from Manchester to Liverpool by the weather.

'That won't have gone down well with Gary Neville!' I tried to cheer myself up.

The inquest into England's failure was bitter and brutal. Even a day out at Wimbledon, and getting the sympathy of the always generous folk who run the All England Club didn't soften the blow. The critics claimed Sven wasn't up to it, his tactics were too timid, Rooney alone up front was too great a burden on him, Walcott was a waste of time and the WAGs were a serious minus. Wrong, wrong, wrong. Theo's inclusion may have proved an unsuccessful experiment but you still must ask whether Defoe or Bent would really have made a significant difference to our World Cup? Ultimately, Sven was too decent and reasonable with everyone over the years, certainly the FA and the Premier League and its clubs and managers. After Germany he had a period of grieving. He shut himself away in Sweden, wondering what more he could have done. As a former club manager himself, Sven bent over backwards to help everybody else. The truth is that the FA and the clubs failed to give the national team the priority it deserved. Sven should have taken them on, breaking this wall of indifference to the national cause. If the Premier League had agreed a winter break, England's players would not have been running on empty by June. Did the most influential people in English football off the pitch give the guys on the pitch the best chance? No. England's players, not for the first time, were let down by the system. *Mea culpa*; I was part of that system.

Inside and outside Soho Square, people flailed out over the reasons for England's failure. The WAGs were an easy target.

'The players spent too much time with the wives and girlfriends,' said some of the older FA men like Dave Richards and Noel White. 'WAGs have no place at World Cups. The players have a job to do. Oh, and who was paying?'

'Actually, they did,' I countered.

Brian Barwick wasn't a fan of the WAGs, either. Barwick is a man's man. When we had our World Cup inquest, I knew I'd be expected to stand up for the WAGs. So I did. 'Blaming the WAGs for England losing on penalties is a huge red herring,' I told the FA leadership team, people like Barwick, Simon Johnson, Adrian Bevington, Sir Trevor Brooking and Steve McClaren, Sven's successor. 'It's an excuse and it's absolute nonsense. The idea that we didn't get beyond the quarter-finals of the World Cup because of the WAGs defies all logic.' I was quite steamed up over this non-issue. 'Were you really going to go against what the captain wanted for his team? Becks was very keen for the WAGs to be in Baden-Baden. I saw the players with their wives and kids after games, relaxing. Surely, that was better than them hanging about playing cards or endlessly draining their brains on games machines. There weren't WAGs in Sardinia before Italia '90 and I seem to remember a different story came out of there. The Great Hostess Scandal! All bollocks, by the way, but that caused real problems in the camp. And, by the way, who came down the steps of that Alitalia plane first when Italy came home with the World Cup? Fabio Cannavaro and Marcello Lippi. And after them? The Italian WAGs.'

I'd made my point. The WAG debate obscured greater failings, like penalties. Sadly, in our celebrity-obsessed society, the glamourous WAGs were manna from heaven. I suspect that Baden-Baden will prove the high point in WAG fever. When England next qualify for a tournament, God willing, I would be surprised if the WAGs got such a profile. But this perception of Sven's players not being professional was just nonsense. England's 2006 World Cup squad was the most serious England group I had ever known, whether working as a TV reporter or for the FA. They reflected their manager: professional, dedicated and distraught at the outcome.

When Sven finished with England, the easiest thing he could have done was disappear overseas away from the prying eyes of the English media. A resilient man, Sven stayed. He waited for a job to rebuild his reputation in England. He hated his year out of football. He loved being in England. 'I want the right club here, and to be a manager here,' he told me. When Manchester City came along, many people were sceptical. Sven did well. One night, I was with him in the Radisson Edwardian hotel in Manchester and he was bantering with a group of United fans. They respected him. He never hid. He enjoyed England. When he accepted the Mexico job, I very much doubted it was his first choice. It didn't surprise me one iota to see Sven depart City with his dignity intact. Sven is immensely polite but he did express his anger to the Thai owner, Thaksin Shinawatra, over City's treatment of him, which was shabby in the extreme. Through no fault of his own, he found the right club at the wrong time. I suspect he'll be back.

One night after he left City in the summer of 2008, Sven went to the House of Commons for a dinner. He stood up to take some questions from MPs. 'As a former England manager, what is your view of foreign owners?' Sven was asked. 'The Glazers have done well for Manchester United,' Sven replied. 'Roman

Abramovich has done well for Chelsea. Randy Lerner's done well for Aston Villa. I can't say what they have done for England!' His audience laughed. Several weeks later, even Sir Dave Richards, the Premier League chairman, echoed this view: 'Does the Premier League hurt the national team? Yes.'

Sven had learned the hard way that English football's refusal to give the national team the priority it deserves means that winning the World Cup or Euros remains highly unlikely. Sir Trevor Brooking has even questioned the FA's new objective of reaching tournament semi-finals at least, and whether that's realistic. Good fortune, not good preparation, will be a more likely explanation of any success unless we change our ways. Meanwhile, Sven is gone. English football will miss him.

10

Death by Shoot-out

When it comes to taking penalties at World Cups and European Championships, England's serial failure resembles Groundhog Day scripted by the Devil. After a good display, often battling stoically against the odds, England surrender meekly in the shoot-out time and again. OK, England outlasted Spain over twelve yards at Euro '96. Otherwise the dates, places and opponents are scarred in the memory of England players and fans: Turin in 1990 against West Germany; Wembley in 1996 against Germany; St-Etienne in 1998 against Argentina; Lisbon in 2004 against Portugal; and Gelsenkirchen in 2006 against Portugal. Again. Every time, my heart breaks and my voice screams frustration. When will we ever find the answer?

In fitness, speed and agility, the players available to the England manager have made huge advances. In developing the mental strength required to survive shoot-outs, the England pro has gone backwards. Famous names adorn the list of England players to miss in a shoot-out: Stuart Pearce, Chris Waddle, Gareth Southgate, Paul Ince, David Batty, David Beckham, Darius Vassell, Frank Lampard, Steven Gerrard and Jamie Carragher. Before France '98, in the non-competitive King Hassan II Cup in Casablanca, Rob Lee and Les Ferdinand both failed this test of nerve and technique in a shoot-out against Belgium. Of course I am not saying it's easy. Ask yourself how you would handle the pressure in front of thousands inside the stadium, and millions watching on TV. But the brutal truth is the English seem hopeless at penalties, and the rest of the world has noticed.

Chances squandered from the spot have been compounded by opportunities wasted off the pitch. If England had listened to Clive Woodward before Euro 2004, the players might have significant medals hanging round their necks. The brains behind England's triumph at the 2003 rugby World Cup, Clive knew what it took to prepare players for the cauldron of tournament life. 'Leave nothing to chance' was Clive's creed. More recently, the 'aggregate of marginal detail' has been the mantra of Britain's all-conquering Olympic cyclists. Practise, practise, practise. Hone the mind as well as the body. On 4 June, just as Sven's players were going through a series of friendlies before Euro 2004, Clive emailed Mark Palios, the then chief executive of the FA. 'Why are you not having penalty shoot-outs after each of these warm-up games, regardless of the result at full-time?' Clive asked. 'Think you have missed major opportunity of rehearsing this in a pressure situation with crowd and TV all watching. Should somehow have built this into the friendlies. Vital you go into the tournament with the mindset you have the best penalty-takers in the business. It can clearly be rehearsed in training in a variety of ways but even better to expose players whenever possible to this. Just an idea. Keep in touch and good luck, Clive.' He copied the email to me, so I talked to Mark. As a former player himself, Mark understood the thinking behind Clive's proposal. Sadly, it never happened. Another tournament came and went with failure from penalties. Even Portugal's goalkeeper, Ricardo, had the confidence and expertise to convert his penalty in Lisbon.

Glenn Hoddle always argued against practising penalties. 'You cannot recreate what it's like in a match so why are we going to spend hours and hours doing it?' Glenn told me three or four times during France '98. 'You can even deepen the tension.' Glenn's view was shared by players and coaches. But a week before

England embarked for the 2006 World Cup in Germany, I brought it up again with Sven.

'Why don't you stage a penalty shoot-out in front of the crowd during one of the friendlies,' I suggested.

'OK, let's do it after the Jamaica game,' Sven replied. 'Can you get permission?' The match at Old Trafford was only seventy-two hours away, so I had to move fast. I explained our request to the Jamaican FA.

'If we want to have a penalty shoot-out at the end of the game, whatever the score, would you be party to that?' I asked.

'Yes, no problem,' came the reply. Good. I felt that this chance to practise before a full house might help the players. For some reason I'll never fathom, Sven, the players and coaches decided against the shoot-out at the last moment. The England dressing room apparently felt it would illustrate their intentions. Paraguay, Trinidad & Tobago and Sweden, our group opponents in Germany, would record the game, so their keepers would have a better idea of where Sven's players like to put their spot-kicks if we won a penalty. Opponents we might meet in knock-out games would have help with their research if the game went to a shoot-out. But I still thought practising penalties in front of a full house at Old Trafford would have been worthwhile. 'Bonkers' was my private verdict on the decision. Wrongly hiding my disappointment, I was still delighted to watch the players practise penalties during training at Baden-Baden. This made a change from previous regimes.

Similar grief with penalties has afflicted Holland, yet they are tackling their problem. Johan Cruyff hails from the Hoddle school that shoot-out drama cannot be recreated, but the Dutch FA insist on their younger age-group sides conducting shoot-outs at the end of games. Surprise, surprise, Holland under-21s beat England's on penalties at the 2007 Euros.

Before Euro 2008 kicked off, the *Sunday Times* published some fascinating research on penalties. Around 25 per cent of knock-out games in major tournaments are decided by skill from twelve yards. Two World Cup finals have been settled by penalties. The gist of the article was that while it is impossible to prepare completely for the moment, for all that stress and noise, technique can be sharpened. More thought, less haste is one improvement. Figures revealed that kickers who took longer than 2.8 seconds to place the ball found the target 77 per cent of the time. Those who rushed it, taking 1.7 seconds or less, scored with only 58 per cent of kicks. That is an incredible difference. The Dutch are taught to place the ball, breathe in, maybe check their laces, anything to slow down the moment. England must learn such tricks of the shoot-out trade. Just imagine what we might have won had our players been able to convert penalties. For now, any opposition heading into a shoot-out with England think they are on to a winner. England's mental block with penalties is worsening. No one has resolved the problem. Until someone does, England will continue to screw up in tournaments. Teams who lift World Cups are almost certain to have survived penalty shoot-outs on the way. Spain defeated Italy on spot-kicks in the quarter-finals *en route* to winning Euro 2008.

England should have listened to Clive. In fairness to Mark Palios, he was keen for Clive to take on some role with the FA, bringing his winning expertise from rugby. 'Go and talk to Clive, see what we can learn,' Mark told me. I did. My audience with Clive Woodward was a compelling experience; he brimmed with ideas and enthusiasm, talking about how the clubs and governing body must work in tandem for the national team's benefit. The Rugby Football Union and the clubs all came together and supported Clive in 2003. Clive had everything he wanted and England won by a drop goal in the final seconds. That's the fraction between success and failure. Clive had trained England to get there, to have the nerve and technique to deliver come the crunch. He was a treasure trove of information. He talked about England's solvable problems with penalties. He urged us to appoint a vision coach to improve England footballers' spatial awareness. Sadly, Clive was also being courted by Rupert Lowe, the chairman of

Southampton and an FA board member. Rupert took me aside one day, berating me for showing an interest in Clive. Rupert even claimed I was trying to hijack his hiring of Clive. I never blamed Rupert. He was looking after Southampton but England would have benefited from Clive Woodward's involvement. The FA and the clubs could both have used Clive's talents to create an environment in which players practise penalties and in which England footballers are toughened up mentally. England managers had long been vexed over this flaw in their players' DNA. Concerned about the players' fortitude, Glenn Hoddle wanted to take Eileen Drewery to France '98.

Sven wanted to take a sports psychologist to Germany. 'Not having somebody was a mistake,' Sven told me. 'It would have helped the players.' Respected sports psychologists can be found out there, doing extremely good work. Keith Power has increased the concentration levels of David James and Rio Ferdinand. They have matured as players in front of our eyes. After forty years of hurt, England needed to wise up. Clive Woodward's recruitment, and the practising of penalties, might have saved England continually checking into Heartbreak Hotel during recent World Cups and European Championships. The FA's loss has been the British Olympic Association's gain.

11

Blame It on Rio?

Rio Ferdinand sat in my kitchen being fed Battenberg cake by my wife Susan while his future was decided in the next room. One of the more surreal scenes in the history of the England national team was played out in my Worcestershire home. The moment it was decided the West Midlands was most convenient to all those from Soho Square and Old Trafford seeking to sort out Rio's missed drugs test, we prepared for distinguished company. Susan popped to the shops and returned with the cake. 'It's all I could get quickly on a Sunday afternoon,' she said. 'Rio might be peckish.'

As I waited for the guests to arrive, I reflected on the extraordinary events that had set the scene for what the media called the 'Crisis Summit' at my place and which was later dubbed by Mihir Bose in the *Daily Telegraph* as the 'Battenberg Summit'. When it came to stepping out of line, Rio had form. Glenn Hoddle left the promising centre-half out of one England team for a drink-driving offence. In May 1998 at La Manga, Rio went for a walk and forgot to attend a team meeting, sending Glenn berserk. Although a wonderful bloke, Rio was forgetful. When the FA were informed that Rio had missed a routine drugs test at Carrington on 23 September 2003, they had to act decisively. Sven-Goran Eriksson was due to announce his squad on 5 October for the critical Euro 2004 qualifier against Turkey a week later. The recurring nightmare was that the story broke while England were in Istanbul, with Rio in the side. UEFA, let alone the Turks, would go spare over the inclusion of a player guilty of missing a drugs test. At worst, England risked expulsion from the competition.

On 2 and 3 October, I talked constantly to United's lawyer Maurice Watkins and the club's chief executive, David Gill. Both are highly intelligent men, who could see beyond the parameters of their beloved club. 'We understand the seriousness of the situation,' both Maurice and David said. 'But the FA need to understand Rio's version of events. He forgot because he went shopping for bed linen. When he heard the drug-testers were looking for him, he offered to come straight back to Carrington.' I was desperate for the bed-linen line to be true. Rio was a hugely important player for Sven. If England were ever to win a trophy, Rio would need to be in the thick of it, making tackles, intercepting the ball, perhaps even sliding a killer ball out from the back. In football and in life, Rio had been known to take his eye off the ball. Concentration goes. He gets caught out. Rio's focus let him down badly here. One moment of amnesia tipped a sport into meltdown.

Mark Palios, Nic Coward, Paul Barber and I had conversations about what to do. Still relatively new to the chief executive's job, Palios said: 'We've got to be strong. We've got to be seen to be taking a lead. We cannot even tolerate suspicion.' Recreational drugs exist in English football but finds of performance-enhancing substances are thankfully exceedingly rare. The FA rightly took some pride in the anti-drugs programme operated throughout UK Sport, and run by Alan Hodson, based at Lilleshall. Never be complacent, but the amount of drug-testing for players at the top level, and the scarcity of positive samples, is reassuring. From the start, in my heart I believed Rio's protestations that he was not a drug-taker but the FA had to show their anti-doping system worked. The World Anti-Doping Agency were understandably taking a keen interest. As we searched for a solution, Palios told Sven to postpone his squad announcement, setting tongues wagging in football and Fleet Street.

On the Monday morning, I was scheduled to fly to Turkey with Lawrie McMenemy and Gordon Milne for a goodwill visit, pressing the flesh before the tense Euro 2004 qualifier. First, we needed to sort out Rio's situation, so a meeting was convened on Sunday afternoon at my place just off the M42, a half-way house for all concerned. Whether we'd all meet in the middle over such an emotive issue as Rio's missed test was less clear-cut. Maurice Watkins and David Gill travelled down from Manchester. Rio was driven up from London. Nic came up from the south. The Battenberg was brought in from the village shop. 'If we're going to keep Rio in the squad, one of us had better come up with something radical,' I said to Nic, the first to arrive. 'The facts of what happened are not going to change. For whatever reason, Rio missed a dope test. Bed linen or no bed linen, he's missed a drugs test.'

As Nic and I talked, an elaborate arrival plan was under way. Just to complicate our rendezvous for this noteworthy moment in England's footballing history, the road between the M42 and our house was blocked as a bridge was mended. Reaching our house required a detour via the village, a few double-backs, followed by some tight squeezes down country lanes. When Rio, Maurice or David came off the M42, they were told to pull into a little lay-by and await Susan. She would then guide everybody along this tortuous route. At times like this, as expensive cars purred through the village, I was grateful for my neighbours' generosity of spirit and lack of curiosity. David and Maurice arrived after Nic, followed by Rio, who seemed remarkably relaxed. Looking at Rio as he strolled in, I wasn't sure whether anybody had fully explained to him the seriousness of his predicament. Rio faced a long ban from football. The FA's drug programme could not be messed with. As the Battenberg Summit around my dining table began, Susan took Rio off for a walk, the pair returning through the back door into the kitchen. She offered Rio tea and cake as the debate raged next door.

'It's pretty clear what the problem is here,' I said to Maurice and

David. 'We cannot risk taking a player under suspicion of a doping offence to a vital European Championship qualifier. Mark Palios is adamant that Rio cannot be in Sven's squad for Turkey. Rio cannot come to Istanbul.'

David and Maurice fought hard for their player. That's what I admired about United. Right or wrong, they stuck together. 'Rio has not been proven to have done anything wrong so any exclusion would be draconian,' David and Maurice said. Draconian. The word hung in the air. United's view elicited some sympathy from me. Rio just forgot, I honestly believed that, but the credibility of the FA's doping policy was at stake. How could the governing body allow Rio to be picked under such suspicion? I hated all this. It wasn't a pro-United thing; I just loathe wrecking the dreams of good guys who make innocent mistakes. But Rio couldn't go to Istanbul while the disciplinary process was under way. The FA wouldn't budge on this. David and Maurice realised their fight was over. Rio was called in from the kitchen. Nic quickly pulled me to one side and said: 'David, I'll tell it to Rio like a lawyer and you tell it to him as a friend.'

Rio ambled in. By then, I was seriously upset. I hated doing what I had to do. Rio sat down at the table and looked around. Our eyes caught. 'Rio, you have to know this is a serious thing,' I said. 'You could face a long ban for missing the drugs test. In those circumstances the view of the FA is that we can't take you to Turkey.'

Rio was devastated. 'I can't believe it,' he muttered, his eyes moistening. In his autobiography, Rio remembered ranting at me. My recollection is that he showed a quiet dignity. He was in tears, fearful for his future. Maybe because I'd known Rio for a few years, he didn't go ballistic. Insults never flew across the table. United were angry, understandably.

'This is draconian,' Gill repeated.

'This is wrong,' added Maurice. But that was as heated as it got. The meeting was civilised but deeply sad. As they left, the United boys wondered out loud whether Mark Palios shouldn't have been there to deliver the bad news. On reflection, Mark probably wishes he had been. Shaking hands with Rio, I said: 'Rio, I'm really sorry. I'll have to inform Sven now.'

Eriksson was shocked the FA could do this to him, Ferdinand and England. 'So I am expected to get a point in Istanbul without one of my best defenders,' said Sven. 'This could only happen in England, leaving out one of your best players.'

'Sven, it's complicated.'

'What about the English principle of "innocent until proven guilty"?' asked Sven. That sentence got a few airings over the following traumatic days.

'Sven, if we took Rio to Istanbul and then the story broke, there is enough jealousy of English football in other European countries for them to have a major go at us,' I said. 'Rio missed a drugs test for whatever reason. If there is a stick to bash England with they'll bash us. There are people on the UEFA executive who aren't always supportive of England. Other major countries aren't necessarily sympathetic to us. We have to be cautious.' Sven didn't understand the politics. He just felt his employers were making the so-called impossible job even harder.

Even later that Sunday evening, when we announced the squad would not be named for another twenty-four hours, news had already begun seeping out that Rio had missed a dope test. A week of anarchy began. On the Monday morning, as England players began reacting angrily to Rio's exclusion, I flew to Istanbul, a haven of tranquillity compared to events unfolding at home. I kept in touch with Palios and the new Director of Communications Paul Barber, who were deciding exactly when Sven's squad could be announced. With Lawrie McMenemy and Gordon Milne, I attended the centenary dinner of the Turkish FA, a triumphalist event where it was made very plain that a great Turkish team would beat England this coming Saturday. On the Tuesday morning we did a PR visit to an Istanbul school. Lawrie excelled at such charm offensives. Gordon spoke the lingo and was still a popular figure in Turkey, following his time managing

Besiktas. Normally, on departing Istanbul, English football people heave a sigh of relief, glad to leave such a chaotic city. Not this time. I was flying back into a war-zone.

When the players gathered at Sopwell House, the mood soon turned mutinous over what had befallen their great mate Rio. Poor Sven was caught in the middle. Employed by the FA, Sven's loyalty lay with his players. 'Can you come and see if there is any way through this?' Sven asked me. Rushing from Heathrow to Sopwell, I was informed that Gary Neville was leading the charge against the FA. Somehow, this news did not surprise me. Gary was a leader, who cared passionately about those who sat alongside him in the dressing room. A United die-hard who expressed his opinions forcibly, Gary was labelled 'Red Nev' by the players and press alike. The media quickly zeroed in on Gary's involvement, slaughtering him for standing up for Rio. Again 'innocent until proven guilty' was Gary's riposte. England's players were outraged at Rio's omission from the squad before he'd even been charged, let alone tried by any disciplinary commission. Gary was accused of backing Rio only because he was a fellow Red. Not true. He would have defended a Liverpool player afflicted by similar woes. Representing England was an honour Gary took very seriously, and he would fight those who stood unfairly in a player's way. Some at the FA were stunned by the scale of the revolt stirred up by Red Nev at Sopwell. Paul Barber went in to talk with Gary, and was almost knocked back by the strength of feelings. Such was the players' indignation that there was even talk of a strike. No Rio, no game, came the message from Gary Neville. It sounded like there could be some empty seats on Thursday's flight to Istanbul. The players' desire to stick by one of their own was understandable. Collective responsibility and all that. But the idea of a strike was far-fetched. Some of Sven's players confided to me that they would never turn their back on England. At one of the players' several meetings at Sopwell, David James stood up and urged everyone to consider the potential ramifications if they did go on strike. Their vilification in the press was already at fever pitch. 'They will go to Istanbul,' I reassured Sven.

The impasse was broken when Rio told the players not to boycott the game. Just in time. I don't think I've ever been more relieved to see Gary Neville, David Beckham and Wayne Rooney running out of a tunnel. If Red Nev had persuaded the squad to strike, the FA would have instructed Sven to call up new players. The FA were simply not prepared to forfeit the game. Bonded together, they withstood a brief Turkish storm to qualify for Euro 2004. That was the one positive to emerge from the pre-match air of negativity. Relations between England players and the FA sunk to an all-time low, tensions exacerbated by the players not knowing Mark Palios. They understood Palios was a former player, at a lesser level to them, but he was new, and he certainly wasn't the popular Adam Crozier. Adam had charm. Palios had a somewhat brusque exterior. Palios's handling of the Rio saga angered many of the players. To add to the tension, the period between Rio's missed drugs test and his disciplinary hearing was far too long. I really felt for Rio. During that time, Rio persistently tried to contact Palios. In his autobiography, he complained about being continually fobbed off by Mark's secretary but Palios had to be elusive. If the chief executive of the FA talked with someone who was effectively a defendant then it could be deemed prejudicial.

Shortly after Istanbul, Sven and I were in a car, travelling to the Cambridge Union. 'David, Rio just wants to meet someone from the FA to explain what happened,' Sven said. 'Rio wants people to know how strongly he feels about being left out of the squad. Mark will not talk to Rio. Will you?'

'I want to, Sven,' I said. 'I need to find some way of seeing him without anyone, particularly any clever lawyer, being able to say the FA is prejudicing its own case.' The meeting never happened. Like Palios, I was under pressure from lawyers at Soho Square to avoid any action that could be deemed to influence the case. Now, I regret not meeting Rio. I should have ignored lawyers and procedures and shown some compassion to a guy I liked in the grip of despair. I let Rio down.

At one point I asked myself: 'Is Mark Palios an unlucky chief executive?' First he had Rio, then the Alan Smith case. Still at Leeds, the striker was in trouble for throwing a bottle into the crowd. Sven was advised by the FA to omit Alan from his squad to face Denmark at Old Trafford a month after Istanbul; James Beattie was hurriedly called up instead. So much confusion now coloured selection for England that Mark wanted to draw up some criteria, attempting to clarify a player's eligibility if he were embroiled in any disciplinary or legal process. Before Mark travelled to Manchester to outline the new plans to the England players' committee, I wanted to reassure him. 'Look, Mark, before we get completely hung up on the new criteria, you must understand these things have never happened before,' I said. And they hadn't. I don't think they have since. Missed drugs tests were not a common occurrence in football, thankfully. Still, Mark was determined that some selection criteria came into force. So he sat down with Beckham, Gary, David James and Sol Campbell at the Lowry Hotel, looking for some common ground. Red Nev immediately shifted into overdrive, telling Palios exactly what he thought of his treatment of Rio. Palios had a young assistant with him called Mark Gosnall. At one point, Gosnall said something and I saw all the players looking at each other, thinking, 'Who is this?' But Palios would not be brow-beaten by the players. He stood up to Red Nev and supported young Mark. Palios was tough, telling them there would be strict new selection criteria.

Palios then had a news conference twenty-four hours before the Denmark game, during which he was grilled over Alan Smith's absence. 'Mark, did you know that Smith's replacement, James Beattie, is in the middle of a driving ban?' Palios was asked. 'How does that fit with any new criteria?' Palios was stunned. Beattie's ban was news to him. He felt ill-briefed and hung out to dry by those around him. The next day's press was bloody. Mark rarely volunteered for media duty after that.

The fractious state of FA–player relations stretched on until after Rio's hearing. Rio was punished with an eight-month ban, incensing him and Manchester United. The lawyer Mark Gay, who led the FA prosecution, called for a longer suspension at the appeal on 18 March 2004. Even with the shorter ban, Rio missed Euro 2004, a particular frustration for him. His anger at the FA and me eventually dissipated enough for him to accept my invitation to him, Gary Neville and David James to come on a trip to Malawi to raise awareness of HIV/Aids. 'I appreciate you coming to Malawi,' I said to Rio, over a couple of drinks in the hotel in Lilongwe. 'I'd have understood if you'd not wanted to come. The whole saga of Istanbul and your ban should have been handled so much better. That will always be a regret of mine.' Fully in confessional mode, I added: 'I also think the eight months was too harsh. I believe you genuinely forgot.' And I do.

Adversity makes people stronger and Rio is now respected as one of the world's leading centre-halves. Newspapers even wrote that he would have walked into the UEFA all-star XI from Euro 2008. The missed drugs test may have acted as a wake-up call to Rio. Perhaps some good came out of it after all. People praise Rio's new maturity these days. The whole saga also showed the FA's drug-testing programme worked. Since the Rio fiasco, I am not aware of anyone missing a drugs test.

12

Flying with Rooney

As the Learjet cut through the clouds over Europe, I looked at Wayne Rooney, sitting there, headphones on, eyes closed, oblivious to the bedlam surrounding him. On 7 June 2006, it seemed the whole country held its breath as Rooney left England's base in Baden-Baden to fly home for a scan on his metatarsal injury. Everybody knew how important the Manchester United striker was to England's World Cup adventure. As I watched Rooney, I reflected on his incredible journey into the hearts of England fans. This tough Scouser was their sort of player, strong, brave, passionate, hard-working and blessed with phenomenal skill and an eye for goal. People did genuinely offer up prayers that England's no. 9 could make the World Cup. He was special. No doubt. Long before he made his international debut in 2003, there was talk within Soho Square about this brilliant teenager at Everton. The whispers became shouts of excitement when Rooney rammed that wonder goal past Arsenal's David Seaman at Goodison Park.

Sven had long been aware of this young bull rampaging around in Everton blue. For all the criticism of Sven being a 'cautious' coach, he didn't hang back with Rooney. 'I'm thinking of going with Rooney in the squad,' Sven told me before the friendly with Australia on 12 February 2003. No under-21s. Straight in. After forty-five minutes against the Aussies and a cameo against

Liechtenstein, Rooney started in the cauldron of a Euro 2004 qualifier against Turkey. I feared this was a gamble too far by Sven but I was wrong. Rooney took the Turks apart in Sunderland.

I found Rooney very polite, certainly to those of us substantially older than him. He was an engaging mixture of confidence and amazement at discovering himself alongside David Beckham in the England squad. Stevie Gerrard looked after him. The pair were inseparable at Euro 2004, a tournament that gave me a fascinating insight into Rooney's psyche. England's base was a hotel called the Solplay, a new if slightly functional place on the edge of Lisbon with a friendly little newsagent's in reception. Usually when a team takes over a hotel, shops shut down. This paper shop stayed open. The morning after Rooney scored twice against Switzerland, the shop did particularly good business. Looking over the railings outside my room, I spotted a somewhat furtive figure below me. Like some secret agent darting between pillars, Rooney made his way to the newsagent's. In a flash he was through the door, emerging moments later, stuffing all the papers up his jumper and hot-footing it back to his room. Maybe he didn't want other England players to read the gushing reports of him, or he simply wanted to devour them in private.

A brutal symmetry then defined Rooney's life. He limped out of Lisbon with a broken metatarsal, a sickening blow for him and England. If he hadn't got injured we would have won the European Championships. I genuinely believe that. Fast-forward two years and Rooney hobbled towards, rather than from, a tournament. At Stamford Bridge on 29 April, my unhappiness at United losing to Chelsea was compounded by the sight of Rooney fracturing the fourth metatarsal in his right foot. As I left the ground, feeling downcast, I knew England were in for another 'will he/won't he make it?' saga akin to David Beckham before the 2002 World Cup. The early prognosis seemed pretty bleak; Rooney would struggle to be involved at all in Germany. As the bone knitted, the assessments became more upbeat. To my alarm, I became conscious of a difference of opinion between United's doctors and the England medical staff. Our doctor, Leif Sward, believed there was a very real chance Rooney could play a part. United didn't.

'I sense a row brewing,' I said to Sven. I understood both sides. United fans wanted our star protected. As an England fan too, I knew how much Sven needed him. My initial scepticism over Wayne's chances began lifting during one pre-tournament session at Carrington. Still doing rehabilitation work, Rooney was training on his own an hour before the other players arrived. Suddenly, he whacked a ball with all his usual power. 'Bloody hell!!' said the few people present. This heartening development for England was soon public knowledge.

Talks intensified between the medical men, between Brian Barwick and David Gill. Three days before England flew to Baden-Baden, Brian said to me: 'David, I want you to get involved in this. It has been agreed that Rooney will travel out with us and then fly back forty-eight hours later to have a final scan.'

'We're not exactly going to the most isolated part of the world,' I replied. 'Can't Wayne have his scan in Germany? Or stay in England, have the scan, and then fly out?' Symbolically it was important to Sven that Wayne travelled with the squad. Rooney wanted to come, to be with his mates; arriving at a tournament as a team is always special. As the England coach pulled up in the cobbled courtyard outside Schloss Bühlerhöhe on 5 June, Rooney and the rest of the players were greeted with folk dancing and music. Hotel staff leaned out of windows, waving and applauding their guests from England. Rooney smiled. I sensed he wouldn't have missed this for anything. Schloss Bühlerhöhe was so magnificent that the Gestapo claimed it as a base during the war. The facilities were extensive, including a notable set of buildings at the end of the driveway. Intrigued, I poked around and found it was a world-renowned clinic, containing the latest scanning machines. 'Why can't Wayne have the scan here?' I asked Sven. 'You know there will be a huge circus if we fly him back to Manchester.' Sven shrugged. The key thing was this: Manchester United wanted the scan to be a home game. I'm still not sure anyone was ever fully aware just how good the medical facilities at Schloss Bühlerhöhe were.

So at nine a.m., UK time, on 7 June Rooney climbed into a minibus with me, Leif and our security man Terry Wise. Sven had a final instruction for me.

'Make sure you come back with him!' said Sven, only half-jokingly. I was not overly impressed with my situation, piggy in the middle between my two footballing loves, England and United. From the start of the trip, I was apprehensive, ready for a ruck if anything went wrong. Some people suggested it was unfair of Barwick to land me with the job. I didn't. Fighting fires was my vocation. My only concern was that this was not primarily a football dispute, this was medical. My qualifications for resolving a medical disagreement were non-existent.

Shortly before ten a.m., we took off from Baden-Baden airport. Cameras pointed through the fence, following the Learjet as it taxied along the runway and then climbed to the skies, carrying its precious cargo back to Manchester. As Wayne settled down with his music, I chatted to Leif. 'Wayne has a real chance of taking part in the tournament,' said Leif. 'We shouldn't deny him that chance. I am convinced the injury is now OK.' Like me, Leif remained concerned how the day would pan out, how the inevitable battle with United's medical staff would unfold. 'Wayne can play at a very early stage of the tournament,' insisted Leif. 'Possibly not the first game but certainly the second game.' We knew United's doctor thought it very dubious whether he could see any World Cup action at all. United's concern was based on the fact that metatarsal injuries had sidelined Beckham for eight weeks and Gary Neville for sixteen weeks.

On landing at Manchester Airport an hour and a half later, with cameras again recording our every movement, we soon linked up with Wayne's agent, Paul Stretford, and the United medical team of Dr Tony Gill, their physio Rob Swire and consultant Mr Ashok Paul. Photographers chased our minibus all the way to

Whalley Range hospital. The scan took only a few minutes, after which Wayne was driven to Coleen McLoughlin's parents' house in Croxteth, leaving the medical men to decide his fate. After examining the scan, Leif, Gill, Swire and Paul couldn't agree, so two independent medical experts were called in. The top men in their field, Professor Angus Wallace and Professor Christopher Moran worked at the Queen's Medical Centre in Nottingham. No one knew more about metatarsals than these two. The feeling was that if Wallace and Moran were satisfied the bone had healed, and there was no risk of it splintering again, then everyone would be satisfied. Brought in by the FA, Wallace and Moran were thrust into the public spotlight and didn't enjoy it very much, especially Professor Wallace, whose wife was unamused by England disturbing her holiday. Wallace and Moran told me they felt under pressure from us to clear Rooney for World Cup duty. Yet the whole nation was screaming for Rooney to be passed fit. Placed under great scrutiny, the professors were phoned constantly by reporters, an unprecedented and unpleasant experience for them and their families. More than once I apologised to them. The crazy circus that follows England had upset these two distinguished medical professors. Commendably, they put aside all their angst at the intrusions and travelled to Whalley Range.

While waiting for the puff of white smoke, I spent most of the afternoon at Stretford's office in Wilmslow. Stretford is larger than life, a real character. At the time, Paul was embroiled in a dispute with the FA, which complicated matters. One moment the FA were arguing with Stretford, the next they were asking if they could borrow Wayne for some commercial venture. As I was pacing up and down Stretford's office, the call from the hospital came. We dashed back to Whalley Range, racing through suburbia, almost running over a cameraman standing in the middle of the road. Fortunately, he jumped out of the way at the last second. I didn't fancy another scan on a broken foot.

Around half past five, I followed Wayne into the medical meeting room. My worst fears were realised. Sward and United remained apart on when Rooney should next kick a ball in anger. They agreed some World Cup involvement was possible, but when?

'At a very early stage,' said Leif. 'His recovery is accelerating.'

'Possibly if England qualify for the knock-out stages,' said United. Concerned for their star striker, United still played fair with England. There was no attempt to stop Rooney going back to Germany. United never disputed England's right to call players up. So it was over to Wallace and Moran, who asked Wayne his opinion. 'I want to play,' said Rooney unsurprisingly. The two professors consulted again. To Wayne's delight and my relief, the independent experts cleared Rooney to return to Germany but he was not, repeat not, to play in the first game against Paraguay in three days' time. He was unlikely to be fit for any of the group matches, they maintained. The professors added that they would fly out to give Wayne the final OK to start. After the inevitable discussion about insurance, Rooney headed out of the hospital at just gone 7.45 p.m. Show-time! Rooney emerged to hundreds of shouted questions and requests from photographers. I followed behind, a huge smile lighting my face. My sunny demeanour was instantly taken as good news for England. Rooney was fine! Here we go! TV reporters outside Whalley Range began speculating that Rooney would soon be starting for England again. Surely the man from the FA would not be laughing if Rooney was staying behind. In truth, the smile had nothing to do with Rooney. Just before walking out of the hospital doors, I'd bumped into a porter whom I'd known while presenting *Look North*.

'Where's your mate Stuart Hall?' he asked, referring to those happy, less-pressured days in my BBC youth.

'We don't need City supporters like him involved!' I replied. And laughed. Out to the cameras. Smiling. Bingo.

Inside the people-carrier, my mood changed. As we tried to put together a statement from United and England, I had to deal with United's inevitable sensitivities. Call upon call was made and received as we raced to the airport. I was anxious to sort out the wording of the statement before climbing on to the plane. The Learjet had a phone but the connection hadn't been that good on the way over. 'I might have to let you go on without me,' I said to Wayne and Leif as we reached the runway. 'There's so much still to be sorted I can't risk being out of contact.' I actually boarded the plane, then got off before deciding to risk it. Mark Whittle, a top media man from the FA, was trying to agree a joint statement with United's Phil Townsend and lawyer Edward Canty. The pilot started up the engines, and that was it. No turning back. Rooney's World Cup dream was alive. As Wayne went back to his music, Leif and I slumped into our seats, shattered. An honourable man, Leif had felt under huge pressure, too; medical people don't like sitting around a table, disagreeing with other medical people.

As we arrowed towards Baden-Baden, I knew there were still some tough phone-calls to be had with Sir Alex Ferguson. He and I had been through rough times before, like Rio Ferdinand's missed drugs test, and this Rooney saga was awkward. In the main, Alex has always been very affable to me. 'I wish you'd retired after the Treble,' I had the temerity to say one day in his office in 2001. 'That was the very best. How do you beat it?' I was wrong. Sir Alex has built another great team, as good as 1994 and 1999, and won the European Cup again. He is the best manager of my lifetime, now ahead of Bill Shankly and Bob Paisley. He has never been afraid to blood youngsters, never been afraid to change winning teams. And he is fascinating to talk to. But I didn't envy Sven his looming conversation with Fergie later that evening.

Darkness had fallen by the time we reached Schloss Bühlerhöhe. I never heard Wayne make his famous 'the big man is back' comment but apparently it was true. Others heard it. Rooney was popular with all the players, who were delighted to see him back and gave him a great reception. As the high fives were going on, I went straight in to see Sven, Clem and Steve McClaren. They'd got wind of all the difficulties we'd had.

Ferguson soon phoned Sven, making his feelings known forcibly. Sven was left in no doubt that United's treasured asset must be handled with care, whatever the independent medical men said. Sven held his own with Ferguson, though once or twice he held the phone away from his ear. Sven wouldn't be bullied by anybody. My conversation with David Gill wasn't much smoother. 'I understand the position you took,' I told David. 'But we have to give Wayne every chance of playing in the World Cup, and as soon as possible.' Relations between United and the England camp remained strained. Fortunately, Dave Richards, the Premier League chairman, helped significantly to ease tensions.

Three days later, Rooney sat on the bench in Frankfurt, itching to get on. Rooney stormed into the second game as a substitute, against Trinidad & Tobago, to an amazing reception in Nuremberg, and was then passed fit by Wallace and Moran to start against Sweden and then Ecuador. Controversially, Sven used Rooney up on his own against Portugal in the quarter-finals. Michael Owen was injured, Theo Walcott too inexperienced, and Sven didn't want to start with Peter Crouch. Although he appeared not really happy with the role, I'd seen Rooney play on his own before but I understood the criticism of Sven's decision. Isolated, Rooney became frustrated and was eventually sent off. But I will defend to the hilt Sven's complete commitment to taking Rooney to Germany, whatever United's misgivings. He was nearing peak fitness and a fully fit Wayne Rooney could have won England the World Cup. The flying visit home was worth it, even though the famous Rooney scan could have been done at the end of the hotel driveway. Funny business, football.

13

Goldenballs

David Beckham was an inspiration for England on the pitch and a marketing dream for the FA off it. FA turnover has grown inexorably over the past decade, increasing twelve-fold during my time to almost £240m in 2007, in no small part due to Goldenballs's worldwide appeal. Why is the FA's international TV deal so lucrative? Partly because of the Beckham factor. Why were England never short of opponents for friendlies? Again, Beckham's glamourous presence was an influence. My sadness is that David's phenomenal talent and superhuman endeavour for England were never rewarded with medals.

The inclusion of Manchester United's rising star in Glenn Hoddle's first England squad in 1996 did not go down well with Alex Ferguson. Tension always existed between Hoddle and Ferguson. They were never close. Why should they be? Glenn and Alex hailed from different generations. Fergie felt Beckham was called into the England squad too early. He was also angered when we put Beckham, accompanied by Glenn, in front of the media at Bisham Abbey. Alex did not need to worry. We cared for his young talent. 'David seems at ease with all the fuss and attention,' I said to Hoddle after day one. He was. Beckham had supreme belief in his own ability. Such an unbelievable talent, Beckham was clearly going to represent England for years to come.

He knew it. We knew it. When he first strolled into Burnham Beeches, my immediate impression was of a very polite, rather self-effacing southerner happiest being with northern lads like Scholesy, Gary and Phil Neville. They protected Becks. They knew he was a thoroughly decent person blessed with special gifts.

I soon learned to read his moods. Beckham's body language revealed instantly when he was fretting over anything, professional or personal. He looked forlorn, eyes distracted, walking slowly. When he was fired up before a match, Beckham moved in a very determined way, almost marching forward. I first noticed his changing moods as England trained at La Baule before France '98 started. Something was not right with Beckham. Watching David around the hotel, it was obvious his body language was wrong, too introspective. He was late for the bus once, a cardinal sin in Hoddle's eyes. Relations became strained between Glenn and David. Talk even surfaced of Hoddle showing Beckham up at free-kick practice. Amateur psychologists proffered the view that Glenn was jealous of Becks. Glenn definitely pined for his playing days but he'd never let that distort his ability to manage. He wanted to drive down the road to World Cup glory, not disappear down memory lane. The real problem was this: having played well in qualifying, Beckham was frustrated to pick up vibes that Hoddle might leave him out of the first World Cup match against Tunisia in Marseilles. I sympathised with David. Football is a theatre for him and he wanted to perform on the world stage. The thought of being kept back-stage wounded Beckham.

The gloom surrounding Beckham on the eve of France '98 worried me, although the sunshine came out briefly when David spent several hours with his new girlfriend, Victoria, before Marseilles. It was not this burgeoning relationship with Posh Spice that distracted Beckham. He was just upset at the thought of being benched.

'I love playing for England,' he told me. 'I'm desperate to play.'

'David, Geoff Hurst didn't start the World Cup in '66,' I

replied, trying to give him hope. 'And Geoff finished as England's hero with a hat-trick in the final. Think of that. You'll get your chance. And when it comes, take it.'

During difficult times, David always impressed me with his willingness to think of others. England got inundated with charity requests, particularly during tournaments, and usually I preferred to let players focus on the football. One letter I received in France I couldn't put down. Written by two distressed parents in England, the letter began: 'Our son is seriously ill in hospital and it would mean the world to him if he could speak to David Beckham.' I immediately went to see David in his room. He was at a low ebb, but I thought I'd ask. 'Of course I'll talk to him,' said David. 'Let's call him now.' So I rang the hospital, and David was put through to this poor lad. David had troubles of his own but they were nothing compared to those of the person on the other end of the phone. He spent five minutes just chatting to this boy, lifting his spirits. A few days later, I received a letter from the very emotional parents, wanting to pass on their eternal gratitude to David for giving their son hope in fighting his illness. David had that gift for cheering people up. He cared. Again and again, he showed that.

Just as David helped others, so those around David stood up for him. When Glenn remarked that David was 'not focused', Fergie hit back. The United manager wrote a piece in the *Sunday Times*, having a pop at Glenn for his handling of David. I knew the missile was on its way and it caused considerable anger in the England camp. I wasn't surprised and actually expected it. Fergie fought for his players. On reading the article, I went to see Glenn. 'You must be careful,' I warned Glenn. 'The press will want you to hit back at Fergie. Then he'll react again. We can do without that.' Glenn agreed. Having aired his concern over David's 'focus', Glenn did not wish to become embroiled in a major dispute with the leading club manager in England. 'I'm still disappointed with Alex,' Glenn said. 'We know David is distracted.'

Elsewhere in the *Sunday Times* article, Fergie criticised us for letting an emotionally raw player be put in front of the media at La Baule. That was my fault. I wanted to get things out in the open. Becks was clearly upset over something. Whether it was Hoddle, whether it was Ferguson, whether it was some problem at home, I felt David needed to get it out of his system. Talk about it. Move on. So I mentioned the idea to Glenn. 'David's mood is getting to everybody,' I said. 'Let's put an end to it, let's get him talking at a press conference.' Glenn agreed. Drastic action is often required. Yet Fergie was essentially right. Beckham was not in the right frame of mind to deal with a barrage of cameras and questions early on at France '98. It was the wrong decision. Although he was unhappy, David usually coped OK with the media inquisition. Whenever I put David up in public he performed well. I laugh when people declare now: 'My goodness, doesn't David Beckham speak well? Hasn't he improved?' They sound surprised. David always has done his best talking to the media.

No one needs reminding how David's World Cup finished. We all know he was provoked into that red card by Argentina's Diego Simeone in St-Etienne. David was culpable for putting himself at risk of dismissal. In the modern game, if a player flicks out a boot at an opponent, he is asking for punishment from pressured referees. The head says David was wrong, but I can't find it in my heart to blame him. Point one: it was a soft dismissal. Point two: who are we to criticise a wholehearted player when we have no understanding of the pressure he was under? David had waited for this moment: starring in a massive World Cup showdown against top opposition in front of a global audience probably touching a billion. The atmosphere inside St-Etienne's ground was electric. Thousands supported England and Becks. Thousands of Argentinians directed vitriol at England's dashing new prince. David felt wronged by Simeone and paid an unbelievable price for his reaction. He snapped. Sitting in the dressing room afterwards, David was in pieces. Terry Byrne, one of England's masseurs, was the person to begin putting David back together. Terry eventually went to work for David, and that night in St-Etienne was where their friendship really grew. David never forgot Terry's support. I muttered a few sympathetic words. Nothing, really, could soothe his pain. As David headed off to deal with the fall-out from St-Etienne, I took comfort from knowing he would be in good hands. I discussed the situation with Steve Double, one of our press officers.

'Tony Stephens will look after David,' I said. Tony was logical, sensible and honest, like Jon Smith, Jon Holmes and Sky Andrew, other agents I admired. 'And Fergie will circle the wagons around him.' No one, though, predicted the backlash against Beckham. Burning effigies and mock-ups of David's head in a noose sickened me. A silly mistake on the pitch never justified such hostile repercussions off it.

Euro 2000 was difficult, too, for Beckham. A few England fans singled him out for abuse. As he walked off the pitch following England's opener with Portugal, one shouted: 'I hope your kid dies of cancer.' As any parent would be, David was deeply upset. The FA reacted strongly, aggressively by our standards. We sought to name and shame those who insulted David. He rightly expected us to stick up for him.

David's full England rehabilitation came under Sven-Goran Eriksson. Those who decried England's first foreign coach banged on about his being in thrall to Beckham. Yet Beckham's star was high when Sven took charge. David had won the Treble with United. Peter Taylor, the caretaker before Sven arrived, made Beckham captain against Italy. He was a fixture in the England team. Why should Eriksson not continue with Beckham? When Sven came in, the chief executive Adam Crozier had published his strategic plan for the so-called 'Golden Generation' of players to win a major tournament by 2006. Rightly or wrong, it had been me who pressed Adam to include that objective. Who should England build around? Beckham, obviously, the top player. When Beckham broke his metatarsal before the 2002 World Cup, the whole country had prayer mats out.

'David's popularity is very high, he is one of our top, top players,' Sven said. 'He is the leader. He is my captain.' I heard rumours that some players were jealous of the player dubbed Goldenballs, but I never detected any envy. Maybe some grew tired of the frequent ballyhoo around David, especially abroad. But they knew he always gave 100 per cent for England. Closest to the United boys he grew up with, Beckham still had the respect of the Liverpool and Chelsea players. David made a good captain. He was certainly not from the 'up and at 'em' school that produced Tony Adams, Paul Ince and Alan Shearer. Just as Sven was not a manager who ranted or raved, so his captain brought a quieter touch to leadership. Sven worked with top players in Italy and immediately connected with Beckham. They felt comfortable in each other's company. He made the perfect captain for Sven. 'I want a captain who I can talk to easily and who can give me the feeling amongst the players,' Sven said. 'David can.' Beckham inspired the team through deed rather than word. In preparation for the epic make-or-break World Cup qualifier against Greece at Old Trafford in 2001, England stayed at the Marriott Worsley, a friendly place on the outskirts of Manchester. David was never noisy around the hotel, and on this occasion he seemed even more focused than usual.

'Good luck, David,' I said to him, as I always did before big games.

'Thanks,' he replied. 'This is the day.' And he meant it. His eyes told me he meant it. His body language showed his appetite for the challenge ahead. Beckham made dreams happen. Before kick-off, David was introduced to an incredibly brave little girl called Kirsty Howard, who was born with her heart back to front. David was insistent Kirsty accompany him on to the pitch. He absolutely fitted into what Crozier and I wanted from the England players – using the power of football to build a better future. If that sounds pompous, I make no apologies. Beckham brightened people's lives. Particularly that day. One touch from Beckham guided England to Japan and South Korea. When that unforgettable free-kick curled into the Greek net, all those who questioned whether Sven was right to back him as captain disappeared into the darkness. With England playing poorly, Beckham dragged them over the line. It was a sensational individual performance.

A star on the field, David was most definitely a star off it. His arrival in Japan triggered hysteria of Beatlemania proportions. In places like Sapporo and Saitama, the moment David stepped out of the hotel towards the team coach, the screams were deafening. Young boys and girls threatened to destroy their larynges. 'Beck-Ham. Beck-Ham.' This was idolatry, pure and simple and very loud.

'I have never seen anything like this before,' remarked Doug Ellis, one of the senior International Committee members in Japan. Doug was bemused by Beckham's effect on the locals. Beckham, the rest of the squad and all the staff went out to a hamburger place in Kobe one night and word spread fast. Thousands of people were soon spilling off the pavement, stopping the traffic. The police were forced to close off all the nearby roads.

As Beckham-mania raged, I feared somebody would be hurt. Japanese kids had this crazy habit of running alongside the coach to catch a glimpse of Beckham. He sat at the back, occasionally opening the window to wave to people, which encouraged more to join in the chase. I talked to Sven about it. 'It's great David acknowledging the fans but I have this nightmare that we are going to run someone over,' I said. 'It's not just the coach. It's the outriders weaving in and out.' Sven nodded. He accepted David's immense fame brought such problems. We talked to our security man, Ray Whitworth, but there was little we could do. We just prayed nobody got hurt.

During the most manic years of Beckham-mania, around the time of Japan, David enjoyed a very good relationship with the FA's marketing chief, Paul Barber. Beckham was the face of England football, generating millions for the FA. David was bright, acutely aware of his lucrative appeal. Brand Beckham was big business and David knew how to milk it. But England was never about the money for Beckham. Representing England meant so much to him and he ran himself into the ground every game for his country. Only in the latter part of Sven's reign did any significant number of people start to question whether David should be in the team at all. As dissenting voices grew, Sven remained loyal. 'Why should I leave Beckham out?' Sven would say. 'There is no one better.' This idea that Beckham enjoyed special privileges under Sven was wrong. England players all got the same type of rooms. Michelle Farrer, the mother hen of the England squad, allocated rooms and was scrupulously even-handed.

Under Beckham, England were the quietest team of my experience. They were more serious. Depicting them as a Hollywood XI, as some critics did, was nonsense. Other than Beckham, it was difficult to think of any show-business types in the side. Gary Neville? No. Steven Gerrard? Definitely not. Scholesy?? No chance!! For one of the most celebrated people on the planet, David is very approachable, always willing to sign autographs or pose for photographs. All the fame and fortune hasn't changed David from the likeable character I first met in 1996. George Best and Paul Gascoigne couldn't cope with fame. David could but he expected perfect organisation around him, leaving him to focus on what he did best, moving a ball around a piece of grass. On a certain unfortunate occasion in Japan, local children were invited in to an event and it was chaos. David complained, directing harsh words at Sir Brian Hayes, the FA's security adviser. 'This is a cock-up,' was David's view. This was one of the rare occasions when I thought David over-reacted. In turn Sir Brian responded angrily but then bit his tongue. England's security guys liked Beckham but his fame placed a burden on them, more than the rest of the squad combined. Would Beckham be crushed by fans? Was there a nutter out there? Sir Brian and his security team were permanently on a state of heightened alert because of Beckham-mania.

Some of the United players took the piss out of David for the world he inhabited. 'It's circus-time, David,' they said whenever England stepped into the public's gaze. Those who had grown up with him were astonished at the Beckham phenomenon, how it took off. I looked at David, at his career, and wondered whether the hysteria would have been so intense if he hadn't married Victoria. Susan met Victoria more than I did, and warmed to her. Victoria had a terrific sense of humour and she and David were clearly besotted with each other.

The attention the pair received was phenomenal, and much of it they cultivated themselves. Victoria enjoyed the attention more than David, which was little surprise. Publicity was important for her career. They endured some rough times, certainly early on in Spain after he joined Real Madrid in 2003. There were times when his life drove him potty. Yet given all the pressures they've had, some of them self-inflicted, David and Victoria have come through it pretty well. David's a family man, that's clear from the way he dotes on his children. Life could be complicated for the Beckhams. One day, he had to rush home from training because of a kidnapping threat. Thankfully, that didn't happen to other England players.

When David eventually retires, I just hope he never becomes a manager. His strengths do not lie in the direction of the dug-out. Instead of restricting himself to one technical area, David can contribute so much more to football around the world. As a global icon, Beckham has already shown what he can achieve as an ambassador for London's successful 2012 Olympic bid. He must be given the chance to repeat that achievement, and help England win the battle to stage the 2018 World Cup. David Beckham won't let his country down.

14

Cup Balls and Balls-ups

Hot balls, cold balls, I've heard all sorts of balls talked about the FA Cup draw. One day in 2004, just before the semi-final draw involving Manchester United, Arsenal, Millwall and Sunderland, this cabbie dropped me off at Soho Square. 'Come on, David,' he said, 'you know you'll be keeping Man U and Arsenal apart, why don't you just say so?'

'We don't,' I replied. 'I promise you. Hand on heart – the FA Cup draw is straight.' I walked into the FA, irritated that too many people seem convinced the draw might be rigged. I'd fought hard to give the FA Cup credibility after the fiasco four years earlier when United hadn't defended their trophy, heading off to the Club World Championship in Rio instead. For a period, the Cup seemed in terminal decline. Protecting the Cup was vital, which was why I bridled at criticism.

So as I prepared for the rehearsal, my mood was pretty gloomy. At the run-through, the four balls were pulled out of the bag and, hey presto, the ties were: United–Millwall and Arsenal–Sunderland. That taxi driver came speeding into my mind. This would fit his conspiracy theory. When the draw was conducted live, I prayed United and Arsenal would come out together. That would kill off any belief the draw was bent. When Fergie and Arsene were pitted against each other, I almost did a jig around Soho Square. Thank God.

The FA Cup obsesses the English. Having commissioned research on what the public associate with the FA, I knew their three main thoughts were 'discipline, England and the FA Cup'. In 1994, though, the Cup draw needed urgent surgery. Back then it was a godsend to TV comedy scriptwriters, who regularly lampooned it. According to the research, the Cup's poor image reflected badly on the FA itself. 'We have to get away from the image of blazered buffoons,' I told my colleague Mike Parry. 'Punters think the Cup draw is just about two elderly gentlemen, Sir Bert Millichip and Gordon McKeag, standing around, looking self-conscious while Graham Kelly stands around, looking startled. It didn't matter when we were young, listening on our crystal radio sets, but the draw's on TV now. What people see is from another age – the ancient FA. Changing the draw will improve the image of the FA.'

The power of television money meant the Cup draw would never stay on radio. At the start, TV conducted the draw badly. One infamous night, *Match of the Day* came on late after the blessed Eurovision Song Contest and the third-round draw did not occur until after midnight. 'That's bonkers,' I told Mike. 'Let's bring the draw to life. Let's get some players in. Let's get a studio audience. Let's make the draw fun.' I knew the risks. Playing with the traditions of the FA Cup would upset some people. So I pulled together a small FA working party, involving people like Ken Bates, who supported the idea of polishing up the Cup draw.

Keeping the traditionalists onside was important. 'We have to stage it at Monday lunch-time on TV, as in the old days, but make it more fan-friendly,' I explained to the working party. 'You'll never touch the FA Cup,' retorted Alan Burbidge, from Cheshire FA. Having Alan on our working party reassured the traditionalists. 'Change is essential,' I told Alan.

Step one in this revolution was a call to the BBC to borrow a designer, who transformed the set. Step two was a visit to Sir Bert's office. 'Chairman, we need to make the FA Cup draw more vibrant, more appealing to a TV audience,' I began. 'So, I don't really think you should be involved any more.' It wasn't the easiest message an FA new boy ever delivered. Sir Bert wasn't terribly pleased he'd been dropped. Fortunately, he was an immensely civilised man.

'I understand what you are saying, David. Things do change.'

'Thank you for your understanding, Chairman.' Sir Bert was a very good person to have on my side.

Step three was a trip to the chief executive's office. Not being seen to undermine Kelly was something I was very sensitive about. 'Graham, what we're recommending will liven the draw up.' OK, so far. 'The broadcasters want me to introduce it.' No reaction. 'But I'm insisting you still oversee the draw and play a major role.' I could see Graham was relieved still to be involved, standing in the middle with the bag of balls.

'I see you've made Graham "Head of Balls", then!' remarked an FA Council member from my old patch in the North West. Happily, it seemed enough people were content with the proposed changes.

'The chairman has agreed to step aside,' I said to Parry. 'The chief executive will still have a role. The blazers are going out. Players and managers are coming in, people like Denis Law, Terry Venables, Bobby Robson, John Barnes, Ronnie Radford, Ricky George.' Attracting the stars was never any trouble and, certainly during my time in charge, they were never paid. These well-known names of the game just loved being part of a great FA Cup tradition, particularly now the draw was more fun. Before the first new draw, I told Denis and Terry: 'Ham it up a bit. Grown men pulling sixty-four balls out of a hat can be very boring, so have some fun. And don't cock up! There are enough people out there, and in the FA, who want this to fail.'

Full of nerves, I clutched the bag full of balls as the programme began and announced: 'In here, I have sixty-four balls which the media are hoping will end up all over the floor!' Fortunately, it didn't happen, but mistakes can occur. No Plan B exists, no safety net. Soon after I left, my successor on the draw, Trevor Brooking, slipped up when he read out the wrong team. No doubt, my suspicious cabbie would have been listening on the radio, shouting: 'There, I told you it was crooked!'

Accidents happen. One year, Martin Peters left a ball in the bag, which luckily we spotted. Another year, we had a tired and emotional Tony Adams doing the draw with Peter Beardsley, a model of sobriety. Tony has achieved so much in his life and I know one of his remaining ambitions is to do the FA Cup draw sober. 'We might have to do the draw with just Peter pulling the balls out,' Graham Kelly said as Tony tottered into the studio. Kelly went pale as this unco-ordinated England legend launched himself towards the FA Cup. All credit to Tony, he was fine when the programme started. He didn't slur his words or try to head any of the balls.

'I'm tempted to bring in eye-tests as well as breath-tests for some players,' I told Parry one year. 'Some of the older players are struggling to read the numbers on the ball!'

To spice up the draw further, supporters' organisations were invited in. 'Keep an eye on the lads from Brighton,' I told a TV director. 'We don't want a bloody demo in the middle of the draw!' They were as good as gold. People respected the sight of the FA Cup and felt honoured to be involved in the whole draw process. The interest was massive. The Cup draw is the only programme in this country, sporting or otherwise, that goes live on terrestrial and satellite TV, and live on commercial radio and BBC. Only a huge royal occasion comes close.

Even with all this intense scrutiny, everybody from cabbies to coaches still likes to allege subterfuge. 'Don't you leave the Man U ball on a radiator, warm it up a bit, so you can get a plum draw?' another taxi driver asked me.

'You are not serious, are you?!'

'We know you're at it.'

'Nonsense. I'd never be party to that. It would be a betrayal.'

I was even told that Alex Ferguson was utterly convinced Manchester United were drawn away from Old Trafford an incredibly large number of times. Brooking and I always laughed about it. 'United actually get a remarkable number of home games!' Trevor said. 'David, I dare you to say: "Manchester United at home – as usual!"' Quite how that would have gone down at Old Trafford I can only imagine.

After some draws, my phone would ring and it would be Sale of the *Mail*. Charlie Sale is a top operator, a fantastic digger of stories, but he could find conspiracy in a cub camp. 'Something's going wrong with that draw, David,' said Charlie. 'Look at the sequence of numbers: no. 4 v no. 5, no. 6 v no. 7. They must be looking into the bag.'

'Rubbish, Charlie,' I'd reply. 'Are they trying to look in? No, they bloody aren't.' Knowing Charlie was watching so closely, the entrance to the bag was tightened. That worked, except we couldn't use players with large hands, so the goalkeeper count dropped. Eventually, we installed a camera inside the bowl and the whole process couldn't be more transparent.

Controversies have dogged the FA Cup over the past decade, with two extraordinary episodes in 1999, one brief, the other lengthy, occurring after I succeeded Graham Kelly as 'Head of Balls'. On 13 February 1999, during a fifth-round tie at Highbury, the Sheffield United keeper Alan Kelly kicked the ball into touch so that his team-mate Lee Morris could have an injury attended to. Etiquette demanded the other side returned the ball from the throw-in. Following dressing-room protocol, Arsenal's Ray Parlour threw the ball towards Sheffield United but Kanu seized it and crossed for Marc Overmars to make it 2–1 to Arsenal. Sheffield United were outraged, Arsenal greatly embarrassed. Both managers, Arsene Wenger and Steve Bruce, wanted the goal ruled out. As acting chief executive, I rang the then FA Cup Committee chairman, Terry Annable, and got his approval for a re-match. We made the decision public within twenty-five minutes of the final whistle. Symbolically, it was an important moment because it showed the FA could take decisions swiftly. I relished the odd headline and some internal criticism of the 'FA TOO QUICK TO

REACT' variety. Less amusing was FIFA's reaction. Initially supportive, FIFA then prevaricated after it was claimed we might be undermining the referee in ordering the re-match. Sepp Blatter had been lobbied along those lines by some of the other British football associations, I learned later on. We stood firm, FIFA relented and justice prevailed.

The following season brought even greater controversy, and a new question for Trivial Pursuit lovers. Darlington were knocked out in the second round but were reinstated as a 'lucky loser' to cover for a famous absentee in the third-round draw. The missing name was only the biggest in English football. The holders Manchester United's non-appearance unleashed a storm of criticism that buffeted the Cup and the FA for months. Some critics claim the Cup has never recovered. Even looking back now, my heart fills with anger and my head with bewilderment over how we could have handled an impossible situation better. The countdown to a disastrous fixtures pile-up began the previous season. My natural excitement about United progressing in the Champions League was tempered by a looming dilemma. Victory meant entrée to FIFA's Club World Championship, beautifully sited in Brazil but badly timed right in the thick of third-round Cup action. As the clock ticked down in the Champions League final at Camp Nou, with Bayern Munich looking in control, I felt at least one silver lining would cling to a United defeat: as acting chief executive, I wouldn't have to sort out a hugely sensitive clash of priorities. Sitting in the posh seats next to the then general secretary of FIFA, Michel Zen-Ruffinen, I ran through the speech I'd prepared for a post-match UEFA event. Two speeches, actually: the good-losers' one and the modest-winners' one. With United trailing 0–1 and time running out, the UEFA president Lennart Johansson walked past me to go down for the presentations.

'David, there's always next year,' said Lennart, patting me on the head. I dug out the good-losers' speech. Then, gloriously, Teddy Sheringham and Ole Gunnar Solskjaer ripped a few scripts to bits. Amidst the celebrations, I knew England's Treble-winners were now double-booked in January, giving me the mother of all headaches.

'What would it mean to our World Cup bid if United didn't go to Brazil?' I asked the 2006 bid director, Alec McGivan. 'Bad, bad news,' Alec replied. Supporting the Club World Championship was vital to keep FIFA sweet, Alec stressed. That message was reinforced by FIFA executive Chuck Blazer, who made it clear that if United didn't represent Europe in FIFA's major club competition it would be impossible for the FA even to dream of hosting 2006. It was my responsibility to negotiate a path through this minefield. What could I say to FIFA? 'I'm so sorry, United can't come to your party in Rio, they are far too busy defending their FA Cup but please we'd still really like to host your World Cup in 2006.' How could I say that? If United snubbed FIFA's invitation to Rio, they would have been replaced by Bayern, who made it absolutely clear they would say 'yes'. No wonder. Guess who else were bidding for 2006? The Germans. Bayern replacing United would be a PR coup for Germany and a disaster for us. The Germans loved our predicament. 'We could see what an awkward position you were in,' two of my friends in the German FA, Horst Schmidt and Wolfgang Niersbach, have told me since.

I never envisaged United's withdrawal from the FA Cup originally. Their chairman, Martin Edwards, was pretty adamant. 'We can't do it,' Martin told me, referring to Rio. 'The rules say we have to play in the FA Cup. They are your FA rules.' Countless conversations took place involving Martin, Maurice Watkins and Sir Roland Smith. Government was included, too, with the Sports Minister, Tony Banks. After all, £3m worth of public funds, taxpayers' money, was invested in the World Cup bid. Much of that cash had already been spent. Even now, I'm unsure who first suggested that the FA amend its rules for one year to allow Manchester United to exit the FA Cup. If it was Martin, I don't think he expected me even to consider such a proposal. But I said I would. In my heart, I believed if we announced the holders' exit in plenty of time, public and media pressure would force United to reconsider and enter teams in both tournaments. United were completely torn, agonising over the decision. They seriously considered entering their youth team to defend the Cup. But the view of some of the coaches was that if United drew Liverpool at Anfield and got stuffed 0–5, some of their kids might never recover. United also felt it would demean the Cup.

So I went up to see Martin and Fergie. Walking into Old Trafford, quite a number of United supporters stopped me to say: 'David, we want to play in the Cup. What you've got to understand is we much prefer playing Man City and Arsenal than all these foreign teams.' This sentiment reflected the public mood. Right from the start, Fergie was shocked about even the thought of forsaking the Cup for a season. His respect for the Cup ran deep; that famous Wembley victory over Crystal Palace in 1990 may even have saved Fergie's job. Bobby Charlton, the United director, felt particularly uneasy as he was part of the 2006 bid team. And so my sleepless nights began, weighing up the pros and cons. Having grown up listening to the debate about United and Chelsea not taking part in the European Cup in the Fifties and then Sir Matt going out on a limb to enter, I understood the significance of new competitions like the Club World Championship. Unlike my friend David Dein, I believed it had a future but, at that time, Rio was all about 2006.

Starting at the FA summer meeting at Carden Park, I set about discussing how United could compete in both the third round and Rio. On the Saturday night, the day before the board meeting, I raised the issue with Ken Bates, chairman of the FA Challenge Cup Committee. Astounded by the dilemma, Ken's attitude was that if United chose not to be in the Cup then OK, so be it. Ken's attitude was refreshing; he understood very quickly the problem. Perhaps he also had a crystal ball. Who won the FA Cup in United's absence? Yes, Chelsea! After another night of disturbed sleep, I rose early and prepared to face the board. I did feel I was betraying the FA Cup by giving United the option of withdrawal. Even though I'd spent my life besotted with the Cup, I couldn't see any other way out, at least in the short term. The long-term impact on the Cup worried me but should I just ignore the £9m including that public money we'd devoted to the 2006 bid? After explaining to the board and the Councillors why United should go to Rio, everyone understood. There was no split. Soon after, the Department for Culture, Media and Sport backed the plan. They knew what it meant to 2006.

Waves of dissension began rolling in, as I'd expected. On succeeding Tony Banks as Sports Minister that summer, Kate Hoey's opening gambit was that Rio was the wrong move. I was furious. Hoey clearly had not been briefed by the DCMS about a decision approved by her new department. They understood the dilemma, Hoey didn't. Ringing the DCMS, I ranted about Hoey's comments. Hearing Hoey would be at the Charity Shield, I smiled. Good. Martin Edwards was waiting. United's chairman told her in full and frank terms the predicament we all struggled with. As we built towards the third-round draw, the criticism flowed faster. In the *Mirror*, their editor Piers Morgan was especially virulent and campaigned against this perfidy towards the Cup. The *Mirror* even floated the suggestion that 'Manchester United should play their FA Cup tie in Brazil'. I wasn't surprised and desperately hoped a new solution might present itself. No joy. Even now, nobody has presented a way out we didn't consider. Ken Bates came up with the best idea, proposing the 'lucky losers' place in the draw that gave Darlington the chance to lose in successive rounds.

'Why did this happen?' Adam Crozier asked me shortly after becoming chief executive. 'Adam, please believe me, I'd have done anything to find a solution,' I replied. In the future weeks and months, whenever Adam wanted to irritate me he'd make some remark about the Cup. He felt it was wrong. So did I but I also believed the Cup, blessed with a long and rich history, was resilient.

Football politics closer to home also surrounded the Cup in the build-up to the 2006 World Cup. During Sven-Goran Eriksson's battle for a four-week preparation period, options proposed included sacrificing replays in the fifth and sixth rounds, and even playing the final on a Wednesday night. One memorable morning, the FA board supported losing the replays only for the FA Cup Committee to vote against. To the surprise of some people, Manchester United's David Gill was amongst the most vociferous defenders of replays. Those of us who supported Sven's campaigns always believed his aim could be achieved without losing replays, but for just one season playing the quarter-finals mid-week. The success of that campaign owed much to the latest FA Cup chairman, Barry 'from Barnsley' Taylor. 'I'm getting killed in Yorkshire for this,' said Barry, just after the 'FA Cup final on a Wednesday night scandal' hit the headlines. 'Stick in there, Barry,' I pleaded with him. And he did.

Nowadays, the Cup is trapped in the long shadow cast by the Champions League. Even those of us who care passionately about the Cup accept the landscape has changed. In these days of a hugely expanded Champions League, the Cup will never again be as high a priority for the elite clubs. Successive chief executives of the FA have recognised the competition would be transformed by the annual award of a Champions League place to the FA Cup winner. So far, the Premier League clubs have resisted this proposal, and it will take remarkable powers of persuasion from the new generation within Soho Square to change things.

To showcase the Cup more, Crozier wanted the round's big televised tie to kick off on Sunday at seven p.m., prime-time viewing. The Met kyboshed that. During my time at the FA, we often fought the police over Cup kick-off times. Their position was not always logical. 'How can every major city in Europe stage a match on a Sunday evening at seven p.m. with the exception of London,' I asked the Met. 'Stretched resources,' they bleated. 'And drinking.' Frustratingly, the Met had the final word. Greater Manchester Police were similar. At least the draw was confirmed in its traditional Monday lunchtime slot, although it will be interesting to see where ITV, owners of the latest FA television contract, choose to schedule the event.

If the Cup is to reclaim all its old magic, the FA must consider a third-round revolution. The draw should be reworked to ensure all Premier League clubs play away. The sight of Manchester United, Chelsea, Liverpool, Arsenal and the rest visiting far-flung outposts would generate amazing excitement. Before chairmen complain about revenue, what about potential replays? London cabbies, and conspiracy theorists, would love it.

15

Ungentlemanly Behaviour and the Gentleman's Agreement

The FA were offered votes for cash during the bidding to host the 2006 World Cup finals. A bribe. An irregular payment. A sweetener. Call it what you like, those of us at the FA who heard this corrupt proposal were shocked. The offer was made on 17 March 2000 by an individual well connected in international footballing circles to Adam Crozier, our chief executive. After a brief exchange, Adam said he'd call the guy back. Adam immediately got FA security people to see if our phones had devices for recording calls. Unfortunately, they didn't. We quickly contacted a private security company to see whether they could install a device in time. Sadly, they couldn't. Adam asked two of us to listen in on an extension. Along with Frank Wheeler, a highly respected former Foreign Office official brought in to help England's 2006 campaign, I eavesdropped as Crozier returned the individual's call at 5.15 p.m. We believed the offer was serious. Again Adam was offered World Cup votes in return for a substantial payment. Quite rightly, Adam showed his outrage and disdain. 'England's bid is a clean bid,' said Adam, 'and will continue to be. In no circumstances would we ever contemplate a deal involving irregular payments.'

At seven p.m., the individual then contacted Frank, who reiterated Adam's emphatic message that the FA had never countenanced bribery and never would. Frank then put the phone down. 'It was a pretty brazen offer,' Frank said. Frank, Adam and I then convened to discuss the calls, noting down what was said to Adam in a one-page memo. Frank also recorded what was said during the call to him. These two memos were then retained by those of us present. All of us were stunned. Neither Frank, Adam, myself nor the 2006 campaign director Alec McGivan were left in any doubt. Financial sweeteners could help bring in 2006 votes. That would never be the FA's way. Some other countries could take short cuts, could walk in the sport's shadows. Not us. We were the FA, guardians of the game's spirit and ethics. However pompous that mission statement can sound, it defined our attitude. In order to protect the good name of the FA, I understand this individual's scandalous proposal was reported to FIFA. To this day, I have no knowledge of what they did or didn't do about it.

England's 2006 campaign was fraught from the beginning. The so-called 'Gentleman's Agreement' dogged the FA throughout the bid process. At times, it felt like swimming against a rip-tide current with lead weights in both hands. The nub of the 'Gentleman's Agreement' was that our chairman, Sir Bert Millichip, was supposed to have promised Germany backing for their 2006 bid if they supported England for Euro '96. This was always denied by Sir Bert, who was good friends with Egidius Braun, the German FA president, and the UEFA president, Lennart Johansson. History has occasionally been rewritten over the 'Gentleman's Agreement', unfavourably and unfairly in respect of the English, and the record needs to be set straight. Along with the testimony of Sir Bert, many other indisputable facts shred the idea that what most people would consider an actual pact ever existed between Germany and England.

Point one: no one ever recorded anything about any concordat. No document. No memo. No letter. No scribble on the back of an envelope. Nothing. If the veracity of the 'Gentleman's Agreement' had ever been debated in court, a judge would have thrown it out for lack of evidence. Come back with something concrete. In deciding the venue for the biggest event on the planet after the Olympics, surely open bidding was required, not hearsay.

Point two: but there surely was a conversation late at night, possibly in the Black Forest, possibly after quite a few brandies, when Bert, Egidius and Lennart discussed 2006. Afterwards, it became clear to me eventually that Egidius and Lennart believed some form of 'agreement' had been reached. Sir Bert, though, signed various letters to confirm this was not his view. In November 1999, I talked to Sir Bert to compile a statement. 'There was not, and there could not have been, a gentleman's agreement that meant England would support Germany as the host nation for 2006,' said Sir Bert, who stressed he had no authority to make such a promise anyway. The reality was that the Gentleman's Agreement was the Gentleman's Cock-up.

Point three: two days after England exited Euro '96 at the hands of our German chums, the FA announced a bid for 2006. So why weren't the Germans on the phone immediately, shouting: 'But what about the Gentleman's Agreement?' Only later did they and UEFA mention it. When we made our announcement, all the senior UEFA officials were in London for the final of Euro '96, attending FA dinners, talking to English officials. None of them raised the 'Gentleman's Agreement'.

'Why did no one say anything when we announced the bid?' I asked Lennart, a great friend of mine.

'No one thought the English were serious,' he replied.

Point four: the FA would surely never have done a deal to step down for 2006, when we had already done one not to bid for the 1998 World Cup. The minutes of the FA executive committee meeting of 3 September 1991 at Lancaster Gate contain a hugely significant fact. After detail about 'County Association Boundaries' and the 'Sports Turf Research Institute', Item 15 revealed: 'Following various discussions within UEFA, the Chairman and Vice-Chairman had reached the conclusion that The Football Association should drop its bid to stage the 1998 FIFA World Cup Finals and concentrate instead on an application to host the European Championship Final Tournament in 1996.' It's ludicrous to believe that we wouldn't bid for TWO World Cups in return for one European Championship finals. One maybe, never two.

The truth is that eventually the majority of the UEFA leadership, led by Lennart and Egidius, genuinely believed there was a gentleman's agreement and poor Sir Bert found himself isolated. I knew how much it pained him. Bert's successor as chairman, Keith Wiseman, and the then chief executive Graham Kelly continued to champion the bid backed by Alec McGivan's enthusiastic campaign team. The success of Euro '96 was the catalyst. The bid train had left the station. By the time Geoff Thompson became FA chairman and wanted to halt it, it was too late.

'But Geoff, nothing was written down,' I told him when we discussed the 'Gentleman's Agreement'. Geoff accepted that, politically, the bid was past the point of no return. As chairman, he needed to defend the FA corner. 'And who knows in a long race what can happen to other people's campaigns?' I added to Geoff. With all his misgivings, Geoff rebuilt bridges with Lennart and UEFA, but kept his distance from the bid.

As England struggled, Alec contacted me. 'We want you more centrally involved,' he said. England's bid was in deep water, with South Africa and Germany pulling clear, so I tried to help. Contacting Lennart, I floated the idea of a joint bid with the Germans. The 2006 World Cup that was eventually such a success from Berlin to Munich could have been shared with Manchester and London. Lennart was certainly keen for a short time. So, too, according to the media, was the most influential man in German football, Franz Beckenbauer. The German FA thought over the possibility of a joint bid until it became clear they could win 2006 on their own. Question marks hung over South Africa being ready in time. Europe always had a great advantage. In World Cup bidding, Europe owns 8 votes and only 12½ are required. The Germans fancied their chances, and duly won the vote in 2000.

The failure of England's bid was more cock-up than conspiracy – and it was a very expensive cock-up, around £9m of FA and public funds, though crucial lessons were absorbed ahead of London's 2012 Olympic bid. When the FIFA delegates visited England to assess facilities, the FA threw an extravagant party at Hampton Court, near London, including speakers like Hugh Grant and finishing with a fabulous firework display. The FA had to lavish money on the event. When FIFA dignitaries come from across the globe, they expect more than a pie and a pint. That's how you treat guests who've travelled a long way. FIFA people expect to stay in nice hotels and be entertained. Every other candidate looked after them well. We had to follow, although it was exorbitant.

During and after the campaign, the House of Commons held two select-committee enquiries into the bid. This independent group of MPs concluded that the FA campaign had been well run but was innately flawed because of the 'Gentleman's Agreement' farrago. England should never have bid for 2006.

16

Uncle Albert and the Pantomime Horse

Life at Soho Square often seemed a daily soap opera crammed with contrasting characters like 'The Lollipop Man', 'Mr Five Agendas', 'Tonto' and, of course, the most senior Englishman in world football today, 'Uncle Albert'.

FA nicknames generally originated from the renowned 'Heardy', Peter Heard, FA and Football League bigwig for a generation, long-time FA board member and president of Colchester United. After one FA summer meeting in Torquay, 'Heardy' and I travelled back with David Dein and his wife Barbara. The journey was long, hot and usually interminable but it flew past when David mentioned he knew nothing of the re-named FA cast-list.

'Go on, "Heardy",' I laughed, 'list them all!'

'Well, there's "The Lollipop Man",' Peter began. 'That's Dave Richards.' On any issue, the Premier League chairman and FA board member was, rightly or wrongly, legendary for changing directions as suddenly as the lady turning her lollipop around at a zebra crossing, so you were never sure which way around it was.

'Ken Bates is "Captain Birdseye",' continued 'Heardy'. The white beard guaranteed that. 'And Barry Bright is "The Badger".' Dein laughed. The chairman of the FA's disciplinary committee did indeed resemble a badger, particularly a badger who was the life and soul of the party.

'Robert Coar is "Bob the Builder",' added 'Heardy'. Blackburn Rovers' then chairman is a hugely witty man given to sending lengthy gags via email. 'Heardy' stopped.

'What about my husband?' asked Barbara Dein.

'He's "Mr Five Agendas"!' replied 'Heardy'.

'You see, Barbara,' I explained, 'in meetings nobody is ever sure which agenda David is on: his UEFA agenda, his Arsenal agenda, his FA or Premier League agenda, his G14 agenda, etc., etc.' David and Barbara burst out laughing but he was still astonished. David never knew staff and officials called him 'Mr Five Agendas'.

'Heardy' had a name for most people. When Simon Johnson joined the FA in April 2005, the new Director of Corporate Affairs followed chief executive Brian Barwick everywhere so he was dubbed 'Tonto'. Simon himself is a top-class mimic, capable of a wonderful two-minute impression of each board member and a particularly accurate 'Uncle Albert'.

'Uncle Albert' is Geoff Thompson, FA chairman from 1999 until 2007 and now vice-president of FIFA. Not since Sir Stanley Rous was FIFA president fifty years ago has there been an Englishman as high-ranking in world football as Thompson, a lookalike for the fabled boat-sinking character from *Only Fools and Horses*. When Geoff was elected chairman at the FA summer meeting at Carden Park, near Chester, in 1999, it was a pivotal day for the organisation and the future of English football. On the same day, Dave Richards was rejected as the FA's vice-chairman, a major surprise. Both events shaped what followed dramatically.

Thompson had become acting chairman when Keith Wiseman resigned over that controversial deal with the Welsh FA. Now Geoff needed to carry the FA Council with him to be installed permanently. He was up against David Sheepshanks, the Ipswich Town chairman exuding all the charisma Thompson was perceived to lack. Sheepshanks enjoyed much good publicity during the campaign, which I fear had a negative impact. 'Unfortunately good publicity is sometimes bad news in the contest,' I told Sheepshanks after Geoff won by twenty votes. If eleven

Councillors had voted the other way, the history of English football would have been very different. David was let down by the Premier League, who didn't support him, thinking they could get on better with Thompson. To my knowledge, some of the old guard like Sir Bert Millichip voted for David Sheepshanks. Sadly, a new chairman made no difference to the widening splits in English football. Could Sheepshanks have united the game any better? He would certainly have been seen to try harder than the man who beat him. But would the Premier League have forgiven Sheepshanks for taking them on and winning?

Sheepshanks, almost certainly, would have recruited Richard Scudamore as chief executive. A driving force behind the Premier League's phenomenal success, 'Scud' was the most talented chief executive the FA never had. Even Richard's biggest critics would acknowledge that his achievement in bringing billions of pounds in income into the Premier League has been breathtaking. But nothing upsets Richard more than the perception that his job is just about money-making. There is much more to Richard than clever commercial and broadcasting deals. He is focused, meticulous about detail, occasionally obsessive. Prior to Friday morning's summits of the FA, PL and FL, Richard would meticulously prepare his lieutenants, Mike Foster and Philip French at Starbucks in Soho Square. Blessed with a better sense of humour than he sometimes lets on, Scudamore can still be somewhat intimidating. Complaints that he doesn't listen enough to others aren't unknown but I have huge respect for his considerable intellect. He doesn't lose many battles, as I found out to my cost over the fights for a winter break and then a four-week preparation period for the 2006 World Cup. Along with Sheepshanks, Richard might have reinvigorated the FA, though the demands on him would have been very different from those at the Premier League. Only now, a decade on, can the FA begin to assess whether it made the wrong decision at Carden Park in 1999. I suspect a majority of Council members think they did. I know Geoff Thompson, the beneficiary of Carden Park, thinks he was forced out somewhat shabbily in 2008.

One evening shortly after that FA meeting in 1999, I took Richard for a drink in Park Lane. Geoff had asked me to pass on some important news to him. 'Geoff doesn't want you as chief executive,' I told Richard, still irritated that the chairman had given me the job of telling him.

'I'm not surprised,' Richard replied. 'I don't think I'd want to be chief executive under Thompson anyway.' Richard's gut instinct was maybe right. I fear Geoff Thompson never built proper relationships with his chief executives, Adam Crozier, Mark Palios or Brian Barwick. I thought that damaged him and them. The chairman also exasperated several members of the board consistently and certain senior members of the management team too, particularly Nic Coward. 'You should step down, you're not up to the job,' Nic wrote in exasperation one day.

Whisperings about the chairman continued throughout his years in office, not only from Councillors – the blazers upstairs – but also the senior management – full-time staff, us downstairs. But no formal challenge to Geoff's position was ever launched, to my knowledge. Ultimately he was even re-elected unopposed as those who had sometimes railed against him failed to coalesce behind an alternative.

I believe Thompson felt most at home on the magistrates' bench in Sheffield, in his homely office at the Sheffield & Hallamshire County FA or as the popular chairman of the FA's disciplinary committee. When he actually became chairman of the FA I thought he was daunted by the job. Geoff is a complex and thoroughly decent character, deeply religious and often guided by his wife. Capable of considerable generosity, an ambitious streak lurks beneath the surface. Some culpability for Geoff's poor public image must rest with me. When his many critics called him 'Mr Invisible', for several years I was responsible. Appearing on TV and in the media was never Geoff's scene. Soho Square offered up other friendlier faces, like Adam, the elegant Brooking, Sven, whoever. Geoff Thompson never wanted to be the public face of the FA. 'Tell me the things you really love,' I asked Geoff one day. He talked passionately about cricket and the story goes he was a very good wicketkeeper. A safe pair of hands? Not everybody thought so at the FA. On at least one occasion, he told me Ken Bates went to his hotel room and asked him to step aside. Thompson stood up to Bates. I fear that wasn't always the case. Geoff was the ghost in the FA machine. Sven coached England for six years, was regularly at Soho Square, but he never went into the office of the chairman of the Football Association once! He was never invited!

Maybe Geoff was shy. The six a.m. train from Sheffield via Chesterfield to St Pancras was also the subject of much humorous debate at the FA. When Geoff boarded at Chesterfield, Dave Richards and the former Sports Minister Richard Caborn were already *in situ.* This train was known to FA staff as the 'Sheffield Mafia Train'; whatever they discussed would influence the football agenda in Soho Square that week. Occasionally, Richards and Caborn gave Geoff quite a hard time on the train and I learned he would breakfast on his own just to avoid them. He hated confrontation.

As England coaches and FA chief executives came and went, 'Uncle Albert' continued his remarkable rise into football's global stratosphere. In 2000, the FA launched a campaign to get Geoff on to the all-powerful UEFA Executive Committee. In the three months leading up to the vote, Geoff canvassed 47 of the 51 members. Their reaction was invariably positive, so Geoff felt buoyant. He needed 26 votes to get elected.

'Well, I'm going to get forty or forty-two,' said Geoff the day before the vote at the UEFA Congress in Luxembourg. He was that confident.

'No, Chairman, you'll get somewhere between twenty-three and twenty-eight,' I replied.

'But I've seen forty-seven people and almost all agreed to support me,' said Thompson.

'Yes but they always say that.' Looking at me aghast, Geoff genuinely seemed to believe that when somebody told him they would back him they meant it.

'Right!' He had a very uneasy night but scraped in with 28 votes. Understanding what a coup this was, I rang 'The Lollipop Man' and 'Mr Five Agendas'.

'How did Geoff get on?' Richards and Dein both asked, expecting me to reply 'badly'. This was at the height of England's unpopularity because of the 'Gentleman's Agreement' and hooliganism.

'He got in!' I said. There was silence down the phone.

'You're joking,' both said eventually. Neither believed me. Both were absolutely astonished. Richards himself had wanted the seat on the UEFA Executive Committee for the Premier League.

Four years later, when Geoff was up for re-election in Cyprus, he started to worry again. 'Chairman, the future is Eastern Europe,' I assured him. 'There are more countries like the old Soviet countries. Get them onside.' Geoff made sure he became very popular in Eastern Europe, chairing a number of committees to help them develop their football, and he eventually received 46 votes out of 52. By tapping into those nations, Geoff's star shines in the international galaxy. For a period, Geoff even aspired to replace Lennart Johansson as UEFA president, an ambition that inevitably soured his relationship with Lennart. Someone close to Lennart made it very clear to me that he felt Geoff was after his job. When the presidential election came, Geoff had no chance against Michel Platini, a European champion with France. He would have had no chance against Franz Beckenbauer, a world champion with West Germany. But if those two footballing legends hadn't been in contention, Geoff might even have replaced Lennart to become UEFA president. It could have been 'Uncle Albert' handing the Henri Delaunay trophy to Spain's captain, Iker Casillas, in Vienna on 29 June 2008. Platini won, and built a relationship with Geoff Thompson along the way. I hope Geoff's support will be reciprocated one day when the battle over who will host World Cup 2018 comes to a head. It will be the ultimate test of Geoff's influence in the corridors of power at UEFA and FIFA.

Geoff knows how to work a committee room and is now well

regarded within UEFA and FIFA. In 2006, Geoff seemed to have made a mess of getting the FIFA vice-presidency, which went to John McBeth, the Scot who then made some injudicious comments about other nations so that the position fell into Thompson's lap. First Wiseman, then McBeth. Some people in history get lucky once. Geoff got lucky twice. Platini may seek to be the next president of FIFA with Sepp Blatter's blessing, which would be good for the FA as he gets on with Thompson. Remarkably, 'Uncle Albert' is one step away from football's top job.

Whenever I travelled abroad with Geoff, assisting his various campaigns, I always felt uneasy. The ancient FA problem of the parallel universes, of upstairs and downstairs, accompanied us. It was not unknown for us downstairs to have to run minor errands for those upstairs, as I did for the chairman and his wife. Perhaps that's as it should be but I believed in a team effort.

A team effort worked very well for the FA, and English football, when Nic Coward, Michael Cunnah and I acted together running the organisation for more than a year between 1998 and 2000. Richard Scudamore says relations between the FA and the Premier League were never better before or since. It could have lasted. Sadly, it didn't. 'We need one chief executive,' Nic insisted. So, aided by headhunters, the FA went out and recruited Adam Crozier from Saatchi's. Things appeared good. Adam was a bright spark, just what the FA required. The mill-pond tranquillity was swiftly disturbed by an almighty depth charge. While Adam worked his period of notice at his advertising agency, we had the nightmarish moment when Mihir Bose called from the *Daily Telegraph*. Calls from Mihir tended to quicken the sweat glands. They were not social calls. They were business calls with alarm bells on.

'David, is the FA aware that Adam Crozier was reprimanded while at this newspaper for altering his advertising figures?' Mihir enquired. Quite a bombshell.

'Mihir, I'll get back to you' was all I could stammer, shocked by this development. Some of the FA Councillors, Joe Lovejoy's 'Blazered Buffoons', thought I enjoyed these moments a little too much, fighting the fires during a Cathay Pacific or a Sven saga. Some conflagrations I could do without. How the hell hadn't the headhunters unearthed this fact? I called Crozier. He sounded in a wind tunnel.

'Where are you?' I asked.

'On a ferry going over to Bute,' he replied. Bute? I remembered. The Isle of Bute was where Adam hailed from. 'David, what's up?' I broke the news about the *Telegraph* story. Adam didn't deny it. Clearly distressed, he fell quiet for a while. All I could hear were the waves and the wind. The scene sounded as raw as Adam probably felt.

'How will people at the FA react?' Adam asked eventually.

'I don't know, Adam. Leave it with me.' I was at a 2006 World Cup bid event at Claridge's, being serenaded by Chris de Burgh. Standing up the 'Lady in Red', I dashed in and out, fielding calls. I phoned Geoff, who sat on the fence. I called Sir David Hill-Wood, chairman of the FA finance committee, now sadly passed away. 'We should support him,' said Sir David. He saw Adam's mistake as mere youthful exuberance. The right view, I thought, but not everybody's. Cunnah felt Adam couldn't survive. Overall, there was no blood-lust and Adam made it through choppy waters to Bute and the FA. He recovered quickly, impressing people at the organisation with his energy and vision. In the early days, Adam was a huge breath of fresh air, blowing away many FA cobwebs and moving the organisation out of Lancaster Gate and into Soho Square, out of the nineteenth century and into the twenty-first.

'You will get on well with Crozier,' Thompson had said to me and he was right. Adam made lively company. Significantly younger than me, Adam used to enjoy having fun at my expense.

'David's not a detail man,' he said, winding me up. Initially funny, when Adam kept bringing it up, it did weary me a bit. He was the one who had been lax with his details at the *Telegraph*. A massive Celtic fan, Adam wasn't bound up in the minutiae of football politics as Graham Kelly sometimes seemed to be. I just wished I'd warned Adam more of the need to keep all parts of the FA happy. He spent so much of his time with the FA staff, and perhaps not enough with the blazers and the powerbrokers of the professional game. Perhaps I should have done more to help. It proved his downfall.

Becoming FA chief executive is a full-on commitment. It is like being PM; the scrutiny is extreme and crisis lurks around each corner. Adam had family responsibilities at weekends which made it difficult for him to go to as many games as he would have liked – and needed to. The chief executive of the FA had to become a familiar face in the boardrooms of Old Trafford and Anfield, and an occasional visitor to lesser locations on the English circuit. When the going gets rough in football, people needed allies in different parts of the game. Adam never had enough allies. 'We don't know Crozier,' people in the game complained to me. Adam's domestic situation was such, I never felt it right to suggest he got out to matches more.

The need to take the FA out of London, visiting people, was something I understood. When the former West Brom striker Jeff Astle tragically passed away from a degenerative brain condition on 19 January 2002, I resolved to go and see his widow Lorraine. The suggestion was that Jeff's persistent heading of those old lead-like balls contributed to his death. I hadn't a clue, and I knew Lorraine Astle was considering legal action, but I felt it important to show respect to the widow of a former England international. The legal advice from within Soho Square was not to but I had to. West Brom kindly provided Lorraine's number, so I called her, went up and spent an afternoon with her and her family in the Black Country.

'Look, I'm not here from the FA,' I said to Lorraine. 'Your husband gave me a lot of pleasure as a fan. I thought he was a great player. He used to forever be scoring against my Manchester United!' We chatted about Jeff's career and whether the old leather balls could have harmed him. As I left, I gained the reassuring impression that Lorraine Astle was just grateful somebody in authority had bothered to come and listen to her concerns. The FA owed it to the families of former England players. They owed it to the memory of Jeff Astle. FA executives had to put themselves about in football, see people, talk to people.

Fairly quickly, Adam's relationship started to fracture with professionals like Scudamore. At those Friday summits Adam used to host, full of wholesome food like yoghurts and fruit, the atmosphere primed like a brainstorming session at Saatchi's, the idea was to spread goodwill and share thoughts. Richard, after his Starbucks team talk with his lieutenants, was always right up for these meetings; he would come flying in with fourteen issues he wanted raised. Disagreements grew between Adam and Richard. I often wondered whether there was a hint of envy on Richard's part. Adam had the job Richard had albeit briefly coveted. I always wondered if he might seek it again.

With a background in advertising, Adam perhaps inevitably drew the accusation of being all style and no substance. The substance was his tireless work untying the knot that was the red tape wrapped around Wembley. The substance was the plan for the National Football Centre. Politics, not lack of substance, accounted for Adam. Dave Richards felt there was too much spin coming from Adam's office. The professional game lost confidence in Adam, reacting to his very successful early days with a degree of jealousy and venom that I felt I could almost touch.

'Crozier never consults us,' they ranted.

'Crozier acts beyond his authority,' they raged. By the time he reached England's Awaji base in Japan in June 2002, Adam's relationship with the Premier League was as rocky as a Zen garden. Wembley took up all his time, preventing him from cultivating relationships with key FA International Committee people like Richards and 'Deadly' Doug Ellis. Rumblings emanated from some committee people about who was paying for the England players' wives to fly to Japan. Adam found questions like that petty in the middle of a World Cup. 'The players have to feel everyone is backing them,' said Adam.

Sven was very closely identified with Adam, who'd appointed him. England's early promise in Japan inevitably reflected positively on Adam as well as Sven. When England overcame Argentina and Denmark to reach the quarter-finals, Adam wondered aloud whether Richards and Ellis appeared less jubilant than the rest of us. 'Surely, everyone in the FA wants England to win,' was my response. It was impossible to believe otherwise, wasn't it? Contrasting with the unity in the dressing room, this division in the FA meant a blow-out was probably inevitable once we got home from the World Cup. I suspected 'The Lollipop Man' and 'Deadly' had unfinished business with Adam.

The pair were fascinating characters, true servants of the game, and steeped in the highs and lows of football politics. Chairman of the Premier League, Richards was an enigma. Capable of huge kindness and *bonhomie*, he was also infuriatingly unpredictable. 'The Lollipop Man' tag was richly deserved. Richards was once confronted by Adam and the Durham FA Councillor, Frank Pattison, who effectively blamed him for the civil wars raging inside the FA.

At board meetings, Richards sometimes wound up colleagues by picking up his papers as if he were about to walk out in outrage over some perceived slight. His tactic of sitting immediately opposite the chairman was often effective in unnerving Geoff Thompson. The more tense board confrontations could be enlivened by some of 'The Lollipop Man's' legendary sayings: 'You can't have penny and bun, son' and 'Off you go and play on railway tracks' were among the milder rebukes some of us got used to. If the going got really tough, this knight of the realm condemned us to 'get off and piss in Scarborough harbour'. I was pleased his knighthood from the Queen recognised his significant contribution to the wonderful work of the NSPCC.

'Deadly' Doug Ellis also loved England. Villa's chairman got on with the England players, although Gareth Southgate wasn't his greatest fan. Amusingly on international trips, Doug was always on the look-out for players for Villa. After England faced the legendary Hong Kong Select in 1996, Doug sidled up to me at the post-match do aboard a floating Chinese restaurant.

'Did you see that number six playing for Hong Kong Select?'

'No, Doug. He didn't make a huge impression on me.'

'He was the one in pink.'

'They all were, Doug, except the keeper.'

'I rate the number six. Can you introduce us?'

'OK. Leave it to me.' I went off to find Micky Duxbury, one of the HK players and someone I'd known from his Manchester United days.

'No problem,' said Micky. 'I'll get the number six into the gents. Tell Doug to come into the gents in a few minutes.' So this bizarre meeting took place between 'Deadly', Duxbury and a Chinese player, although no deal was ever reached.

Doug was great. He used to play up to his super-scout image. 'Gazza, can we have a quick word,' Doug would say to Paul Gascoigne on England trips. They'd disappear around the corner, and Doug would return smiling, as if he'd signed Gazza for Villa. Doug wasn't tapping players up. I don't think so anyway. He was just revelling in the England experience.

When England returned from Japan in 2002, few people were laughing. For several months, Adam endured a relentless barrage of briefings from certain board members to journalists that spending was out of control, that the FA might be bankrupt. There was no truth in that. Keen to build Wembley and the National Football Centre, Adam had good financial advice that the FA could afford both. Adam's enemies in football allowed the perception to grow that the organisation had become recklessly extravagant, overstaffed and overpaid. FA salaries, and not just that of the England coach, did increase under Adam but some had been relatively low for too long. There was extravagance but also penny-pinching to extremes I'd never experienced before. Again, the parallel universes collided. The Blazers complained about what they saw as lavish Christmas parties for the staff at places like the Royal Geographical Society near the Royal Albert Hall. I seem to remember Sven enjoyed such events almost as much as the paparazzi outside. Incidentally, tell me another organisation that attracts the photographers to its seasonal festivities. The staff responded by highlighting the cost of the annual FA summer meeting for Councillors and their wives. Up to £250,000 covered a five-star hotel, food, drink, cabaret, generous mileage, and the wives' outing while meetings took place over three days. 'Don't volunteers deserve some reward at the end of a long season,' the Blazers exclaimed. Not that such events in places like Torquay, Brighton and Harrogate were always peaceful. In Cambridge one year, the FA summer knees-up was accompanied by a non-stop rock festival in the park next door.

The endless leaks from the FA and Premier League grew into a wave, crashing into Adam. Eventually, life became intolerable. On the day he left Soho Square, I talked to Adam and he told me it wasn't worth the struggle anymore. The whole experience had scarred him. Adam had hoped to make a difference, to improve English football, and had been brought down by people with their own, more limited agendas. 'What I have learned in football is that people who say they are your supporters are not necessarily your supporters and they are the worst,' Adam said wistfully. 'At least with your enemies, you know where you stand.' I realised this was also meant as a warning to me.

'Be careful, David,' were Adam's last words to me. My mind immediately strayed towards who at the top of the organisation would support me if I came under fire. Geoff Thompson? Dave Richards? I suspected the list, as in Adam's case, wouldn't be very long. Anger swept around Soho Square at the board's treatment of Adam. Paul Newman, appointed by me as senior spokesperson, went out on to the steps of Soho Square and expressed his frustration, a move that predictably outraged some members of the board.

On his way out of Soho Square, Adam spent an hour talking to his good friend Sven, telling him to stick with England. When Nic Coward and I assumed temporary control again, everyone worried about how Sven would react now that perhaps his biggest ally had left. Emerging from the board meeting, I told 'Uncle Albert', 'The Lollipop Man', 'Bob the Builder' and 'Mr Five Agendas' that they needed to act quickly. 'You need to reassure Sven,' I said. We all trooped into Sven's office, and they voiced their support for him. As always he was polite, though he was angry inside.

Crozier's departure was followed by an avalanche of negative media coverage concerning his alleged financial legacy. 'REGIME OF EXTRAVAGANCE', 'MONEY MESS', 'FINANCIAL MELTDOWN', '£90M BLACK HOLE' and 'PANIC STATIONS' were amongst the plethora of bad headlines. For Nic and me, installed as joint acting chief executives, those months were traumatic and ultimately brutal.

Deloitte and Touche were called in to advise on why the FA board had received one set of financial forecasts at their August 2002 meeting, and a significantly different, and more depressing, set just three months later. Thankfully, the accountants concluded there had been no deliberate intent by anybody to misrepresent the truth. Income from broadcasting rights, licensing and sponsorship as well as cashflow forecasts for the new Wembley had been 'incorrectly processed' in the August presentation. Nobody was blamed.

Nic had always been sceptical about whether the FA could afford to proceed with Wembley as well as the proposed NFC at Burton simultaneously. His view hardened after more than £20m was committed to create the high-quality pitches at the NFC. 'We just can't do it,' Nic kept saying. But Adam had convinced the board it could. With his departure, and then the revelations about inaccurate financial forecasting, a problem very rapidly deteriorated into a crisis. Before the NFC could be ready for players and coaches, an additional £70m was required.

As now, the real burden was Wembley with its huge loan repayments. By March 2003, Jamie Magraw, our latest finance director, was forecasting a 'significant funding gap' amounting to £28m per year between 2004 and 2006, and £13m per year over the four years up to 2010. Real worries about a significantly reduced future TV deal shook confidence further. Sitting in his office, Jamie found himself regularly under pressure from passing board members. The FA's dysfunctional nature worsened matters. The staff were convinced board members leaked information to the press, often using figures even worse than the real ones, and then wringing their hands. The board blamed the staff for doing the same. My worries revolved increasingly around Nic, who bore the brunt of responsibility for finding a way through the nightmare. Along with Paul Barber, Nic reassured sponsors and banks. At times Nic seemed in despair. 'I'm fine,' he told me repeatedly. He wasn't, developing a dreadful cough that went on for months and signalled his inner stress.

At a series of lengthy and tetchy management meetings, we eventually concluded our cashflow issues meant significant cost-cutting measures. The board ordered us to chop jobs. Several years earlier, Paul Barber had managed through a redundancy programme at Barclays Bank. 'This is far worse,' Paul told me of the FA bloodletting. 'People love football and love working here. This is about shattering people's dreams.' Paul was right. Over several days, department by department, those being axed were called to Room 520, 'a discreet room' as Paul Nolan, our HR director, put it in his top-secret memo to the management team. A passionate Evertonian, Paul is a caring man who'd overseen the expansion in staff numbers authorised by Crozier. Now Paul was asked to reverse much of it. 'Shit happens,' said Paul stoically.

The killing field, the 'discreet' Room 520, was immediately next to the chairman's office, where months earlier Adam had negotiated himself a bumper pay-off. Generous severance terms were not available now. Those being dismissed, some in tears, were escorted unceremoniously from the building. A heavy responsibility hung in my heart for every single person sacked. Some I had recruited. Some were good friends. It was a miserable time.

Was there another way out of this mess? Led by Dave Richards, some members of the board championed a long-term financing agreement with Bear Stearns International. In 2008, when Bear Stearns went under in the worldwide financial turmoil, I wondered about the problems that deal might have caused the FA. Instead, at the behest of the incoming chief executive Mark Palios, a smaller and more flexible short-term loan was arranged with Barclays and the crisis passed. Mark had not even formally taken up his role but he considered the Bear Stearns proposal to be madness.

'The numbers man with a football background' was how Palios was hailed by Charlie Sale in the *Daily Mail*. Mark played 400-odd games for Tranmere and Crewe, some of which I'd reported on for the BBC, and his debut for the FA could not have been more assured. This gritty midfielder was not the first choice. In typically surreal FA fashion, their number-one target was 'the Man from Mars'. This was no 'Heardy' moniker. The headhunters actually found 'the Man from Mars', confectionary executive Peter Littlewood, who promptly turned the job down for family reasons. The public scrutiny was too much. Following Littlewood's withdrawal, Palios appeared a top-class alternative. Having built a fine name for himself at accountants PricewaterhouseCoopers, Palios's early actions were impressive, although he was very much a systems person. No one just ambled into a meeting with Palios. Detailed preparation was the order of the day. 'This is what I've done this week, this is what I want to do next week,' all written down in neat memos. Yes, sir, no, sir, three bags full, sir.

Palios was not the easiest person to get to know. Anyone who managed to get past his sometimes brusque manner did find a warm human being but they had to put the hours in. After Adam Crozier's vision statement 'to use the power of football to build a better future' we had Mark's philosophy that 'the fish rots from the head downwards'. Palios even took the FA management team, or leadership team as we now called ourselves, on a bonding session near Reading. All the way down the M4, I prayed for the weather to intervene. Rain stops play. Please. No luck. Under Palios's eagle eye, the first day involved middle-aged limbs creaking around a commando course. Brooking excelled at these high-wire walks, of course. As someone who'd always hated heights, I struggled. I just thought: 'I'm fifty, will climbing through trees sixty feet above terra firma make me better at my job?'

The organisers then led us into the middle of a field that had a circle in it. 'Get into the middle of the circle without walking there,' we were ordered. So the great brains of the FA management – sorry leadership – team were put to work finding a route into the middle of this bloody great circle without touching the ground. I'd dealt with dentist chairs, riots, and stroppy Argentinians, and now I was auditioning for *Gladiators*. Palios's idea was to make us bond more. For two days, I ricocheted between laughter and terror.

Palios did set me more interesting tasks. He asked me to give priority to the FA's relationships with Westminster and Whitehall. Soon afterwards, I wrote a private letter to the Secretary of State Tessa Jowell in early 2004. I noted 'the rumblings within the Treasury and elsewhere in Government for an inquiry into football and its corporate governance'. I also pointed out that 'the gap between rich and poor in football is as wide, if not wider, than ever. It is the belief of people like myself that this is perpetuated by the structure of the sport which builds in conflict between the various sections of the game'. Within months that structure was to be under scrutiny as never before.

I had always wondered for how long the Premier League would be able to continue with a board of just two directors who were its chairman and its chief executive.

Now students of corporate governance principles were to be horrified by events at Soho Square after Mark Palios left the FA in 2004. Suddenly, the FA had two acting chief executives, Dave Richards and Roger Burden, both of them effectively seconded from the board. Digby Jones at the CBI told me proper corporate governance precluded board members becoming day-to-day chief executives. Once again, the FA had ripped up the rulebook – and stirred in some farce for good measure. Roger and Dave decided to meet the leadership team. Roger, formerly a very senior figure at the Cheltenham and Gloucester Building Society, arrived first and insisted he was working in tandem with Dave. Good. Here was one end of the pantomime horse. Burden chose some interesting words to inspire a depressed leadership team. 'Here in Soho Square there are too many televisions and too many tits,' said Burden. Apparently people were not properly dressed. Apparently, Crozier had allowed the installation of too many flat-screen TVs. After a dispiriting time, we could all do with a good laugh, and Roger cheered us up no end. A note of Burden's remark was solemnly taken by Jonathan Hill, the commercial director. Shortly afterwards, Richards walked in to address us. Unlike Burden, 'The Lollipop Man' insisted he should not be regarded as joint acting chief executive. Brilliant. We had one half of the pantomime horse but not the other.

We cried out for one chief executive, for the pantomime horse to return to its stable. An experienced TV executive, Brian Barwick was dead keen on the job, although he didn't realise how split the board were. Some members wanted to keep the pantomime horse. Knowing Brian from the BBC, I met with him several times and helped him in terms of factual information about the structure of the FA. 'You're running Barwick's campaign,' insisted 'The Lollipop Man'. 'That's news to me!' I replied. Brian was not an overwhelming favourite. Some of the board were set against him but he convinced a majority in the end. Despite surviving no more than three-and-a-half years at the FA, I hope he doesn't regret seeking the role.

On the night Brian negotiated his terms at Soho Square, the leadership team had coincidentally arranged a farewell dinner for Palios in a private room on Charlotte Street, 300 yards away. When Brooking and I came out of Soho Square to walk to this dinner, all the camera crews followed us. We had to shake them off. The stroll was scarcely a minute or two to Charlotte Street, but we embarked on a healthy detour. After fifteen minutes bobbing and weaving around Soho, we slipped unnoticed into the room on Charlotte Street to greet Palios. He was in great form. We talked about Barwick. Would he sign up? We all knew he was very unhappy about the financial terms being offered that night. Briefly, a fear gripped the FA that Barwick might turn the job down. We felt it must have been resolved. Paul Nolan should have been with us in Charlotte Street but was elsewhere, sorting it out.

At about ten p.m., after quite a few wines had been consumed, a Sky reporter suddenly walked in. His cameraman waited just outside the door.

'I thought Brian Barwick might be here,' said the reporter, looking around.

'Well he isn't, right, and this is actually a private dinner,' I said, pretty politely.

'Oh, sorry,' said the man from Sky. Fortunately, the reporter didn't spot Palios.

The following morning, heading in to Soho Square, I was slightly more expansive with Sky. 'David, you must be disappointed that the board was split on your friend, Brian Barwick,' asked another reporter.

'Be that as it may,' I replied, 'everybody at the FA will get behind Brian Barwick and Brian will have the same aim that we have, we all have, which is to be successful for English football.' With that, I walked in, thinking nothing more of this brief interview. Declaring we were all going to get behind the newly appointed chief executive was hardly controversial. Within ten minutes of that short clip being screened, I received a phone call from a senior board member. 'You speak for yourself, David,' he said. 'Don't think we are all getting behind Brian Barwick, because we're not.' That's how big the internal battle was around Brian's appointment. I doubt Brian and Lord Mawhinney are on each other's Christmas card list. Chairman of the Football League, Brian Mawhinney may not be everybody's cup of tea. Bristling with that Ulster edge, he wouldn't pretend to be the easiest character but he has sharpened up the Football League no end.

Barwick has found the job much more difficult than even he anticipated. In the early days, the phrase he used to describe it was 'quite daunting'. He has had good days, bad days and some he won't forget. David Gill, United's chief executive, asked one day whether he could bring in the club's new owners, the Glazers, to meet Barwick at the height of the fury against the Americans. Brian immediately called me.

'I want you to be with me this afternoon,' Brian said. 'We've got company. The Glazers are coming.'

'I need someone who knows United really well,' said Brian. I didn't know much about Malcolm Glazer or his sons, apart from the fact that whoever was advising them should find more flattering pictures of Malcolm, who resembled a Beverly Hillbilly with his trousers hitched up. The Glazers were immensely polite, very interested and slightly shy. Impressively, Brian really got over to the Glazers that they had bought a football club and an institution that mattered in English life. It was the FA at its best. What a contrast to the way I felt Brian, and the FA board, acted over the scandal surrounding Faria Alam that engulfed the organisation and my own life.

17

Faria

When my former PA, Faria Alam, accused me of sexual harassment, my world turned upside down. Emotions and questions raced through me. How could Faria do this? What dark demons inhabited her mind to inflict such a slur on me, of all people, the person to whom she'd turned for help at her lowest ebb? How would my wonderful wife Susan react to her husband being accused of trying to force himself on another woman? How would my beloved daughters Amanda and Caroline, who in my worst moments made life worthwhile, cope with the brutal publicity hurtling the family's way like a runaway train? From the moment Faria made her poisonous claim in October 2004 after quitting Soho Square, nightmares stalked my sleep. I'd wake suddenly, shaking and sweating. But when did the nightmare ever really end? All night, all day it went on. While I waited the eight long months for the employment tribunal that could clear my name, doubts assailed me constantly. Had I done anything wrong? Did I ever do or suggest something that could have been misconstrued as sexual harassment? No, never. I wouldn't. I couldn't. I respect women too much. Since a childhood bereft of a father, women had shaped my life.

Women often told me of their frustration at the glass ceiling that exists in many organisations, of how they felt they could rise only so far. Whatever role I filled at the FA, whether Director of Communications or executive director during the Faria fiasco, I determined to help them smash through that glass ceiling at Lancaster Gate and then Soho Sqare. I promoted Jane Bateman, who has given such fantastic service as the FA's head of international affairs. I helped launch the career of Kim Fisher in sport, who's worked successfully at the FA, FIFA and now lives in Zurich. Clare Tomlinson was given her first break by me, and is now a successful Sky presenter.

When I interviewed Faria in room 513 of Soho Square on 26 June 2003, I thought she would do well for me and the FA. Little did I realise I was opening the door to a malevolent whirlwind that ripped through the building. Ambitious, smart, outwardly confident and fun, Faria seemed perfect for the FA. I warned her she was walking into a demanding office. 'You're not working in a nine-to-five, five-days-a-week job,' I explained. 'It'll be stressful. I need a PA who understands that while the FA is an exciting place to work, there will be times when you'll be required to work excessive hours. I need someone to project a professional image and deal with a variety of figures from public life, from football managers to politicians.' On my interview notes, I noted that Faria was 'not big on football knowledge' but I liked her 'personality'. Wrong.

Faria came highly recommended. She'd been temping as PA to Mike Richardson, the construction director of Wembley. If there'd been a permanent position, Wembley assured us they would have considered keeping her on. Joining us on 21 July, Faria quickly enjoyed the fact that I had this cross-section of contacts in politics and show business as well as football. She loved it when Sir David Frost pulled up outside Soho Square in his Rolls-Royce and popped in for a cup of tea.

After several months, I noticed she was tremendously engrossed in writing emails that I was pretty clear weren't to do with me or FA business. 'You seem very busy,' I said. She brushed it aside. Initially concerned, I dismissed the matter. It seemed to cease anyway. Faria, after all, was engaged in FA activities beyond my office. One day, Dave Richards wanted Faria's help in arranging an NSPCC event. Eventually, I read in the media she was bragging to people about who she knew at the FA, the famous people she had talked to on the phone. Working at Soho Square turned her head. She would often walk past TV cameras outside the building in the morning. The FA were always in the news.

I never asked Faria about her private life. It was none of my business. One day, Faria did mention an unwanted sexual overture from another female member of staff.

'I object to it,' Faria told me.

'Faria, I suggest you report the matter to Human Resources,' I urged her. Which she did. Nothing came of it.

Overall, Faria seemed happy in her work. She sat outside my office, chatting to anyone who passed by. Soho Square was like that: people were very friendly. Sven-Goran Eriksson and the new chief executive, Mark Palios, would wander in and out of my office, but I never noticed any frisson between either one of them and Faria. I trusted the people I worked with. I didn't expect them to be leaping into bed with one another. But again: it was none of my business.

On 18 January 2004, I took my usual table at the Football Writers' Association ladies' night at the Savoy. Always a good evening, I was pleased with the table I'd put together. Susan was abroad so my daughter Amanda accompanied me. Richard Keys, Ray Stubbs and Adrian Bevington were there with their partners. I invited Mark Palios, who was single, so we were a woman short. Other PAs of mine had attended in the past, so I asked Faria. Thus into this very glamourous setting walked Faria, looking stunning. She sat between Richard and Mark, who was incredibly attentive. Later on, Faria claimed that was the night when her affair with Mark began. And so what? The room was crammed with journalists, so people were hardly hiding from the press.

One day, I was told Faria was distressed about something. When she was next at her desk, I tried to cheer her up. 'We all get upset, don't worry about it, you do what's necessary for you,' I said. She didn't want to talk about it. Much later, I heard she'd had a ruck with Mark in his office. I never suspected anything was going on at the time. Nor did I know there was anything happening between Faria and Sven.

To understand fully what was going on in 2004 it is vital to hear what Faria subsequently said to the employment tribunal on 21 June 2005. I couldn't believe my ears. Faria stated she had a brief affair with Palios, beginning in October 2003, which confused me as she also then said it started at the Savoy. She said the relationship ended after a weekend trip to Paris in April 2004. On returning to Soho Square, Faria went into Mark's office. 'I do not want to encourage the relationship,' Mark evidently told Faria. It was over. She was livid.

Giving evidence to the tribunal in 2005, Faria was very frank about what had happened between her and Eriksson. 'Sven expressed his interest in me from an early stage of my employment at the FA,' Faria claimed.

> He would often appear on the floor where I worked and give me compliments. He would telephone and ask what I was wearing. He would tell me that I was beautiful. He would often say: 'You have never tried me, give me a chance.' He was always very charming and very persistent in his advances towards me. At that time, I was involved with Mr Palios and did not encourage Mr Eriksson. Indeed Mr Palios had noticed Mr Eriksson paying attention to me on several occasions and said to me later whilst I was still involved with him that he knew Sven wanted me.

This was incredible. Sven and Palios were not mates – I knew that. Palios inherited Eriksson when Sven's star was pretty high. Palios approved an extension of Sven's contract, although he said he regretted it soon afterwards. But I never had an inkling of the love triangle being played out on the upper floors of Soho Square.

'In time, I found Mr Eriksson's attentions more welcome,' Faria continued to the tribunal in 2005. 'I was flattered that he was so interested in me. Our relationship began shortly before Euro 2004. He then telephoned me regularly during Euro 2004.' This was all news to me. 'I had told Mr Eriksson that I would not want to embark on a relationship with him whilst he was still involved with his long-standing girlfriend, Nancy Dell'Olio,' Faria went on. 'Mr Eriksson told me that he and Miss Dell'Olio had been leading separate lives for over a year. After Euro 2004, at Mr Eriksson's invitation, I went to his home in Sweden for two days. I was falling in love with him and thought that he felt the same way. We had two wonderful days together. I found him very understanding, caring and very attentive. As well as the physical side of our relationship, we talked and talked.' Unfortunately for them, and the FA, someone else close to Faria talked to the *News of the World*.

Bombshell no. 1 dropped at 3.30 p.m., on Saturday 17 July 2004, the reverberations of which were still being felt eleven months on at Faria's tribunal. The bombshell came in the form of a phone-call from Andy Coulson. I've come to learn that when the editor of the *News of the World* calls on a Saturday afternoon, just before his mighty presses are about to roll on the first edition, he is rarely the bearer of good news. Hearing Andy's voice, I immediately retreated with the phone to a favourite bench in our front garden in Worcestershire. This was my 'bad news' bench, and the place giving the best mobile phone signal. Andy had a pretty forthright question.

'Is Sven's relationship with Nancy over?' Andy asked.

'I don't know,' I replied honestly. 'If I can help, I'll get back to you.' Susan and I were close friends with Sven and Nancy, but were never sure of what stage their relationship was at any particular time. Sven was in Sweden, his phone ringing out, so I left a message.

At five p.m., Andy rang again, his tack changed. 'Is Sven having an affair with Faria Alam?' Andy asked. 'Because I have access to text messages and emails to prove he is.' I was stunned.

'Faria?! Sven?! Texts?! Emails?! I'm not sure whether Sven has sent a text or emailed anyone in his life. I've not got a clue what you're talking about, Andy.' I told him I felt it very unlikely. Ringing off, I called Colin Gibson, our latest Director of Communications, alerting him to the Screws' story. Again, I left another message for Sven, and one for Faria as well.

An hour later, Sven called. 'Are you having an affair with Faria?' I asked, launching right in. 'The *News of the World* are convinced you are. I'm not sure how much information they have, but they definitely think they are on to something.'

Sven convinced me there was nothing to worry about. 'It's nonsense,' he said. Sven left me in no doubt there was no affair with Faria.

Later, Faria returned my call. I told her about the *News of the World*. I told her that her relationships were nothing to do with me. But I said I needed her help.

'Is the story right, Faria?'

'No,' Faria replied. 'Sven does not even know how to text.'

'OK. So I can go back to the *News of the World*, tell them nothing is going on, and I won't be made to look a complete idiot?'

'Yes,' Faria insisted.

Little did I know that Faria was with Eriksson at the time. She claimed later that Sven told her to deny having an affair with him, if the FA ever grilled her. Faria also declared that I never asked her whether she was sleeping with Sven.

The whole story seemed just a red herring. Coulson, though, is a serious tabloid operator, who would not be making calls on a Saturday evening unless he was running a big story. So I talked with Colin again. 'Both Sven and Faria deny anything is going on,' I told Colin. 'But the Screws are clearly running something. It might be worth a call to Palios to warn him something's brewing.' Colin said he would phone Palios while I called Andy to put out any fires or ask him not to name Faria.

'You've asked me as a mate of Sven's what I think and I don't think this stands up, right?' I told Andy. As Colin and I agreed, I also asked Andy not to name Faria. I never thought she was involved anyway, so that made sense.

'I can't guarantee anything,' Andy told me. As I climbed into bed that night, I wasn't sure what the morning would bring. False alarm or full sirens? The verdict was a score draw. 'SVEN'S SECRET AFFAIR, ENGLAND BOSS CHEATS WITH NANCY DOUBLE' announced the Screws with trademark subtlety. Sven was named, but the blurred picture of Faria would not have revealed her identity. 'She is a sexy brunette he met through his work,' was the limit of their revelation. When I talked to Colin later, he said that journalists were chasing the mystery woman's name.

On Monday, Faria called me at seven a.m., sounding troubled. 'I've had to leave my flat,' she wailed. 'It's besieged with reporters. I'm in the office. I need your help.' Two papers had outed Faria as the mystery brunette. When I reached Soho Square at 8.30, Colin and I immediately had a chat with Faria. She was obviously distressed, so we were firm but considerate. 'I'm not having an affair with Sven,' she told us.

I worried about Faria. She was my PA. At the FA, I hoped I was a decent boss, believing in pastoral care of employees. Seeing Alistair Maclean, the FA's lawyer, in the canteen, I told him about my concerns for Faria.

'We need to protect her,' I told Alistair. 'She's being hassled by reporters.'

'I'll get Addleshaw Goddard on the case,' replied Alistair, walking off to scramble the FA solicitors.

At noon, Sven wandered into my office. 'Faria has been named by the papers,' I told him. As always, Sven seemed very relaxed. 'I will never make a comment in public on my private life,' said Sven. 'It's my private life.' I sympathised. Why should the public be titillated over what Sven got up to? It was nobody's bloody business but I knew the world we lived in. We still had to clear the mess up.

When Sven left, I was needed in Colin's office. Alistair and Faria were already there, talking to Colin. 'It's not true,' Faria kept saying about the claim that she was entangled with Sven. She wanted the FA to deny the story. Continually repeating how troubled she was about the press intrusion, Faria wanted us to take action on her behalf.

'We just want to be sure of the truth, Faria,' said Alistair. 'You won't be in any trouble if you've been having an affair with Sven.'

I waded in. 'If we're going to spend a lot of money instructing lawyers on your behalf, we need to know you're telling the truth,' I told Faria. Twice I asked her this.

Twice she replied: 'There is no affair. I had a meal with Sven, at Kettners and Yatra, but nothing more.'

Now listen to this: 'Nobody asked me straight out whether I was having a relationship with Mr Eriksson,' Faria subsequently claimed to the tribunal in 2005. That defied logic. Faria also alleged that 'she found the whole process very intimidating'. Rubbish, again. We went out of our way to calm her down and support her, stressing how much the FA would protect her. Faria later complained she 'felt bullied throughout the meeting' with Colin Gibson, Alistair Maclean and me. Laughably, she added that she had never spent time with 'three such senior people at the FA' before. Well, she worked for me and slept with Sven and Mark. Faria didn't just lie to us about her affair with Sven, I learned later. She also insisted her innocence to Jane Bateman and Phil Smith, the FA's head of policy.

Later on that Monday 19 July 2004, with the media camped outside Soho Square, the FA issued a statement, defending Faria, and insisting there was no affair. Faria approved Addleshaw Goddard's letters to newspapers, which were written 'on behalf of our client Faria Alam'. It contained one fatal flaw that was to have massive repercussions: Faria's lie. As she herself confessed later: 'I did not want to admit to anything because I was protecting Mr Eriksson.' What more could we have done? We asked Faria time and again. She stonewalled with lies. As for Sven, to this day he insists he never deliberately misled me.

That Monday evening, Sven and I went to a London Olympics

do in the garden of Number 10. The tranquillity of the setting reflected my mood. The Faria story seemed to be fizzling out.

The next day, Tuesday 20 July, I headed off on holiday to La Manga with Susan and Caroline. Amanda was travelling elsewhere. After all the drama and confusion at work, it was good to clear the head. On the Thursday, Faria texted me details of her new mobile phone number. She'd had to change the old one. I was disappointed to learn later that she felt '*persona non grata*' at the FA, that she 'was being left to fend for herself'. Her evidence to the tribunal did not tally with the reality that the FA lawyers went in to bat for her. Believing her innocence, I cared for Faria as any boss would. But knowing she was in pieces, should I have rung her a couple of times from La Manga? Probably.

Everything seemed calm. On Saturday 24 July, I strolled off to the La Manga *supermercado* to buy the family lunch. Back in our rented apartment, I cooked for Susan and Caroline, who then headed back to the pool. My halo polished by some good work in the kitchen, I now enjoyed some 'dad time'. I sat on the balcony without a care in the world, just a book, a cup of coffee and a chunk of chocolate. Perfection. Which lasted five minutes. Bombshell no. 2 was whistling its way down. Almost a week to the minute since Andy Coulson's dramatic phone-call, his deputy, Neil Wallis, called. He sounded exasperated.

'David, will you intervene in discussions that have been going on between us, Colin Gibson and Faria? David, you've got to sort out this mess.'

'What mess?'

'David, we know Faria had affairs with Sven-Goran Eriksson and Mark Palios. There are emails to back this up.'

'What?!' I replied, astonished. This was supposed to be fizzling out. 'What the hell is going on? Palios?! I've no idea what you're talking about. Neil, I'd better ring you back.'

Since departing on holiday, I had no knowledge of what had been going on in Soho Square. After a series of heated phone-calls involving Colin Gibson, the *News of the World* and myself, I had only one piece of advice. 'Publish whatever you like,' I told the Screws editor, Andy Coulson, with whom not long before I'd lunched in London with Mark Palios. This was not defiance on my part, just exasperation with the whole sorry mess. In my absence, Mark had admitted to Gibson that he'd slept with Faria. Together they chose not to tell me on holiday in Spain. Lucky me.

On Friday, the FA had felt forced to go through Faria's emails and discovered she had lied. She had been sleeping with Sven. Little did I also realise that Palios asked Gibson to try to keep his name out of the news. In retrospect, I believe Mark feared it might scupper his attempts at reconciliation with his children's mother. God, this was a nightmare. I went bananas. Eventually putting my anger at all this deception to one side, I switched into damage-limitation mode. Working swiftly, Gibson produced a statement for the Screws to carry, which read: 'Earlier in the week, the FA made statements on behalf of Faria Alam denying that she had a sexual relationship with the England coach, Sven-Goran Eriksson. New evidence has been presented to us in the form of emails which Ms Alam has sent to friends about the relationship and, having made further enquiries, we can confirm that a relationship did take place. With regard to Mark Palios, we can confirm that a brief relationship did take place.' As I went to bed that Saturday night, I was livid with my PA, and just about everybody else. The FA looked complete fools. The morning's Screws would be complete carnage for us.

Rising early, I nipped to the shops to buy the English papers. On the way, I thought of the tactic used by one club chairman whenever his name appeared splashed across the Sunday tabloids. He went around all the shops near his village, buying up every incriminating copy. The thought of purchasing every *News of the World* in La Manga briefly crossed my mind. Sod it, let's just read it and weep. The Screws didn't let me down. 'I BEDDED SVEN AND HIS BOSS' screamed its front page. The FA's cack-handed attempt to manage the situation had turned a minor drama into a crisis. Gibson phoned the FA chairman Geoff Thompson, offering to resign. Geoff refused his offer. Two days later, Geoff ordered an inquiry into why the guardians of English football issued statements on misleading information. We were trapped in a nightmare of our own making. The press couldn't get enough of the story. Sex sells papers. Football sells papers. Mix the two into the same story and it was dynamite. Faria was also said to have claimed to have had an affair with a 'Third Man' at the FA. That titillated interest even more. Our nightmare became a soap opera with daily episodes.

At the height of the scandal, I had a phone-call from a friend at FIFA, Jerome Champagne, while I was still in La Manga.

'David,' Jerome said, 'will you correct me if I'm wrong: a single person has had a relationship with a single person and also has had a relationship with another single person, right? And the result is worldwide publicity, right?!'

'That's pretty much it,' I replied. 'But unfortunately none of them had very good memories.'

A thousand miles from home, I soon had Her Majesty's press corps shadowing me around La Manga. One day, I was back in my favourite *supermercado*, wandering around, collecting ingredients for a Caesar salad. Suddenly, I became aware I was being watched by some guy in a raincoat. This was sheer farce. It was ninety degrees! I giggled to myself. My good humour evaporated when the Man in the Mac approached me.

'David, can I have a word?' This was an expression that rarely prefaced good news. He was some freelancer sent over from London.

'If you'll excuse me, I'd like to finish buying my Caesar salad before we have a word.' The Man in the Mac was not put off.

'David, I have to put it to you that you are the Third Man.'

I just stared at him in disbelief. I was standing in a Spanish supermarket, hunting bits of salad, and being accused of involvement in a sex scandal rocking England. 'Right, off the record: bollocks and garbage,' I told him. He looked crestfallen, needing a quote for his story. 'Now I want to tell you something on the record,' I added.

The Man in the Mac got really excited. 'On the record: bollocks and garbage.' Such language had served me well with the media before, and could do so again. With that, I strode to the check-out, paid for what I had, and sped back to the flat. For the first time, I thought: I could be in the bloody firing line here. Faria worked for me. Perhaps I'm the obvious target. Having employed a woman who had unleashed pandemonium through Soho Square, should I resign? I rang two friends I trusted with my life.

'Am I responsible for this mess?' I asked them.

'Absolutely not,' they replied. 'You employed her in an open competition with good references. You can't beat yourself up about this.'

The temptation was to fly home early. 'Do you want me back to help out?' I asked Mark.

'Stay,' he said. 'Try and enjoy your holiday.' Gibson again sounded optimistic. 'The story might have run its course.'

Thank God for Kenny Dalglish and Gordon Strachan. They were at their places in La Manga at the same time and looked after the girls while I spent hours on the phone. One afternoon as I fielded call after call, Kenny took Susan and Caroline out on a boat. The warmth and support of Kenny and Gordon will always be remembered by me and my family. On the Thursday, Gordon and I travelled on the La Manga minibus to the airport. Gordon was heading back to Southampton, me to Gatwick. Steve Curry of the *Daily Mail* was also with us. He too had been trying to have a holiday, but had found himself in proximity to a worldwide story. Finally boarding the plane after a two-hour delay, I looked forward to relaxing in my seat, perhaps leafing through a newspaper. To my horror, on each seat lay a copy of Steve's paper displaying the headline: 'Is Davies the Third Man?' Terrific. Another hint of the gathering storm came at Gatwick. Some friendly soul who'd gone through into Arrivals managed to slip back to find me in the luggage hall. 'There are TV crews out there,' he said. The kindness of strangers continued when a Gatwick official smuggled me out of the airport's back door.

Hiding was pointless, though. Having arrived home at two a.m., by eight a.m. I was pushing my way through all the cameras outside Soho Square. Business as usual. That was my message. But walking through the building, I was shocked by the low morale. Everyone was so down. Some were worried for me. Forget that, I thought, my job was to lift the staff. On my desk lay a memo from Palios. Before heading off on his own holiday the night before, Mark sent me and the rest of the FA leadership team a note, thanking all of us for our support. He wrote that the media would love to run the FA. 'They don't' was Mark's message. 'We do.' Mark also wrote to Geoff, assuring the chairman that his affair with Faria was conducted out of office hours. Mark stressed he'd never denied the relationship with Faria. Mark also suggested to Geoff that he assume a more visible role. When I read this, I thought it hysterical. Geoff Thompson was as likely to do 'visible' as Howard Hughes. Mark also asked me to be acting chief executive while he was away.

Later that day, I'd agreed, against my instincts, to talk to Peter Norbury, the man from Eversheds solicitors leading Geoff's famous inquiry. The tenor of his questioning was so aggressive, I thought: Hang on a minute, I need a lawyer here for myself. This was my own organisation questioning me! My suspicions grew that my enemies within Soho Square were ganging up on me. Paranoia maybe. After such a ghastly day, I decided to make a dash for Euston and the train to Birmingham. Having ordered a black cab to wait outside, I knew I'd have to run the gauntlet of photographers and journalists. Normally I'd stop and give them a few lines. Today was different. Infuriatingly, I fell for the old trick of two snappers standing up against my taxi, so I couldn't shut the door. While at the BBC, this was a stunt I'd used myself, very effectively at times. As I yanked the door to, I caught my finger, grimaced and the photographers had a field day.

My mood blackened more than my finger the following day, another day of fire-fighting. Colin Gibson rang. 'I've done everything to keep it out of the paper, and I've failed,' he said.

'I'm holed beneath the water. I don't think I'll survive the weekend.'

I soon discovered why. On Sunday 1 August, Bombshell no. 3 dropped on Soho Square. Astonishingly, the *News of the World* claimed Gibson had tried to broker a deal with them about Faria giving 'chapter and verse' on Sven, but only if they kept Palios's name out of the story. It made grim reading. Gibson described Palios's relationship with Faria as a 'two-week fling with a secretary'. Gibson issued a statement, saying he'd acted for Palios to protect his family. Where that 'chapter and verse' deal originated from remains a mystery to me to this day. During my time as FA Director of Communications, I did a few deals with papers, usually to get a negative story on an England player out of the way before a tournament started. Never, never, did I come close to anything like the 'chapter and verse' pact. Blame for this suicidal idea generally gets dumped on Palios and Gibson. I don't know. By Saturday morning, various lawyers had been crawling all over the story.

As a member of the FA leadership team, I would have expected to be consulted if people were doing a deal that would shaft the England coach to save the chief executive. Looking back, I assumed I was kept out of the loop because everyone knew my friendship with Sven. Apparently, Gibson and Palios didn't want to disturb my holiday. That was kind of them, but Soho Square was going up in flames and I did have a reputation for putting out media fire-storms. That might have helped. Having been a journalist skilled at lighting fires for twenty-two years and then FA Director of Communications adept at extinguishing them, I was amazed Mark and Colin didn't ask my advice on whether a deal with the Screws was wise.

Sadly, Colin soon resigned. I talked to Palios, who was very low. Later that afternoon, Mark also fell on his sword. As usual, the issue was not the event but the aftermath. He couldn't survive. Neither Geoff nor Dave Richards would support him. A ring-round of board members revealed little backing for Mark. I think

Palios realised the attempted cover-up had gone too far, although he felt pretty hard done by. Some sympathy followed Mark and Colin out of the door of Soho Square. Two men who had worked incredibly hard for the organisation had left. Those of us who remained at the FA felt like battered boxers who did not know when the punches would stop raining down.

After agreeing the wording of Mark's resignation with him, I called a meeting of the leadership team at my flat in Craven Hill, Paddington. I was still acting chief executive. Strangely, every address containing senior FA staff was doorstepped except mine. Craven Hill seemed the safest venue. Andrew Halstead, Jonathan Hill, Alex Horne, Paul Nolan and I sat there eating pizza, drinking red wine and watching Mark's resignation statement on the evening bulletins. It was the lead story on Sky and the BBC. The key part was Mark's belief that 'personally I do not accept that I have been guilty of any wrongdoing. But it has become clear to me that my action tonight is essential to enable the FA to begin to return to normality.'

To find some normality we needed Trevor Brooking, the FA's director of football development, currently held up on the M25. In his absence, the leadership team decided the elegant Brooking should be acting chief executive with my full backing. 'Look, the attention is going to be on me because of all this "Third Man" bollocks,' I said. 'Trevor's perfect in this situation.'

Trevor phoned in.

'I'm still on the M25,' he said.

'I've got some good news for you but you may think it's bad news,' I told Trevor. 'We all think you should be acting chief executive and I am going to inform the chairman in the morning.'

'You must be joking,' Trevor replied. 'Anyone thinking of nominating me can think again. It's not for me.'

Someone had to stand up for the FA, so I did. Arriving at Soho Square on the Monday morning, I stood on the steps and made a short comment to the assembled media: 'It's a time for us to rally the staff and Sven is very popular and respected by the players.

Sven has a consistent track record everywhere he has worked.' Some board members were incensed by my support for Sven. I'd saved him. They couldn't get rid of him now, not with a senior FA executive like myself declaring Sven had done nothing wrong. Some board members felt this had been a chance to axe Sven cheaply. People were calling for his head, but any beheading was now scuppered.

I was trying to unite the FA. Instead, my employers turned on me. Clearly believing Faria might say something damaging about me, the board sought to distance the FA from me. They got wind that I was concerned by their lawyers' attitude, and was bringing in my own. My lawyers said that at the very least I deserved some apologies from people at Soho Square. At a later stage, I was even urged to consider legal action against my own employers.

Geoff's famous inquiry was cranking into action. On 3 August 2004, Sven was interviewed by Peter Norbury. The 2005 tribunal's report into those meetings makes fascinating reading.

> During the course of the interviews, Mr Eriksson had said to Mr Norbury that he had not been specific about his answer to David Davies but that he had used the word 'nonsense' when the allegation was put to him by Mr Davies and that he told Mr Davies that 'his private life was his private life'.
>
> We are satisfied that comment from Mr Eriksson supports Mr Davies' account that when he first raised with Mr Eriksson an allegation about an affair his firm view at the end of the conversation was that Mr Eriksson was denying the affair. Of course, Ms Alam also denied it to him and it was with that background that the Football Association through Mr Davies and Mr Gibson had issued the statement denying the affair.

The tribunal vindicated my stance that I believed nothing had gone on. Sven had said the Screws story was 'nonsense', and Faria had also denied it. At the tribunal, people spent three and a half hours trying to get me to say Sven lied to me. The truth is I don't know whether Sven deliberately tried to mislead me, whether he was unclear about it or whether he thought it was none of my business.

Drawing on the Norbury report into everyone's conduct, the board called an emergency meeting for 5 August 2004, at a supposedly secret location in London, to discuss whether Sven had been in breach of contract and to discuss the role played by executives like me. The venue was so hush-hush that a hundred journalists were on the pavement outside the Leonard Hotel near Portman Square within minutes of the start. Eventually, after discussing the Norbury report, the board concluded that Sven had not been in breach of his contract. 'No case to answer' was the verdict on Sven. No mention was made of me. I couldn't believe it. Palios had gone. Gibson had gone. Sven had been backed. I was left dangling. The board ignored the opportunity to clear my name. I was absolutely hung out to dry by my employers. Nobody contacted me. This had to be payback for my supporting Sven. Thompson, predictably, was silent, although he rang Sven to offer him his support. 'It's good you've had a phone call from the chairman because I certainly haven't,' I told Sven.

Soon afterwards, a fax appeared at Soho Square from the offices of Max Clifford, Faria's new media adviser. 'I have decided in view of recent events I have no alternative but to resign my position as PA to Mr David Davies,' came the statement from Faria. 'I believe that the company has behaved in a way that amounts to breach of contract and/or has completely undermined my trust and confidence.' Faria's behaviour continued to confound me. She decided to sell her story to the *News of the World* and the *Mail on Sunday* for £150,000 each and do an interview with Granada TV in *Tonight with Trevor McDonald* for an additional £110,000. Total – £410,000. So she had to resign. I did raise an eyebrow when she concluded in her statement that she 'had decided that to try to kill the story, I would speak to the

Press'. Hello?! That was like pouring petrol instead of water on a fire.

The cold war intensified between me and the board. I sensed a whispering campaign in the media, with unattributed stories trying to damage my reputation. Separately, Dave Richards invited me into his office and, without warning, broached the subject of resignation. 'Why would I want to do a deal?' I asked. Richards said he knew I intended leaving the FA in 2006, which was true. He wondered whether I might not be tempted to bring the day forward, picking up a nice pay-off on the way out the door. Absolutely no way. To resign would be to admit guilt. Richards's stance shocked me. Leaving his office, I realised I was on my own now. By not taking the Richards shilling, I knew my future was unpredictable. Betrayed by the board, I fell out of love with the FA, and even questioned my passion for football. Physically, I left Soho Square in 2006. Emotionally I left in 2004.

These were bleak times. On the day of the board meeting I took a phone-call from Mark Palios, who sounded so desperate I feared for his mental state. I was alarmed enough to ring two good friends of his, Trevor East and Nigel Doughty. 'I'm worried about Mark,' I told them. 'You'd better keep an eye on him.' For myself, I had some desperate moments, too. Much worse was to come.

With Faria's 'kiss and tell' weekend looming, various women at Soho Square made their way, completely unprompted, to my office at 4.45 on the Friday afternoon. Led by Jane Bateman, they had a point to make. 'Whatever appears this weekend, if she attacks you we will stand up for you,' they said. 'We will speak out in your defence.' At a time when the board had turned their backs on me, the support of these colleagues made me very emotional.

The day had not been without light relief. At one point, everyone on my floor began peering out of the windows. Down below, a big furniture van had pulled up and was blocking Soho Square. Intrigued, the photographers gathered around it. On opening the back, the furniture delivery men hauled out a double bed! They placed the bed outside the entrance to the FA, lobbed some sheets and pillows on it, stuck two flags of St George in the pillows and sped off. The Met Police soon arrived and took the bed away for questioning. Some men's magazine did it for a gimmick, a skit on recent goings-on at Soho Square, and it certainly cheered us all up for half an hour or so.

The following morning, 7 August, Sven and I headed down to Cardiff with Gibson's successor, Adrian Bevington, an honest guy and massive Boro fan. We were due at the St David's Hotel before the Community Shield on the Sunday. Saturday was awful, like waiting for a bomb to go off. Throughout the afternoon, I received various tip-offs as to the content of Faria's interviews in the *Mail on Sunday* and the Screws. FA board members knew how frantic I was, how I craved a show of support. Only David Dein, to his great credit, called. If any of them had ever suffered such an ordeal, I would have let them know they had my backing. Other than David, presumably they'd concluded there was no smoke without fire or just weren't bothered. That coldness I have never forgotten.

Adrian got the first editions and we pored over them. Faria spared few blushes or details on her romances with Sven and Palios. Sven was quite relaxed. Fortunately, there were few references to me. On the Monday, I still had Faria's Granada exclusive to survive but that contained little new. One hundred and fifty thousand pounds each from the two papers, and £110,000 from TV was not a bad few days' work for Faria. 'With a speed which is perhaps unusual in other areas of commerce invoices were sent to the media for these large sums of money by 10 August,' the Tribunal noted wryly.

'The story could be blowing itself out,' I said to Adrian. I prayed it would. I needed to concentrate on work. When Sven returned to Soho Square, I warned him about the inevitable scrum on the pavement. 'Just keep walking,' I said.

Sven ignored me. He stopped amidst the assembled journalists. 'You will excuse me for saying this but you are all completely mad,' Sven said and carried on into the building. Sven was right and I was wrong. When he left the building three hours later, only one snapper maintained a lonely vigil. The hilarious moment when Sven lectured the reporters was not repeated on Sky News!

Things seemed to quieten down. The new season was under way. People talked about football, not bed-hopping. My pulse-rate began to slow, my smile began to return.

The following month, Faria called. 'How are you?' she asked.

'It makes no difference how I am,' I replied. 'How are you? I hope you are well. But I can't talk about what happened leading up to your resignation.' The ice was broken, though.

Faria soon called again. 'Can you help me get another job?'

'Of course, I can. What sort of job are you looking for?' She wasn't sure, and rang off.

A third phone-call was more distressed. 'No one is helping me. I have no friends at the FA.' Faria sounded very emotional. She sought my assistance in securing a settlement with the FA. She never mentioned I was to be the target of her case. That was the last I heard from her until I saw her at the tribunal.

Shortly after those phone-calls, Max Clifford had dinner with Dave Richards and the agent Jon Smith, where they uncovered that Faria had another surprise for us. She was taking the FA to an employment tribunal for wrongful dismissal and sex discrimination. To my horror, I heard that Faria was also going to allege sexual harassment against a senior FA person that could only be me. On 5 October, I was attending a British Olympic Association meeting at Queen's Club when Peter Heard called, requesting I come to his office as quickly as possible. Peter, a senior FA board member, had been asked by the organisation to deal with the Faria tribunal. I sensed bad news. 'Faria has named you as having sexually harassed her,' Peter told me. 'She has given no details.'

Faria had dropped another bombshell. This time the pieces I had to pick up were bits of me. One Sunday afternoon, I took Susan for a long walk in the countryside and broke the news about Faria. Susan took it remarkably well. First, she trusted me. Secondly, she wasn't surprised. 'David, you were always naïve about Faria,' Susan said. 'I saw her at that International Board event at Claridge's, pushing herself forward.'

My marriage with Susan has always been strong. I worried more about the girls. Caroline and Amanda reacted in characteristically different ways. Caroline, a born fighter, wasn't remotely bothered; she just told me to go and fight Faria in the tribunal and anywhere else. Amanda was upset but also aware of the perils of public life. Beginning to acquire a media profile of her own in TV, Amanda understood that flak flew in this business. It was particularly awkward for Amanda, working in a journalistic environment. At one stage, Sky were looking for me while she was working for them. I hardly hid. Most decent reporters had my number. One day, a camera crew appeared at the end of the drive of our house in Worcestershire. Sitting in London, I watched some rolling news service. Their reporter, rather breathlessly, announced that I was inside the house in Worcestershire, having a showdown with my wife. I called Susan. 'This is silly. Just go outside and tell that fool to ring my mobile,' I said.

Without the love and support of Susan, Amanda and Caroline, I might have collapsed under the crushing weight of all the pressure. The torture would have been easier to bear if the tribunal had been quick. The delay was disgusting. From learning on 5 October 2004 that Faria was smearing my name, I had to wait eight desperate months to challenge her in the tribunal, which began on 21 June 2005. My life was on hold. Relaxation was impossible. Enemies lurked in every shadow, real or imagined.

One Monday night before Christmas, some friends invited Susan and me to see the Irish comic Frank Carson. Frank would cheer me up, my friends thought. He usually did. But I was too morose, and headed home early. Only two glasses of wine had crossed my lips, a modest amount for me at that tense time, but I was bushed. Susan stayed behind at the do. Hailing a black cab, I returned to our ground-floor flat in Craven Hill. Walking up the short pathway to the front door, I pulled out my key, and as I was about to locate the key-hole, I heard a woman's plaintive voice behind me. 'Oh, please help me, please help me,' she said. I glanced down the road. My cab had gone. Parked slightly away from the kerb in front of my house was a car, with a woman sitting in the front. Winding down the passenger window, she said something else. Instinctively, I would go to help. That is my nature. She might have been lost, run out of petrol, whatever. Something stopped me. Don't go. Danger. I turned back to the house.

'I'm terribly sorry,' she shouted through the window. 'It's a new car and I've run out of petrol, could you lend me ten pounds?' I never moved.

'Sorry, I can't but I'll try to find someone who can,' I eventually said, and ran into the house. Shaking, I rushed through the door and called the police. This woman-in-car situation could have been a pure coincidence, completely innocent, but when Susan appeared twenty minutes later the road was full of flashing lights, police, but no woman, no car. She cannot have run out of petrol. The next day, I consulted the FA's security adviser, Sir John Evans. We came to the conclusion that it was probably a trap. The hope was that I would hand some money through the window, while someone snapped a picture of me. The area was Paddington, prostitutes weren't unknown, and that photograph could have destroyed me. That was what I was up against. I never thought it was Faria's people. My stalkers were journalists. My former PAs were contacted by freelance reporters on what I knew as fishing expeditions, hoping to net some information. 'You'll just have to live with it until the tribunal,' Sir John advised me.

My life was so grim, I had to escape. Disappearing to Dubai for a week, I walked down the beach, enjoying the sun warming my face, and the sand between my toes. Wherever I was, though, one question took up permanent residency in my mind. Why was Faria putting me through this? I knew I couldn't ring her to seek some explanation. Again, some pretty dark thoughts went through my mind. Most days, I was tempted to stand on the steps of Soho Square and scream my innocence. Lawyers forbade that. Frustration also mounted with my employers' attitude. The FA concentrated on defending their name against Faria, not mine. Until the tribunal actually opened, I did not meet the FA's barrister once. One chat on the phone was the sum total of the FA barrister's contact with the only FA employee guaranteed to be at the forefront of the case. It was crazy. I suppose I should have been grateful the FA allowed me to carry on working for them. The work was important, too, with the battle to get England a four-week break for the 2006 World Cup.

Wary of the FA lawyers, I found someone to represent me, Paul Herbert, from Goodman Derrick. As well as having the good taste to be a Manchester United supporter, Paul is a man of principle, who realised the injustice of the case against me. Without Paul, I would have struggled big-time. Paul kept me going, kept me sane.

The FA contested Faria's claim on the grounds of gross misconduct. Fearing more damage, some members of the FA board were actually keen to settle in advance. Two meetings of the leadership team unanimously believed there should be a settlement out of court. David Dein tried to cheer me up. 'You know who the Third Man was? It was Sven twice!' The mood of certain other board members I found less amusing. The board was split. In my suspicious state of mind, I even questioned the motives of those board members, including friends like David Sheepshanks, who wanted to fight Faria. The tribunal would inevitably see my name up in glaring headlines. I would bear the brunt of the abuse on the FA's behalf.

'You would think that someone who had already done twelve years' service for the organisation in good times and not so good times was owed some degree of pastoral care,' I told Paul. In truth, I half-understood the FA's dilemma. I was torn myself. I wanted to fight this scurrilous allegation, but did I really want my name dragged through an employment tribunal and then splashed all over the more sensational newspapers? But if the FA was to fight, surely I deserved real and visible support?

Case 2204627/04 at the employment tribunal on Kingsway, Holborn, central London, was scheduled for 21 June 2005. As I'd planned, I was away with the Australians at the Confederations Cup, gaining experience of situations in Germany in case England qualified for the World Cup the following year. My plan was that the Confederations Cup would run into the start of the tribunal, so I would be out of the country until required to give evidence. Unfortunately for me, Australia got knocked out at the first stage!

At 12.45 on 10 June, I finally attended a meeting with the FA's lawyers. I arrived armed with a memo from Paul Herbert, containing a question that I immediately put to Simon Johnson, the FA executive in charge of dealing with the tribunal. 'Are we actively seeking a settlement?' I asked Simon. 'Yes or no?' 'We are not actively seeking a settlement,' Simon replied. That was it.

Flying to Germany on the Sunday, I knew the fight was on. On Tuesday morning, Faria's witness statement was faxed to me by the lawyers. Sitting in the Frankfurt reception of the Australian team hotel, I watched the twenty-eight pages fall one by one from the fax machine, wondering which contained the most damaging material about me. I tore through them, looking for my name. To my relief, her allegations against me were fairly limited. Maybe all the pages hadn't come through. I checked. No, they all had. Seeing a phrase like 'sexual harassment' in print next to my name was still pretty repugnant. To my horror and amazement, Faria named my former PAs, Sarah Ford and Kim Fisher, as also claiming sexual harassment by me. Faria's fantasy world knew no boundaries. Paul Herbert immediately got on to Kim and Sarah. Kim was in South East Asia on holiday and Sarah at home in London. They responded fantastically, volunteering to make statements on my behalf, which they did through Paul. My debt of gratitude to Kim and Sarah remains as deep as my admiration for their strength of character.

I rang Susan, and read out Faria's claims about me. 'Is that it?!' she replied.

The following Saturday evening, I was with the Australians travelling to Leipzig for their game against Argentina when Simon

Johnson called.

'Faria's statement has been leaked to the *Sunday People*,' said Simon. 'I don't know if you will be named.'

'That means everyone will know it is me,' I replied. Simon couldn't spare me any more time because he was dashing to the Theatre Royal Drury Lane to see *The Producers*. As he rang off, I was apoplectic. In tears, I rang Paul Herbert. 'Paul, I'm stranded. My name is about to appear in what will undoubtedly be seedy headlines, and Simon Johnson can't talk because he's off to *The Producers*.' Paul was astounded. I'd had enough. I flew home from Germany the next day.

With the tribunal starting in two days, I began to prepare myself properly. As the complainant, Faria had her version of events heard first, which gave her all the coverage. I made the decision that Faria was not going to have those headlines all to herself. My response to her claims needed to be in those headlines, stealing her thunder, even though I was not due to give evidence until Friday. After studying some previous cases at the tribunal, I outlined my plan to Paul.

'The moment my name is mentioned I'm going to issue a statement through the Press Association from outside the court,' I told Paul.

'That could be seen as contempt of the tribunal,' Paul replied.

'I'll risk that,' I said.

That Tuesday, I sat in my office at Soho Square, watching the Sky pictures of Faria cavorting down Kingsway to the tribunal, less than a mile from my childhood home off Euston Road. This was where my love of football had brought me. Inside the building I knew the FA lawyers, to their credit, were putting forward legal arguments to keep me from being named. That, predictably, failed. The clock ticked ever louder on when I would be named. I was ready. My response was in place.

Beginning her evidence, Faria's conduct in that tribunal can only be described as venal. How dare someone whom I had encouraged, employed and trusted seek to destroy me so callously?

How dare she throw such grief through my front door? 'During my time of employment with the FA I was sexually harassed at work on several occasions by David Davies,' Faria told the tribunal. She claimed I'd tried it on with Kim and Sarah. She claimed she wrote incidents in her notebook, which then conveniently disappeared. Ludicrously, she claimed that I seriously urged her that 'we should run away together'. In her statement, Faria claimed I 'tried to hold' her. 'I also recall a time at an FA party when I was sitting near a column and his arms sneaked around me from behind.' The idea that I would force myself on a woman in public or private repulsed me. Almost hilariously, she told of being harassed in my office – which she had presumably forgotten had wall-to-ceiling windows.

Mendacity and malevolence characterised Faria's allegations against me. When she had returned from a break in New York, she claimed I told her: 'I missed you.' What employer wouldn't tell his PA he'd missed her during a busy time of the year? She claimed I told her to turn her cab around one night and come back 'because I need you'. Absolute nonsense. Faria visited my flat twice, just as previous PAs had done when I was working from home. PAs would drop off or collect correspondence. Twice, I had meals with Faria. But it was Faria who invited me to dinner at Yatra, a restaurant in the West End of London whose owner she knew. Her imagination became particularly wild when she alleged I held 'her close' and kissed her on the lips. All this rubbish about trying to kiss Faria, it was so pathetic, so obvious what she was trying to do with her allegations. She hoped to scare the FA into paying her off.

At 16.10, a message came through from inside the tribunal that I'd been named by Faria. By 16.15, my statement was handed out outside the tribunal. 'I was immensely saddened to hear these cruel and grotesque allegations against me,' it read.

> They are deeply hurtful and will be refuted vehemently not only by myself but by others. It is now public knowledge that I have been dragged into an employment dispute

> between the FA and my former PA, who I trusted and respected, and with whom I enjoyed an excellent professional and friendly relationship while she worked at Soho Square. She left the organisation almost 11 months ago. Her story was then sold by her to several newspapers and to a television company. Absolutely no mention was made of these allegations at that time and indeed until very recently.
>
> So I can only try to imagine why she would choose to say these things. I can only try to imagine why since last year she would have sought my help to settle her case on three separate occasions without ever mentioning these sorry tales. Beyond all else, if she truly believes any of them, it is beyond comprehension that she would also have said the highly complimentary things about me that she did in broadcast interviews last August. How could I have been a 'fantastic' boss who was 'great to work for', as she described me then. After 22 years at the BBC, and more than 11 years at the FA – and after working with countless wonderful professionals, female and male – I trust Faria Alam is aware what she has done to people who tried to support her. Just for the record, there is more, very much more, I would like to say. I look forward to saying it at the appropriate time when I can defend myself against this cowardly and callous attack on my integrity and reputation.

Every news organisation ran it – with one exception. The organisation I served for twenty-two years, the BBC, decided it was contempt. The BBC apart, Part One of my plan to stop Faria from dominating the agenda had passed off well.

Fair play to the FA, they at last rallied behind me, releasing a statement at 18.41: 'The FA is fully supportive of executive director David Davies following claims made by former employee Faria Alam at an industrial tribunal today. We strongly refute the allegations made by Faria Alam and will be mounting a vigorous defence against these claims when presenting our evidence during forthcoming days. David Davies is a hugely respected figure and enjoys the organisation's total support.'

Part Two of my response was then abandoned. It involved attending the tribunal with Susan, Amanda and Caroline. I wanted Faria to know and see what she had done. But Paul Herbert dissuaded me. He was right. I was wrong. Nothing would stop Part Three, though. On Wednesday, I decided to pop into the tribunal when least expected. Just as Faria was being cross-examined, I turned up. The room was small and the press seats were full to the gunnels. Good. I would be noticed. The message I wanted to send was that I had nothing to hide or fear.

After Thursday was taken up with Colin Gibson and Alistair Maclean giving evidence, my turn arrived on Friday to step in front of this legal firing squad. Sleep was impossible the night before. As I lay in bed, wondering what tribulations lay in store, I realised nobody from the FA board had called to wish me luck. Typical. When I arrived at the tribunal, Simon Johnson was conspicuously notable by his absence. He'd attended most of the sittings on behalf of the FA but not today. He couldn't have been at *The Producers*. Too early. Brian Barwick, the latest chief executive, was absent, too. Many staff members wished me well. Adrian Bevington, to his everlasting credit, chose to come, an act of kindness I'll never forget. Some of the leadership team rang to offer their support. Trevor Brooking was fantastic. So were Paul Nolan, with that cheery Scouse wit, and Jonathan Hill. They all felt the board had deserted me. Messages of support also flowed in from senior people in government, and from friends abroad. Even strangers sent good-luck messages. But my own people? The FA board? Not a word.

I knew my life would be defined by how I came through that day. The morning session was taken up by my evidence and then cross-examination. Talking to Paul Herbert beforehand, I'd predicted the opening gambit from Faria's barrister. He'd try to discredit my evidence, insinuating my career had been built on putting on a show, whether in TV or in PR. Faria's barrister didn't let me down.

'Mr Davies, you have been a performer for twenty-five years,' Faria's barrister began. 'You are very highly regarded as a performer, aren't you?'

'Thank you very much, some people have been kind enough to say that but that was my job,' I said. 'This is nothing to do with that whatsoever.'

After that, most of the time was taken up with Faria's counsel trying to get me to say that Sven had lied. I stood my ground. As I gave evidence in what was more a classroom than a courtroom, Faria sat close by. I deliberately never looked her way. I never wanted any eye contact. Engaging with her was not something I craved after eight months in purgatory. At lunch, I was told I couldn't speak to anyone, family, friends, lawyers, no one.

'Would you like a sandwich?' they offered.

'Please.' The choice was cheese or cheese. I went for cheese. They brought me a rather elderly sandwich, an inedible apple and a glass of warm water and left me in a room that made saunas seem air-conditioned. I wondered how much lower I could go. So close to where I'd been brought up as a child, where my love of football began, it had led me to this temporary prison. For a moment, I wanted to escape out on to Kingsway and away. What would happen then? Who cared? It was a brief, mad and quickly discarded thought.

As I waited in this grim room, I thought of the women in my life. Susan, Amanda and Caroline have made my life worthwhile. Caroline is strong-willed, hugely amusing and not interested in football. Amanda loved football from the moment I left her in the pouring rain of the family enclosure at Vicarage Road while I reported on the game. United won, Norman Whiteside scored, and Amanda didn't care about the rain.

As I lost the will to continue with the cheese sandwich, I thought of the moments in life when I had reached crossroads and could have taken a path that would have led me away from Faria.

In late 2003, Greg Dyke had offered me a job as the first sports editor of the BBC, the position now filled by Mihir Bose. 'Why are you wanting to do this?' Sven asked at the time. 'It is going backwards.' Out of loyalty to Sven, I stayed. The Hutton Report was then published, Greg Dyke went and Faria happened. By October 2004, my rejection of the BBC offer looked to have been about the worst decision ever.

I thought of how I could now be a politician. I was offered the possibility of succeeding Cyril Smith when he was thinking of standing down in Rochdale. I even talked to Cyril about it, but he wasn't in a rush to go. Later, in the build-up to the 1997 election, I was offered the chance of fighting a seat in the West Midlands. For twenty-four hours, I was interested, but I was too committed to the FA, Glenn Hoddle and the upcoming World Cup in France.

My reverie was broken by a knock on the door. Time to go again. The afternoon session involved continued cross-examination about Sven. Come on, I thought. What about me? Finally, Faria's QC mentioned the allegations against me. On the harassment that had ruined my life for eight months, I was cross-examined for all of four minutes nine seconds. That's it? All those sleepless nights, those awkward chats with family, those suspicious looks from people, those awful headlines. And that was it? Her barrister didn't even try to prove the case against me. Scarcely four minutes. Nausea swept through me. Faria had trampled all over my family for a year simply to try to get a few quid out of the FA. Disgusting.

Taking innocent comments and spinning them for her own ends, Faria's accusations were laughable. Did I say at any stage to Faria 'You would be better off with an older man'? Absolutely, I did. But the jump of faith to me being that older man was hilarious. I was friendly with my staff, I bantered with them, even, shock horror, bought them Christmas presents out of my own money. My staff were well treated. I tore up their clocking-on slips. 'This isn't about nine to five,' I told my staff, 'this is about getting the job done, getting in early, staying late, and if you need to disappear mid-afternoon to do a quick spot of shopping, that's fine by me.' My anarchic approach appealed to some, and appalled one or two others. Faria enjoyed it.

At the tribunal I was asked to describe my working relationship with Faria. 'During her time here, I am happy to say that I trusted and respected her, enjoyed an excellent professional relationship with her, and regarded her as a friend,' I said. Not now.

My testimony delivered, I stepped out into the Kingsway sunshine, still smarting over the injustice of it all. Everyone felt we were going to win. Faria had been so unconvincing. Life would go on, after all.

The FA's summer meeting was being held in Brighton that weekend, starting with a dinner with partners that evening. Should I go? Could I face them all? Sod it. I don't hide. 'Come on, Susan,' I said on getting to our flat. 'We're going to Brighton.' Everybody had gone into dinner by the time we arrived. Inevitably, our table was across the room, so we had a very long, very conspicuous walk to our seats. Half-way across, somebody stood and started to applaud. Then many more rose and clapped. I glanced at Susan. Extraordinary. I looked around the room, searching for certain board members. Too late, I thought. You blew your chance to back me when I really needed it. The charge of hypocrisy could not be levelled at all in the room. Some Council members were fantastic, and their applause was very generous. Others in the room must have found it difficult acknowledging my presence when they had clearly wanted me gone.

Strange events moved quickly. In the morning, I received messages to ring the Screws and the *Mail on Sunday*. 'For goodness sake,' I said to Susan. 'What on earth can they want now?' Amazingly, the Screws wanted guidance on a totally different story! Newspapers glide from one car crash to the next. Fortunately, the *Mail on Sunday* call was far more significant and agreeable. Their excellent correspondent, Sarah Oliver, had some magnificent information. 'I did all the interviews with Faria for the original story and what she said about you we left out because she had nothing critical to say, actually the opposite,' Sarah said. 'I've got it all on tape.'

'Can you tell me what was said in more detail?'

'Yes.' Sarah did and, more importantly, promised to run it in the *Mail on Sunday* the next day, completely blowing Faria's case out of the water. I was jubilant.

Feeling more positive, I accepted Brian Barwick's offer of a walk and a cup of tea in a café down on the beach at Brighton. He apologised for not supporting me more visibly. 'Thank you,' I said. I was too angry to tell Brian what I felt about him. Having decided to dispute Faria's claims, the FA should have said: 'Bring it on, we'll defend our man.' Don't say 'bring it on' and then all disappear. Support me. Perhaps they believe I should have been stronger. Perhaps they would have been. Whatever. The fact is I did not believe that Brian Barwick, Geoff Thompson and Simon Johnson were there for me when I needed them.

When the tribunal resumed on the Tuesday, the *Mail on Sunday* tape was raised. When Sarah Oliver asked Faria: 'Did he ever come on to you?' Faria replied 'no', and actually praised me for being a great boss. What also destroyed Faria's allegations of sexual harassment were complimentary comments about me on certain radio shows. Faria went on James Whale's late-night programme on TalkSPORT on 29 August 2004, saying I was 'fantastic' and 'great to work for'.

Evidence completed, the three members of the tribunal retired to consider their verdict. How long? No indication. I just waited, filling my time with work, a strained holiday and then, on the weekend that England won the Ashes, Simon Johnson called. I was checking in at Heathrow for a flight to Marrakech for the FIFA Congress. 'We'll have the judgement this afternoon,' said a very jolly Simon. Hurriedly hauling my bags off the belt, I managed to put back my flight. So I sat at Heathrow, waiting for my life to be allowed to start again. When Simon rang back with the verdict, I punched the air. Faria's 'inconsistent accounts' were lambasted by the tribunal. I felt the storm clouds passing.

Even now, three years after first hearing them, the tribunal's evisceration of Faria sounds so sweet:

> She denied in evidence that she had lied to or been deceitful with the *Mail on Sunday* reporter despite the fact that it was absolutely clear to everyone other than apparently Ms Alam that she had said one thing to the *Mail on Sunday* and another completely different thing to the Tribunal with regard to the allegations against Mr Davies. The veracity of the Claimant with regard to the allegations of sexual harassment is seriously in doubt. Mr Davies, on the other hand, appeared to us to be an honest and straightforward witness. We have no doubt that we prefer the evidence of Mr Davies and we are entirely satisfied that none of the incidents of alleged harassment which the Claimant refers to took place.

In the detailed judgement, one of the other allegations against the FA, not relating to me, was only lost by two to one. Miss Lapierre, the female member of the tribunal, sided with Faria on that, but she certainly didn't take any female line with the allegations against me. They were unanimously thrown out. The tribunal absolutely shredded Faria's evidence. 'There is no support for the Claimant's contention that Mr Davies sexually harassed her,' said the tribunal, dismissing the suggestion of a 'third man' as a lie.

> The full details of the allegation were not in fact provided until the exchange of witness statements a week before the hearing commenced. The Tribunal considers that was a very unusual way for an honest person to proceed. We are inclined to the view that it was no doubt intended to put some pressure upon the Respondent to settle the claim being brought against them by holding over the head of the

> Respondent the threat of further disclosures which would embarrass the FA. A significant factor in our view is that the Claimant repeatedly contradicted herself to the Press in connection with Mr Davies.

Sarah Oliver at the *Mail on Sunday* had come up trumps. So had James Whale's show.

Faria's accusations never led to me being placed in chains, or incarcerated in any cell, but now I felt truly liberated. I was a free man, my reputation restored. My legal fees amounted to £7,000 but that was irrelevant. I appreciated when the FA eventually agreed to pay the bill. Freedom and respect were qualities money couldn't buy. A couple of newspaper columns had been written about me that were plainly actionable. Susan was furious about them. If I'd had more energy, I would have taken action against them.

Later, when the dust settled, I was asked by an all-party group of MPs about employment laws. I was well placed to give them some choice thoughts. 'In a magistrates' court, the magistrates can say "there is no evidence against this person" and throw the case out early,' I told the politicians. 'In the Crown Court, the judge can say "there is no evidence against this person" and throw it out. In employment tribunals, once the process is set in motion, no one steps in, even if there is no evidence.'

People appeared fascinated by my ordeal.

'How did you come through all that?' asked John Birt, the former director general of the BBC. 'Congratulations for the way you handled yourself.' I was grateful to John. There were wonderfully generous letters and messages again from people who went to unbelievable lengths to contact me.

Faria's act of calumny taught me a lot. I am not a vindictive person. I am not a saint. People have suffered far worse experiences than mine. Faria's inability to value loyalty has made me cherish loyalty. But I am more wary of being trusting, more cynical. When I hear allegations against somebody, I pause before judging them.

Just because there's smoke doesn't mean there's fire. My view of Faria is disdain shaped by great sadness that she should have stooped so low. I don't wish ill on her. I hope she finds a new and a happy life somewhere. Faria craved love and attention, but found only attention. Walking into Kingsway, she enjoyed being the star of the soap opera. I didn't enjoy the soap opera, but at least I survived with, I hope, my credibility intact.

18

The Magnificent Money-pit

Before joining the FA I wasn't exactly Wembley-friendly. I'd witnessed glorious occasions with England and Manchester United there, some incredible FA Cup finals, but the whole Wembley experience had become miserable beyond comprehension, and not just for fans of the losing team. Getting in and out was a nightmare. Getting wet was a regular hazard and not just from the leaking roof. Torrents of urine seeped from too few toilets. The catering was poor, the seating uncomfortable and too many views were restricted. Wembley had lost its allure.

In my later years at the BBC, I made several films about the merits of a new national stadium in Manchester or Birmingham. In 1995, John Major's government and Sport England were keen to spend some of the new-found lottery riches on a modern national stadium. In a twelve-year saga riddled with doubts and debts, the first question was: where?

People like Doug Ellis, Aston Villa's strong-willed chairman, campaigned tirelessly for a Birmingham solution. Having a house in the West Midlands and local friends who passionately agreed with Doug, it was a difficult time for an FA employee like me. As the FA moved steadily towards a new Wembley option, I was subjected to harsh words late at night at parties near my Worcestershire home. Tact stopped me from pointing out that

Birmingham's bid was damaged by being based in Solihull, let alone the horrendous traffic. Queues around Wembley can be bad but the M42 is hardly the open road.

'Do we actually need a National Stadium?' some people asked me. 'Why not keep England on the move, using the Premier League's many splendid grounds?' The Three Lions road-show was fun for a while, but it was becoming England at Old Trafford with the odd game elsewhere. Southern clubs and supporters also moaned about trekking 200 miles up the clogged M1 and M6 for Cup semi-finals. 'It's embarrassing having Arsenal against Spurs in Manchester in the FA Cup semi-final,' London cabbies told me and I nodded in agreement.

What really swung me behind keeping the national stadium in its natural Wembley habitat was talking to other associations when we proposed friendlies. 'And we will be playing at Wembley?' asked the men from Cameroon, Japan, and Saudi Arabia as fixtures were arranged through my early FA years. Wembley evokes so many images, so many memories to millions. Whether it is grainy photographs of a White Horse, footage of a famous World Cup final, or the sight of Ricky Villa dribbling to glory, Wembley inhabits the hearts and minds of billions around the globe.

'I can't believe there is any question about what you are going to do with Wembley,' Franz Beckenbauer told me as the debate intensified in 2000. 'You have to rebuild it.' Years before, I visited Dennis Tueart at New York Cosmos, and he introduced me to Pele, who'd just stopped playing. We got talking about Wembley. 'It is my greatest regret that I never played there,' Pele said. Wembley means so much to so many people, young and old, fan and legend alike. The nation that invented the greatest game owed the world the greatest stadium.

Slowly, the FA set to work on one of the most complicated and expensive property deals in British construction history. We had to deal with central government, the London Development Agency, the mayor's office, Sport England and Brent Council. Under the chairmanship of Ken Bates, Wembley National Stadium Limited was formed. Using lottery money, this FA subsidiary bought the old stadium for £106m and managed Wembley through its last FA Cup final in 2000. Few present failed to appreciate the irony and significance of Ken's Chelsea beating Doug's Villa, London defeating Birmingham.

Arguments raged over the grand design for the new Wembley, a design many felt more grandiose than grand. WNSL and Ken sought the necessary finance from the City to begin the redevelopment. When the banks stalled, the FA froze. On 7 December 2000, football's governing body faced up to possibly its most embarrassing moment, and there had been a few. A momentous board meeting was preceded by headlines like 'DOME-STYLE FIASCO FEARED AT WEMBLEY', 'FA COULD KEEP WEMBLEY AND DITCH NEW STADIUM' and 'DARE THEY SHUNT CHAIRMAN BATES INTO THE SIDINGS?'

Drastic action was required. Ken seemed to believe that several of us had ganged up to oust him in favour of Sir Roland Smith, the chairman of HSBC as well as Manchester United plc. I certainly talked to Sir Roland about the merits of bringing someone from the construction industry on to the WNSL board. What Ken has never known was that months earlier I'd defended him strongly against criticism by senior government figures. They believed Ken's brusque style was partly why the banks' appetite to lend to WNSL was so limited.

'The FA has to replace Bates,' they told me.

I hit back. 'Wembley would never have got off the ground without Ken Bates,' I told them. I'd had some huge run-ins with Ken but football always needs men like Bates. He could be rude, awkward, and was always calling for my sacking but, overall, Ken was a positive influence because he roughed things up, often when that was needed, and banged heads together. Eventually, Ken did step down but whenever I walk into Wembley now, I give thanks to him. Without Ken, and Adam later on, the new Wembley might never have risen from the ground to dominate the London skyline as it now so majestically does. At the very least, it would have taken even longer.

Ken was succeeded initially by Sir Rodney Walker, who always seemed to have more hats than that legendary visitor to Ladies Day at Ascot, Mrs Gertrude Shilling. Sir Rodney was chairman of UK Sport, chairman of Leicester City plc and chairman of the Rugby League and World Snooker. How he managed them all and stayed sane I never fathomed. Sir Rodney boasted a handshake straight out of WWF wrestling and made mere mortals quake as he loomed into view. Ultimately, a construction man, Michael Jefferies, became its chairman.

That FA board meeting of 7 December was of seismic significance. Among the options presented to the board were refurbishing the existing stadium or, even worse, baling out and handing back the stadium keys to the government. What humiliation that would have been. The FA would have been the laughing stock of world football. Due to the lack of bank finance, the FA couldn't proceed with the new Wembley project. But it also couldn't afford to abort it with costs totalling £150m including the return of £120m to Sport England. The dilemma took ten months to resolve.

German footballers like Didi Hamann closed Wembley down. German bankers helped open it up. Westdeutsche Landesbank agreed to lend £426m under a series of stiff conditions: one, government must be supportive; two, a guaranteed fixed-price contract had to be confirmed; three, the FA must stump up £150m as equity capital; and four, the long-term business plan had to be convincing.

The question of visible and audible government backing dogged the project from early on. The FA's strained relationship with the Sports Minister Kate Hoey at one stage certainly didn't help. One morning at the BBC, I appeared on the *Frost on Sunday* show coincidentally with Tony Blair. Before we went on air, I mentioned to the PM how vital the government's positive support to Wembley was. 'Anything you can say today could make a real difference,' I told Blair. When David Frost then asked Blair about Wembley, the PM replied: 'I want it to happen. It's essential it does.'

Blair's backing was well timed, but much needed to be done, particularly by Adam. At the World Cup in 2002, I walked into Adam's room at England's hotel on Awaji Island and found him submerged under piles of fax paper. Adam worked night and day as we moved gingerly towards a final agreement with Sport England on completing the new Wembley project. Not until 19 May 2007 did the FA Cup final return home. Criticism of the delay was intense but, in comparison with the Dome, let alone Terminal 5 at Heathrow, the opening of Wembley was a triumph. Our country doesn't do big projects easily and they take their toll on careers. Ken Bates, Adam Crozier and Michael Cunnah, Wembley's CEO for several years, are only the better-known names who know what Wembley cost them. The Aussie builders Multiplex might also wonder how they came to make a reported £200m loss on building somebody else's national stadium.

'David, how come those Japanese and Koreans can build ten stadia each and we muck up Wembley,' one London cabbie asked me on my return from the 2002 World Cup.

'Well, the honest answer is their governments made it happen in Japan and Korea and some are going to be knocked down and replaced with shopping malls,' I replied. The British government would never pay for a stadium as they did across the Channel for Stade de France or Down Under for the Sydney Olympic stadium, both of which have struggled financially.

Despite the ongoing costs, Wembley has already been hailed as the 'best stadium on the planet' by Franz Beckenbauer. Despite its precarious financial beginning, Wembley boasts a real commercial value and sponsor appeal. The 17,000 Club Wembley seats and boxes have generated £500m in revenue after probably the most successful marketing programme of its type anywhere. 'I want to buy two seats myself,' I told my wife, Susan, in 2003 as I planned for life after the FA in 2006. 'Not the poshest, not the cheapest.

But let's try and find a couple where I can shout "Sack The Board" at the Royal Box and get heard.' Having bought the seats, I still held my tongue that miserable night of 21 November 2007 when England lost to Croatia. Looking up to the VIP seats, I knew there were FA people there hurting just as much as me.

Having survived a difficult beginning, Wembley still faces an unclear future. The governing body of English football shouldn't be a property company. The FA must ask itself whether it really is in the business of owning and running a venue that stages up to fifteen football games a year but also needs to attract P. Diddy, the Miami Dolphins, the Foo Fighters and Madonna and allow the motor Race of Champions to speed across its hallowed turf.

The FA could float WNSL on the Stock Exchange, letting a wider public own the national stadium. The FA could sell WNSL and let another company run it while guaranteeing its matches remained there. If the FA did sell up, some of the money, in some form, would have to be handed back to government. Meanwhile, Brian Barwick, its latest former chief executive, talked about moving FA staff from Soho Square to Wembley. An idea debated many times in the past, that Big Move was always rejected in my time. Sponsors, some Council members and marketing types wanted to be in the centre of town. 'If you come to London, you want to come to central London,' Adam Crozier always observed. And of course there will be a cost to leaving Soho Square. Maybe times have changed. Maybe Fabio Capello, the latest England coach, fancies his office in dear old Brent; it is certainly convenient for the odd opera at Wembley Arena. It never would have bothered me where the FA was based.

Lord Triesman, the latest FA chairman, must find the right answers for the next stage of Wembley's development. If he doesn't, Wembley risks continuing to be a huge financial burden for English football in the next generation. But one thing is for sure: the magnificent new Wembley has been worth all the pain.

19

Prejudice and Pride

England supporters are no longer the lepers of Europe. Watching the 200,000 England fans partying at the 2006 World Cup, it was impossible to believe they had once been pariahs. Hooliganism was the English disease. Everyone said so. We invented travelling trouble-makers. Not now. An unbelievable amount of hard work has been done by the FA and fans' organisations to eradicate the stain on England's reputation. People even remarked that England fans had been missed at Euro 2008. Such sentiments would have been unimaginable a decade earlier. Back at Lansdowne Road on 15 February 1995, war broke out on the terraces when England played the Republic of Ireland. It was supposed to be a friendly match but the trip was a disaster from start to finish.

England's arrival in Dublin was hardly auspicious. The driver kindly took Terry Venables and me the long way round to our hotel. 'I know Dublin, this is very interesting, but get us to the hotel, please,' I said. On finally arriving we found England's base undistinguished, the food even less so. We also found Adrian Titcombe, the FA head of security, arguing with our senior press officer, Mike Parry, not for the first or last time. What on earth was our head of security doing in the team hotel when he should surely have been in the city centre, checking for any trouble? That was the crux of what Mike was asking, with his usual bluntness.

On reaching Lansdowne Road, my sense of foreboding deepened. The stadium was decrepit, the atmosphere already bad. When Ireland scored after twenty-seven minutes, England fans rioted. Bedlam. England supporters were on the upper tier, lobbing missiles down on to largely innocent Irish fans. 'No surrender to the IRA,' came the chant from the English, who launched into the Irish fans, forcing them to flee. Briefly, I feared another Heysel. 'The match is abandoned,' announced the referee, to no great surprise. Down in the tunnel, mayhem reigned. Players ran past, dazed and confused, racing to escape the carnage outside.

I convened a quick meeting with Mike Parry. 'We must be on the front foot,' I instructed him. 'This could scupper Euro '96. I bloody believe that. Listen, Mike. Is a country whose fans are incapable of sailing across the Irish Sea without rioting worthy of staging the second-biggest football tournament on the planet?' Security arrangements were poor in Dublin. Segregation was minimal. I'd no idea who'd agreed to where in the ground the England fans were positioned. But England's fans were England's problem. We had to acknowledge that. First, we had to smuggle England's players out. 'Get on the bus quickly and away' was the instruction. 'But surely the pitch is clear now?' one player replied. Amazing. They would have played on. Footballers are remarkably resilient. 'We have to leave,' I replied. 'The match has been abandoned.' I knew how bad it would have looked if England and Ireland resumed kicking a ball around while the police tidied up after a riot.

Everyone on the bus, we drove at speed towards Dublin Airport. 'The plane will not be ready yet,' the charter company then informed us. 'But it is being brought forward from its scheduled slot.' Damn. We had time to kill.

'Let's stop off at a hotel for something to eat,' Terry said.

'We'd better not do it too publicly,' I replied. At around nine p.m., when the game should still have been in progress, the England bus drew up outside a hotel and I nipped inside. 'Could you give us something to eat?' I asked. As they checked with the kitchen, I looked around. Incredibly noisy, the hotel heaved with Irish fans. Twenty England footballers trooping through the foyer might have caused another riot, so we made a sharp exit. The players, staff, none of us ever got that meal.

Eventually we arrived home, and the following morning I was in sharpish at a besieged Lancaster Gate. Clare Tomlinson, our new press officer and now the well-regarded Sky presenter, was already hard at work with Mike, putting out media fires ignited in Dublin. Typically, the FA email system was soon preoccupied with a less-pressing issue than rioting England fans.

'What is all this about Mr Rushden's raincoat?' I asked Clare.

'Mr Rushden has lost his raincoat after a committee meeting and everyone is looking for it,' explained Clare sarcastically. So there we were, gripped by a major hooligan crisis that threatened our hosting of Euro '96, searching for Mr Rushden's raincoat. I knew Percy Rushden, a great character, one of journalist Joe Lovejoy's 'Blazered Buffoons', and proud of it, but still capable of having a debate about the FA's strengths and flaws. His raincoat was, I'm sure, a cherished possession of Percy's, but English football had more important concerns.

As we sorted the media debris from Dublin, I wondered whether the fixture had ever been a good idea. We tried hard to avoid potential minefields. The previous year, when I learned the FA had fixed up a friendly with Germany on 18 April in Berlin, I went spare.

'We have to cancel this game,' I said to Terry.

'Why?' Terry asked.

'It's bloody Adolf Hitler's birthday,' I said. 'Terry, we're not having this. The potential for mayhem is enormous.'

Terry had understood. The Germans didn't. They were very upset. 'This is not what gentlemen do,' the German FA president, Egidius Braun, told Sir Bert Millichip. That word 'gentlemen' was soon to poison Anglo-German relations again in the battle to host World Cup 2006. Bert appreciated the sensitivities. He had a very distinguished war record, including landing on the beach at Salerno, where he met Barbara, his future wife. Having called off the England away game against Germany, people at the FA were less keen on cancelling another fixture. So we flew into Dublin to fanfares and left to sirens. Dublin was our first wake-up call. The ugly scenes at Lansdowne Road reminded me of the truly unpleasant nature of the flotsam and jetsam of society that sometimes followed England. For the hoolies, England trips were seen as an easy touch. Sometimes our fans were innocent and were ambushed by malevolent locals. The English are coming. Let's get them. The usual drill. Sadly, too many times our supporters were guilty of throwing the first punch, the first bar-stool. Only a minority tarnished England's reputation, but enough to cause significant problems. England's hooligans were split into two groups, ringleaders and followers. Now and again, I had the nasty experience of encountering these obnoxious characters. 'Fuck off,' they shouted at me in Dublin, 'you're in with the police.'

The FA were out of their depth against these people, a feeling strengthened during Euro '96. We survived but it still wasn't very pleasant around Trafalgar Square the night England lost to Germany. Then came Rome, 11 October 1997, a day of joy on the pitch and misery off it. The night before the World Cup qualifier, Adrian Titcombe again seemed to spend much time in the sanctuary of the team hotel, rather than venturing on to Rome's streets where the predicted scuffles materialised. I didn't know why, but also knew how nightmarish his job must have seemed. The Italian police hit back the following evening. Inside the Olympic Stadium, the treatment of England supporters by the baton-wielding Carabinieri was disgraceful. Rome proved our second wake-up call. The moment the game finished, we should have been jubilant. After all, Glenn Hoddle's side had qualified for France '98. The urge after a match like that is: get on the plane, have a few drinks, celebrate. But I looked around the Olympic Stadium, seeing all the England fans penned in. The Italian police were in belligerent mood, following the trouble the night before.

The Carabinieri even held the team coach up for ages. We finally landed at Luton at 4.45 a.m. I was fuming.

Preventing such situations happening again was now priority no. 1. Pat Smith, the FA deputy chief executive, and I went in to see Graham Kelly. 'The FA are not a police force,' I told Graham. 'We need top-level professional assistance. We can't fight this low-life with an internal staff member.' The FA employed dear old Adrian Titcombe as head of security. As competent as he may have been, we needed reinforcements. The situation was so frustrating that I would probably have resigned if the FA hadn't moved to take on the hooligans. My blood boiled over the issue. 'We're putting at risk all the good work of the team and the staff,' I told Graham. 'We're trying everything to give the guys on the pitch and Glenn the best chance, and these thugs are ruining everything. We must take our share of the blame.'

We were architects of our problem. Sir Bert, the old secretary Ted Croker and that generation at the FA in the Eighties surely must have comprehended how awful this hooliganism was. But we seemed reluctant, even frightened to confront the issue. England players would never criticise the fans. They travelled around the world supporting the team, often in hostile places. The England squad appreciated that loyalty and sacrifice.

Finally, thanks to pressure from Pat Smith and myself, very senior security advisers arrived to help England. Former deputy commissioners of the Metropolitan Police like Sir Brian Hayes and Sir John Evans began the fight-back against the hooligans. It took time. England endured painful scenes at the 1998 World Cup and Euro 2000. Facing Tunisia at France '98 in Marseilles was always going to stir local tensions. We warned UEFA. 'Playing a North African team so near to North Africa at the end of a weekend with a Monday 1.30 p.m. kick-off is a big worry,' we told UEFA. 'It's the English again, isn't it?' UEFA replied. They were fed up with England fans ruining their summer parties. 'There's nobody else who would have a problem playing this game.' I couldn't argue. We were the problem. I arrived in Marseilles, dreading the stay. In stifling weather, the fans drank and drank and then fought. England's name was blackened further.

After the riot in Marseilles, our new security adviser, Sir Brian Hayes, disappeared on a scheduled short break to Majorca with his wife. On discovering this, the *Mirror* lambasted him. Despite having been in the Met for a long time, Sir Brian was sensitive to criticism. He then went straight to Toulouse to check on security arrangements before England's game with Romania. When the team landed, Sir Brian greeted the players at the bottom of the steps. 'Had a good holiday, Sir Brian?' enquired Alan Shearer, usually to the forefront of any mischief-making. Sir Brian was absolutely livid. Working with England was a hard school at times. Security advisers like Sir Brian were vital, though, and brought much-needed professional advice.

Euro 2000, another of our wake-up calls, showed time and persistence were still required to eradicate hooliganism. The style of policing was key. England fans rioted at Euro 2000, but only in Belgium, not Holland. When we played in Eindhoven, there were few issues. Dutch policing was more subtle, more skilled. When England arrived in the ancient Belgian town of Charleroi to face Germany, our fans clashed with Belgian police. Hostilities were brief. The damage to a few bar-stools was minimal, but the damage to England's reputation was massive. The TV pictures beamed round the world looked terrible. 'It was never as bad as Marseilles,' fans told me, 'it only lasted thirty seconds.' Sadly, that was enough. A half-minute of skirmishing was shown almost on a constant loop on the rolling TV news services. 'Not the English again,' was Europe's reaction.

After beating Germany in Charleroi, we returned to our base at Spa euphoric over England's performance. The next day, we staged a triumphant news conference with Kevin Keegan, who talked away about England's great display and what an impact Steven Gerrard made. I sat next to Kevin, enjoying the moment, when my assistant, Joanne Budd, sidled up and whispered in my ear. 'UEFA want you,' she said. As inconspicuously as possible, I slipped out of the room and called UEFA. Europe's governing body was in uproar over the rioting. England were in danger of being thrown out of Euro 2000.

'David, what are you going to do about your hooligans travelling around Europe?' UEFA's Gerd Aigner asked me.

'Look, we have a problem,' I replied. 'There's no secret about it.'

'We're having an emergency meeting of our executive committee,' Gerd added. 'If you want to send a representative, you can.' The tone in Gerd's voice told me how deeply in trouble we were.

'We'll send our security chief, Sir Brian Hayes,' I informed Gerd. I went back to Kevin, who'd finished talking to the press. 'Kevin, there is a serious risk we could get kicked out,' I said. 'I need you to appeal to the fans for calm. We are back in Charleroi to meet Romania. We cannot afford another disturbance.' Kevin took on board how serious the situation was. His appeal to the supporters was perfect, and they responded well. But we all knew the hooligan problem needed addressing further.

'We cannot go on like this,' I said to Adam Crozier, the FA's new chief executive, after Euro 2000. 'We need legislation to stop these yobs travelling.' Banning orders were debated in Parliament. 'I fear they may be thrown out on human-rights grounds,' I said to Adam. 'Removing people's passports because you suspect they may do something is a big thing to do.' Amongst the sceptics were Tories like my near-namesake, David Davis MP, eventually to become shadow Home Secretary. The Tory party has a libertarian wing and they were concerned. We had to convince them of the need for action. I also went to see the Lib Dems' Charlie Kennedy, whom I'd known for years. 'Banning orders have got to happen because our country is being dragged through the gutter,' I said to Charlie. 'We have to bring in legislation that, normally, I would be very uneasy about. But I've seen what goes on in places like Charleroi.' Charlie nodded. He understood the gravity of our problem. English football was on the brink, risking another Heysel ban. Despite some opposition in the Lords the legislation went through. That was a turning point.

A few scuffles broke out in Munich in 2001, but unsavoury incidents became less serious, less frequent. The 2002 World Cup in Japan and South Korea never worried me – the hoolies wouldn't have travelled that far. But goodness knows the mess we'd have been in had banning orders not been in force before Euro 2004 in Portugal and the 2006 World Cup in Germany.

As well as removing passports, the campaign against hooliganism was being waged on other fronts. CCTV drove trouble out of English grounds. Paul Barber, the FA's marketing man under Crozier, and then Jonathan Hill, the FA's Commercial Director, worked hard to broaden football's fan-base, encouraging families and women to attend games. Their increasing presence diluted tension. Portugal in 2004 was marvellous. Most fans stayed on the Algarve and the Portuguese were fantastic hosts. They were used to large numbers of young Englishmen invading their country. They welcomed the English, and their warmth was reciprocated with better behaviour. At the 2006 World Cup, the Germans estimated that the crowd could be up to 40 per cent female when England played.

Self-policing on the terraces was essential. A decade ago, there seemed loads of different supporters' groups, their leaders coming and going with considerable speed. I wanted the FA to fund fans' organisations. Some supporters were against that, fearing they would be in the authorities' pockets but we managed to develop links. The Football Supporters' Federation under Malcolm Clarke has proved excellent. As has Kevin Miles, who initiated the fans' embassies abroad. The official Three Lions support, englandfans, engage with the FA so much more. They come into Soho Square, meet the manager, air grievances.

People talk about a right-wing element amongst England's hooligans, which was undeniably true, but the political edge is nowadays more significant amongst other countries' troublemakers. The German FA asked me to chair the Daniel Nivel Foundation, named after the policeman paralysed in Lens tackling German hooligans at France '98. Poland have a problem. Italy's

Ultras have a big political element. One day, I was sitting at a Daniel Nivel Foundation meeting, talking about English anti-racism campaigns with a member of the Italian FA.

'David, stop going on about racism because you're only highlighting it,' this Italian told me.

I was apoplectic. 'What do you mean?' I asked.

'If we kept talking about racism as you do in England we'd merely make it worse,' he replied.

'That is exactly the attitude we had in England,' I retorted. 'We had to change the attitude that allowed racism to flourish. We've tackled it now.' Along with people like Gordon Taylor and David Dein, I helped develop the Kick It Out campaign. Talking to Ian Wright and John Barnes, I was made aware of the horrific abuse they endured. John told me in graphic detail about playing in matches, running down the wing, with bananas being thrown at him.

The FA now protest swiftly and vehemently when our players are racially abused. We voiced our outrage when Yugoslavia fans aimed monkey chants at Emile Heskey during an under-21 play-off game on 29 March 2000. Kevin Keegan and I were both watching, and couldn't believe what we were hearing. Shaun Wright-Phillips then took unbelievable abuse in Madrid on 17 November 2004. These are dates that shame European football. Back then, UEFA were slow to deal with racism, reflecting the attitude of the rest of Europe. Now that Michel Platini is president, UEFA are far quicker to stamp down on racism.

We're still not angels. Racism can be found in English football, particularly in some public parks on a Sunday morning. And for Turkish supporters wandering up to the Stadium of Light on 2 April 2003, it wasn't a ball of fun. 'I'd rather be a Paki than a Turk,' some England fans sang in Sunderland. Even with Platini's impressive stance on racism, UEFA still needs to be tougher, imposing harder punishment on people who step out of line, English or whoever. Fines are meaningless. The only penalties that matter are point deductions or exclusion from cup competitions. That threat would encourage authorities in other countries to accelerate their anti-racism campaigns. And role models help. In England, Paul Ince's rise up the managerial ladder is fantastic news. Incey's a brilliant role model. I applauded Blackburn Rovers' decision to make Incey their manager in June 2008 and will continue to follow his career closely whatever happens as I think with proper support he has the potential to manage England one day. But there are still far too few black, let alone Asian, coaches.

Eventually, after many years,the FA reacted well to the problems of racism and hooliganism. Realistically, England's problem with trouble-makers has been contained, not solved. Hooliganism feeds on social ills and those ills remain. Like booze. Go into any English town-centre on a Friday night and observe the trouble caused by alcohol. Education and parenting skills need improving. We are breeding feral youths oblivious to respect. Some form of compulsory community service, like VSO, to be completed at home and abroad, might teach the yobs some respect. It's costly but, I believe, essential. Having witnessed Dublin, Rome, Marseilles and Charleroi, I will never be complacent about England's hooligan problem. It's a fragile peace. But week in, week out, English clubs now compete in Europe, generally without major incident. Slowly, ever so slowly, the English are losing their unwanted mantle of world champion hooligans.

20

Olympic Heights

Walking into the British Museum for a news conference to launch London's bid for the 2012 Olympics, I looked admiringly at all the famous relics collected in the heart of the capital. Could we possibly bring the celebrated five-ringed circus from ancient Greece to London? Could we turn all those barren stretches of East London into a gleaming Olympic village and stadium complex? Could we really pull off such an unbelievable feat? I fervently hoped so. So when Simon Clegg, the British Olympic Association chief executive, invited me to represent football in those first days of the London 2012 campaign, I leapt at the chance. Football was one of just five sports asked to front up a BOA announcement of the bid at the museum. Even at that stage I realised we had no official government backing, no money, but we had some powerful weapons. Also London offered the huge enthusiasm of Simon Clegg and the political clout of BOA chairman Craig Reedie. The bid had the encouragement of the national game. In that amazing race for 2012, the power of English football helped London overtake Paris.

The FA could have killed off London's chances before the race even started. At the time, Downing Street was divided on the Olympics. 'Would England be staging the 2018 World Cup?' I was asked by No. 11 when London first requested government money. 'We're reluctant to provide funds for the Olympic bid because Paris and Madrid seem too far ahead. We need to know whether we should be focusing more on the football at 2018? If we're going to get the World Cup the next time Europe hosts it, shouldn't we concentrate on that? The World Cup is less expensive. Why bother getting involved in this Olympic thing?' Chancellor Gordon Brown may have been initially sceptical about London 2012, as opposed to PM Tony Blair. No. 10 was wholehearted from the outset. As acting chief executive of the FA, when I heard No. 11's question, my heart wanted to cry: 'The FA will bid for 2018, and we will win.' As football's representative on the BOA, I knew the danger of such an announcement. Critics of 2012 would use it to destroy the Olympic bid there and then. 'I don't know whether the FA will win 2018 or even get the chance to bid,' I informed the Treasury. The seed of doubt was planted in their minds. Government didn't want a decade with no great sporting event on our shores. No. 11 began to back the Games.

Other sports were jealous of our influence. 'The government are only interested in football,' the chief executive of another sport told me during bidding for 2012. 'Thank you,' I replied. 'I'll take that as a compliment.' As the bid grew in strength, English football's big hitters were lined up behind London 2012. The London bid guys, encouraged by the Premier League chairman Dave Richards, wanted to call on the charm and global appeal of David Beckham, who was born in Leytonstone, close to the Games site. 'He should do it,' I told those close to David. 'He'll really be a great plus for London.' David agreed. England's captain flew into Singapore, venue for the International Olympic Committee final vote on 6 July 2005, and the pictures of his arrival were very potent. Thousands flocked around this athletic symbol of London's dream. Probably the most recognised football person in the world after Pele, Beckham bowled everyone over with his charisma. David sprinkled star-dust all over London's campaign. The IOC love glamour and Beckham has become part of Hollywood. He is also a very human star. His natural charm hypnotised everyone in Singapore. Paris may have felt confident going into the final ballot, but Beckham helped tip key votes London's way. He smiled at everyone, glad-handed the IOC powerbrokers. He went to several schools, spreading happiness and goodwill, creating a fantastic image for London 2012.

Sven-Goran Eriksson's involvement was called for, too. The sight of a sophisticated Swede backing London helped. Sven added to the cosmopolitan feel behind the Olympic bid. Whatever people in England say about Eriksson as a coach, he is considered a star overseas. Whenever I accompanied him to gatherings of coaches, Sven was always fêted. 'God has arrived!' the French coach, Raymond Domenech, would say as everyone rushed to greet Sven. Jurgen Klinsmann said the same. Sven was a celebrity coach even among coaches. He radiated charm – and not just with women. Everyone was impressed with Sven in Singapore.

If my heart felt London had a chance, my head calculated the many difficulties. Dave Richards would give me his assessment – sometimes optimistic, sometimes totally negative. That was Dave. Paris appeared miles ahead (in the event, perhaps too far ahead for their own good). London was the underdog and had to fight. It had to put on a great show. Everyone contributed. London was driven by the bizarre alliance of Tony Blair, Ken Livingstone and Seb Coe, all points of the political spectrum. Was it Tony's finest hour? Probably. Here was a charismatic prime minister and his wife throwing themselves and the whole country behind the bid. Tony was approachable, making IOC delegates feel how valued they were. I wondered whether the world had ever seen a big-city mayor like Ken before? Definitely not! Seb was Seb, effortlessly charming, an Olympic legend, eloquently converting people to London's cause. When he talked, Seb's speeches blended substance, humility and humour. Watching back in London, I stood and applauded when Seb delivered his final speech in Singapore – it was brilliant, so exciting. I felt the whole world seized by Seb's vision. Wavering voters must have been seduced. Would it be enough? Paris were still favourites on the day of the vote. To my great shock and delight, London won. A campaign of inspired leadership, perfect timing, some footballing glamour and Parisian arrogance swung the vote London's way.

Winning the right to host the Games was straightforward compared to finding an agreement between the home nations over fielding a Great Britain football XI in 2012. The task has proved hellishly difficult, and still hasn't been resolved. The FA are in favour. Scotland, Wales and Northern Ireland aren't. As it stands, English footballers alone will represent Britain at 2012.

'The politics in football are more complicated than the politics at Westminster,' Lord Tom Pendry told me. He was right but I was determined to fight to give young Brits a chance of Olympic glory.

'I want British football teams participating in the Olympics,' I told Tom. 'I want a men's team – probably under-21 plus three over-age players. I want a women's team plus two paralympic teams, cerebral palsy and blind.' English football at least is hugely committed to this. Sir Dave Richards, the chairman of the Premier League, showed his support by appearing in Singapore. Surely the Scots, Welsh and Northern Irish don't want to deny their players the chance to take part?

'But our independence as individual FAs will be threatened if we agree to a Great Britain Olympic team,' they all replied when I asked them.

'It's ludicrous to think FIFA will strip you of your independence,' I argued back. 'You've had guarantees from Sepp Blatter and he runs FIFA.'

'Blatter may not be in charge in 2012,' they replied. And sometimes Blatter himself had seemed ambivalent.

'Who was the manager of the Great Britain football team at the 1948 London Olympics?' I asked the others. 'A certain Matt Busby. And who do we want to manage Great Britain at the 2012 Olympics? Alex Ferguson. If Alex says yes, and I hope he will, what will you Scots say then?'

On 28 May 2003, at the Midland Hotel in Manchester, I made a lengthy attempt to convert the Scots. David Taylor and Jack

McGinn, great friends and respectively the then chief executive and chairman of the Scottish FA, seemed to believe a compromise was possible. 'If London win the bid for 2012,' the Scots said, 'we will work with you for a solution and a one-off British team. But David, they won't win, will they? Paris will.' And they laughed. After London's stunning victory, I reminded the Scottish FA of our agreement at the Midland. McGinn's successor, John McBeth, replied: 'That wasn't me who agreed it.' And in the Scottish Parliament, the political landscape had changed too. I'd hit a brick wall again.

Perhaps the inspiration of Team GB's performance at the Beijing Olympics – 47 medals, 19 golds – when it comes to the crunch will move a few stone hearts in Edinburgh, Cardiff and Belfast. The opposition of the Scots, Welsh, and Northern Irish has nothing to do with sport. I hope sanity will prevail. That young Scots and Welsh and Northern Irish players won't be denied the chance of competing at the greatest show on earth by stubborn narrow-mindedness. When London won the bid, we committed to our teams' participation in all the major sports in the Games. We must field a football team, and we'd have a great chance of winning, particularly if Sir Alex is involved. Sir Alex would be the perfect footballing statesman to unite Britain. He's won just about all of football's medals. What a way to complete his collection, with an Olympic gold. If this famous Scot did manage an all-English Olympic team in 2012, now wouldn't that be the ultimate irony? How would they feel in Cardiff, Belfast and Ferguson's native Glasgow then?

21

Blue Bloods and No. 10s

English football now has friends in very high places. Prince William, the future king of England, is president of the FA and Gordon Brown, like Tony Blair and John Major before him, is hugely supportive of the national game. Never again will English football hold the pariah status it did in the Eighties. Over the past decade, the FA have worked assiduously to build up relations with Downing Street and Buckingham Palace, ensuring we made the right response to assorted crises when they arose, as when Princess Diana died.

When Diana was introduced to the players of Spurs and Nottingham Forest before the Gazza FA Cup final of 1991, I was on the Wembley pitch, reporting for the BBC, and observed the impression she made on the players. Diana radiated star quality. She looked magnificent. I could see twenty-two lustful young footballers thinking this woman was pretty hot. Diana exuded natural charm and incredible beauty. Everyone fell for her. That image of the bewitching Diana sprang into my mind when I learned of her tragic death. Waking early on 31 August 1997, I switched on the TV, and saw the news of the car crash in Paris. I nudged my wife Susan. 'For God's sake, look at this,' I said. Like millions of others across the country, we watched and listened in horror to the bulletins.

'Football cannot go ahead today,' I said to Susan. 'The right thing has to be done.' Port Vale were playing Stoke City at one p.m. and Liverpool were due to meet Newcastle United at four p.m. I phoned Graham Kelly.

'We must postpone today's games,' I said.

'OK,' replied Graham. 'I'll leave you to sort it out.' I called the Home Secretary, Jack Straw, to find out the government's stance on public events in these tragic circumstances. Ever since joining the FA, I'd been nurturing contacts with Downing Street for moments like these, when English football could have quick access to government ministers. Jack agreed football games should not go ahead. Rugby played on. Cricket played on. I didn't care what other sports did. That was their judgement call. English football made the right decision.

In the lead-up to Diana's funeral on 6 September, the FA made it very clear that there should be no football that weekend. The Scottish FA initially took a very different tack. Our 'no games' stance put pressure on the SFA, and I wasn't sure they were very happy. It was a really difficult time. In the end, no football was played anywhere that weekend. England's players were supposed to be preparing for a World Cup qualifier with Moldova but Glenn Hoddle gave every player the weekend off. I know some of them were deeply upset by Diana's death. They all admired her. Talking to the players on their return to camp, I wasn't surprised to hear each one had watched the funeral.

We were very conscious of this match with Moldova coming up at Wembley on the Wednesday, 10 September. This would be the first London occasion of any public note after her funeral. The responsibility of getting our approach right was a pressure I felt keenly. Having heard Elton John sing his 'Candle in the Wind' tribute to 'England's Rose' in Westminster Abbey, I contacted his manager, John Reid. 'Would Elton possibly be interested in performing "England's Rose" at Wembley?' I asked. 'Elton's abroad,' Reid replied. That was that. The *Mirror* wanted everyone to take a candle to Wembley. Health and Safety kyboshed that though many still did. Eventually, the evening went off well, with the fans paying a moving tribute to Diana. Even though England won, I felt the whole emotion of the occasion got to the players. Inevitable, really. That does happen.

Some within the FA were often uneasy at games being affected by outside tragedies. Pat Smith, Wembley's overseer, believed I was too quick to postpone games or order a minute's silence. I preferred to be criticised for having a minute's silence, than for not having one. It's about respect. One year, I ordered a minute's silence at an FA Cup final for a stadium tragedy in Africa, a decision questioned by a number of FA Councillors.

'Are we going to have this for any tragedy anywhere in the world?' enquired one Councillor.

'I believe if you trumpet the fact that our Cup final is seen live by 180 countries, and one of those nations has just been hit by a terrible tragedy, the least we can do is show our respect,' I replied.

On becoming executive director at the FA, I inherited the whole question of football's relationship with the Royals. As president of the FA back then, the Duke of Kent would come with the Duchess to Cup finals. Their presence was more visible at Wimbledon, coming down on to the court to meet the winner and loser after the men's and women's finals. The Duke was not a football fan and eventually he made it known he wanted to stand down from his FA duties. I didn't know what was going on between the Duke and Duchess but the situation had become complicated. Before one Cup final, we received a letter from the Duke saying he wasn't attending and another from the Duchess's office saying she was. It was very awkward. Keen to avoid a diplomatic incident, we went back to each, pointing out the other's intentions. In the end, neither came.

Over several months, I had visited the Royal Household to talk through who might be available to become president. 'We are very keen to have one of the young Royals,' I said to Sir Michael Peat, Prince Charles's private secretary. Both William and Harry, particularly William, had shown an enthusiasm for football. Harry enjoyed football but was more of a rugby fan. Sir Michael, a big Arsenal fan, listened sympathetically. Prince Charles had never been a huge fan of football but the people around him were supporters of the national game. Sir Michael relayed the message from Charles that the young princes would not take up any public duties until their education was complete. Clarence House did come to an unwritten understanding with the FA that when William finished university they would seriously consider his becoming president of the FA.

In the interim, Prince Andrew was given the position. 'Doesn't he just like golf?' someone at the FA remarked. Andrew had this public image of running around the world, playing golf and having a good time, but he was easy to get on with. He never had a great knowledge of football but he was interested in what the FA did. Andrew was helpful, giving good speeches on the right occasions, but his period as president was always going to be short.

The day it was announced that William would be president of the national game, some of us went down to Clarence House with the FA Cup for some ceremonial pictures. The FA's new president was not the type to stand on ceremony. He's good fun. One year, I even considered asking him and Harry to make the FA Cup third-round draw. I'm sure the princes would have loved it. Perhaps rightly, some people within the FA were against the idea. The Prince threw himself into his first high-profile role. We took him to Charlton Athletic, a real community club, and William enjoyed it. Whenever I talked to William about football, he always knew his stuff. The Prince was not briefed. He just knew it. 'Of course he knows his football – he's a Villa fan,' said Doug Ellis, the then Villa chairman. 'We fired up the future king's enthusiasm for football.'

When William then visited Soho Square, he was introduced to board members, who were slightly fazed at meeting such glamourous royalty. William sat in on one of Trevor Brooking's youth-development presentations. I hoped he understood! Keen to see all of Soho Square, William went on a tour and met everyone, the boys in the post room, the secretaries and Sven-Goran Eriksson, charming everyone. Before the 2006 World Cup, William attended an England training session at Manchester United's Carrington base with his press secretary Paddy Harverson. Paddy used to be United's Director of Communications before a surprise transfer to Clarence House. Knowing his way around Carrington, Paddy led William over to where the players were training. I was there, watching and laughing as all the players egged Peter Crouch on to do his well-known robot dance for the Prince, who loved it. Afterwards, William came back to the Lowry, our hotel in Manchester. He wanted to meet the England backroom staff, medical men like Gary Lewin and Steve Slattery. William was relaxed. There was no formality. Everyone called him William. He was about to leave the Lowry when David Beckham and Wayne Rooney came haring down the corridor. 'William, can we have your autograph?' they asked. William laughed and obliged.

During the World Cup in Germany, William was an enthusiastic supporter of the team. Before England's first game in Frankfurt, he met fans outside the stadium. He has this easy manner with people. After the win over Paraguay, he went down to the dressing room, very excited. He walked around the room, shaking hands, chatting away. 'How are you? Wasn't it hot?' Small-talk, certainly, but much appreciated by the players. William is of their generation. He was bound to be more at ease than Charles in those surroundings.

Having William as president made me realise how far English football had come since the dark days of the mid-Eighties when the elite shunned English football. Ensconced in No. 10, Mrs Thatcher certainly looked down on the national game. After the Heysel disaster in 1985, Thatcher summoned the FA's chairman Bert Millichip and its secretary Ted Croker to Downing Street. All she did was lecture them. I know that meeting with Thatcher profoundly depressed Bert. Her government's membership-card scheme for football was a classic example of well-meaning non-sense emanating from No. 10.

Thatcher's slightly disdainful stance towards football was partly the FA's fault for failing to develop connections in government. 'We have to nurture a rapport with politicians, even when there is no big issue,' I told FA staff shortly after joining in 1994. 'I don't want a situation like 1985 when we go head to head with government at exactly the time we need to be working shoulder to shoulder.'

The first PM who understood football's importance to the nation was John Major. He realised it could be used as a force for public good. In the run-up to Euro '96, Major held meetings with some of us in the Cabinet room and was really supportive. He certainly knew his football, particularly Chelsea, although friends of mine who were Bridge regulars in the Nineties always moaned about Major. 'Major is always here when we lose,' they complained. 'He's a jinx.' Whatever effect he had on Chelsea, Major was good for English football, welcoming regular contact with the FA. Shortly before the 1997 general election, I visited him at No. 10. Walking through the door into the Majors' private domain, I noticed Norma measuring the curtains. 'Norma's being bloody optimistic if she thinks she is staying on at No. 10,' I told Susan later. 'The opinion polls are awful.'

Tony Blair was miles ahead and swept to a landslide Labour victory. For two years, the FA had been building up a bond with Blair in Opposition. Blair and his adviser Alastair Campbell, a friend of mine from my Westminster Lobby days, were hugely enthusiastic about football, particularly Alastair, a passionate Burnley fan. A cynical perception has arisen of Blair being interested in football only for PR reasons. Maybe he would never win the Wallsend Working Men's Club quiz on the history of Newcastle United, but he liked football, and enjoyed the occasional kickabout. At the 1995 Labour party conference, Blair and Kevin Keegan headed balls to each other. A career politician was never going to be in the same league as a former European Footballer of the Year, but Blair didn't embarrass himself.

English football was boosted by Blair. When England set off for a tournament, the manager always received a personal letter from the PM, wishing the team good luck. On special occasions, such as before World Cup and European Championship knock-out matches, Blair would call Glenn Hoddle, Kevin Keegan or Sven-Goran Eriksson. The calls sometimes came through when we were on the bus to the stadium. After another miserable quarter-final defeat, Blair would still invite the England team to Downing Street. Critics could never understand what the players had done to deserve the honour. It was not our shout! It would have been churlish to turn down invitations to Downing Street or Buckingham Palace. I believe almost all the players wanted to go. Football is such a transient profession, each player knew he might not get another chance. OK, they lost on pens again, but England deserved some recognition. They entertained millions of people on the way to the quarter-finals. Most players enjoyed Blair's company.

Unlike Blair, nobody questioned Gordon Brown's footballing roots. During his time at the Treasury, Brown ensured that, if they were working late, meal breaks coincided with the evening match. The Brown set of Gordon, Charlie Whelan and Geoffrey Robinson would gather round the TV, watching a European or Premier League game while wolfing down their takeaways. Brown is passionate about football. He took great delight in staging a reception for the 1966 English and West German World Cup teams.

Another ancient rivalry we always talked about was the possible revival of the Scotland v. England fixture. 'It should happen, it is such a great historical event,' Brown told me. He still remembers Slim Jim Baxter playing keepie-uppie at Wembley in 1967, humiliating the world champions. I'm afraid I always disagreed about a resumption of Anglo-Scottish hostilities, just as I always did when the subject came up inside the FA, where the commercial boys and girls were particularly keen on the fixture. 'If England draw Scotland in competitive games, as in the Euro 2000 play-offs, then fine,' I argued. 'But recreating the fixture artificially is of benefit to nobody. And I'm not sure the police would go with it.' Police on either side of Hadrian's Wall wouldn't want the hassle. Nor would the FA security advisers. 'Not the brightest idea,' Sir Brian Hayes said to me one day. Sad events in Manchester city centre before, during and after the 2008 Uefa Cup final involving Rangers show why England–Scotland, for all No. 10's enthusiasm, is unlikely to be high on the FA's agenda in the immediate future. But Downing Street's huge interest did show how far English football has come from the dark days of the Eighties.

22

Steve and Fabio

Guus Hiddink was my first choice to succeed Sven-Goran Eriksson as England manager in 2006. Knowing Guus from his days as Australia coach, when I travelled with the Aussies, I'd long admired this inspiring, intelligent coach. When the FA began laboriously drawing up a short-list of candidates to be interviewed, Guus's interest waned. Someone who had achieved so much in football didn't wish to join a beauty parade to show off his talents. Guus thought the FA process would be a circus, which it inevitably turned out to be, descending into farce eventually. If the FA had been quick and enthusiastic, Hiddink would probably have agreed. But they insisted on CVs and 'prove yourself' interviews. What happened next? Hiddink's Russia qualified for Euro 2008 instead of England, earning lavish praise for the tactical sophistication of their football in reaching the semi-finals. That's football fate.

Brian Barwick and Simon Johnson knew how they wanted to recruit for 'the impossible job'. Rightly, I played no significant part in the recruitment of Sven's successor. By then, my retirement plans were well advanced and well known inside the FA but I helped organise the famous interviews at Sir Victor Blank's estate in deepest Oxfordshire. Otherwise, I looked on with amusement, sometimes bemusement. Why all the secrecy? What Brian and

Simon tried to do was well-meaning and probably straight from the Wall Street guide to making major appointments. Running the process like the recruitment of a chief executive of a Footsie 100 company was the FA plan. Long-list, short-list, days of interviews. Barwick and Johnson followed normal recruitment practice for an abnormal job. The England manager is not the head of ICI. Different rules apply. Different pressures arise. The FA's new tactics were radically different from how we recruited Keegan and Eriksson: target him, get him. The obvious flaw in Barwick's and Johnson's tactics was that the public and media are not particularly interested when a normal CEO is appointed. The scrutiny for an England manager is massive, so playing secret squirrels in the Oxfordshire countryside was always going to be risky. But no one wanted a public circus in Soho Square either. After Johnson had approached Luiz Felipe Scolari, Sam Allardyce, Martin O'Neill and Steve McClaren, they were all invited to interviews. Alan Curbishley came later. The whole event resembled *The Apprentice*.

'Have you any suggestions for a discreet venue?' I asked Digby Jones, now Lord Jones of Birmingham. He suggested talking to Sir Victor, the outgoing chairman of Trinity Mirror. 'Is this going to cause you any embarrassment?' I asked Sir Victor. Clearly not. He was happy to lay on his place. Some of the managers were followed in their matching black Mercedes MPVs, and people found out what was going on.

Things really became messy when Barwick and Johnson homed in on Scolari and flew to his Lisbon base. The trip itself wasn't ill-judged. But I think they'd agree that they shouldn't have returned home without a firmer commitment from Scolari. Immediately news broke, it seems Scolari's children at school in Portugal were told their father was a traitor. His wife was doorstepped by reporters. As Scolari travelled to Germany to look at the Portuguese training camp, he was hounded by journalists. Infuriated by the intrusions, Scolari dramatically withdrew and Brian was absolutely slaughtered in the press. I sympathised with Brian. He and Johnson followed through this process they believed in despite all its flaws.

Having finally identified their first choice, they went to see him, and were given enough encouragement to come back and be positive. Within forty-eight hours the whole thing had blown up, smearing egg on their faces. Scolari hardly emerged as a hero. He'd got out of the kitchen even before the real heat was turned up. Chelsea will be an interesting challenge.

Bruised, battered and on the rebound, Barwick and Johnson went for McClaren, Sven's no. 2. Five years earlier, Adam Crozier made great play of bringing through an English coach in Sven's slipstream, and by accident rather than design this now happened. McClaren succeeded Eriksson. The FA will now hope Stuart Pearce will develop under Fabio Capello. This plan of English no. 2 learning under foreign no. 1 always worried me. The no. 2 will forever be tapped up by clubs for far greater reward. Howard Wilkinson's dream of this conveyor belt of English coaches coming through has, I fear, proved inherently flawed.

In my view, international management is usually not a young man's game. My concern about Steve was his youth, that he hadn't been through the mill enough and he had a young family. He entered a brutal realm where his children would be abused at school because of their father's job. The odds were stacked against McClaren, whose reign was compromised from day one by him not being first choice. Scolari's shadow hung over Steve. Being manager-in-waiting during the World Cup was also not easy and I discussed the situation with Eriksson.

'Sven, we had a slight problem at Euro '96 when Terry didn't want Glenn Hoddle around training,' I said to Sven.

'Well, Venables was totally and utterly right,' Sven replied.

'Now we have the situation with Steve, how are you with that?'

'Well, I am uneasy, but what can I do?' said Sven. He knew it would be strange having his successor right at the heart of every training session but Sven couldn't tell his main coach to stay away. He never thought Steve disloyal but he felt his presence might distract the players. 'What does the new coach think?' they could worry. Typically, Sven bit his lip and got on with it – except once.

One day, Steve went out for a coffee in Baden-Baden with three reporters, talking about England's future. Sven was too much of a gentleman to go ballistic but he let Steve know his disappointment. Focus on the present, not the future was Sven's message to Steve.

When McClaren finally started, I was pleased, if surprised, by his decision to call on Venables's expertise. They barely knew each other. But Terry's involvement won me a small bet. Terry joked when he left after Euro '96 that I would be at the FA until I retired.

'Utter bollocks, Terry,' I replied. 'You'll be at the FA after I've left!'

'Rubbish!' said Terry.

'Tenner on it?'

'Done!' And Terry was at the FA after I left.

Terry was horrified by the vilification McClaren endured from England fans and media in places like Barcelona at the game with Andorra. England's qualifying hopes for Euro 2008 were on the line but no one should be subjected to that sort of spiteful abuse. Steve's a very likeable guy, a good friend of mine now, but fans' patience was undoubtedly being tested. Sitting in my flat, watching England slip up in Moscow in 2007, I became so angry I threw a cup at the wall when Steven Gerrard missed a great chance. I prayed and believed Steve McClaren and his players would come through all the adversity. When England needed Israel to do us a favour against Russia, I knew a proud nation wouldn't lie down in their Tel Aviv citadel. Having led England's delegation that organised the fixture schedule, I understood there was no love lost between Israel and Russia. England dreamed of Hiddink's side being held to a draw, and Russia actually lost! The Great Escape was on. Rarely can England's spirits have been lifted so high and then so quickly dashed. I was at Wembley for Croatia's visit. They'd qualified, they'd spent lunch-time shopping on Sloane Street, we needed just a point . . . and yet. That defeat to Croatia hurt deeply.

The morning after, Steve behaved with incredible dignity. Having talked to Steve since, I was impressed by his philosophical reaction to defeat and dismissal. It happened. Move on. I wish him well at Twente Enschede. Terry meanwhile was treated shabbily by the FA; not for the first time, his admirers might argue. Terry discovered he had been sacked on TV. A reporter announced his fate. He deserved better. Any employee deserved better. All's fair in love, war and England but the FA should behave with some class when the battle is won or lost. Maybe McClaren and Venables didn't work out. I suspect neither would rush together again, which is sad.

Twenty-four hours after the latest blood-letting at Soho Square, I was asked by various TV stations who would be the next England coach. 'Fabio Capello,' I answered on Sky News. Capello was available, a huge plus. The question was when and how much? Familiar tunes must be danced to. After a sacking, FA officials always say the same thing: 'We're going to take our time. We're going to look around. There's no pressure.' Wonderful words, words I've uttered myself, but it isn't really like that, though. Take your time? With the public craving reassurance and a marquee name?! So the England dance begins. After about ten days people start to ask: 'What's happening?' After another ten days, people shout: 'The FA are dithering.' At that stage, if somebody's available, then the FA tend to go for them. Missing the boat scares them. After fouling up with Scolari, they rushed into McClaren. When he flopped, the FA could have gone for Scolari again, but it would have meant waiting until the end of Euro 2008. 'Big Phil' might have embarrassed Barwick again.

The English option in McClaren having failed, the FA went foreign again. We'd considered Capello before, notably when Kevin Keegan walked out of Wembley. Capello was well known to the FA and very well regarded. Before Eriksson arrived, Howard Wilkinson had a meal with Capello and, by the time they reached coffee, Capello thought he'd been sounded out for the England job. People around Capello told me that when he realised he wasn't going to get the job in 2000, he determined to get it one day in the future. At the time, the major factor against him was his lack of English. Fabio was considered again when the whole question of Eriksson's contract renewal came up as well. Mark Palios asked me to assess potential successors and my document praised Capello's credentials. It was difficult not to. From Milan to Madrid, Fabio has impressed wherever he has gone. Managers of Capello's substance have no difficulty moving from major football country to major football country. They love big stages, big stadia. The leading stages are found in Spain, England and Italy. Capello has the hat-trick now.

I hope Capello proves to be a great appointment and all behind his appointment deserve to be congratulated. My one surprise with this experienced Italian is that he doesn't tell the England players the starting line-up until the last minute. Though for sure it avoids the legendary leaking of the team that outraged so many of his predecessors, England players don't like grey areas. They want black and white, in or out. In wishing Fabio well, it needs stressing there's a distinct risk England may not qualify for the 2010 World Cup. Only one qualifies automatically per group while the eight second-best are thrown into the play-off lottery. People bang on about South Africa being perfect for England because the World Cup is being staged in winter-time but as breathless players may soon discover, a number of those 2010 games will be at altitude. Preparation and time to acclimatise will be crucial in South Africa.

In May 2008, Lord Triesman and Brian Barwick published their vision for the FA and English football. Some of us had seen one or two such documents before. Similarly, some of us had been regularly chastised over the previous seven years for the temerity of aspiring for 'England to win a major tournament by 2006'. It became a burden, we were told. Here was the new leadership setting their sights merely on England reaching semi-finals at least over the coming generation. Trevor Brooking was even reported as thinking this was over-optimistic. When I mentioned it to

Wolfgang Niersbach, CEO of the German FA, he roared with laughter. 'Not the German way,' he said. But maybe it's realistic unless English football decides its real priorities. One day some England coach, and possibly Capello, might get lucky, as Greece did at Euro 2004. Or England will finally perform at full capacity as Spain, our rivals as perennial underachievers, did so memorably at Euro 2008.

Fabio Capello arrived with a great reputation but what of the long-term English alternatives? Everyone at Soho Square says Middlesbrough's Gareth Southgate is a talented coach, a good judge of people but needs more experience. As I have mentioned, I hope Paul Ince comes through eventually. He has the strong personality. But when a cold-eyed look is cast over the situation, we may well have foreign coaches for the next ten years. At 2018, we might host the World Cup but not have someone who speaks English in the dug-out. The public's hunger for an English manager remains immense, comfortably in the majority. Even though I've left the FA, I get assailed constantly in the street by people saying: 'We want an English coach.' They may have a long wait.

23

Tackling the Taliban

Just weeks after the Taliban were expelled from Afghanistan's major towns and cities in 2003, I found myself on a mission as 'the President of FIFA's Special Envoy to Kabul'. We'd managed to persuade the most powerful man in world football, Sepp Blatter, that the brave and bloodied Afghans needed a show of support from the international football community. The Taliban committed brutal acts inside the Olympic Stadium in Kabul and it was time to reclaim it for sport. So began the countdown to the 'Match of Unity'.

If not quite the Dirty Dozen, the Enterprising Eight gathered at RAF Brize Norton one evening. Joining me and our two coaches, Lawrie McMenemy and Gary Mabbutt, on the eighteen-hour flight to Kabul were my former PA, the intrepid Kim Fisher, plus the Premier League referee Peter Jones and his three match-official colleagues. Boarding the American C16 military aeroplane up a rear ramp, we squeezed past a huge tank that occupied half the plane, and took our seats along one side beneath several tiny portholes. 'We're in the posh seats!' laughed Lawrie.

As this flying bus climbed with some difficulty into the sky, I reflected that organising the 'Match of Unity' in Kabul had seemed like a good idea at the time.

'You are barmy,' my younger daughter, Caroline, told me the night before.

'Good luck,' said Sven-Goran Eriksson as I left the England hotel for Brize Norton. 'See you soon – I hope!' Sven's voice contained a degree of scepticism that was hard to avoid or appreciate. Tord Grip merely shook his head and laughed. As we journeyed towards Afghanistan, stopping briefly in Bahrain, I mused on how someone who loathed flying as much as me was now hurtling towards a war zone in an uncomfortable military plane. Adam Crozier made me an offer I couldn't refuse. In the wake of England's failed bid for the 2006 World Cup finals, Adam called me into his office.

'You've told me you want to do something different,' said Adam.

'This could be it,' I thought. 'The bullet. My P45.'

'You've got two options,' Adam went on. 'Either stay in charge of communications or take on responsibility for international matters. We'll think of a title. The lesson we've all learned from 2006 is that we are not hacking it in UEFA and FIFA.'

'Good idea,' I answered, 'and not before time. The Germans have been schmoozing the world for a generation.' In my new role as Director of International Strategy, we developed a plan intended to increase our influence inside UEFA and FIFA and enhance English football's image around the world. I recruited two highly talented women, Kim Fisher and Jane Bateman, both strong linguists, and we set out to win the world over to England. Sadly, our work was not without critics within Soho Square.

'Why do we spend so much money in Africa when we need a new changing room in Bognor Regis?' one board member asked.

'In spending terms, the FA's money goes 99 per cent on England, the rest on the world,' I replied. 'Personally, I don't think the world gets a very good deal.'

Determined to keep costs down, we hitched a free lift to Afghanistan in an American plane. As we neared a darkened Kabul, we observed flashes of light on the hills below. We later learned these were Taliban remnants taking pot shots at passing planes. Welcome to Kabul. During our four-day stay, the new

Afghan minister of tourism was murdered on the very tarmac on which we arrived. Suddenly Soho Square seemed a haven of smiling faces.

Our accommodation at the multinational force HQ in a former Taliban government building was the level below basic. No heat, no electricity, no running water, no glass in the windows. No danger here of even the FA board complaining about senior staff living in luxury. As 'the President of FIFA's Special Envoy to Kabul', I was accorded the honour of my own room. Others were not so fortunate. Gary and Lawrie shared. Gary, eternally positive, and Lawrie, rightly proud of his Guards background, made the perfect travelling companions. Both were constantly upbeat, making light of the difficult conditions. 'What have we got here, lovely boy?' Lawrie quipped as we passed a series of long plastic tubes sticking out of the ground inside our compound. This was our bathroom and toilet. The British troops loved Lawrie and Gary with their wonderful stories, not least about winning the FA Cup at Wembley. As we settled down for our first night on Afghan soil, the mind became numbed by the cold. After battling in vain with the wonky zip on my sleeping-bag, I finally drifted off to sleep at around four a.m. Minutes later I was awoken by the local mosque summoning the faithful to prayer.

Later that morning, grisly discoveries awaited at the Olympic Stadium. At either end of a rough, straw-strewn pitch were goalposts pockmarked with bullet holes. Blood stained the dressing-room floor and ceilings. Human remains lay in one corner. During the brief periods that they had sanctioned football, the Taliban found their own version of half-time and post-match entertainment: executions.

The 'Match of Unity' was contested by a local team and representatives of the countries forming the multinational force. After Friday prayers were completed, 30,000 Afghans crammed inside the Olympic Stadium while an equal number milled around outside, cutting frustrated figures. Those who tried to sneak in were treated pretty brutally by the stick-wielding local security forces.

Inside the ground, I had a choice to make. 'We invite "the President of FIFA's Special Envoy to Kabul" to sit in the VIP box,' pronounced one of the Afghan organisers. 'Thanks, but I really need to be pitch-side, near the teams, to check everything is going smoothly,' I replied. The thought of being in such an exposed position as the front of the VIP box didn't excite me. Snipers were not unknown in Kabul. If I really was the FA's 'Great Survivor', as so many people insisted, now was the time to live up to the title. As I made my way to the dug-out, Peter Jones and his match officials received some memorable advice in the tunnel.

'If firing starts from outside the stadium, which it may do, just throw yourselves on the ground,' they were told.

'No problems,' Peter replied. 'I've refereed at Stamford Bridge and Anfield, you know!'

Passionately received by the Afghans, the 'Match of Unity' was never going to change the world, but there was a legacy. Along with FIFA and the ubiquitous Germans, we set up a project that began the process of rebuilding football in Afghanistan after twenty-five years of almost incessant conflict. For ninety minutes, we also brought some pleasure to a population who've suffered unbelievably. Before going home, the eight of us were taken on an armed tour of Kabul. None of us had ever witnessed such devastation. Whole areas of the capital had been razed. Amidst the rubble, young children kicked tatty balls about. Amidst chaos, a ball provided hope. We all looked at each other. I wasn't the only one in tears.

Emotionally drained, we all fell fast asleep on the flight home from Kabul, although not until the gunfire from the surrounding hills had been left behind. My sleep was soon disturbed. 'We have a problem, Mr Davies,' said one of the pilots, who'd left the cockpit to come and talk to me. 'Look out that window.' The view was not reassuring. The wing had a flap open that was pointing upwards. Even to an untrained aeronautical eye, this did not look good. 'We don't know why it won't close,' the pilot added calmly. Then came the sting. 'We're trying to contact the designers in the

States. But if it doesn't go down soon, we may have to return to Kabul.' Words failed me.

'Do you want to wake your colleagues and tell them?' the pilot said. Still speechless, I shook my head. Thankfully, half an hour later the pilot returned. 'Crisis over,' he announced. Relieved, I dozed off until Paris, when some of the guys shook me awake. 'Look out the window,' they said. Oh no, not again. This time, as the Seine snaked far beneath us, a plane flew almost alongside. Evidently the French military wanted to check our credentials. 'It's great here!' laughed Lawrie.

Thankfully, other trips were less hairy. Africa became the main target for the FA's international strategy and, with Sven's backing, I travelled to Johannesburg with a team of England over-30s, real stalwarts like Ian Wright, Chris Waddle, Terry Butcher and Viv Anderson, raising money for the families of those killed in a stampede at Ellis Park. While in Jo'burg, I committed to Sven taking the full England team to South Africa and that 22 May 2003 visit to Durban included the famous meeting with Nelson Mandela. Sadly, I had to withdraw from that chance of a lifetime because of a recurrence of my long-running back problem. When I heard that some England players declined to meet Mandela, I was speechless. I hope they don't regret it in days to come.

After that South Africa trip, a debate erupted over whether England had promised David Beckham would be involved. Such are the vagaries of a footballer's form and fitness, England couldn't guarantee anyone. We pledged to take the best available team at the time, and did so. When England travelled to Port of Spain for the 2008 friendly with Trinidad & Tobago, I was relieved more was not made of Fabio Capello's exclusion of most of the Chelsea and Manchester United players. Mind you, the inclusion of star names like Beckham, Steven Gerrard and Rio Ferdinand satisfied even Jack Warner, the president of CONCACAF.

Ferdinand was particularly impressive. He charmed Warner and the Trinidad people. He had loved meeting Mandela. With Gary Neville and David James, Rio and I flew to Malawi in 2005 to highlight the HIV/Aids epidemic that has reduced life expectancy in some African countries to less than forty years. The simple message they were to deliver to people who love English football was 'get tested for HIV'. To my annoyance if not surprise, the FA were not prepared to sanction a goodwill visit that hadn't been in any budget for a year. Short-sightedness almost stopped play. The trip was finally rescued by the Elton John Aids Foundation and other smaller but generous benefactors like Peter Gandolfi at Nationwide, Martin Protheroe at Umbro, Stephen Hall at McDonald's and a marvellous man I met by chance with Charlton Athletic, Sir Maurice Hatter. These principled individuals stepped in with donations when the FA ducked out. Rio, Gary and David all contributed. So did Gordon Taylor at the PFA. When the FA trumpeted Capello's journey to Lesotho in 2008, I didn't forget those in Soho Square who'd been so lukewarm to some of us going on similar trips three years earlier.

In Malawi, Rio, Gary and David visited Lilongwe general hospital, seeing dying children lying forlorn on decrepit beds with their mothers sleeping on the floor underneath the beds. 'Forty-eight hours ago, we crowded around this old TV and watched both of you in the FA Cup final,' the senior doctor said to Gary and Rio. 'And now here you are in our hospital. It means everything. Thank you so much.'

'No, thank you,' Gary and Rio replied. Rio has returned to Africa several times since Malawi, most recently to Nigeria in 2008. These conscientious men are not the uncaring multimillionaire prima donnas portrayed in the papers. John Terry, Joe Cole and Frank Lampard among others also use their fame for the wider good. Perhaps nobody has taken up the baton more than David James. England's charismatic goalkeeper took the Lilongwe experience so much to heart that he set up his own foundation, which has a special project helping to improve irrigation in Malawi. Two of David's friends have moved to Malawi to lead the work.

Football can reach out and touch people's lives. On one goodwill trip to China, Sir Bobby Robson made light of the 90°F heat in downtown Beijing to coach street kids. Tony Blair looked on admiringly. After the PM's success at head tennis with Kevin Keegan at that Labour party conference in Brighton in 1995, Blair found converting a number of goal chances in front of the Beijing cameras rather time-consuming. Chance after chance went begging. 'It wouldn't have happened in Alastair Campbell's day,' one political correspondent muttered. 'One missed chance and he'd have been off.'

From Kabul to Malawi and Beijing, my job was to spread the word that England and English football cared for the world. The charm offensive needed to be cranked up when Sepp Blatter came into view; we needed to build bridges after a spectacular falling-out with him in 2002. During all the relentless rows over FIFA finances, Crozier spellbound a FIFA Congress in Seoul with his 'time to go, Mr President' speech attacking Blatter's leadership. Persuasive and ferociously intelligent, Blatter held on, even strengthening his FIFA power-base. We English had to rebuild a seriously damaged relationship.

The annual International FA Board meetings provided the best opportunity to talk to Blatter. Unheralded by the British media, IFAB is incredibly important. The Board agrees on the laws of the game and any changes to them.

As the founding fathers of football, the British boast a privileged position on the Board. Each association, England, Scotland, Wales and Northern Ireland, possesses one vote each. The world, through FIFA, has four votes. No wonder Jack Warner of CONCACAF once railed against what he called this 'colonial anachronism'. As if to underline its historic roots, IFAB events have been staged at venues like Stormont, Cardiff Castle, Cliveden and aboard the royal yacht *Britannia.* Slumming it was never on the IFAB agenda. Hillsborough Castle, formerly the Northern Ireland base for the royals, always seemed a perfect setting for an IFAB meeting to me. Several of us, including Sven, stayed there on the eve of George Best's funeral. Sven slept in the Queen's bed. Thank God, she was not there.

I quickly learned that all the vital IFAB decisions were sorted out the day before its formal meeting. Only in recent times have significant disagreements, and votes, taken place. At Claridge's in 2004, Blatter decided the number of subs in friendly matches had reached ridiculous proportions. 'Is he talking about us by any chance?' I wondered aloud to Sven, who had notoriously replaced all eleven players at half-time in the friendly with Australia a year earlier. To the delight of the Scots in particular, we FA delegates found ourselves caught between a Swedish rock and a Swiss hard place.

'We have two options,' I told our FA group. 'Support Sven and snub Blatter. Or support Blatter and snub Sven.' When everybody else in the room made clear their support for Blatter's limit of six subs in friendlies, I did not detect Mark Palios, Geoff Thompson or Dave Richards being exactly distraught at this embarrassment to Sven. Blatter won and it was left to me as usual to tell the England coach. 'They're all mad,' observed Sven, not for the first or last time in his FA career.

Giving the English a hard time at IFAB was nothing unusual. The FA were always much keener on experimenting with goal-line technology than the rest of the world. Blatter believed in what he grandly termed 'the universality of the game', essentially that football's laws must apply to jumpers-for-goalposts kickabouts and the World Cup final.

'You cannot equate park football with Brazil v. France in front of a billion viewers worldwide,' I argued at one IFAB meeting. 'Refereeing decisions that technology quickly shows are wrong can cost managers their jobs. One day, a World Cup final like 1966 will be decided by a wrong decision and technology will prove that the decision was wrong and this board will be responsible.'

'This is emotional,' said Blatter, rebuking me.

'Mr President, remember how Romania were denied a good goal in Euro '96,' I repeated, thinking back to when Dorinel Munteanu thought he had scored against Bulgaria.

'Controversy over refereeing decisions is part of the game, too,' Blatter countered, clearly unimpressed by my stance. Other than the English, the rest of IFAB always agreed with Blatter, so I became determined to persuade them of the need for technology. When FIFA agreed to a 'microchip in the ball' trial at two under-17 World Cup matches in Peru, I travelled out with David Taylor, David Collins and Howard Wells, chief executives of Scotland, Wales and Northern Ireland respectively. The technology appeared simple. When the ball crossed the goal-line, the microchip transmitted a message to wristbands worn by the referee and the fourth official to confirm a goal. For the first match between Mexico and Holland, I deliberately stationed myself next to the fourth official. At half-time his wristband confirmed the score as Mexico 3, Holland 1. Unfortunately, the real score was Mexico 1, Holland 0. The ball had landed three times on top of the goal and the relevant piece of equipment had been impounded by Peruvian customs. Technology has some way to improve but its time will come. I hope Lord Triesman and Brian Barwick's successor will continue to champion technology. Maybe a replay of the 1966 World Cup Final might persuade the Germans.

So far, Blatter has won the battle to keep technology out of football. Whatever his many critics say, FIFA's president is a remarkable man, a politician of high calibre to the ends of his fingertips. He has this incredible capacity to make up policy on the hoof. Ideas are floated, and sometimes disappear almost as quickly. Blatter came up with the idea of staging the World Cup every two years and women players wearing tighter clothing. In July 2008, Blatter stunned many people by describing players' contracts as 'modern-day slavery'. My own view had grown steadily that Uncle Sepp enjoyed the controversy and profile that came with his flights of fancy. We were in Scotland once, ready for a post-IFAB news conference in a hotel, when the fire alarm went off, forcing everyone on to the streets. When the all-clear sounded, Blatter immediately delivered this bravura performance before the cameras, announcing the arrival of professional referees. This was news not only to everybody who'd attended the meeting but also to Blatter's staff. It had never been mentioned inside IFAB. But never underestimate Sepp.

Blatter has countless countries in his thrall. FIFA now have 208 members, more than the United Nations, and few see the world through English eyes. At one FIFA Congress in Marrakech in 2005, all these delegates were gathered in a hotel which had Sky News pumped into every room. Understandably, Sky were rather obsessed with the fifth and final Ashes Test, an event that bemused most of the delegates from around the world.

'David, what on earth is this Ashes?' they kept coming up and asking me. 'How can the lead story in world news be the Ashes? We don't even know what they're talking about.' So I patiently explained the joys of cricket, and listed the nations that played it seriously. 'But there's only eight countries playing it!' they replied. This Ashes contest provoked most debate during the Congress. Amazingly, there was not one speaker from the floor during the various votes on certain legal issues and FIFA statutes. No dispute. No debate. Even Blatter stood up and said: 'You agree with your president?' This style of leadership used to be hugely popular in Eastern Europe in the 1950s. I doubt it will survive after Blatter leaves the FIFA president's office. Meanwhile, I hope future FIFA events will include fringe meetings with a better chance of debating football's big issues.

Having failed in the past, the FA almost certainly must win over Blatter if they are to gain the right to host the 2018 World Cup. Staging the tournament should be a serious prospect for England. By then South Africa and Brazil will have had their turns. Enthusiasm to bring the World Cup back to Europe after a gap of twelve years will be considerable, particularly amongst the powerful broadcasting and marketing lobbies. But England have their work cut out. Spain, the new European champions, may well put in a strong bid. Russia boast the necessary deep coffers to finance a bid. The European block vote could be split, with Australia a likely beneficiary. Australasia have never hosted a World Cup and the legacy for 'soccer' Down Under would be immense. Led by their country's second-wealthiest citizen, Frank Lowy, the Aussies will make a compelling case for 2018.

In late 2005, the FA leadership reacted warily to Gordon Brown's enthusiasm for a feasibility study of England's preparedness to host 2018. By 2007, it was the decisiveness of FA board members like David Gill and David Sheepshanks, not of the chief executive or his senior staff, that committed the FA to press ahead immediately. If England are to play a winning hand, they must learn from past mistakes. The bid must be a full-time project with full-time leadership semi detached from the FA. FA and Premier politics mustn't be permitted to influence decisions or tactics. Lord Triesman will need 100 per cent support, and no backbiting. Geoff Thompson's presence amongst the twenty-four FIFA executive-committee members must be exploited; the 2018 challenge is a huge chance for Thompson to make a difference and to prove his critics wrong. English icons like David Beckham, Kevin Keegan and Alan Shearer must be used to promote the bid. So must legends like Sir Alex Ferguson and foreign players whose careers were enhanced in England. I hope the FA seek and listen to the advice of Seb Coe and Keith Mills. With those goodwill trips to Kabul, Malawi, Beijing and many more, I know the perception of English arrogance still exists in foreign eyes. The FA has plenty to do to convince Planet Football that the World Cup should come home in 2018.

24

The Future

England's absence from Euro 2008 provoked an intense debate about our footballers' technical standards. Why are we not breeding players of the technical class of Cesc Fabregas? Surely our vaunted, well-funded academies were designed to provide a conveyor belt of talent? Evidently not. 'The academies are becoming no more, no less than finishing schools for foreign talent,' Sir Trevor Brooking told me. Fabregas's footballing education was completed at Arsenal but the nation that benefits is Spain, now the European champions. England's dream of emulating Spain will be impossible unless the technical level of our schoolboys is raised.

Conceived by Howard Wilkinson, academies were deemed the future. 'Howard's a top man,' Alex Ferguson told me when Wilkinson was appointed technical director, as we sat in his old office at the Cliff. 'It's a real step forward.' But Alex had spotted what he perceived as the main flaw in Howard's plans: 'the ninety-minute rule'. Academy players must live within an hour and a half's travelling distance of their club. Howard wanted to ensure clubs all over the country had a chance of attracting local talent, preventing all the best youngsters being lured to the glamour teams. Clubs like Fabregas's Arsenal just looked outside the UK for young talent unaffected by the restriction, moving them and their families to England for a new life. Alex predicted what would happen but by then the rules had been agreed. The damage had already been done.

The deep conflicts within English football are highlighted by the endless debates about youth development. These arguments played a significant part in driving Howard out of the FA. In exasperation I missed him. When Howard left for Sunderland, temporarily Les Reed filled the gap. Les and I quickly experienced the almost annual frustrations involved in England entering an under-20s team in the prestigious Toulon tournament. In 2003, England failed to get beyond the qualifying group stage, performing miserably. Portugal, one of our opponents, had a bloke named in the programme as C. Ronaldo who ran rings round everybody and scored goals for fun.

Problems were bound to occur when Toulon coincided with senior and under-21 commitments. No overall selection policy existed. Sven-Goran Eriksson and David Platt, then in charge of the under-21s, demanded large squads so Les was left in Toulon 'giving a fantastic tournament experience to the wrong players'. Ronaldo's presence alongside other future international stars illustrated how seriously their nations took tournament football in contrast to England. Portugal proved England's nemesis at Euro 2004 and the 2006 World Cup.

The politics that frustrated Howard drove Sir Trevor Brooking into almost daily bouts of apoplexy. Trevor had been Charles Hughes's fiercest critic, believing the *Winning Formula* was anything but a recipe for success and actually damaged England's chances. Trevor craved the chance to revitalise the youngest age group, the seven- to eleven-year-olds, but he quickly found himself swallowed up by the continuing battles between the game's different factions. Trevor never managed to build the close relationship with Sven or Steve McClaren that some of us had hoped. As I was close to all of them, that saddened me; somehow I should have done more to bring them together. As long as he stays at Soho Square, I pray Trevor manages to build a bond with Fabio Capello. Problems abound, though. Several of the board men, not least Lord Mawhinney of the Football League, criticised Trevor for wanting to tell their organisations how to spend FA-provided resources and for his frequent outbursts of frustration. 'I can't stand much more of this,' Trevor told me regularly. Sadly, I'm not convinced Trevor will win his wars.

So much needs to be done to give English football the best chance of winning. Lord Triesman must bring together the FA, the Premier League and Football League and agree priorities and a concordat for English football over the next decade and they must stick to them. A highly intelligent football fan who won't be pushed around by the Premier League, the FA's new independent chairman is scheduled to be a one- or two-day-a-week chairman. Ultimately I believe the chairman should be full-time and very hands-on. The FA may be better off with a charismatic, authoritative, decision-making chairman in Triesman assisted by a chief operating officer. After Brian Barwick, I suspect the logic of that happening may find some support. But if it proves too radical, and I fear it may for now, I am certain Barwick's successor will be a very different character.

My future executive chairman would need to serve a maximum of two four-year terms, and then ensure he or she has the staff around them they want. In this way, the flaw in how the FA operates, upstairs and downstairs, staff versus volunteers, would at last be addressed. Meanwhile, uniting English football should be Lord Triesman's top priority, along with ensuring England and our top clubs are given the best chance of success. England and the clubs could work better in tandem if internationals were played in blocks of three or four at specific stages of the season. They must put money and energy into the National Football Centre. A winter break will surely come with the League Managers' Association planning to campaign for it.

Change is in the wind. I think there'll be a Premier League Mark II in the foreseeable future and Premier League Mark I may then go to eighteen clubs, easing the crazy workload on the leading players. I also hope a new football task force will reassess corporate governance in English football as a whole, and finally force through non-executive directors on to the boards of the FA and Premier League. Formed with strong-minded individuals, it must learn the lessons of the well-intentioned David Mellor task force of the late 1990s. For sure the resources are there to revolutionise the game. FA turnover increased twelve-fold during my time to almost £240m in 2007.

And let's give the referees – the Ellerays and Durkins and Howard Webbs and, yes, Jack Taylors of the future – all the backing in the world, including technology at the top level. In the parks, find some limited money surely from the TV bonanza to make it rather more lucrative than £20 or so a game to put up with the pressures of refereeing in the modern age. At the same time, why not revolutionise high-profile disciplinary proceedings by implementing Lord Terry Burns's proposal for opening them up to public scrutiny?

Other issues must be addressed. The Community Shield, contested on 10 August 2008 by Manchester United and Portsmouth, has outlived its usefulness, raising only about £1m a year. We live in the age of Sports Relief and Children in Need, so football could make a much more substantial contribution with a four-team tournament, involving the champions, Cup holders and two invited sides, at Wembley on the eve of the new season. Imagine Inter Milan, Real Madrid, Portsmouth and Manchester United colliding at Wembley over a weekend followed by 'Football Relief' on the Sunday night. And do our biggest clubs really need to get their expenses for such occasions?

On the wish-list of changes English football must work towards, a women's league must be moved to the summer, maximising rising interest levels and ultimately turning professional. 'Football's future is female,' Sepp Blatter said. The increasing numbers of women becoming involved in the game, on and off the field, has been one of the most astonishing trends in English football over the past fifteen years. When I went to see my daughter play a hockey final at Milton Keynes, this woman from the

English Hockey Association told me in no uncertain terms that I was wrecking traditional girls' sport in schools by championing football for girls. I wish I could tell you everybody at the FA, and in the top clubs, supported girls' and women's football in my time. Actually they didn't.

Now, I'm on the outside of Soho Square looking in. I left the FA on Thursday 28 September 2006. Riding down in the lift from the fifth floor, walking out for the last time through the foyer with its chrome and glass and televisions, I thought how different it was from entering dowdy Lancaster Gate almost thirteen years previously. I don't miss the politics and infighting of Soho Square but, despite all the troubles and tensions, it was a privilege working there. There are good people in English football like David Gill, the Manchester United chief executive. If he fancies the grief, David could be a future FA leader, providing the balanced leadership English football craves. So too could David Sheepshanks. David Dein still has much to offer English football at the top level as well. I do miss FA people like Graham Noakes, its fantastic fixtures guru, and Steve Clark, without whom the FA Cup and all the other competitions wouldn't work year in, year out. I miss Sue Ball, my first PA, who knows more about grass-roots football than I ever will. I miss great servants of the game like Andy Williamson and Glynis Firth at the Football League. But I stay in touch with the many friends at home and abroad that football gave me. As a freelance pensioner, I'm still involved in a football-development and event-management company called Alexander Ross that operates across the globe. I am lucky. I have a new life.

I still enjoy going to matches, and revelled in Cristiano Ronaldo's remarkable contribution to Manchester United's Double-winning season of 2007–08. Ronaldo could ascend to the pantheon of greatness if he acquires the consistency. Of the modern generation of players, Ronaldo entrances me most, followed by Kaka of AC Milan and Brazil, who graces the game with his elegant talent. The memory burns strong of Thierry

Henry at his very best, scorching away from opponents, cutting in from the Arsenal left and scoring. I have never seen speed off the mark quite like Thierry's. Johan Cruyff captivated me during his Total Football days. But none of these special talents can eclipse my memory of George Best in his prime, gliding through defences to embarrass another keeper.

I dream of more glory for Manchester United. My tickets from Wembley 1968, Barcelona 1999 and now Moscow 2008 are all encased in a frame and there's always room for more. I have another frame preserving my 1966 World Cup tickets. The colours may fade. The memories don't. Please let me live to see England triumph again.

Index